CROSS PURPOSES

CR⊕SS PURP⊕SES

The Violent Grammar of Christian Atonement

Anthony W. Bartlett

TRINITY PRESS INTERNATIONAL
Harrisburg, Pennsylvania

Trinity Press International, P.O. Box 1321, Harrisburg, PA 17105

Trinity Press International is a division of the Morehouse Group.

Cover art: *Four Leaders of the Crusades*, copyright © Leonard de Selva/Corbis

Cover design: Jake Haas

Library of Congress Cataloging-in-Publication Data

Bartlett, Anthony W.
    Cross purposes : the violent grammar of Christian atonement /
Anthony W. Bartlett.
      p. cm.
    Includes bibliographical references and index.
    ISBN 1-56338-336-5 (alk. paper)
    1. Atonement. 2. Violence—Religious aspects—Christianity. I. Title.

BT265.2 .B37 2001
232'.3—dc21   00-066316

Printed in the United States of America

01 02 03 04 05 06   10 9 8 7 6 5 4 3 2 1

To
Linda, James, Christopher, Susannah, Liam
and
"Wood Hath Hope"

CONTENTS

INTRODUCTION

For two thousand years the story of the Crucified has been with us, giving rise to a series of interpretations filled with profound tension; and alongside these, keeping pace with them, has been the astonishingly violent history of the Christian religion. The message of the Crucified has disturbed the order of planetary time, helping form a Western culture and placing its ever-expanding zone of influence under an arc of judgment and expectation that has rendered it deeply conflictive, and yet full of hope for final transformation. There is no historical parallel to the tensions generated by this story. They are singularly formative for our world as it has just traversed two millennia measured from the temporal frame of that story. Those who own this story, who identify with it and with its diverse traditional and institutional expressions over those years, have a unique responsibility for its impact, above all as they look out at a world relentlessly pressured by Western culture. And also those who do not own this story, yet recognize it as part of their cultural account, they too have a need to think about it, to seek to understand its strange, disruptive paradoxes, and perhaps to take up a considered response in face of it.

In the late eleventh century Abbot Anselm of Canterbury wrote a document, the *Cur Deus Homo*, that may well be described as the master hinge in the whole two-thousand-year tradition of interpretation of the Crucified, and which I present in this book as displaying some of the most destructive tensions in that tradition. He wrote it because monks were coming to him with "perplexing questions" on the meaning of Christ's death. Such questions have not gone away, instead they have increased in urgency, and rather than being asked by monks they are perhaps voiced by the very times in which we live, by their remorseless content of violence, which is somehow reflected in and by the violence of the Christian symbol of redemption.

1

For, as a study of the meaning of the cross, this book is predicated on sensitivity to contemporary human crisis—to such an extent that, if someone feels for one reason or other that this crisis is tolerable, that an invisible hand is still guiding the depredations of global commodity culture, or that an individual can somehow separate himself from the suffering of every other, then he or she should stop reading straightway.[1] In the terms of this inquiry that person would have no relevant question to ask of the Crucified. However, the same crisis is interior to the Christian faith, which may for a moment feel itself comforted by the thought that a world in crisis is part and parcel of its traditional preaching viewpoint, as if the world as the human living space were somehow different from its own destiny. To let the Crucified speak originally from the cross, in its scene of raw violence, is a shocking thing. Perhaps he has not been heard clearly before. The cross, if it means what Christians claim it means, should become always again a question to Christians, and thereby Christianity a question to itself. Perplexing questions, confounding, destabilizing, provocative . . . re-creative.

My study sets out to pose these questions in a coherent way, seeking the grammar or set of logical rules by which the Christian event of salvation has been understood in the history of the Christian tradition. It shows how this grammar is inflected or formed by violence, so that violence in turn is validated by it. At the same time it at once begins to suggest an alternative viewpoint, wherein the grammar of violence is demolished and a new, radically refigured grammar is opened up in the very scene of the cross itself. This is what I term the abyssal meaning of the cross, a dynamic that has always been there in the Gospels and represented in the less obvious contours of the Christian tradition, but that now reveals itself in its oblique power with increasing insistence and persuasiveness. It runs as a kind of basso continuo throughout this book, yet one that progressively develops its deeper line to become the only truly credible note in a message of redemption.

The overall method I use is a type of general anthropology, which is more particularly a biblical anthropology, and might properly be called an anthropology of the cross.[2] It implies that we do not seek answers in terms of metaphysical propositions, but in a structure of human relations that

---

1. A statistic of our time, its global frame a picture of unparalleled inequality, is a snapshot of contemporary human crisis. According to the *United Nations Human Development Report* (Cary, N.C.: Oxford University Press, 1996), the assets of the world's 358 billionaires exceed the combined annual incomes of countries with 45 percent of the world's population, approximately 2.5 billion people.

2. The term *anthropology* means primarily the scientific study of the human species, but it includes also a philosophical reference concerning basic human structures of relationship in world history. The idea of a biblical anthropology suggests that the complex of the biblical narrative provides both data and a pregnant outline of the ways human beings do and may shape their human world.

can be seen to have controlled historical explanations of the meaning of the cross. However, it is the significant collapse of this structure itself that is the true redemptive achievement of the cross. My approach is by no means indifferent to formal Christian theology, and some of the connection with the latter will become clearer in the final chapters of the book. However, the methodology begins always from the human side of the matter, from what might intelligibly be reported from *within* a continuum of human responses, these responses interpreting and yet also being reinterpreted by the focal Christian event of Christ's death.

All reflection is selection, especially when we deal with the complexity of cultural processes. This will inevitably be the case when we come to analyze the historical patristic tradition in the second chapter, and then, in the third, a particular set of events and themes making up an episode of medieval Christendom. But forming this selection helps to establish a certain evident clarity and clarity of evidence in Christianity's relation to violence. It communicates a certain established complex of emotions in Christian culture that is not, I believe, unfamiliar. Moreover, providing as much as possible a textured description of the tradition and history of Christianity will enable us to perceive the function of violence both in the full cloth and also precisely in the folds of its story. According to this model, the overall goal of my book is not the victory of a thesis by dialectical force and necessity, but the demonstration of a certain ambience that may in itself be persuasive. For it is perhaps only in the free response to a rhetorical ethos, but one also constructed on singular claims about history, that violence may be overcome.

The general name in the English language for the saving function or meaning of the life and death of Christ is *atonement*. The word has no parallel in romance languages, where *expiation* generally fills this semantic space. The etymology of *at-onement* gives the English a certain abstraction, seeming to set it apart from the very direct sacrificial connotations of the romance term. At the same time the back-formation, "to atone," is clearly associated today with expiatory meaning. Generally the phrase *atonement doctrine* implies a chain of related themes and ideas with a subtle shading between them: namely, sacrifice, expiation, propitiation, penal substitution, vicarious suffering, satisfaction. However, all these usages in respect of the Crucified imply an exchange value in Christ's death, whereby something is gained in return for the life lost, and by means of an eternal order or economy that demands it. This is sacred order, something constituted essentially by violence in the definition of the concept I will propose. To reduce the meaning of Christ's death to a negotiation with sacred order has been a way of validating human violence and at once neutralizing the full human, transformative impact of the cross. Such an interpretation removes the historical-apocalyptic tone and content of the New Testament account of Jesus' death, and transfers the dynamism instead to some eternal presidium of judgment. This is an absolutely key point. *Apocalyptic* here means the opposite of an absolute judgmental violence on the part of God. Rather it is the undoing of all violence by the radical gentleness of the Lamb entering and transforming the depths of the human condition. The attendant violence of history as in one way or other it resists this very forfeiture of violence is graphically described in New Testament apocalypses; but it has been mistaken for the terminal anger of God and so has been able to coexist with an exchange meaning of Christ's death precisely in terms of an eternal order of violence.

The prince of exchange theories of the cross is the treatise of Anselm of Canterbury, which introduced the notion of "satisfaction" into atonement, and this has remained there ever since, forming and fixing the idea of Christ's death as sacrifice.[3] It is this complex that currently represents the immediate default sense of "doctrine of atonement" for most people formed by Western traditions of Christianity. Behind this, historically, stood another dominant version, the so-called "rights of the Devil"; and these two dominant explanations of atonement provide the main focus in our study of those traditions in the second chapter.

Since the time of the Enlightenment the actual violence and contradictions of the Christian tradition have become a byword, serving for rapid intellectual dismissal of the claims of the Crucified. Such a viewpoint would perhaps consider a renewed discussion related to "atonement" as supremely redundant. From another angle, the thought worlds we inhabit are sufficiently structured by broad-brush Freudian notions to make us believe the only things worth repeating are interpretations of guilt, anxiety, and repression.[4] Furthermore, within the practice of Christian religion

---

3. See, for example, Timothy Gorringe, *God's Just Vengeance: Crime, violence and the rhetoric of salvation* (Cambridge: Cambridge University Press, 1996), 29: "From Anselm onwards satisfaction and sacrifice were read together, and sacrifice was understood as propitiation. Even today such a connection is felt by many Christians to be self-evident. . . ."

4. For example, Paul W. Pruyser Miller, "Anxiety, Guilt and Shame in the Atonement," *Theology Today* 21 (April 1964): 15–33. Here Pruyser Miller argues that intrapsychic conflicts interpreted on Freudian lines can serve as a model for the main theories of atonement. The theory of ransom (from the Devil) is "a typical expression of conflict between the Ego and the Id," whereas the later satisfaction theory is "typically modelled after conflicts between the Ego and the Super-ego" (20). Jean Delumeau's *Sin and Fear, The Emergence of a Western Guilt Culture 13th–18th Centuries*, trans. Eric Nicholson (New York: St. Martin's Press, 1990) includes a constant undertow of references to atonement theology and is predicated on the cultural break provided by Freudian thought. "Psychoanalysis enables a discussion of files opened by history" (296). He quotes Antoine Vergote: "Can one imagine a more obsessional phantasm than that of a God who demands the torturing of His own Son to death as satisfaction for his anger?" (300, from *Dette et désir: Deux axes chrétiens et la dérive pathologique* [Paris: Editions du Seuil, 1978], 161).

itself, the continuing evocative power of the Passion story, and its seamless rehearsal week after week, seem to have dispensed with any need to subject traditional explanations to analysis. These are in fact so interwoven in the received version of the tale that they have become unreflective, precritical, second nature to its telling.[5] Yet as regards this Christian rehearsal surely there is one striking feature of the death of Christ that should prove a difficulty, even on a popular level, and yet has never in itself been the subject of comment in the traditional accounts. Rather it is also taken completely for granted, as something that in itself seems self-evident and self-explanatory. I am talking here of the brutal violence inflicted on the protagonist of the Gospels, and the way this violence always functions to bring about the desired goal of human redemption. Why is it so obvious that a violent death should "work" as a form of ultimate resolution? Why is that violence itself not an outrage, beyond any possible formal effect that theologians might apply to it? In fact, one of the prime motives for Anselm of Canterbury in writing his seminal exposition was to rebut the charge by Jewish critics that the death of Christ was by its violent character necessarily demeaning to the God-man. But this charge was not answered by questioning the violence. On the contrary, Anselm dealt with the violence by reinforcing its necessity. Here and now, however, a question about violence seems profoundly appropriate. The evidences are too diverse and insistent

---

5. Theologians are, however, well aware of stresses implicit in these traditional viewpoints. In reference to the satisfaction theory G. Greshake states, "There is probably no other so fiercely controversial theological theory that has yet formed the consciousness of so many Christians—while never being the object of official Church teaching" (*Erlösungslehre Anselms von Canterbury*, ThQ 153 [1973], 323), quoted in Raymund Schwager's *Der wunderbare Tausch* (München: Kösel, 1986), 161; my translation. Joseph Ratzinger proposes that a "coarsened" version of this theory has deeply affected "universal Christian consciousness" to the extent of communicating a "sinister wrath" that "makes the message of love incredible" (*Introduction to Christianity* [New York: Herder & Herder, 1969], 214). It is also true that, beginning with Gustav Aulén, this century has witnessed a reaction against the dominant satisfaction theory. His theory of *Christus Victor*, characteristic of the early church and sounding the "note of triumph" against the spiritual enemies of humanity, was relevant against a background of World War "in a European culture aware of demonic forces" (John R.W. Stott, *The Cross of Christ* [Downers Grove, Ill.: InterVarsity, 1986], 229). The same awareness of spiritual forces is to be found, centered now in the Americas, in Walter Wink's *Powers* trilogy (*Naming the Powers: The Language of Power in the New Testament* [Philadelphia: Fortress Press, 1984]; *Unmasking the Powers: The Invisible Forces that Determine Human Existence* [Philadelphia: Fortress Press, 1986]; and *Engaging the Powers: Discernment and Resistance in a World of Domination* [Minneapolis: Fortress Press, 1992]). The difference here is that there is much more direct consciousness of the social-political dimension of the demonic. Attempted repristinations of an early-church redemptive viewpoint are certainly welcome, but so far "victory over the powers" has failed to dislodge the satisfaction model, perhaps because it is in fact less rooted in anthropology than the latter construction. Dealing at the abstract level of the "powers" it does not respond to the profound need for a sense of personal transformation.

to need repetition. It has become in fact a question of the survival of the human species, both on an obvious, evilly banal "macro" level, but also on a more intimate level, of the possibility of integrity and meaning to the human condition, of its resistance to fracture and fragmentation. The violence manifested in the cross poses itself the question of the human species and its capacity for relentless, abusive violence. Thus it is a profoundly anthropological question, and this principle of thought guides our discussion of atonement both as starting point and consistent methodology.

Another glance at stereotypical Freudian critique of atonement doctrine tells us that it centers predominantly on the Freud of individual psychology and the array of forces related to the individual psyche, unconscious drives, Oedipal repression, and the ego ideal. The Freud of *Totem and Taboo* and of *Moses and Monotheism*, the Freud of collective violence at the heart of cultural origins, is not invoked.[6] This less-fashionable Freudian perspective is related in fact to something of a commonplace among theorists of religion and culture around the end of the nineteenth century: the crucial significance of killing in group ritual and mythology reported from a large variety of times and places in human history. There is perhaps an implicit inheritance of this perspective that informs a further level of decision about the atonement—it is already fundamentally interpreted in terms of a cultural theme or typology, the "death of the god."[7] So, that which in the Christian context seems consistently ignored as an issue—the shocking violence of Christ's death—is precisely another leading factor in enabling detached observers to dismiss it as a question needing a solution.

But in *Totem and Taboo* Freud was not dealing with a supposed primitivism lost in prehistory. Everything for him was related to actual human psychology and relationships. The background of his reflection comes

6. Sigmund Freud, *Totem and Taboo: Resemblances between the psychic lives of savages and neurotics*, trans. A. A. Brill (New York: Vintage Books, 1946); *Moses and Monotheism*, trans. Katherine Jones (New York: Vintage Books, 1967).

7. Joseph Campbell provides a parade example of merging together sacrificial killing and motifs garnered from a globeful of religions, including of course the cross. He describes a New Guinea fertility sacrifice of a young woman and man crushed under a fall of logs while they engage in intercourse. "Then the little couple is pulled out and roasted and eaten that very evening. The ritual is the repetition of the original act of the killing of a god followed by the coming of food from the dead savior. In the sacrifice of the Mass you are taught that this is the body and blood of Christ. . . . In the hunting cultures, when a sacrifice is made, it is, as it were, a gift or a bribe to the deity that is being invited to do something for us or to give us something. But when a figure is sacrificed in the planting cultures, that figure itself is the god. The person who dies is buried and becomes the food. Christ is crucified, and from his body the food of the spirit comes. The Christ story involves a sublimation of what originally was a very solid vegetal image. Jesus is on Holy Rood, the tree, and he is himself the fruit of the tree. . . . Jesus on the cross, the Buddha under the tree—these are the same figures" (*Joseph Campbell, The Power of Myth, with Bill Moyers* [New York: Doubleday, 1988], 106–7).

from thinkers like James George Frazer and W. Robertson Smith, who both propose theories of the killing of a key individual, human or animal, at primary levels of social existence. Freud especially used Robertson Smith, who saw the totem animal as a kinship member of the group, killed and eaten in solemn events that demonstrate communion between them and their god. Freud then traced this killing as a ritual substitute for the original killing of the father, by the group of subject brothers within a Darwinian primal horde. Then, at this point, his argument vigorously rejoins the Oedipal complex, showing that its actual repressed wishes correspond to taboos awakened in the brothers as a result of the original murder.[8]

In the same work, Freud then goes on to see the death of Christ as another permutation of guilt and expiation for this original murder, and so his voice returns to the general chorus seeing the atonement as explained by universal human themes, and so without remainder. But Freud's reflection is certainly not to be ignored, nor should we fall prey to the general disregard with which *Totem and Taboo* is treated among professional psychoanalysts.[9] It has its difficulties, not least relating an original breaking of the power of the father to a permanent institution of the same power. The thin thread that makes this possible is the "filial sense of guilt" of the brother assassins postmurder, but presumably guilt depends on the psychic power of the father, which itself depends on the Oedipus complex! Freud was prepared to leap this ditch in experimenting with the idea of an original murder. But perhaps, after all, it is the idea of an original murder itself that provokes the most offense. So long as we remain on the level of Oedipal fantasy, of childhood ideas of revenge, then human culture is largely in the clear. The moment Freud proposes an original act of murder, determined simply by rivalry, then a certain real complicity in bloodletting appears inescapable. It is not possible to dismiss as ethically negligible a panhistorical conspiracy simultaneously to commit murder, regret it, and make use of it.

The French literary theorist and anthropologist René Girard consciously reprises this late-nineteenth- and early-twentieth-century

---

8. W. Robertson Smith, *The Religion of the Semites* (New York: Schocken Books, 1972). See also James George Frazer, *The Golden Bough*, abridged edition (New York: Collier Books, 1963), 309–45.

9. See, for example, the Jungian scholar, Erich Neumann, *The Origins and History of Consciousness*, trans. R. F. C. Hull, Bollingen Series, vol. XLII (Princeton: Princeton University Press, 1973): "Freud's illogical and anthropologically impossible hypothesis of a gorilla father" (153). Citing Robert Briffault (*The Mothers*, 3 vols. [London: George Allen & Unwin Ltd.; and New York: Macmillan, 1969]), he also argues: "The conjectural originality of the patriarchal family is . . . caused by excessive reliance upon Biblical research" (Neumann, 182).

stream of thought, returning deliberately to the notion of generative acts of violence at the base of human culture. My study is decisively indebted to his thought, and I will seek to give adequate account of its development in the first chapter. For the moment it is useful to sketch a preliminary view to point the direction of the book. Girard may be read as a kind of radicalization of Freud, into a much more self-consistent theory of "violent origins." He is able to do this because he attains to a layer of human relationship that is at once more open, more anonymous, and more dangerous than the hypostatized sexual or erotic drive that Freud stated as the source of the brother's violence. At the same time it is less confidently rationalist and evolutionist than the attribution of primitive "magical thought" that Frazer makes. The layer he points to is imitative desire, or what he calls *mimesis*, and Girard's hypotheses can be considered under the general title of mimetic anthropology. As I make use of this thought I will also seek a deeper exploration of the field Girard was the first to open up, and at the same time establish crucial general differences from his approach. Remaining just now with the overall question, we may suggest in advance that pursuing the implications of this general anthropology will quickly make apparent violence at the core of atonement theories and so force a demand that they be reexamined thoroughly by its analytic. If mimetic anthropology can indicate a certain substantive violence in the traditional constructions of Christian redemption, then surely this is a momentous disclosure. And if atonement theories tend to consecrate or consolidate processes that may be seen as forms of human violence per se, not simply processes on which human violence is attendant, then it is vitally urgent once more to raise questions related to them.

Girard's mimesis is a significant conceptual breakthrough. It enables a startling reflection on human relationality, and at a primary level. For someone like Jacques Lacan, the psychoanalytical theorist, the area of relationality certainly focuses key problems, including the problem of desire that seeks to find itself as the object of the other's desire, and so desire itself with that desire. This dynamic, however, appears under the dispensation of a more general problem, which is that all psychic movements are locked in the "imaginary," the narcissistic and unreal projection or mirroring of the self in all experience. It is only the function of symbol and language, of speech, that rescues desire from "cannibalistic" solipsism, negotiating for it a tolerable, boundaried existence alongside others in a social world. With this stress on knowledge, however imaginary, and then language as a kind of deus ex machina resolving the "speculative" impasse, Lacanian theory situates itself within an intellectualist, epistemological frame, heir in its way of the Cartesian *cogito*.[10] On the contrary, when we see desire controlled by mimesis, as in the Girardian hypothesis, then the problem suddenly exceeds the Cartesian frame completely, and demonstrates the anthropological radicalism of his approach. Desire in itself is mimetic; it does not simply seek another desire, to mirror its monadic solitude in the world, but primordially imitates the other desire in order to know what to desire in the first place. It is originally "triangular," consisting of the subject, the model, and the object signaled as desirable by the model. Desire as such remains whole-bodied, prereflective, always already "other," simultaneously as it discovers itself in relation to the world around it. It does not arise in a private misconstrual of "reality," but rather is an original alterity, or otherness, that may be seen both to subtend and then create the primordial conditions for reflective knowledge itself.[11]

This latter becomes clear when we see that the imitative quality of desire links contemporary humanity, born into sophisticated language worlds, to hypothetical very early hominids, characterized by inchoate or nonexistent symbol systems. Among these mimesis can be understood to have exacerbated appropriative tendencies in the group, step by step as mimetic potential increased with the increasing size of the hominid brain. We can easily grasp the huge potential for conflict in hominid groups when a spiraling ability to imitate appropriative actions of others outstrips instinctual dominance patterns and group hierarchy. Girard thus moves to a hypothesis of endemic crisis among our first ancestors precipitated by conflict over the possession of food, mates, territory, objects of any sort. However, this in turn is resolved by the "miracle" of the surrogate or emissary victim, when one individual is made to bear, and discharge, all the force of the collective crisis of violence. These resolutions, experienced as "the sacred," are primary moments of culture formation, subsequently preserved and elaborated in sacrificial ritual. The potential for conflict is unchanged in modern humanity, and the "sacred" quality of violence is even now not hard to discern in much of given culture, which is always at root a tool for controlling and canalizing this violence. Nevertheless, one thing is certainly different: another name Girard uses for the surrogate

---

10. Jacques Lacan, *Ecrits: A Selection*, trans. Alan Sheridan (New York: Norton, 1977), 1–2, 106, 197–98.

11. Three key works in which these ideas are developed are René Girard, *Deceit, Desire and the Novel, Self and Other in Literary Structure*, trans. Yvonne Freccero (Baltimore and London: Johns Hopkins University Press, 1966); *Violence and the Sacred*, trans. Patrick Gregory (Baltimore and London: Johns Hopkins University Press, 1977; paperback 1979); and René Girard, with Jean-Michel Oughourlian and Guy Lefort, *Things Hidden since the Foundation of the World*, trans. Stephen Bann and Michael Metteer (Stanford, Calif.: Stanford University Press, 1987), hereafter *Things Hidden*.

victim is the *scapegoat,* and it is at once synonymous with a certain contemporary vindication of the human object of collective violence. The
cultural force that has uniquely sided with the victim, helping to publish
this vindication and thereby demythologize the sacred, is the biblical narrative, the Hebrew and Christian Scriptures. But it is also immediately evident that the actual record of historical Christianity is no exception in
terms of the making of victims, anything but! The purpose of this book is
to recruit mimetic anthropology also to the cause of understanding
Christian violence, particularly in reference to atonement doctrine and its
validation of sacred violence by framing of the cross within its categories.

This summary description now begins to point up key concerns that
are methodological in character. Girard clearly breaks from the
Cartesian, and behind that Platonic, assumption of a mysterious "heavenly origin" of ideas and meaning. He links consciousness substantively
to the material universe and its processes, including cultural processes
that "spill over" from biogenetic developments. This continuity is a primary tone in the discipline of understanding I adopt. Mimetic anthropology talks of a consistent material and cultural genesis of the human kind,
of its typical religious and cultural structures, and then of the fragile constitution of these structures, of their aboriginal, uneasy collusion with violence. Now, it is not too hard to identify here a type of biblical pattern:
namely, the production of humanity in continuity with the material
order, their own generation of language and meaning, a primordial fall,
and a subsequent dispensation somehow both enshrining and ordering
that fall. The pattern becomes manifest, and indeed more than a mere
pattern, when Girard arrives explicitly at the biblical narrative as thematic
disclosure of the victim. The contention I wish to make is that in the
Girardian pattern we are in fact dealing with a biblical typology in a technical sense—*a biblical typology of human violence.* But this typology is not
simply the repetition of internal motifs throughout the biblical narrative. It
simultaneously bears reference to an external, rational frame, to what in
fact we have just seen as a free-standing progression of ideas independent
of the Bible. A full account of the status of mimetic anthropology as discourse will emerge in the fourth chapter, but at once it can be said that the
analytic of mimetic desire and violence may be read either constitutively in
the biblical narrative from Cain and Abel onwards, or as squarely based in
an intellectual history of its own.

The double nature of the discourse must pose a particular problem as
to where exactly anyone using it takes their stand, and an important critique of Girard is that he himself does not distinguish these discourses
but in fact deliberately seeks to hold a leg in both camps, or even conflate
the two completely, via a higher claim arising from the origin of the bib-

lical pattern.[12] On the one hand, Girard protests that his thought should be evaluated on criteria drawn from scientific methodology, in particular that of scientific hypothesis.[13] He is adamant that there is a true rational basis to his thought, which in his most revealing statements he compares with Thomistic philosophy.[14] Simultaneously, however, he says that the rationality at the heart of his own work is one provided dynamically and uniquely by the Scriptures, what he calls the "intelligence" in the text of the Gospels, or an original "evangelical anthropology."[15] The question then is pressing: how can this revelatory anthropology be truly comparable to Thomistic philosophy, as well as other forms of Christian theology, which derive their form from a Greek tradition that stands fully outside of the biblical scriptures? *Fides quaerens intellectum* uses dialectical methods and concepts deeply embedded in Greek thought. Its inheritance is manifestly at work in Girard's own writing; but when he claims that the final source of mimetic anthropology is the biblical narrative, especially the Gospels, then surely he is dealing with an altogether different form of reason or, shall we say, *logos*, from anything in Greek philosophy. In fact what Girard is talking about is a rationality generated by the

---

12. "[T]he end of philosophy brings with it a new possibility of scientific thinking within the human domain; at the same time, however strange this may seem, it brings with it a return to religious faith. The Christian text returns in a completely new light—not at all buttressed by some existing science that would be exterior to it, but as identical with the knowledge of man that is surfacing in the world today. . . . There is no contradiction in (1) offering the scapegoat hypothesis as a scientific hypothesis and (2) stating simultaneously that this hypothesis has come to the fore in the course of a history governed by the Christian text in which the hypothesis figures in its original formulation . . . . (*Things Hidden*, 438–39).

13. Ibid., 438–39. See also *Diacritics*, March 1978, "Interview with René Girard," 42–44: "When the failure of all dogmatic methodologies is fully acknowledged, the scientific threshold is close. . . . This is the threshold of hypothetical knowledge."

14. "It is not me, but the Gospels that read myths starting from the scapegoat. The Gospels are inspired by an intelligence that is not that of the disciples, and that I clearly see to be beyond anything, you, me, all of us, could conceive of without them: a reason so superior to ours that after two thousand years we are discovering new things from it. We're dealing with a process that exceeds us since we have not been able to grasp it by ourselves; yet all the same we are capable of assimilating it, or we will be soon. It is therefore perfectly rational but with a higher reason than ours. In my eyes we're dealing with a new example of a very great traditional idea: reason and faith that undergird each other mutually. *Fides quaerens intellectum* and vice versa.

"This is a Thomistic type of reasoning, I believe, but applied in an area, anthropology, which at the time of Saint Thomas did not exist in the sense it has in the modern world. And therefore it is once more a question of the Light that is simultaneously that which must be seen and that which permits us to see, *Deum de Deo, Lumen de Lumine*" (from René Girard, *Quand ces choses commenceront. . . Entretiens avec Michel Treguer* [Paris: Arléa, 1994], 146–47; my translation). We need to pay attention to the *vice versa* in the above quotation and what it seems to imply—the sense of an interchangeability of reason and faith.

15. See footnote above, and ibid., 141. Also René Girard, *The Scapegoat* (Baltimore: Johns Hopkins University Press, 1986), 162–64.

Bible itself, which is its own authentication, precisely because we could not have reached it by ourselves. Therefore, it might well be said that Girard is invoking a new, biblical rationality or science, which is not precisely the same as faith, but which appears very much to tend toward the same results as faith; as Girard indeed suggests, an *intellectus quaerens fidem*. That is why Girard talks of this rational "biblical anthropology" as being able to rehabilitate orthodox Christian theology.[16]

My approach here seeks to escape from possible biblical rationalism, with its tone of exaggerated apologetic. At its worst it would create a monstrous hybrid of reason and faith. The anthropology of the victim might be understood as bringing every intellect to submission, without invoking the profound and ultimately "undecidable" conversion of heart that presumably is the traditional sense of the dynamic of the cross, and one in no way necessarily dependent on a historical-cultural disclosure of the victim. The dynamics of conversion are in fact another area in which I depart significantly from Girard, and for ultimately the same reasons. I will refer to this also in a moment, but first I wish to reinforce the statement of a conscious biblical heremeneutic adopted here. I wish to read mimetic anthropology predominantly within a biblical narratological and rhetorical continuum. If a certain independent rational argument supports or illuminates it, or even provides key structural features of its hermeneutic, then well and good; but this can never be to equate the biblical pathway with rationality or science as such.

What results from this is a fairly sophisticated methodology that needs to be attended to carefully at each turn. There are in effect two separate discourses that tend to overlap but nevertheless should be kept separate and, despite parallels of theme and content, moving from one to the other must always be understood as a leap. Thus the frame of mimetic anthropology rationally understood may help to illuminate biblical anthropology embraced as a religious rhetoric. Reciprocally, the biblical text preserved by a religious community may very well be understood to have influenced the courses of Western history, including intellectual, but without implying any necessary acceptance of the faith of that community. The latter, as I present it, arises in an abyss without foundations, discovered absolutely in the event of the cross. Thus, from the core vision of my argument the idea of a rational necessity to the Christian message of redemption is impossible, even as I also make use of several frames of rationality, including philosophy, to illustrate precisely this persuasion. The drama of these tensions will perhaps be clearest in the sixth chapter

---

16. See René Girard, "A Conversation with René Girard," *The Girard Reader*, ed. James G. Williams (New York: Crossroad Publishing, 1996), 288.

when I engage in conversation with some aspects of the philosophy of deconstruction. On the one hand, the biblical narrative may be seen to drive reason into its own abyss. On the other, reason itself, out of the whole philosophical tradition in the West, is well aware of the abyss, and so needs to be recognized and dialogued with on its own terms, if only then, in a self-consistent move of faith, one may be moved to meet Christ in the very place of the abyss.

This may occur because a positive, redemptive meaning of the cross is articulated by the Crucified's endless response of love in the foundationless depths of human life infected with violence. The experience of conversion is proportionately the alteration effected by meeting this response in a personal depth that is stripped of all foundations. I extend the scope of mimetic anthropology to provide a new account of atonement in this sense. Through a radicalization of the mimetic model, a picture of the human "self" and its relationality emerges that is open, always "alternative," and so potentially transformative. I want to advance the possibility of mimetic transformation in this sense, based in the figure of the Christ and the moment of the cross. The proclamation of the bottomless response of Jesus in the human abyss breaks the chains of violence even exactly as it plunges humanity into the possibility of a new creation without foundations.

The redemptive act of Christ is approached from the standpoint of biblical anthropology, rather than from any dogmatic position. In other words, it takes the biblical narrative from a concrete human perspective, but without reducing it purely or necessarily to that perspective. This is where the separation and signaling of the discourses is even more important. To talk of the anthropological dimensions of conversion may seem to move in the direction of a rationalization or science of faith; however, the description in this mode still essentially takes place within the overall tradition of the biblical story and its self-consistent status as divine revelation. In contrast, because Girard makes rational and scriptural processes inseparable, when it comes to conversion his remarks tend to suggest an external conformity or a formal rational awakening, albeit at a deep level, more than a radical human transformation at the foot of the cross. He calls attention to the "intelligence" of the text of the Gospel, but this indeed remains a kind of intelligence almost in the sense of information. The scandal of the cross is seen continually in the key of demystification rather than a challenge to a foundationless abyss of love. Instead, in chapter five, I attempt a hermeneutic of the historical protagonist of the Gospels that represents this dimension as much as possible, while it seeks to set free New Testament interpretation from the accumulated baggage of "sacrificial" atonement doctrine. I believe that it is the abyssal response of the Crucified that is primary to any intelligence or demythologization read later in the Gospels. The disclosure of the sacred in textual terms is always secondary and depends ultimately on the event of the cross to break the hold that violence has on the human mind, even though it is the text itself that mediates the process.

The preference for rational disclosure over transformation is also evident in Girard's treatment of the history of Christianity. At one point in his writing he explicitly concludes that the "sacrificial concept of divinity must 'die', and with it *the whole apparatus of historical Christianity*."[17] However, he has never expanded on such ideas, but rather exercised himself to take the part of the Christian tradition in the face of "modernist" critiques against it. This suggests a kind of ecclesiastical privilege that makes an exception, from the destabilizing effects of the Gospel narrative, for the very institutions that claim most closely to represent it.[18]

In conclusion, therefore, I may characterize Girard perhaps as a "biblical rationalist" for whom the rational truth of Christianity is vindicated and repristinated by mimetic anthropology. As such he fails to see through the radical consequences of his own thought, what might be termed the deconstructive potential of the cross, both in respect of inherited Christian traditions that petrify the Gospels themselves within a sacred system and, more essentially, in respect of the profoundly challenging, humanly re-creative effect of the Crucified. In short, while the project engaged here owes an irreplaceable debt to Girardian analytic, it differs from his thought on methodological, psychological, and theological grounds. It is true perhaps to say that my work sets biblical mimetic anthropology in motion again, progressively redrawing the map created by the first thinker in the field, and turning it so that its provocative and indeed revolutionary effect may be felt in the very stronghold from which it emerges.

A central aspect of biblical anthropology is the tradition of *stories* that the Bible represents, stories that are engrained in Western culture and form part of its symbolic world. That is why there is a certain affinity between the thought developed here and theories of narrative theology, and this discussion is engaged in chapter four. However, we can at once recognize that the irreducible focus of biblical mimetic anthropology is the reality of suffering, of murder, the brute fact of the victim in human culture. The claim of biblical rhetoric is to identify and speak through and

---

17. *Things Hidden*, 235–36 (my italics).
18. For a forthright defense of traditional Christianity against the possibility of "modernist faith," see René Girard, *Quand ces chose commenceront...Entretiens avec Michel Treguer*, 113–15, 147–51. As far as I can tell Girard has never applied such subversive statements as the following directly to inherited Christian institutions: "In the long run, it [the Gospel narrative of the Passion] is quite capable of undermining and overturning the whole cultural order and supplying the secret motive force of all subsequent history" (*Things Hidden*, 209).

on behalf of this concrete figure, and this breaks the bounds of a purely regulative theology of narrative. That is why Kierkegaard's concept or category of *repetition* becomes central to reflection at that point, providing a means of talking about life moments whose experience completely exceeds a locked narrative system or sequence. In this context the theme of compassion begins to take on its full resonance; it is the assumption by Christ of the situation of the victim, which becomes both a matter of disclosure and bottomless gift, the preparedness of one to hand himself over for and as the other at the deepest point of individual abjection. This abyssal act itself welcomes the other into an alternative, life-giving mode of being "self," producing a repetition of the same that is constitutively new. Thus, mimesis becomes truly alternative, above all to the conflictual version that is seen to structure the regnant accounts of atonement throughout the Western Christian tradition. In the fourth chapter this other mimesis is illustrated by means of exemplary accounts from literature. Such an approach certainly relates to the nonfoundationalism of narrative theologies, but its final source is an existential endlessness of compassion rather than the immanent endlessness of a narrative world.

One of the objections to "moral imitation" as a basis for atonement is that it offers no necessary purchase on the world; it refers to no ontological change brought by Christ that achieves its goal regardless of human response.[19] However, in a postmodern world the lack of necessity would seem to be a condition of human existence itself. Moreover, if the subversion of cultural order, including the securities of metaphysics, is a product of "deconstruction" brought by disclosure of the victim, then presumably the non-necessary is precisely a circumstance the Christian message has helped in bringing about.[20] More important still, the work of *grace*, of an utterly free gift from God, would seem in itself to imply the

---

19. For example, Luther argued against the sophists who "segregate Christ from sins and sinners and set him forth to us as an example to be imitated. . . . In this way they make Christ not only useless to us but also a judge and a tyrant who is angry because of our sins and who damns sinners. . . . Whatever sins I, you, and all of us have committed or may commit in the future, they are as much Christ's own as if he had committed them. In short, our sin must be Christ's own sin or we shall perish eternally" (quoted by Gorringe, *God's Just Vengeance*, 133, from Exposition of Galatians 3.13, 1535 commentary, *Weimar Ausgabe*, XL).

20. Cf. Mark C. Taylor's *Erring, A Postmodern A/theology* (Chicago and London: University of Chicago, 1984), for a synoptic statement of deconstructive philosophy as fatal to metaphysics. For "deconstruction" brought by disclosure of the victim, see Girard: "The discovery of the scapegoat as the mechanism of symbolic thought, human thought itself, justifies a deconstructive discourse and at the same time completes it. It can also explain the characteristic aspects of this contemporary discourse. Because much of contemporary thought is still without an anthropological basis, it remains given to verbal acrobatics that will ultimately prove to be sterile. . . . If there is really 'something' to Derrida, it is because there is something beyond: precisely a deconstruction that reaches the mechanisms of the sacred and no longer hesitates to come to terms with the surrogate victim" (*Things Hidden*, 64).

non-necessary. If something is truly given freely, unconditionally, or as suggested here, abyssally, then a genuine contingency must be assumed. It may or may not be accepted. It must be possible to refuse an offer of love if it really is love. Or, to state the same thing epistemologically, grace is "undecidable"; there is no way of ever knowing in advance whether it will or will not attain its end. An abyssal account of atonement of itself would seem to demand and in fact celebrate its lack of necessary foundations. The alternative mimesis of the Crucified may be seen to be always bottomless, an offer of love without end, either as ground or limit.

All in all I wish to suggest a radical theology by continuing to work out the anthropological implications of the cross, something that coheres with "the profound this-worldliness of Christianity" as remarked by Dietrich Bonhoeffer.[21] The way forward, as I see it, is via a progressively deeper anthropologization of Christian soteriology. This is based in the redemptive contingency of the message of the cross, attempting to avoid the "sacred" content, in both senses, of ontological and systematic approaches, while holding on to the possibility of "endless" repetitions of its saving message. The attempt is to produce a faithful thought of biblical mimetic anthropology, writing a progressively more consistent grammar of the cross. Once the cross is engaged at the level of humanity, the level of the victim *and* the level of compassion, it does not seem justifiable to stop at a purely illuminative disclosure of violence. Its other, deeper dimension is brought to the table, the disturbing, abyssal vision of the earthly space transformed in peace.

---

21. In a letter from Tegel prison, 21 July 1944, in Eberhard Bethge, ed., *Dietrich Bonhoeffer: Letters and Papers from Prison* (New York: Collier Books, 1972), 369.

Chapter One

THE ABYSS THAT IS NOT YET LOVE

The scene is Thompson's Children's Home in the Episcopal Diocese of North Carolina. Robyn was there with the kids to celebrate their Children's Sabbath. She had the opportunity to sit for dinner with some of the boys, between ages of seven and eleven. Usual dinner conversation, favorite games, favorite subjects in school, favorite books, favorite food, spaghetti of course! While they were talking Cameron, who sat on her right, took a copy of the New Testament out of his pocket and said, "That is my favorite book." Then he looked up at Robyn and asked, "Do you know why Christ died?"

After a quiet pause, she responded, "Cameron, why did Christ die?" He said, "Because no one else but God's Son could die for all the meanness, all the anger, all the hatred in the world." Robyn later learned that Cameron had no one. Neither mother or father, nor aunts or uncles, not even his grandparents, could or would care for him. Cameron's story also included the facts that he had been asked to leave ten public schools and he was only seven years old.

From the Rev. Robyn Szoke,
Episcopal Office of Children's Ministries,
New York, N. Y.

What is the meaning of the cross? What is the nucleus of human and divine affairs represented there, out of which Christianity has always made the astonishing statement "Christ died for us." Traditional answers deeply formative for Western culture—and formed themselves out of raw material that lie culturally prior to the Gospels—will be the subject of critique in the next chapter. Here let me immediately propose a nontraditional answer. My basis for this is twofold. First, theological tradition on this question is decisively not a matter of dogma, but rather a pith of cultural themes that crystallize around the cross and become, apparently, second nature to it. And, second, we are currently in a very nontraditional situation.

A way to express this contemporary situation, and therewith the possibility of a new, radical understanding of the cross, is via a metaphor, a term, a reference that seems at first sight negative, but will over the course of this work prove itself deeply positive. It is that of *the abyss*. Our modern or postmodern situation can justly be construed in and by the image of the abyss. The gospel event of the cross may be understood to take place in the human abyss—the depth of injustice, meaninglessness and horror it can sink to—-indeed, to reveal it to humanity. And at the same moment a redemption by the cross may be glimpsed to arise in the abyss, to change it from within into a place of radically new possibility, to effect an absolute novelty of human selfhood. The final and true referent of this term, its resting place, therefore, is not a darkness, a chasm, a pit in the heart or the world. On the contrary, it is the active moment itself of the gospel, a moment, until then unimaginable, of life, of hope. It is the act or moment of *abyssal compassion*, much more a verb than a noun, in the sense of moment as movement. This is the real starting point of these reflections, and without it the concept of the abyss is of course intolerable.

A GEOMETRY OF THE ABYSS

Let me propose a kind of geometry of our contemporary abyss, composed of four cardinal points or headings. These headings are chosen with reason, and although I do not think it is impossible to describe things in any other way, I do believe they gather together most of what is urgently at issue in our contemporary Western world. They are *abandonment, violence, philosophical postmodernism*, and *the gospel account of Jesus itself*. This chapter will consist of a synoptic description of these points, followed by a theoretical background that then serves to bring them to a historical-cultural depth of remarkable force. Even as this picture takes shape the positive, creative role of the cross as a work of the abyss can begin to emerge. Here, then, is an understanding of atonement, of the work of salvation, that responds intimately to the crisis of the world and of the time in which we live.

Abandonment resonates with the experience of being left behind, of calling out and not being heard, of no longer playing a significant role in life socially, economically, or emotionally. It is that of a child who feels that her parents no longer hold her as visible and valuable. Or of a worker with no work, or whose job is oppressive and for whom there is no way out. Of a socially excluded group whose very skin is sick with exclusion and yet a terrible desire to restore itself in the face of the excluders. Of a partner whose beloved no longer accepts the offer of love, or for whom the emotion of love collapses, it seems, from within. Of the countless poor of the earth, the Third World or the South, whose faces of dereliction are paraded daily on our TV screens, but whose structural relationship with Western wealth and well-being is never a cause for serious reflection. And all this takes place within a world that presses ahead with irresistible force, displaying overwhelming technical and material mastery, as it releases a Babel of information and a jackpot of commodities, continually erasing reflection and memory, merging the cry of abandonment seamlessly with the voice-over of the car salesman.

Within the context of Western culture it is the experience documented by Douglas Coupland, the prophet of end-of-twentieth-century young adulthood, Generation X. Coupland inhabits a landscape of fractured and fragmented relationships, within a larger physical landscape that once had religious meaning but now seems to be empty. The evacuation of God from the world has of course being going on much longer at the level of philosophical culture, but one of the things Coupland registers is the way the material culture effectively deputizes for any sense of transcendent presence in the cosmos, and helps to establish its absence. Matthew Arnold's "sea of faith" become a "long, withdrawing roar" has now been substituted by a storm of commodities, of electronic entertainment, of virtual communication. As the narrator of *Life After God* reports, the cascade of stations picked up by the car radio seek button surges with "those fragments of cultural memory and information that compose the invisible information structure I consider my real home—my virtual community."[1] The function of computers and the World Wide Web confirms again and deepens both the torrent of information and the disintegration of more traditional human memory. Fragments of memory are also in typical disjunctive continuity with fast food, fast cars, money, mobility. Fast military jets, each of which may carry the end of the world, puncture the sky with childhood fears jarred into the moment. War as the abolition of life itself forms an antistructure beneath the world. Solitude fills the heart.

There is no escaping a terminal loneliness at the bottom of the culture, the enigma of human time that seeks the wholeness of intimacy and yet is threatened by catastrophic interruption at every moment. It is not simply the physical fact of the bomb. Or the social fact of marriage relationships

---

1. Douglas Coupland, *Life After God* (New York, London: Pocket Books, 1994), 168–69. Also see *Microserfs* (New York: Regan Books, 1995), and *Generation X, Tales For An Accelerated Culture* (New York: St. Martin's Press, 1991).

ending so frequently in divorce. Or then the threat of AIDS transforming sexual relations into a worldwide vehicle for fatal illness. It is the very possibility of relationship itself that for Coupland is in doubt. People come, people go. Couples "fall" out of love. They simply wake up and no longer love. Siblings disappear without a trace. Children are spread out over households divided sometimes by huge distances. And the past when there seemed to be love remains in memory as a ghost of itself. Only the car radio provides a constant; and that is also filled, alongside everything else, with fervent evangelism. It is the confident gospel of "Jesus saves" that confronts the culture with a literal (and here we should really read authoritarian) version of Scripture and takes its place without complication next to adverts for hair products, cars, and Jacuzzis. As the bumper sticker says, "Got Jesus?" But Coupland's narrative is also affected by the sincere change that seems to have been worked in lives touched in this way. He poignantly asks himself, "What was it that these radio people were seeing in the face of Jesus?"[2]

We might therefore at once intuit that the figure of Jesus does in fact coexist with the abyss of human abandonment—at least as a question, and with that a possibility. But, before we move ahead too quickly, it is essential to underline that as far as the heading itself of abandonment is concerned, it is not to be interpreted morally, as if a generation, or any alienated individual, somehow culpably missed out on a vital element in becoming a person. What I have described is an objective condition of cultural history, one of profound human displacement or loss, something with analogies in any culture or period of history, including the time and place in which Jesus lived. What is special here is the way in which an intensely developed material culture both produces a mode of being in the world that appears to soak up the need for transcendence in the human soul, and simultaneously plunges the individual into an experience of utter helplessness, tantamount to not being at all. If the individual for one reason or another falls below the continuum of fragments, if he or she fails to make the next connection, the next deal, to inhabit the next virtual structure of meaning, then that person is in the abyss, without recourse. The abyss of nonrelationship lies just below the surface of contemporary Western culture.

> When I was younger I used to worry so much about being alone—of being unlovable or incapable of love. As the years went on, my worries changed. I worried that I had become incapable of having a relationship, of offering intimacy. I felt as though the

---

2. Ibid., 184.

world lived inside a warm house at night and I was outside, and I couldn't be seen—because I was out there in the night. But now I am inside the house and it feels just the same.[3]

Violence is the second heading in order. Here introductory comment is hardly necessary, for violence erupts with visceral force that does not so much stake out conceptual explanation in advance but seeks it in the shock of aftermath. This is particularly true of the exponential violence of the twentieth century, with its horrors that seem to exceed the frame of any possible rationality: the gulag, the Nazi holocaust, Hiroshima, and then, in its dying years, Bosnia and Rwanda. These names are invoked not at all for shock value, as if their mind-numbing power would precipitate of itself an apprehension of the abyss. On the contrary, they do indeed fit, in their very excessiveness, a theoretical background shortly to be outlined. To headline them here is to anticipate that understanding: it is to say that incommensurable violence is very much a human capacity, and the story of Western culture seems to have a terrible capacity to spark it into flame.

We can specify two instances that straddle a spectrum of Western experience. In 1994, close to one million people were killed in a planned and systematic genocide in the Central African country of Rwanda. How did this carnage occur when the world declared after World War II that it would never again allow such things to happen? And how did it take place in a country that since the early part of the century had been in the hands of Christian missionaries and educators, the White Fathers, under the aegis of Belgian colonial authorities? Without going into an extended account it seems evident, as Amnesty International claims, that the Belgian system of colonial rule sowed the seeds of Rwanda's future discontent.[4] Yet apart from divisions between Tutsis and Hutus entrenched and exacerbated by colonial adminstration, there is the sheer scale of the killings, involving careful planning, systematic propaganda, and organization and efficiency of execution, that somehow matched on the continent of Africa patterns set in Europe. How much of this was learnt, imitated? How much was the spontaneous result of hatred built up over the course of the century that exploded in such a "modern" way simply because the tools were at hand? And is there a real difference, at root, between sequential and parallel? Modern conditions that permit such

---

3. Ibid., 142.
4. *Forsaken Cities,* Amnesty International Documentary Video on Genocide in Rwanda, (Amnesty International USA, 1997). Also, Alain Destexhe, Alison Marschner (trans.), and William Shawcross, *Rwanda and Genocide in the 20th Century* (New York: New York University Press, 1996).

enormities are a product of modernity, a Western cultural invention, and it is this very modernity, with its simultaneous expertise and loss of inherited boundaries, that is very much the environment of the abyss. Western political powers will always feel obliged to prevent this horror they know intimately from within, but even given the integrity and energy to do so, loss of attention is surely the pendulum swing of eternal vigilance. Perhaps the truly terrifying thing about Rwanda is that it suggests the unthinkable has become possible, again and again. . . .

The other instance is the events of Columbine, and the sequence of high school massacres in the United States over the last decade, for which they provide the horrifying emblem. In less than fifteen minutes on a sunny spring day in April 1999, two student gunmen killed thirteen and wounded twenty-one in a suburban high school in Jefferson County, Colorado, before they turned the guns on themselves—the most devastating school shooting in U.S. history. How could such things happen in the heartland of the most privileged country in the world, and among children who—typically in these instances—are not divided by race or class, and certainly not by inherited colonial grudges? Popular-media reporting in the U.S. frequently asks this helpless question as the terminus of comment. The formally excessive nature of the events makes it inadequate simply to point to civilian access to arms, disruption in the family, or violence in the media, although doubtless these are issues that play somehow into the larger question. Rather, these events stand as a surd in the cultural scene, a mark beyond which one cannot go, where explanation lapses into inarticulacy. The real point of significance *is* the inarticulacy and helplessness: that, parallel to the incommensurability of Rwanda, there is a home-grown incommensurability, smaller in scale but equal (and perhaps more than equal) in excess over cause. Are we not faced here with the possibility that violence is itself significant, not that it requires significance to be given it? That at certain points where abandonment, in one form or another, feels that it has lost all possibility of speech, of ordered social communication, then violence becomes a terrible new speech, a new foundation of meaning? Is there not the awful possibility that even at the expense of countless victims, or rather precisely because of these come-what-may victims—and including therein the loss of your own life—it is "worth it" in order to give birth to a new universe, *your* universe. Children and young people do not really need this to be taught them. Pushed to the edge of human reality by the processes of Western abandonment, they somehow "know" that transcendent violence is the only solution. Is this not a glimpse of the abyss?

A third heading or dynamic point is *philosophical postmodernism*, and its strategy known as "deconstruction." A representative picture of what this implies is given by Mark C. Taylor. He summarizes the condition of philosophy arrived at in the contemporary era as "the death of God," "the disappearance of the self," "the end of history," and "the closure of the book."[5] Probably an even more provocative way of stating this situation comes from the paladin of deconstruction, Jacques Derrida. It is the non-definable concept of "dissemination": this metaphor of the working of a text, in itself a nonreference, illustrates both the way meaning is spread through a text as a kind of violent insemination of itself (with the sexual overtone intended), and simultaneously rendered void of its power by the very opening up of the word—dis-semination—to its (patriarchal) "sem-inal-semantic" content. The semen of meaning can never be recovered in a cup of truth, in some fixed holding of the substance of life. Its ejacula-tion is always sterile, always self-inseminating, disappearing with only the trace of its empty movement, never fertilizing a beginning or an end. Deconstruction describes and is itself "an economy of war" because it reveals the textual violence of meaning as such.[6] This comprehensive loss of all fixed values and references parallels at the level of formal academic reflection the experience of abandonment lurking beneath the destruc-turing of popular Western culture. This is one reason, I think, why decon-struction has taken academia in the United States by storm. It provides the ideological complement for the infinity of difference and play pro-duced by systemic consumerism, for the cascade of fragments that con-stitutes its daily life. It bestows intellectual validation on the riotous fugue of commodity culture.

Nevertheless, it is also clearly the case that philosophical postmod-ernism follows a strict intellectual pathway through Kant, Kierkegaard, Nietzsche, and Heidegger (to choose a recognizable route while not excluding other roads too). This contemporary Western world of thought stands in its own right as a marker of the abyss. It is surely the case that the classical philosophical tradition never before demonstrated such zeal to proclaim undecidability. Deconstruction is not simply world-weary skep-ticism; it is a vigorous program of exposing the conceptual violence of any fixed essence of meaning, and therefore takes its place as a contemporary dynamic funneling our vision toward something we would rather not entertain: the impossibility of any secure reflective existence. Derrida him-self struggles with the ethical consequences of this dynamic, and in the sixth chapter I will look at the significance for theology of his later attempts to retie the knot once it has been unraveled. But here, at this

---

5. Taylor, *Erring, A Postmodern A/theology*, 19–93.
6. Jacques Derrida, *Dissemination*, translated, with introduction and additional notes by Barbara Johnson (Chicago: University of Chicago Press, 1981), 5, 44–45.

moment, the thought world signaled serves once again to construct a sense of existence where the heavens indeed have fallen, where humanity looks to itself and asks in apprehension, "To what are we headed?"

The fourth and final dynamic point continues the direction of fall and yet simultaneously introduces an entirely unexpected element. It is the gospel itself and the figure of Jesus emerging from the gospel as a matter of history. The gospel texts and proclamation are structured intimately as announcement of a historical figure. The Christian creeds echo this with the reiteration "he suffered under Pontius Pilate." The historical specificity contained in this phrase returns us inexorably, as a matter of what the text proclaims, to a concrete person. That is why Coupland can ask in all directness what the radio people see in the face of Jesus, rather than what they see in the idea of Jesus. It is at this point that the classification of the abyss as I have presented it—all its relentless horror and sense of aporia, of no exit—turns into something new, something that could not have been anticipated. It becomes a historical moment, absolutely of abandonment, extreme violence, and the falling of the heavens ("My God, why have you forsaken me?"), yet also, at the same time, and by virtue of these very characteristics, one of possibility, of another kind of life. The existential movement that transforms one into the other is compassion, but not in any sentimental or secondary sense. It is abyssal compassion, one that shares the full dynamic horror of the abyss and then continues the fall in forgiveness and love. This is nothing more than the force of the gospel account, but turned specifically and rigorously toward the human experience of abandonment and violence.

What I would like to press here, and throughout the book, is the strict particularity and contingency of this gospel event. Essentially Christianity as a message erupts in and as the particular, rather than the eternal or metaphysical somehow grafted into history. If not, the meaning of *news*, as in the Good News, is evacuated into philosophy (ontotheology), and the apostles should have been academics strolling in the *stoa*, not road-weary messengers driven to the ends of the earth. The character of that Gospel particular depends on and is vindicated by the contingency of compassion. If there was anything necessary in the abyssal response of the Crucified it at once loses its character as compassion. It is no longer suffering in and with the abyss, but becomes something else, something substantial, a secret essence injected into the human continuum—anything but compassion. Compassion is formally given over to the moment of suffering, to foundationless, free giving and forgiveness. Otherwise it is always condescension, a hand proffered from on high, and in this case a Gnostic vision of Christ. On the contrary, the gospel compassion of the abyss is all contingency. . . and yet it occurs! This is its immense novelty: the eruption of a moment of love from the deepest, darkest place of human abandonment, including the ultimate point of death itself that somehow does not/cannot extinguish it. It is that moment assimilated profoundly or transformatively to the consciousness of the disciples that gives rise to the impetuous character of news in the first experience of early Christianity.

This does not mean that certain images and language in the New Testament do not lend themselves at a second stage of reflection to an essentialized or metaphysical understanding, only that the contingency of the cross is the primordial truth of this development. The abyssal compassion of the Crucified so interrupted human affairs in all their relentless violence that it was inevitable that this interpretation be made. Only God could have done this! And inevitably this becomes the God of philosophy, of metaphysics, of being and its ideal rationality. But we must also remember that it was the God of Abraham, Moses, Isaiah, deeply meditated and mediated by Jesus, that produced this wonderful new contingency, and this is by no means the same thing. The revolutionary truth is that the gospel begins radically and properly in the particular and the contingent.

If there is validity in this position it means that Christianity is also always a memory of the contingent and the particular in its cultural history. The gospel has communicated this special memory when it has been read day by day, week by week in private or public, over two millennia. In its own way, therefore, and perhaps with an inner urgency that is much more culturally productive than metaphysical theology imagines, the gospel returns us to the particular, to human actuality, to the abyss of human life on earth. It is surely correct then to add the figure of Jesus to the structure of the abyss, not only in terms of compassion, but—precisely because of that impossible moment—in terms of an opening up of human life to its inner uncertainty, its lack of ultimate foundations. In which case the gospel anticipated deconstruction, and in a much more challenging (extratextual and nonviolent) form, by the length of its cultural history.

Nevertheless, the four headings need to be taken each in its own right and then together as integral markers of our contemporary abyssal experience. Their constellation can then produce perhaps a downward or inward movement, evoking a contemporary sense of the formless and dangerous underside of human existence, and at one and the same time a profundity of answering love drawing us deeper into itself, changing life and its possibilities out of recognition. This is the way I wish to present the meaning of Christ's death, as opposed to the dominant Western tradition. To allow Christ's death to be understood within this movement is clearly to reverse the direction in that tradition. It is not a matter of sacrifice to a

God above, as in the movement at the altar when a priest using sacred objects makes gestures of elevation that may always be interpreted in that manner. Nor is it a matter of some negotiation or exchange at a cosmic level where God is always the supreme and supernal judge. This vector leads to a reverse of what I attempt to present: the abyss becomes something in God's armory, or within God himself, divinized instead of disclosed. Thus, in his famous sermon, "Sinners in the Hands of an Angry God," Jonathan Edwards could depict humanity suspended like a spider over hell's fire. These dominant themes in Western imagination will be the subject of more detailed critique particularly in the next chapter, and chapter five on the New Testament. However, it is worthwhile to make at least one general comment on New Testament directions of up and down.

Christian Scripture is full of both motifs. The up normally follows the down, but a movement of Platonic otherworldly ascent has been the predominant mode of interpretation for this upward motion. It is more appropriate to read it, I believe, within the frame of the whole New Testament, which actually ends with a final downward movement, of the heavenly city to earth. And then more critically within the language of the cross itself. The Gospel of John explicitly makes the turn, wherein Christ is exalted in and on the cross (3.13–15). The movement of ascent should be understood as a metaphor for the profound reversal *within* the abyss of abandonment that is made by the cross, so that the very depths of human experience become the place of the eruption of the new. In this way to state an image of "going up" is simply to transform the meaning of the down. It is to posit at a formal level of religious imagery a reversal or change within the meaning or construction of humanity itself. It is what will be termed here an anthropology of redemption, in contrast to a nonhuman escapology with another "spiritual" world as its destination.

So the overall attempt underway in this geometry of four points is working toward an understanding of Christ's death that has always been there in the text of the Gospels, but is now increasingly provoked for us by the condition of the world itself. Because of the contemporary condition, this new understanding is perhaps for the first time theologically possible, certainly in any historically rooted and compelling way. The attempt advances forward, out of and by means of faith, toward a set of questions that are reflective of the world as it is, and thereby faith understands itself more profoundly and with renewed freshness and urgency. An approximation perhaps to this method is the praxis of Jesus himself in first-century Palestine. As the fifth chapter will indicate, the historical Jesus can be seen to move out of a committed reading of his own tradition into the specific conditions of the world in which he found himself, formulating in this very move the announcement, "The Kingdom of God is near." The

movement of rereading itself creates a lever of intervention interrupting
the times with a new, nonviolent beginning. But in both instances the
lever is essentially the cross plunged in the depth of the earth—Jesus ending with it, ourselves beginning.

ANTHROPOLOGY FROM BELOW

To the side of this descriptive and to some degree impressionistic account,
I want now to place a set of reflections that will give much greater theoretical depth and perspective on the phenomenon of the abyss and so
underpin the argument of this book. They constitute an anthropology, in
the sense of an evidenced hypothesis of the structure of human relations
and culture, and are the work of René Girard, a uniquely important
thinker of our times.[7] Girard stands fully in the postmodern environment,
and yet also within the biblical tradition, and bringing these two stand-
points into profound conversation, he provides a deeper, more critical
level in every sense to the headings outlined above. Girard takes "deconstruction" in a very different direction from the textual kind, although
there is a provocative convergence between his work and the subversion of
the text. Girard's form of deconstruction is ultimately far the most creative, pointing to culture and history as the arena of crisis, the space where
a new departure is vitally needed—and at a depth never truly plumbed
before. I will now introduce his thought, but do so at once with a theological caveat. What I have outlined so far and what I will continue to
develop throughout the book—the understanding of Christ's death as
abyssal compassion—is a radicalization of Girard's analysis as it bears reference to the meaning of Christ's death. I seek to push Girard's thought to
its logical limits, and then perhaps some way further still. Girardian
anthropology pivots centrally around the death of Christ—and here
Girard himself comes to astonishing conclusions about Western culture

---

7. René Girard's main writings referred to here are *Deceit, Desire and the Novel, Self and
Other in Literary Structure,* trans. Yvonne Freccero (Baltimore and London: Johns Hopkins
University Press, 1966), originally published in French as *Mensonge romantique et vérité
romanesque* (Paris: Grasset, 1961); *Violence and the Sacred,* trans. Patrick Gregory
(Baltimore and London: Johns Hopkins University Press, 1977; paperback, 1979), origi-
nally published as *La violence et le sacré* (Paris: Grasset, 1972); Réne Girard with Jean-
Michel Oughourlian and Guy Lefort, *Things Hidden since the Foundation of the World,*
trans. Stephen Bann and Michael Metteer (Stanford, Calif.: Stanford University Press,
1987), originally published as *Des choses cachées depuis la fondation du monde* (Paris:
Grasset, 1978); *"To Double Business Bound": Essays on Literature, Mimesis and Anthropology*
(Baltimore and London: Johns Hopkins University Press, 1978); *The Scapegoat,* trans.
Yvonne Frecerro (Baltimore: Johns Hopkins University Press, 1986), originally published
in French as *Le bouc émissaire* (Paris: Grasset, 1982); see also *The Girard Reader,* ed. James
G. Williams (New York: Crossroad Publishing Co., 1996).

and history in general. I seek to give that movement a further turn so that it applies more properly to the internal meaning or quality of that death, both in terms of a critical description of the theological tradition and then in the emergence of the new understanding of abyssal compassion. So, in a way, Girardian theory that is largely self-censoring as regards the theological tradition is now turned to apply in the area of its own presuppositions. The deconstructive force of Christ's death serves to deconstruct inherited meanings of that death, and itself posit a dramatically new one.

Girard's thought spans what might well be called a dark trinity in human behavior, that of desire, violence, and the function of scapegoats. It is useful to put it this way because all these terms are immediately recognizable, and together they may communicate already some sense of the workings of his thesis. But it is also necessary to be more precise; so I should at once point out that *desire* for Girard is defined as imitative or mimetic, and this qualification links it structurally to an exponential human possibility for violence. Desire and violence are therefore organically linked. Scapegoating then arises as a further structural moment that resolves the crisis the first two provoke, but still entirely within the scope of the dynamics they serve to generate. It is at this point that Girard proposes a new, interruptive element, a genuine *novum* that challenges the previous construct to its core. It is the biblical narrative, which more than any other text reveals the working of desire and murder in human culture. With the addition of the biblical narrative, and above all the Gospels, the full range of Girard's startling, interdisciplinary reflection is reached. Girard bridges gaps between a number of disciplines—between literature and anthropology and between ethnography, philosophy, and psychology—but his most provocative integration by far is that between this full range of secular thought and the scriptural traditions of the Jewish and Christian faiths. No thinker since Kierkegaard has carried through such a challenging fusion of dialectical thought and biblical Christianity; and Girard is if anything much more subversive because of the concrete historical and cultural application of his analytic. It is well worthwhile to lay out, with some attentiveness to detail, the workings of the hypotheses I have just outlined, but to do this always with a view to breaking open the parameters Girard sets, toward a radical rereading of Christ's redemptive death.

The Girardian thesis emerges self-consciously in the philosophical tradition, with a direct, if polemical, connection to the Plato of the *Republic* and in more recent terms to Hegel, Nietzsche, and Heidegger. There is not the space here to rehearse these roots and relationships, but it is important to signal that Girard's thought belongs in a central stream of Western philosophy, for two reasons. First, he draws from it the substantive role of desire, articulated forcefully of course by Hegel, and then via the more classical theme of mimesis (imitation) he demonstrates desire's structural connection to violence. His work may be read as a pressing of the philosophical tradition to something it would rather forget, its birth in an all-too-human kind of chaos, and from there a history of attempts to shore up the world in one way or another. The family connection to textual deconstruction should be evident, but on the Girardian side the implications are much more disturbing because they bear directly on human relationships rather than abstract questions of meaning.

This reflection leads to the second point of linkage with the philosophical tradition, and one that is deliberately controversial: Girard suggests that the pressure of biblical revelation is a crucial factor in the pathway of modern philosophical development, in the sense at least of a profound challenge. This intimate linkage between philosophical thought and biblical revelation is again something the former would rather forget, but from the side of revelation it has the effect of returning the biblical narrative to center stage as a powerful leaven in Western thought. The dialogue of biblical revelation with philosophy repeats, of course, movements in Christian thought at least from the second century onwards, but there is a highly significant shift of emphasis. This time it is the biblical patterns that progressively set the agenda. And above all it is the function of Christ's death as disclosive of human violence that produces this critical reversal. In this case it seems to me desperately urgent to seek to re-present that death in its transformative or redemptive significance.

Against this background I will now go through the main architecture of Girard's hypotheses, its triple stages, to focus the broader allusions I have made, but specifically to bring us to the constitutive figure of the human abyss they disclose. Even though I have just argued that his thought is to be located in the Western philosophical conversation, Girard in fact does not begin with general questions and propositions within the philosophical tradition. His point of departure is instead the concrete human phenomenon of imitation as observed by outstanding writers and novelists, like Cervantes, Stendhal, Flaubert, Proust, and Dostoyevsky. His first book, a critical interpretation of the work of these artists, was entitled in French, "Romantic lie and novelistic truth." The French title neatly expresses the argument that purely romantic works are based in a falsehood, while the achievement of the great novel is a contrary truth. What is the falsehood? It is "the lie of spontaneous desire," and its opposing truth is the demonstration of "triangular" desire.[8] This latter is the desire for an object that is formed or mediated by a third corner in the relationship: the

---

8. *Deceit, Desire and the Novel, Self and Other in Literary Structure*, 16.

ghostly function of the model whose own line of desire toward the object confers value on it for the subject. Such is the profound effect of this form of imitation that to give it due weight Girard returns to the classical name, *mimesis*. The fantastic nature of this mimetic desire is derived from the doubling and redoubling forces, traveling in the field between the subject and the mediator, below their common object. Romantic works depend intimately on this force, but they never actively reveal its functioning. The genuinely great works of literature are organized in view of just such a disclosure. The great novelists reveal the imitative nature of desire. They discover that desire is "according to the other." From this starting point, provoked by a very particular insight in the narrative world composed by these writers, Girard begins his odyssey into the origins of human culture.

He makes a primary distinction between two forms of mediation. Cervantes demonstrated in a classic way the function of a stabilized form of imitation, what Girard calls "external mediation." Don Quixote in all his madcap schemes never felt it necessary to outdo Amadis of Gaul, to become somehow more chivalrous, more noble than his model. Amadis was a star in the heavens, utterly unreachable in himself but a sure guide to action on a lesser plane. It is the progressive shift from this stable universe of imitation toward another "internal" and conflictual form of mediation that marks the pathway of discovery of the great novels. Here the mediator is not lost in some idealized universe of chivalry, rather the "glorious" individual is a concrete figure and actively desires the object on his or her own behalf. The subjects for their part refuse to admit the role of the mediator and yet at the same time identify more and more closely and desperately with their idol. By the simultaneous proximity and hiddenness of the mediation a qualitative rivalry is set up, producing the most exacerbated forms of the modern emotions: according to Stendhal, "envy, jealousy and impotent hatred." The significant characters here are persons in the grip of "metaphysical desire." They no longer seek the object of desire but the elusive substance of the mediator him- or herself. "The object is only a means of reaching the mediator. The desire is aimed at the mediator's being."[9] In the absence of a fixed universe of value, of an established "vertical transcendence," the subject must needs make gods out of other humans and seek, no longer even the pretext of the mediated object, but the metaphysical figments of desire itself.

A key factor is that "minimum difference" between rivals acts to produce maximum desire, and this occurs within highly rarified social groups, which seem constructed almost for the purpose of bringing about this exquisite combination. Girard's first intuition is related to conditions

9. Ibid., 53.

at the very apex of nineteenth-century "high society," primarily French and Russian, and described at the pens of exceptional novelists. However, by inspired extrapolation using a pattern of evidence from mythology, ethnology, and psychology, Girard carries his insight straight back to pre-history, to conflictual relations among hominid ancestors. In *Violence and the Sacred* he reaches this central axis of mimetic anthropology, the concept that original human development is based on mimetic desire, via primary events of terrible violence resolved in the very crisis by the emergence of religion or the sacred. The evolutionary faculty of imitation provides the concrete bridge from animal drives and restraints into the much vaguer, borderless, dangerous world of desire. The hominids' increased cerebral capacity to imitate automatically spills over into the imitation of behaviors and, crucially, imitation of acquisitive behavior. In this scenario enhanced imitation already implies a cutting loose from instinctual structure—a kind of excess of imitation that leaves the emerging human in a novel "emptiness" of desire, a lack that needs to be filled. It then fills itself, forms itself—knows *what* it desires—only in imitation of the acquisitive act of the other. At once then there is a convergence on the same object. The potential for "human," unrestrained violence is born, an escalation of mimesis bringing the possibility of war, all against all, among primal groups. In this potentially disastrous scenario it is a new imitation, the imitative convergence of all against a single victim, that brings peace and in one act establishes the heart of the sacred.

Substitution is the articulation of mimesis at this point. Mimetic chaos is translated by a very specific figure who is singled out by any arbitrary mark of difference or weakness, and has thrust upon him or her the character of doubling for the whole community in terms of its amassed and massive violence. This is the "surrogate victim," later termed the "scapegoat," who by the effects of a sudden, single collective mimesis by the group becomes the individualized recipient of what was before undifferentiated mayhem. Here it is *violence itself* that becomes the key signifier for mimetic desire, that itself awakens desire, and so almost immediately becomes a collective polarized violence. Violence itself provides its own "miraculous" solution in the shape of the group victim who always appears to be singly to blame for the violence inflicted. With this resolution there occurs the first truly "cultural" moment—the substitute who is guilty and yet brings peace provides the ground zero of meaning, of the sacred, the origin of the god, the emergence of religion that is itself the birth of humanity.

The ancient commonplace of sacrifice, so vastly diffused in history and culture, finds here its source and explanation. It is the gradually learnt repetition of the original crisis, enacting again and again the return to the ordering of the group through human or animal victims. At the same time it permits the progressive development of symbol systems and prohibitions, all posited on the signification of the moment of murder that fixes the attention of the group and simultaneously suggests boundaries of difference that should not be transgressed. Yet there is always the possibility of "sacrificial crisis," by reason of the inherent fragility of the substitutionary solution. The victim must seem both sufficiently alike to the group to figure as its surrogate, and yet sufficiently distant not to threaten a sudden reversal to "one of us," thereby undoing the carefully constructed fiction of an incarnation of violence other than from the group. It is the permanent possibility of the collapse of "difference"—either in this way, from within the sacred order, or because of contingent factors of social crisis like plague or famine—that produces an always present danger to human institutions, family, tribe, or polis. The key to this collapse lies not in any formally structured and broken negotiations between the group and its god, but in the uniquely ambiguous nature of human violence itself. Violence gives the impression of marking a definitive difference, and yet always threatens the erasure of all difference. And the root of this paradox lies in mimesis, which participates without remainder in each phase, and is able to switch unself-consciously from one pole to the other.[10]

By a circling movement these hypothesis bring us to the core of Girard's demonstrative argument, which is a discussion of texts from clas-

---

10. Here is a speculative rendering of the primary scene given by Girard. "A single victim can be substituted for all the potential victims, for all the enemy brothers that each member is striving to banish from the community; he can be substituted, in fact, for each and every member of the community. Each member's hostility, caused by clashing against others, becomes converted from an individual feeling to a communal force unanimously directed against a single individual. The slightest hint, the most groundless accusation, can circulate with vertiginous speed and is transformed into irrefutable proof. The corporate sense of conviction snowballs, each neighbor taking confidence from his neighbor by a rapid process of mimesis. The firm conviction of the group is based on no other evidence than the unshakeable unanimity of its own logic" (*Violence and the Sacred*, 79). The picture of mob frenzy is recognizable—at different levels of seriousness—from any number of situations in given historical and social life. This, of course, is a particular strength of mimetic anthropology: that it posits no extraneous principle, philosophical, psychic, or biogenetic, different from one of the most commonly observed phenomena of human animals in groups. Girard's thesis of "violent origins" coheres broadly with the views advanced by Walter Burkert, who derives cultural genesis from ritualizations attached to the adoption of hunting by primitive hominids. "[Man] became man through the hunt, through the act of killing." He notes the consistent presence in mythologies of a founding act of violence, and states: "Sacrificial killing is the basic experience of the 'sacred.' *Homo religiosus* acts and attains awareness as *homo necans*" (*Homo Necans, The Anthropology of Ancient Greek Sacrificial Ritual and Myth*, trans. Peter Bing [Berkeley, Los Angeles, and London: University of California Press, 1983], 21–22, 23). It is evident also that the primary scene described by Girard is much more autoexplanatory, via mimesis, than a "given" paleolithic transition to the hunt by primatelike hominids.

sical Greek tragedy. For Girard these works illustrate a privileged consciousness of the collapse of sacrificial order. Historically speaking, they
were written at a time of transition between archaic religious culture and
the emergence of a more "secularized" society based in laws and city states.
As such they represent vital texts in the West's cultural repertoire, a kind
of bridge between dimly lit archaic roots and a "modern" drive for critical
knowledge. The crucial feature is the display of reciprocal opposition. "If
the art of tragedy is to be defined in a single phrase, we might do worse
than call attention to one of its most characteristic traits: the opposition
of symmetrical elements."[11] Adversaries square off, they engage in duels,
physical or verbal, and the opposition of protagonists always threatens to
engulf the whole community. It is *Oedipus the King* that always invites
interpretation for any theory of tragedy, and its disturbing ambiguities
provide a rich vein for mimetic anthropology.[12] The central protagonists
engage in verbal skirmishes, each seeking to pin on the other the ultimate
blame for the crisis that is devastating the city of Thebes. At the stage of
sheer adversarial reciprocity—i.e., of the sacrificial crisis—there is no distinction to be drawn between opponents. For Girard this is the significant
innovation of tragedy over myth. Tragedy actively manifests the crisis of
mimetic opposition. However, it is finally the classic themes of prohibition, the "worst possible" charges of patricide and incest, that succeed in
breaking the deadlock of opponents, and at the height of the crisis introduce a new difference. It is the recourse of unequivocally attributing the
blame to Oedipus, because he is "discovered" a monster of familial murder and copulation, that suddenly resolves the situation. Oedipus becomes
the surrogate for the violent undifferentiation of the community, or to use
the word more recognizable now, the scapegoat.

> The crimes of Oedipus signify the abolishment of differences,
> but because the nondifference is attributed to a particular indi-
> vidual, it is transformed into a new distinction, signifying the
> monstrosity of Oedipus' situation. The nondifference became the
> responsibility, not of society at large, but of a single individual.[13]

The mythical work depends precisely not on knowledge, but on
something driven out. This is not Oedipus, who is visibly driven out,
rather *it is the at once unanimous and arbitrary nature of his selection as*

---

11. *Violence and the Sacred*, 44.
12. Sophocles, *Oedipus the King*, trans. Robert Bagg (Amherst: University of
Massachusetts Press, 1982).
13. Ibid., 76.

the guilty party. It is the arbitrary condemnation itself that must be excluded. "In order for the anathema to deploy its full force, it must slip from sight and from conscious memory." This, as should be evident, is a vital structural element in all surrogate solutions to group crisis: a systemic misconstrual or misrecognition of the victim as truly guilty. This is the core meaning of the sacred, of the gods of mythology, an expedient forgetting of the truth of the scapegoat and yet a residual memory of the terrible violence inflicted on it, preserved in the notion of its crime or transgression. It is the genius of tragedy to effect a partial raising of this veil of ignorance. On the strength of this tragic denouement, or denouement of tragedy, Girard announces the hypothesis that the functioning of the surrogate victim forms "the structural mold of all mythology."[14]

As well as this and other evidence from classical drama, Girard offers a raft of ethnographic material to support the claim that ritual and mythological origins are associated with the surrogate victim. He concludes again that "the original act of violence is the matrix of all ritual and mythological significations."[15] There is a natural bridge here to Sigmund Freud and his neglected study *Totem and Taboo,* which constructs a similar causative chain from a primal murder. Girard pointedly rehabilitates this work, appropriating its insight while replacing its flawed architecture with that of mimetic anthropology.

He demonstrates that at a key point Freud comes very near to the concept of the surrogate victim but does not take the decisive step. In commenting on Greek tragedy Freud asks why the hero had to suffer. The answer comes that in essence the hero is the primal father and the Chorus is engaged in a hypocritical unloading of its own guilt (as representatives of the brother-sons) upon him. In other words, he is a scapegoat. Now Girard, in his turn, asks why Freud in this connection does not move to discuss the hero of Greek heroes, Oedipus. And the reason at once presents itself: Oedipus, unlike the tragic hero, *has to* be guilty, he has to carry the thematic guilt of the Oedipus complex. He must "in fact" murder his father and sleep with his mother because this is the psychogenetic mechanism by which desire is translated at the heart of psychoanalytic theory. "If the great advance of *Totem and Taboo* is also a kind of detour and the work seems to end in an impasse, this is due to the heavy burden of psychoanalytic dogma with which the author approaches his text."[16]

Furthermore, the central function of the father's murder works against the overall argument of the book: the institution of the incest

---

14. Ibid., 84, 87.
15. Ibid., 113.
16. Ibid., 210.

taboo. The murder breaks the continuity between the sexual monopoly of the father figure and the later historical strength of the interdictions. Sexual disorder could just as feasibly follow the murder as sexual order. So then Freud is forced to introduce a second motivation for the prohibitions, "a practical basis," again much closer to events surrounding the surrogate victim. As Girard points out, Freud invokes the acute danger of a struggle for women among the brothers, "of all against all." The emphasis thus shifts from the father to the enemy brothers and the possibility of an internecine battle for any of the available women within the group (not just the Oedipal mother). Girard concludes, therefore, that in the "murdered father" theory of *Totem and Taboo* the vulnerable element is not the *murder*, but the *father*. It is the murder that holds the work together and survives the problems exposed by so many commentators. Ultimately the thesis of the surrogate victim gives coherence to the murder and the inner connection to sacrifice and prohibitions intuited by Freud. Once the murder is taken out of the familial (read "paternal") situation of the Darwinian horde and placed in the mimetic conditions of any primal grouping of hominids, then the breakthrough insight of this work can be acknowledged.[17]

Now, with this critical link to an absolutely key thinker of modernity, we can see how the argument reveals the human abyss with a progressive rigor. We are not looking at something in a simply impressionistic way, nor at an isolated set of intuitive reflections, rather it is reasonable to suggest that the truth of the human abyss has been slowly emerging in its stark horror over the history of critical thought. But here, it is not just that the origins of culture are disclosed in violence, but within this frame the profound instability of all human constructs: the self, the other, the world. Mimetic analysis (with its organic link to the biblical narrative always to be held in view) provides us with a shocking account of the human crisis and at the level of a fundamental anthropology. It provides formal underpinning to the descriptions I began with, above all in terms of the eruptive phenomenon of violence, but also in respect of our contemporary accelerated culture in which these eruptions occur. We might say that it is mimetic desire that is for the first time allowed to roam freely on earth, granted its liberty by a prodigious material and technical culture offering an infinite series of objects of desire for acquisition. The infinitization of commodities "contains" the possibility of violence in both senses; it transfers it through money and purchase into an organized way of life, capitalizing on desire and competition, but without changing in any sense the basic anthropology. Rather, as I suggested, it precipitates a sense of abandonment

---

17. Ibid., 212–17.

when, in the absence of both sacred order and the serial satisfaction of desire, the individual finds herself in a world stripped of relationship. It is in this context that the death of Christ needs urgently to be revisited, developing a dynamic understanding of salvation "in the abyss."

But before we rush to conclusions it is important to indicate one further implication of mimetic anthropology. Girard also engages Freud in respect to a general concept in psychoanalysis, that of "identification." Here he enters the central territory occupied by Freudianism, where the issue becomes bluntly mimesis or the Oedipal complex as the primary "structure" of desire. This is not the place to enter the discussion at length but it is essential to indicate the nodal point of divergence. For it is here, I believe, that Girard's hypotheses offer the most creative opportunities for an abyssal theology of redemption, even as I seek to pressure them further to that end.

In a careful examination of the chapter on "Identification" in *Group Psychology and the Analysis of the Ego*, Girard tracks a subtle movement by Freud away from an open concept to one closed by the dogmatic frame of the Oedipus theory. Initially, "A little boy will exhibit a special interest in his father; he would like to grow like him and be like him, and take his place everywhere."[18] This form of identification is not further defined by Freud and he is quite happy to have it subsist alongside "a true object-cathexis towards his mother," which continues without interference until the point when "the boy notices that his father stands in his way with his mother. His identification then takes on a hostile coloring and becomes identical with the wish to replace his father in regard to his mother *as well*."[19] These two words, *as well*, signal for Girard an immediate "correction" by Freud, suggesting now that primary identification with the father somehow did not include a desire to replace him in relation to his mother. Rather the true mother-desire only occurs within the proper Oedipal framework, arising apparently out of nowhere. For Girard this text indicates that Freud, if only in a vague fashion, intuited the role of mimesis in identification and then moved swiftly to censor it within the orthodoxy of psychoanalysis. "[I]t is impossible to elucidate Freud's theory of identification without encountering a mimetic mechanism that makes the father into the desire-model."[20]

This conclusion is strengthened by an anomaly that others also have noted. If the mother was excluded from the initial desire to replace the

---

18. Sigmund Freud, *Group Psychology and the Analysis of the Ego*, trans. and ed. James Strachey (New York, London: W.W. Norton & Co., 1959), 46.

19. Ibid., my italics.

20. *Violence and the Sacred*, 172.

father, it can only be that the child is already aware of the law imposed by his father, but without prior instruction! Here we have not only spontaneous sexual desire but spontaneous legal obedience. For Girard a much more credible explanation must be that the son turns toward his father's objects *because* he is following the example of his father. The convergence results in rivalry, which is itself a mimetic process. In fact the child cannot be aware of the "law" until in some way the adult responds with "violence," and so teaches him; and also teaches him to respond violently. "The son is always the last to learn that what he desires is incest and patricide, and it is the hypocritical adults who undertake to enlighten him in this matter."[21] In terms of mimetic anthropology, then, the Oedipus "complex" is not instinctual but is learnt, and rather than providing an impenetrable knot of destiny is itself a result of open-ended mimetic possibilities.

An Altered Self

These reflections lead us to the very heart of what I am proposing in the theme of abyssal compassion. They are taken up on a pathway that turns sharply in this direction by an author indebted to Girard, Mikkel Borch-Jacobsen. In his important monograph, *The Freudian Subject,* Borch-Jacobsen presents an incisive critique of Freud and the whole apparatus of psychoanalysis. The value here of this work is the way it radicalizes mimetic psychology, pushing the notion of mimesis to show how the "self" is always at some level a "selfish" or violent differentiation of "self" from the "other." It argues that we are always at a basic level in hypnotic identity with the other. Trawling the mimetic critique through a shoal of Freudian concepts (identification, narcissism, object love, the crowd, ego ideal, hypnosis), he catches again and again the theoretical constructs instituted by Freud to shape and fix the Oedipal complex out of primitive identification. Here is his conclusion in relation to the theory of an original intact narcissism:

There is only one "stage," and it is that of the primary opening (the narcissistic wound), which opens me to myself as (the)

---

21. Ibid., 175. This picture comes close to the ideas of another contemporary critic of Freud, Marie Balmary. "[T]he origin of neurosis is not sexual desire alone nor even sexual trauma alone, but all the faults committed by the very people who present the law to the child, either directly or indirectly—faults that have not been recognized" (Marie Balmary, *Psychoanalyzing Psychoanalysis: Freud and the Hidden Fault of the Father,* trans. Ned Lukacher [Baltimore and London: Johns Hopkins University Press, 1982], 164).
22. Mikkel Borch-Jacobsen, *The Freudian Subject,* trans. Catherine Poret (Stanford, Calif.: Stanford University Press, 1988), 93.

38

other. So let us not dream, with Freud, of an ego whose existence would precede sociality (or—and it is the same thing—a sociality that would relate already-constituted subjects to each other). This would be to theorize with delusion, to speculate in line with desire. For narcissism is precisely that: the violent affirmation of the ego, the violent desire to annul that primitive alteration that makes me desire (myself) as the mimetic double. Here we find a sort of instantaneous undertow that makes desire forgetful of its own origin, as Girard sees quite clearly: desire is mimetic and *by the same token* narcissistic, and that means that it launches headlong into a systematic, unreflective forgetfulness of what institutes it.[22]

Borch-Jacobsen does not explain how in these circumstances there is any sense of independent subjecthood at all, and for this we must surely return to mimetic anthropology, to the founding order of the sacred, bringing symbols, rituals, prohibitions, all the apparatus of distinctions by which humanity constructs itself. For Freud, in fact, this function is fulfilled in a critically less satisfying form, but basically in the same direction, by the founding Father, the Absolute Narcissus, of *Totem and Taboo*. There is no need to delay further on this. The cardinal point is primitive alteration, its possibility, or rather its inescapable facticity, underlying at a level of mimetic disorganization the complex cultural superstructure of social order and formal learned modes of relationship.

Here is a much more borderless, undifferentiated notion of the "self," one that carries the function of mimesis into the deepest reaches of that elusive phenomenon. The idea of this "hypnotic" (other-centered) identity appears deeply disturbing, but it also has a peculiar contemporary aptness, in terms of the media-inspired virtual identity reported by Coupland. It is in a way thematic to an age of exponential desire, a current psychology that fits with the collapse of sacred order and its substitution by an infinity of fragments to which we relate in desiring identity. But it is also appropriate to a transformed notion of the meaning of Christ's death, one that in itself replies to the contemporary world from within its abyss of abandonment. For Borch-Jacobsen's concept of a deep "primary opening" to the other, of primitive *alter*ation, carries with it the logical possibility of an imitation that is *transformative*, were it also possible to find a model that was truly other than violent and devouring. Borch-Jacobsen cryptically suggests something along these lines in a later

---

22. Mikkel Borch-Jacobsen, *The Freudian Subject*, trans. Catherine Poret (Stanford, Calif.: Stanford University Press, 1988), 93.

reflection on the (mimetic) predicament of the psychoanalyst, seeking to effect a cure via the mechanism of transference:

> In the end, in this strange rite of passage that today we call "psychoanalysis," perhaps the only stake is this: repeating, repeating the other in oneself, dying to oneself—to be reborn, perhaps, *other*.[23]

It is this possibility that is now the final term in the description of an abyssal Christ who is able to change us abyssally. If the Crucified via the proclamation of his gospel is able to reach us in the depths of our abandonment and therein to confront us in and by primitive alteration, then we can be changed, *altered*, into the very compassion, the abyssal gift of self that he is for us in that moment. The compassion of the Crucified becomes the point at which the foundationless, unconditional gift of love transforms the mimetic faculty from hostile rivalry to a totally new movement of the self. Because it is sensed as foundationless, without ontological grounds or power, because it surrenders itself without remainder, abyssal compassion is able to undo the reserve of "selfish" (conflictual) identification with the other that in every other case remains in relationship. The traditional word for this is *grace*, but the difference here is that it proceeds directly from the phenomenology of the cross and is decisively not the term of an economic redemption based on a cosmic exchange. The name *compassion* is suited to be at the core of this phenomenon because it evokes a double-sided event, an identification working from both sides. On the one hand it is a suffering-with and "mimetic" gift of self on the part of Christ, and then an answering identification on the part of the believer that is both the experience of forgiveness and the birth of love—a mutual passivity that is at once intensely active. Here then is the nucleus of my thesis in this book, and it is evidently important to have traversed the thought of Girard and Borch-Jacobsen in order to reach a cogent expression. It will underlie all that remains, in both the critical and constructive theology that follows.

The final stage of Girard's triad has been with us in all the foregoing and will be easily recognized. It is the unique historical role of the biblical narrative in disclosing the victim at the heart of culture. Rather than repeat the essential gesture of the sacred, that the victims of human groups are always guilty of the chaotic violence of the group, the Bible discloses (reveals) again and again the innocence of the victim. Through Abel, Joseph, Job, Jonah, the Suffering Servant, and of course Jesus, and along with many other stories

---

23. Mikkel Borch-Jacobsen, "Hypnosis in Psychoanalysis," in *Representations* 27 (Summer 1989): 92–110.

exposing oppressive violence, the biblical text undergoes a progressive tra-
vail that announces the culture of murder and rehabilitates its victims. This
Hebrew and Christian revelation is at the heart of the Western history of
concern for the victim, something clearly articulated by Nietzsche, and lies
for Girard at the source of his own anthropology. But the revelation of the
victim itself plunges human culture in the abyss, facing it continually with
the truth of its violence while it endlessly struggles to preserve the old order
based on violence. Although Girard does not use the term *abyss*, he understands that this terrible dilemma is the essence of the biblical apocalyptic
vision. The more humanity kicks and screams in the face of biblical uncov-
ering of original violence, without coming to true conversion, the more the
world arrives at the edge of chaos.[24] The critical problem here is not the
convergence of structural themes from the Scriptures and contemporary
history; it is both (1) the way in which there is no real attempt at a redemptive anthropology answering the crisis, and (2) the fact that institutional
Christianity is largely spared in Girard's work from the consequences of its
own subversive dynamic. Mimetic anthropology is used to vindicate the
astonishing rationality of the Gospels in the face of cynical secular dismissal, but not to apply them in their critical power to the very church tradition that enshrines them. Therefore, at this other point too, following
through the proposition of abyssal compassion, I take a decisive step
beyond Girard. Hand in hand with the radicalization of mimesis into
primitive alteration, and therewith a new notion of the anthropology of
the cross, I seek a real, contemporary encounter (one that fits the abyssal
times we are in) between this new vision and theological traditions that
are still based in the violent sacred.

Analogous perhaps to the famous "overturning of Plato," what is
implied here is an overturning of Girard and at the same time a certain
tradition of Christianity compromised in the structures of violence.
Girard is really already half overturned from within his own thought, but
he does not pursue it to its own radical implications, to the significance of
the abyss. Girard sees Jesus as the point of meaning, the logos of John, that
enters the world but is driven out because he does not/cannot in any way
collude with powers of violence. Yet even as he is driven out, by virtue of
the very act, his meaning is revealed. As Girard says, the Christian logos is
not the traditional Greek logos, it is an "absent logos" and in the structural rather than negative sense, that of actively disclosing violence in its
expulsion.[25] Does this not signify that the logos of Christian truth arises in
the abyss and by virtue of the abyss? However, what in fact establishes the

24. *Things Hidden since the Foundation of the World*, 201, 257.
25. Ibid., 271.

formal necessity of this thought is something that Girard does not say—that it is only there in the abandonment of the abyss that redemptive compassion and forgiveness can truly erupt in human affairs, and that the abyss is the necessary origin of the categorically new. Therefore the formal point of departure for theology must be this term, this place, this contemporary world, the abyss.

We may conclude then with the vision of the abyss strengthened and formalized by mimetic anthropology. It tells us that human beings have founded their world on murder, and that it was the surrogate victim, the scapegoat, who was made to incarnate and yet hide the abyss of human violence. From this the formal structures of social order and meaning flowed, leading to the appearance of the very reverse of the abyss. We could say in fact that all traditional sacred culture actually inverts the abyss by means of the victim, finding there the Archimedean point by which the constellations of the heavens are established in human minds. By deliberate forgetting of the human abyss, and the figure it has abandoned there, humanity is able to avert its eyes to the stars. Meanwhile in its gaze remains all the systemic violence on which it stands, in which case it does not truly see the stars. In contrast, the Christ of the Gospels fully and explicitly exposes the abyss, abandons himself in it in order both to reveal and to redeem it. From this flows the progressive deconstruction of all sacred and metaphysical order, proposing in its stead a terrifying freedom of abyssal love. The cross is both the source and the pathway of this love. It is the fulcrum of the human universe to change it into something we can hardly imagine and yet do dimly intuit, an abyss of love.

Chapter Two

IMITATIO DIABOLI

Soon after the turn of the second century of the Common Era the brilliant Christian polemicist Tertullian declared: "It is warranted by reason (*ratio*) that God should recover his image and similitude which had been stolen by the Devil, by an operation which was the converse of the fraud carried out by the Devil." The immediate background is a debate on the meaning of the flesh of Christ, whether it was the same human flesh as Adam, or an incorruptible flesh. The argument is with the Gnostic Valentinus and a disciple of his, Alexander, who contended that a terrestrial flesh was incompatible with Christ's identity and function. At this point in his discussion Tertullian cites Paul's explanation of Christ as a second and final Adam (1 Cor. 15:45), and insists on this basis that Christ was of true earthly origin. He then inserts the fateful phrase describing a mimesis with the devil.[1]

Christian theology in fact owes the first textual expression of some sort of exchange with the cosmic figure of evil to a passage in Irenaeus's *Adversus Haereses*, and it is useful to signal at once the lapidary role it occupies in the tradition.

> Since the apostasy tyrannized over us unjustly, and, though we were by nature the property of the omnipotent God, alienated us contrary to nature, rendering us its own disciples, the Word of God, powerful in all things, and not defective with regard to His own justice, did righteously turn against that apostasy, and redeem from it His own property, not by violent means, as the [apostasy] had obtained dominion over us at the beginning, when it insatiably snatched away what was not its

---

1. Tertullian, *De carne Christi*, 17, 2, in *La chair du Christ*, Sources Chrétiennes, introduction, texte, traduction et commentaire de Jean-Pierre Mahé (Paris: Les Éditions Du Cerf, 1975), vol. 1, 280–82: "*Sed et hic ratio defendit: quod deus imaginem et similitudinem suam a diabolo captam aemula operatione recuperavit.*" (My own translation given. *De carne Christi* dated 202/203 C.E.).

own, but by means of persuasion, as becomes a God of counsel, who does not use violent means to obtain what he desires; so that neither should justice be infringed upon, nor the ancient handiwork of God go to destruction.[2]

Tertullian was almost certainly aware of this text, given that some of the key expressions in his *De carne Christi* statement appear almost word for word in an earlier, and also seminal, passage of *Adversus Haereses*.[3] In his own treatment Tertullian goes on to develop the theme of a reciprocal action by God, detailing the way in which the life-constituting Word is introduced into the virgin Mary, over against the serpent's word, instituting death, "raped" into the virgin Eve.[4] The key difference from the Irenaeus passage is that in his forceful style Tertullian nails the essence of a theory of mimetic exchange in a single phrase. The Latin is *aemula operatione*, which implies a reciprocal antagonistic imitation by God of the original action of the Devil. Hastings Rashdall paraphrases it as "the converse of the Devil's fraud, *i.e.* . . . a rival fraud."[5] The idea may be immedi-

---

2. Irenaeus, *Against Heresies,* V.i.1 (*The Ante-Nicene Fathers*, vol. I [Edinburgh: T. & T. Clark, 1994].

3. Cf. Irenaeus, *Against Heresies* III. xviii, 1–2: "But when he became incarnate, and was made man, He commenced afresh the long line of human beings, and furnished us in a brief, comprehensive manner, with salvation; so that what we had lost in Adam—namely to be according to the image and likeness of God—that we might recover in Jesus Christ (*id est secundum imaginem et similitudinem esse Dei, hoc in Christo Jesus reciperemus*)." The passage continues: "For as it was not possible that the man who had once for all been conquered, and who had been destroyed through disobedience, could reform himself, and obtain the prize of victory; and as it was also impossible that he could attain to salvation who had fallen under the power of sin,—the Son effected both these things, being the Word of God, descending from the Father, becoming incarnate, stooping low, even to death, and consummating the arranged plan [economy] of our salvation" (*The Ante-Nicene Fathers*, vol. I, 446. Latin original in italics from *Contre Les Hérésies*, Sources Chrétiennes, texte et traduction, Adelin Rousseau et Louis Doutreleau, tome II [Paris: Éditions Du Cerf, 1974]). For full treatment of dependence on *De carne Christi* on Irenaeus see *La Chair du Christ*, vol. 2, 401–4.

4. "*In virginem enim adhuc Euam irrepserat, uerbum aedificatorium mortis; in uerginem aeque introducendam erat dei uerbum structorium vitae. . . .*" (*La chair du Christ*, 282). It is worth noting that Tertullian's rhetorical style is itself often a series of reciprocating and antagonistic tropes, putting into action the *ratio* or "reason" of an exact reversal or inversion, constituting a satisfying (mimetic) symmetry. Irenaeus had already employed this form of rhetoric, and other Fathers including Augustine would continue to use it. The primary idea, of course, is that as the Devil had deceived Eve with his word *in* her, God deceived the devil with the Word *in* Mary: and therefore we are dealing with genuine human flesh in the person of Christ. So mimetic doubling requires the human reality of Christ's flesh. The idea of a fooling of "the prince of this world," but without mimetic imagery, was already expressed by Ignatius of Antioch, *Epistle to the Ephesians*, par. 19 (*Early Christian Writings*, trans. Maxwell Staniforth [Harmondsworth, UK: Penguin Books, 1968], 81).

5. Hastings Rashdall, *The Idea of Atonement in Christian Theology* (London: Macmillan & Co., 1920), 251. (Hereafter *Idea.*) As a comprehensive survey of traditional atonement

ately recognizable as the *mise en scène* of mimetic doubles: Devil/God, God/Devil; it was to be a commonplace of patristic writing and commentary until the end of the twelfth century, and enjoyed an established role in pastoral teaching and homiletics for a great deal longer.

To get a more penetrating grasp of this it is important to take one further step in the field of analysis that mimetic theory opens up. Mimetic rivalry can be demonstrated as itself a primary dynamic in the structure of certain social groups, emerging under certain conditions as the formality of stable relationships. The anthropological theme of "gift exchange," which received its classic exposition in Marcel Mauss's *The Gift, Forms and Functions of Exchange in Archaic Societies*, provides the material basis for this claim. Mauss's key observation is that the gift is in fact an obligation, realized in triple form: the obligation to give, to receive, and to repay. I will return to this topic in chapter six, in respect to the way it has surfaced in certain postmodern thought, and with explicit reference to the death of Christ. But here, against the background of the last chapter, it is possible to deduce that the movement of exchange depends intimately on the content of mimetic rivalry, or threat, in relation to a disputed object. The gift is in fact this object, and the paradoxical obligation of the gift derives from the charge of violent reciprocity arising spontaneously in connection to objects of desire. Translated into "gift," these objects may be passed back and forth without overt conflict, but the latent threat is what maintains the institution itself in vigor. The potential for violence is in fact utilized in fixed forms of exchange, stabilized over long periods and in settings of relative abundance. What is important here is the way the exchange represents a process of proximate then deferred violence. The object is pursued by the proximate mimetic violence of both parties in desiring relation to it, and so the obligation either to give, receive, or repay the gift, and thus defer the violence of the other, becomes organic in the formally structured setting. The process can occur in terms of less tangible or spiritual objects, like prestige and honor, which in fact emerge as symbolic forms out of the established ethos of exchange, and carry within them

---

theory Rashdall's work has not been bettered in the English language. However, Rashdall relies on broad ethical sensitivity in his response to atonement theories and lacks the instrument of mimetic analysis. For *aemula operatione* compare "*aemulus -a -um*. 1: (of persons, cities etc.) Striving to equal or excel, actuated by rivalry, emulous, rival. 2: Jealous, envious" with "*aemulatio -onis*. 1: Desire to equal or excel others, emulation, ambition. 2: Unfriendly rivalry, envious emulation. 3: An attempt to imitate (a person) or reproduce (a thing), imitation" (*Oxford Latin Dictionary* [Oxford: Clarendon Press, 1982]). In the context of this study an appropriate translation of *aemula operatione* could well be "by a mimetic operation," or "by mimetic exchange."

its irrefutable logic or rationality.[6] A slight of any sort demands a compensation, both to recover the precise amount of honor or duty refused and at the same time to defer the proximate violence of the one slighted. It is this rationality that is surely at stake in Tertullian's remark that it is "reasonable" for God to practice a rival fraud on the Devil. So at once the content of relational violence is established in a central image of Christian catechesis, ensuring its validation as a motif of both divine and human reality.

The bulk of this element in Tertullian's writing overall is certainly minimal, and the same may also be said on this count for many of the patristic authors. But a textually minimal item may command a disproportionate destiny given the forces that it invokes and releases. I would suggest at once three historical factors that should be highlighted in an account of these forces:

> 1. A drive in primitive Christian thought to present Christ in a broad hermeneutic of substitution, to make the figure of Christ stand in for whatever was the locus of meaning in the ancient world.
>
> 2. The need on the part of orthodoxy to confront the doctrines of Gnosticism in the latter half of the second century, and the key problematic they revealed.
>
> 3. The distinctive contribution of the Roman legal mindset in the unfolding of Western Christian theology.

These three reflections will together constitute the basis for a mimetic analysis of atonement theory, and from this starting point I will continue to pursue a radical account of the Western tradition through all its major exponents up to Luther. As we proceed on the path we will gain a progressively more devastating vision of the structural content of violence in traditional Western theology of Christ's death.

---

6. Marcel Mauss, *The Gift, Forms and Functions of Exchange in Archaic Societies*, trans. Ian Cunnison, with an introduction by E. E. Evans-Pritchard (New York, London: W.W. Norton & Company, 1967; hereafter *The Gift*). Mauss connects the idea of honor particularly with the exacerbated gift exchange of potlatch, where prestige or honor is tied up with the amount of wealth an individual is prepared to destroy in the face of his rival. It is clarified by his conclusion "that in this system of ideas one gives away what is in reality a part of one's nature and substance, while to receive something is to receive a part of someone's spiritual essence" (10). This hypostasized "spiritual essence" disclosed within a culture of gift exchange probably finds its most powerful manifestation in the phenomenon of honor. Mimetic theory demythologizes the spiritual essence as proximate and deferred violence.

CHRIST AS METAPHYSICS

The first point, regarding the drive to present a hermeneutic of Christ in terms of substitutionary metaphysics, is really a very broad comment on Christian apologetics in the first centuries. This is an extensive subject in its own right, covering the field of late antiquity and patristic thought. I am only concerned here to make a general comment that will assist in developing an understanding of atonement theory. A writer like Clement of Alexandria (?150–?215 C.E.) saw Christ as the Logos, the universal origin and pattern of creation, and he did so against a background of Platonic and Stoic thought, which together characterized the prevailing intellectual climate of that period. Within this philosophical worldview the Christ Logos is understood as a real, active principle undergirding and enlivening all creation, giving to all things their reason and purpose.[7] Like the *nous* of middle Platonism, the Word is at once unity and plurality, comprising in itself the mind and ideas of God and also therewith the active forces by which the world of creatures is animated.[8] The task of the reasonable human life was to place oneself as much as possible in harmony with this principle, in thought, in the emotions, in modes of behavior. The process is one by which the disciple is "fully perfected according to the image of his Teacher, and becomes a God while still walking in the flesh."[9] Before Clement, in what are known as the Apostolic Fathers, the dominant emphasis in descriptions of Christ's saving work came in more general terms of enlightenment and knowledge.

---

7. "We are the rational images [*logika plasmata*] formed by God's Word, or Reason, and we date from the beginning on account of our connection with Him, because 'the Word was in the beginning.' Well, because the Word was from the first, He was and is the divine beginning of all things. . . . The Word, then, that is the Christ, is the cause both of our being long ago (for He was in God) and of our well-being" (Clement of Alexandria, *The Exhortation To The Greeks*, trans. G.W. Butterworth [London: Heinemann; New York: G. P. Putnam's Sons, 1919], 16–17). There is a sense, of course, in which this is present in the New Testament, particularly in the first chapter of John; but what makes it significant here is the progressive way in which the gospel of Christ is made to appropriate the worldview of a rational-spiritual philosophy, what Harnack called "the spiritual culture" of the time. Cf. Adolf von Harnack, *Outlines of the History of Dogma*, trans. Edwin Knox Mitchell (Boston: Beacon Press, Beacon Paperback, 1957), 123–25.

8. J. N. D. Kelly, *Early Christian Doctrines* (London: Adam & Charles Black, 3rd ed., 1965), 127 (hereafter *Early Christian Doctrines*).

9. Clement's *Stromateis*, vii. xvi. 101 in *Alexandrian Christianity, Selected Translations of Clement and Origen*, trans. and intro. John Ernest Leonard Oulton and Henry Chadwick, The Library of Christian Classics, vol. II (Philadelphia: Westminster Press, 1954), 159 (hereafter *Alexandrian Christianity*). For conformity of detailed practical behavior to the pattern of reason that is Christ, see Clement's *The Instructor*, in *The Anti-Nicene Fathers*, vol. II [Edinburgh: T. & T. Clark, 1994], 207–96.

Christ's suffering and death are seen in this key as didactic "models of obedience and self-effacing love."[10]

Justin Martyr (?100–?165 C.E.) belongs to an intervening strand of Christian writers, the Apologists, and it is with this group in fact that the self-conscious presentation of theology in philosophical terms commences. As fits someone persuading at a pioneer stage, Justin's treatment of Logos doctrine is bold and insistent. It was the eternal Logos, immanent in God's mind, who inspired the philosophers and poets of paganism.[11] These possessed the "germinal logos" or "seed of the Logos" within them, the idea deriving from the Stoic doctrine that it was this seed of reason that united all humans to God and gave them knowledge. But the revelation of Christ proves superior to the partial and confused nature of their wisdom, bestowing the knowledge and illumination of the "whole of the Word" on humanity.[12]

In the east Clement's teaching was taken up by his pupil, Origen, in the radical form of the preexistence of rational souls (*ta logika*) in company with the divine Logos.[13] This sealed in eternal form the idea that Christ came into a world that was already his and that his truth would be naturally assimilable by the truth of human reason. For Clement the end of human being was, precisely, knowledge (*gnosis*) of God, and the final goal of Christian faith is a matter of philosophical contemplation, of *theoria*. For the Christian "living in gnostic activity according to the commandments (life) culminates in contemplation." [14] Origen envisioned the same final goal; but, moreover, the Christian's day-to-day existence is already a mode of transformative *theoria*. "Discoursing in bodily form and giving Himself out as flesh, He summons to Himself those who are flesh, in order that He may first of all transform them into the likeness of the Word who has been made

---

10. *Early Christian Doctrines*, 164.

11. See his *First Apology* xlvi. "Those who lived reasonably [or "with the word," *meta logou*] are Christians, even though they have been thought Atheists; as, among the Greeks, Socrates and Heraclitus, and men like them. . . ." (*Ante-Nicene Fathers*, vol. I, 178); and *2 Apol. 13.*: "Whatever things were rightly said among all men, are the property of us Christians" (*Ante-Nicene Fathers*, vol. I, 193). See also Clement of Alexandria: "Mere persuasive arguments are too superficial in their nature to establish the truth on scientific grounds, but Greek philosophy does, as it were, provide for the soul the preliminary cleansing and training required for the reception of the faith, on which foundation the truth builds up the edifice of knowledge" (*Stromateis*, vii. iii. 20, in *Alexandrian Christianity*, 104).

12. See Justin Martyr, 2 *Apol.* viii, x, xiii, in *Ante-Nicene Fathers*, vol. I, 191–93. Also *Early Christian Doctrine*, 169.

13. *Early Christian Doctrine*, 155, 180-81.

14. *Stromateis*, vii. xiii. 83. Cf. *Alexandrian Christianity*, 146.

flesh, and after that may exalt them so as to behold Him as He was before He became flesh."[15]

Within this frame the figure of Christ may clearly be seen as a substitute for culturally established religio-philosophical meaning, what might perhaps be called in contemporary terms a reconfiguring of the transcendental signifier. Early Christian thinkers like Clement and Origen were engaged in a dynamic project of translation motivated by the conversionary goals of the Christian movement. Whatever constituted meaning in the world of antiquity in one way or another could and should be claimed for Christ, in order that those who looked to that meaning might in turn discover Christ. The good and the true received the name of Christ, so all things might reflectively lead to him. At the same time Christ was not simply philosophical truth writ large, but rather the indispensable means for attaining it in a darkling world where truth shone only fitfully for a few remarkable individuals.

There is already, therefore, a distinctive type of "atonement" doctrine at work here. Essentially it is a theory of imitation understood intellectually in the Greek manner, with reference to a realm of essential philosophical truth. The metaphysical framework marks it off most dramatically from the anthropological mimesis of compassion presented in the argument of this book. Nevertheless, in the patristic authors imitation is still brought to historical, human possibility by the gospel account of Christ's incarnation, death, and resurrection, and in this respect it is arguable that the Greek model also contains the nucleus of an anthropological reading of atonement. But this is implicit only, and the "eternal" Platonic ethos remains dominant. From the time of Clement the approach became characteristic of Christian teaching at Alexandria, and later in that city would be given landmark formulation in Athanasius's *De*

---

15. Origen, *Contra Celsum*, 3.28, quoted in *Early Christian Doctrines*, 184–85. See also his doctrine of the *epinoiai Christou*, the aspects of Christ by which the Christian is drawn to imitate the character and image of Christ. Cf. Origen, *Commentary on the Gospel of John*, trans. and intro. Ronald E. Heine, *The Fathers of the Church*, vol. 89 (Washington, D.C.: Catholic University of America Press, 1993), 39–41. The following presents the great paradigms of transformative-restorative contemplation. "One who contemplates the Image of God in whose likeness God made him receives through the Word and his power that form which was given to him (originally) by nature. . . . Matthew was a publican and because of that like to the image of the devil, but in coming to the Image of God, our Master and our Savior, and in following him he was transformed into the likeness of the Image of God. . . . Paul used to persecute this same Image of God, but as soon as he was able to contemplate its brilliance and beauty he was so powerfully transformed into its image and likeness that he was able to say 'do you seek a proof of him who speaks in me, the Christ' [2 Cor. 13:3]?" (*In Genesim Homilia*, I.13, J.-P. Migne, *Patrologia Graeca* [Paris, 1857–1887], vol. 12, my translation).

Incarnatione.[16] Here, again sympathetic with the Platonic ethos, the human problematic overcome by the divine Logos is at least as much death as it is sin, and indeed this is true throughout the "philosophical" tradition of atonement. In the Western doctrine, as we will see it emerging, the problem becomes overwhelmingly that of sin.

A WORLD OF EVIL

The worldview of what came to be known as Gnosis and Gnosticism (not to be confused with Clement's philosophical use of the term *gnosis*) is the second of the major factors behind the typical Western doctrine. It enshrined indeed, and in stark contrast to the foregoing, a dark, polluted sense of existence. In fact, as Harnack notes, the vision of a cosmos permeated everywhere by reason and divine truth was itself in conscious opposition to Gnosticism.[17] Rather, this latter formed a broad syncretist doctrine interpreting the world as the creation of an inferior divine being, or consisting of irredeemable matter. In the assessment of Kurt Rudolph, Gnosis is radically dualist to the degree of being "anti-cosmic": that is, "its conception includes an unequivocally negative evaluation of the visible world together with its creator; it ranks as a kingdom of evil and darkness."[18] In illustration we may cite the tractate *The Apocryphon of John*, part of the Gnostic collection found at Nag Hammadi. It describes the world as the artifact of the monstrous creator-god Yaldabaoth. Humanity was the result of trickery, the possessor of divine particles but a prisoner of matter, and so a battleground between powers of light and darkness.

Whatever its origins, therefore, Gnosticism was much more responsive to what must have been a strong sense of world-despair. It has been described as "a radical trend of release from the dominion of evil . . . that swept through late antiquity."[19] A reflective Christianity that found it easy to substitute for Platonic reason and Stoic immanence was in fact exposed on another front, one on which it would soon be forced to take seriously the consciousness of evil in human existence. Alongside a philosophical and contemplative culture that found God's mark or truth somehow in all things, a much bleaker vision of the material universe

---

16. Athanasius, *Contra Gentes and De Incarnatione*, ed. and trans. Robert W. Thomson (Oxford: Clarendon Press, 1971).

17. Adolf von Harnack, *Outlines of the History of Dogma*, trans. Edwin Knox Mitchell, intro. Philip Rieff, 2nd ed. (Boston: Beacon Press, 1957), 125.

18. Kurt Rudolph, *Gnosis*, trans. and ed. Robert McLachlan Wilson, with P. W. Coxon and K. H. Kuhn (San Francisco: Harper and Row, 1983), 60.

19. *The Nag Hammadi Library*, ed. and intro. James M. Robinson, rev. ed. (San Francisco: Harper Collins, 1988), 10. For *The Apocryphon of John* see this work, 104–23.

saw it as hopelessly alienated from the heavenly good and true. So, on this level too, a substitutionary movement was called for. The Christian message must correspond to the burgeoning sense of evil, as well as the idea of the good. Irenaeus's *Adversus Haereses* may be read then as the first significant attempt at a mediating point between the philosophical vision of the logos and the world of wrenching polarity exhibited by Gnosticism. But even as it undertook to rebut the claims of Gnosticism, orthodox Christianity was deeply affected by the existential tensions to which it spoke.[20] For us this becomes the second main element in the development of Western atonement doctrine.

Previous Christian authors had already understood the work of Christ as victory over the Devil and the host of demons. Jewish apocalypticism had provided precedent for the role of Satan as a supernatural agent of evil.[21] The Gospels themselves, and the New Testament in general, are radically apocalyptic, envisioning a decisive encounter, in the person of Christ, between the Kingdom of God and the powers of evil. There are the classic passages of the temptation of Christ, the binding of the strong man (Mark 3:22-27), and the final conflict with Satan in the book of Revelation. And there is John's description of Christ's death and resurrection as bringing the overthrow of "the ruler of this world" (John 12:31; cf. 13:2). Ignatius of Antioch taught that the incarnation of Christ brought with it the destruction of the power of evil spirits, through the extinction of magic and the oracles as well as by the disappearance of ignorance.[22] A

---

20. Commentators are frequently conscious of this shadowy influence, but it seems exclusively noted in respect of attitudes to the body and sexuality, and a relationship to antagonism and violence, and specifically in connection to the doctrine of atonement. is largely ignored. Cf. Robert Markus for a statement of Christianity's "Other" made in reference to the body: "Mainstream Christianity became infected by the strong undercurrent of ideas which accompanied it, sometimes as an overt rival, more often as its own, dark, shadow" (*The End of Ancient Christianity* [Cambridge: Cambridge University Press, 1990], 58).

21. See, for example, the apocryphal *Life of Adam and Eve* (*The Apocrypha and Pseudepigrapha of the Old Testament*, vol. 2, ed. R. H. Charles [Oxford: Clarendon Press, 1973], 137). Satan is here the tempter, speaking through the serpent, and explains his hatred of humankind on account of his expulsion from heaven by the angel Michael (John L. McKenzie, *Dictionary of the Bible* [New York: Collier Books; London: Collier Macmillan Publishers, 1965], article on Satan). Also Wisd. of Sol. 2:24: "[T]hrough the devil's envy death entered the world" (NRSV; subsequent New Testament quotations are from this translation, unless otherwise stated). The name "the devil" is from the LXX Greek translation of Satan, *diabolos*. There is no functional difference in the New Testament between the titles *satanas* and *diabolos*. See Rev. 12:9 where identification is made between these two terms and "the ancient serpent," the latter being explicit allusion to the story of the fall (literal translation from the *RSV Interlinear Greek-English New Testament* [London: Samuel Bagster, 1968]).

22. *Epistle to the Ephesians*, par. 19. As we saw, Ignatius also gave expression in the same passage to the idea of a fooling of "the prince of this world." It is typical of Christian thought at this point that the way the trick plays out is the disappearance of spiritual ignorance, rather than a mimetic exchange of property between rival powers.

similar connection of defeat of the evil powers and the triumph of
knowledge is present in Justin Martyr.[23] I would suggest, however, that
none of this approached the level of a true metaphysical reality. Until
Adversus Haereses the Devil or Satan had a broad descriptive role in the
Christian economy, evocative on the level of narrative and symbolism,
but lacking an essentialized reference; now he was to receive contractual
or, more accurately, mimetic status, over against God. His role becomes
systemic or metaphysical, fixed by a field of exchange between supernatural rivals. Under the pressure of the account given by Gnosticism,
Irenaeus has moved to elaborate a doctrine that did justice to a sedi-
menting sense of evil, and he does so by giving the Devil a negotiating
role on a par with God. He broached a doctrine of redemption that established a mechanism of exchange between God and an evil "other."
Rashdall describes the pressure that put this doctrine in place. "The religion of the Gnostics was essentially a religion of redemption. . . . If the
Church was to hold its own against them, it must perfect its scheme of
redemption. It had to explain why a God of love should not forgive sin
without demanding the death of His divine Son."[24]

Perhaps the contradiction voiced in the last sentence was more the
long-term result of the doctrine being introduced into Christianity, rather
than its cause. For it is very possible that Irenaeus was responding to the
Gnostic problem by stealing the narrative frame of one of the heresies he
was opposing in *Adversus Haereses*, namely the teaching of Marcion. The
latter drew a fundamental division between the God of the Jews, the so-
called punitive Creator God of the Hebrew Scriptures, and another God,
loving and benevolent, revealed in Christ. This scission had the effect of
excluding the Hebrew Scriptures from the Christian canon even as it
apparently explained how God should do something as monstrous as
bringing about the death of his own Son. A scheme of redemption that
was, in contrast, to remain faithful to theological continuity between the
Old and New Testaments had to provide a convincing reason as to why the
one God should will this death. The sensitivity to evil given currency in
and by Gnosticism had pushed to the surface the difficulty latent in the
story of the Passion. What ultimately necessitated Christ's death? If there
was a design or purpose behind it, whose and what was it? Marcion was
not a Gnostic, in the sense of proposing gnosis as the pathway to salvation,
but he clearly shared in a stream of thought that fixed a separation

---

23. Kelly summarizes: "Having forgotten the truth and having been inveigled into ignorance and positive error by the demons, men desperately need the restoration of the light
they have lost" (*Early Christian Doctrines*, 168).

24. *Idea*, 235.

between the God of creation and another, salvific God, the Christ, and
with that a separation between the realm of creation and a putative realm
of the spiritual. In responding both to Gnosticism in general and Marcion
in particular, Irenaeus appropriated the broad perspective of separation.
In his case it was constituted by hostility between a good God and a metaphysical force of evil.[25]

Part and parcel with this frame was the rationality of a "just" exchange
between the two. For Marcion the God of the Jews, the just but harsh
Demiurge, had violated his own laws in bringing about the death of
Christ. Consequently "it became just for the true and benevolent God to
set men free from the Demiurge. Irenaeus simply substituted the Devil for
the Demiurge."[26] Here is another key substitution, but this time it is for a
negative, violent focus. And it is not just the New Testament figure of the
Devil that stands in for a violent Creator, but the mimetic exchange
between this figure and the good God is both supplied by and supplants
the Marcionite account. I shall return to this in more detail below; for now
it is necessary simply to recognize the sea change it represents for
Christian theology in the West. From now on the Devil had a "rightful"
place in the scheme of things. In effect Marcion had been scandalized by
the cross, attributing its phenomenon of violence to a mimetic exchange
with a violent Creator God. And in response the Western tradition appropriated a good part of that "scandal." To preserve a continuum between
Christ and the God of the Jews, orthodox theology did not deny the
exchange but moved to transfer the metaphysical role of evil to the figure
of the Devil. The rationality at stake in this process is a very different logos
from the one invoked by Clement. We are no longer dealing with a
supreme philosophical principle that serenely communicates order to creation. The *ratio* of redemption is one born out of conflict; it is the logic of

---

25. Simone Pétrement argues that it was the message of the cross itself that hardened
apocalyptic dualism into the "anticosmism" of gnosis. The idea that the Son of God was
crucified in and by the world was intolerable to ancient minds impacted by the Christian
message, and so the world had to be in itself the work of another, evil protagonist. He comments that much of what Jesus taught had already been voiced by other Jewish masters.
"But something really was revolutionary: it was the image of the cross, the image of the
divine persecuted by the world and punished by it, the image that Paul had made the primary teaching of Christ and foundation of Christianity" (*A Separate God, The Christian
Origins of Gnosticism*, trans. Carol Harrison [San Francisco: Harper, 1990] 34–36).
Gnosticism was acutely sensitive to this image. We might conclude, then, that it realized
beyond second-century orthodoxy the radical contradictions set up by the kerygma of the
cross. Its response was equally radical, but amounted to mythologizing or short-circuiting
the difficulty. The evolving orthodox doctrine of atonement may then be understood as
the "cleaned up," orthodox rationalization of that short-circuitry.

26. *Idea*, 245. For Marcionite theology of redemption see Harnack's standard treatment,
Marcion: Das Evangelium Vom Fremden Gott (Leipzig: J. C. Hinrichs, 1924), 123–33, 288.

the "gift," not abstraction. It has the symmetry not of eternal ideas but of mimetic rivalry.

It should be stressed that Marcion's ruthless editing of the Jewish Scriptures was a censorship rejected by the proto-orthodox tradition. Nevertheless, and at the same time, Marcion's sensitivity to the discordance between divine acts of violence and a gospel of love represents an issue that is also present on the pages of the New Testament itself. His attempt at coherence through separation failed but his sensitivity was not misplaced. The tensions within the text of the Christian Scriptures are not to be resolved without a radical hermeneutic beginning and ending with the abyssal love of the Crucified, seeing this as redemptive interruption of cultural history in the thrall of violence, and even of time itself. It could be said that Marcion's attempt at resolution was the first signal of a debate to which this present study seeks to make a further, signal contribution. My final two chapters provide both an exegesis and a theological response in respect to the biblical tradition and its relationship to violence. In the meantime, it is undeniable that the issue of redemption is more critical to the New Testament than a vision of intrinsic order to creation. To that extent Marcion's wake-up call was certainly closer to Christian roots than the harmonics of Platonic contemplation.

LAW AND MIMESIS

The third element in the forces at work in doctrine of atonement is the characteristic tenor of thought contributed by Roman law. The "zealous African"[27] who trained and practiced law in Rome before his conversion to Christianity must be counted the first, most fluent spring by which this element entered Christian theology. The forensic style and vigor of Tertullian's writing produced theological concepts of importance, particularly in emerging complexities related to the Trinity. But what is at stake here is much more an issue of forces and atmosphere rather than abstract definition. Tertullian must be credited with the most brutal notion of primordial sin formulated to that point. He inherited from Stoicism a concept of the soul as refined matter and understood it as generated by the parents of the child along with the body. Solidarity in Adam, therefore, is natural and physical: we all participate in a portion of stem sprouted from the root of the first soul. We have in a realist sense, then, participated in Adam's sin. "The evil that exists in the soul . . . is antecedent, being derived from the fault of our origin (*ex originis vitio*) and having become in a way

---

27. The phrase is Gibbon's, quoted by F. R. Barry, *The Atonement*, Knowing Christianity, vol. 7 (London: Hodder and Stoughton, 1968), 132.

natural to us. For, as I have stated, the corruption of nature is second nature (*alia natura*)."[28] For this reason every child must be regarded as impure until reborn in the waters of baptism. Moreover, procreation was thus linked formally to transmission of fault and insistence on the fault so communicated would be bound to amplify suspicion of the sexual process itself. The link to Augustine here is not difficult to conceive.

Alongside this penal biology is the legal-minded rationale of compensating for personal sin in acts of exchange, making "satisfaction" by penance of confession, fasts and other forms of austerity.[29] And the obverse of this is that good deeds are characterized by "merit," which invokes good reciprocal action on the part of God.[30] We can see here at work a formal mimesis that defers proximate divine violence, or enacts a proximate violence of its own to oblige a divine gift. The following assessment captures the institutional mimetic framework. "Morality is for [Tertullian], as for no previous Christian writer, a doing of the will of God not because what God commands is good, but because an autocratic Deity commands it. . . . It is chiefly by self-inflicted suffering that God can be 'placated.' . . . God is represented almost entirely as a criminal judge—a criminal judge whose decisions were not unlike those of the persecuting magistrates with whom Christians of that age were too well acquainted."[31]

---

28. *Early Christian Doctrines*, 175–76, from Tertullian, *De Anima* 19 and 41. Cf. *De Anima* 39 where Tertullian offers proof of evil attendant on the soul from its birth, citing numerous pagan practices seeking the protection of gods and demons on the child. "In no case (I mean of the heathen of course) is there any nativity which is pure of idolatrous superstition" (*The Ante-Nicene Fathers*, vol. III, 219). But all souls also retain "seeds of good" (ibid., 41).

29. "And the price which the Lord has set on the purchase of pardon is this—He offers impunity to be bought in exchange for penitence. If, then, merchants first examine a coin, which they have stipulated as their price, to see that it be not clipped, or plated or counterfeit, do we not believe that the Lord, also, pre-examines our penitence, seeing that He is going to give us so great a reward, to wit, everlasting life" (Tertullian, *On Penitence*, trans. and annotated by William P. Le Sant, *Ancient Christian Writers*, vol. 28 [London: Longmans, Green and Co, 1959], 24). "We confess our sin to the Lord, not as though he were ignorant of it, but because satisfaction receives its proper determination through confession [is performed, *disponitur*], confession gives birth to penitence and by penitence God is appeased" (*On Penitence*, 31). "Who will any longer doubt that of all dietary macerations the rationale [*rationem*] has been this, that by a renewed interdiction of food and observation of precept the primordial sin might now be expiated, in order that man may make God satisfaction through the selfsame causative material through which he had offended, that is, through interdiction of food; and thus, in emulous wise (*aemulo modo*) hunger might rekindle, just as satiety had extinguished, salvation. . . . " (*On Fasting*, III, *The Ante-Nicene Fathers*, vol. IV).

30. "A good deed has God as its debtor, and a bad deed also, because every judge settles a case on its merits" (*On Penitence*, 17).

31. *Idea*, 253–54.

The mimetic structure of Roman law is reinforced by reflecting on its vocabulary. For example, the term *reus*, the guilty party, derives from a genitive form: the man who is of the thing or possessed by the thing (*res*). So the meaning of the term is rooted in the thing handed over, which puts the one who has received it under an obligation to repay, and thus "guilty." "The mere fact of having the thing puts the *accipiens* in a condition of quasi-culpability (*damnatus, nexus, aere obseratus*), of spiritual inferiority, moral inequality (*magister, minister*) vis-à-vis the donor, the *tradens*."[32] The key concepts of satisfaction and merit can also find original semantic reference as modes of obligation to repay, but in respect of actions rather than objects handed over. Generally satisfaction derives its meaning in relation to deleterious actions by one party against another, with the obligation on the agent to compensate; merit to beneficial actions done for another, with the obligation on the recipient to repay.[33] In every case it is the flux of mimetic violence that determines the obligation, and—-once settled into institutional form—-provides a conceptual matrix. At this point, therefore, we may say that legalism in a strict sense rejoins mimesis, or mimetic violence. We are not dealing at all with two separate realities, one "institutional," the other "relational." Therefore, yet another of the enduring forces underpinning atonement doctrine may be traced genetically to a ground in anthropological mimesis. In terms of Tertullian's redemptive theology, God's *aemula operatione* vis-à-vis the Devil is conceptually of a piece with God's demand for *satisfactio* through human penance. It would be only a matter of time before the two would meld together in what was to become the typical Western understanding of atonement.

A defense given of Tertullian and his successors in the West is that they were inevitably subject to cultural influence in their attempt to translate Christianity in terms intelligible to the Roman world. F. R. Barry says, "the theories [of atonement] were of their own time and place and were part of the risk inherent in the venture of attempting to Christianize the Latin

---

32. Marcel Mauss, *The Gift*, 50–51.

33. In fact "merit" can also bear a negative meaning. The verb *mereri* (to deserve) may denote the act by which the agent earns a legal punishment as well as a stipulated payment; cf. n. 29. The etymology of "satisfaction" is not so immediately found in mimetic exchange via prestation of gifts. *Satis* is related to *satire*, "to satiate," which refers to the filling up of hunger or desire of some sort. But *satis dare* and *satis exigere* also mean to give and demand security, bail, or guarantee for someone or something. Cf. *Oxford Latin Dictionary*, also *Latin Lexicon*, ed. F. P. Leverett (Philadelphia: The Peter Reilly Company, 1931). "Satisfaction" carries a sense more explicitly related to the already awakened mimetic violence of the (other) individual, than the attribute of mimetic power in the "thing" exchanged. Rather than a steady state of deferred violence as implied in the cycles of giving, satisfaction implies an urgent "remedial" action deferring imminent proximate violence in the other.

culture."[34] The same issue arises when we deal with atonement doctrine in the Middle Ages, and a background there of barbarian cultures, involving if anything an even sharper problematic of Christianization. While readily admitting the truth of these cross-influences, I would propose that the question is not so much a matter of condemning or defending, rather it concerns the implications for contemporary theology once these influences are granted. Looking at the preeminent Latin line of theologians after Tertullian, the succession of Cyprian, Ambrose, Ambrosiaster, and the ecliptic figure of Augustine, we see how inculturation hardens into worldview. Cyprian follows Tertullian's lead in his ascription of "the stain of the primeval contagion," and creates what was to become a standard metaphor of original sin as "wounds."[35] Pressured by the need to reintegrate numerous Christians who showed willingness to offer sacrifice in the Decian persecution, he vigorously expands the currency of satisfaction in a penitential system requiring confession, fasting, tears, suffering, and almsgiving.[36]

---

34. *The Atonement*, 131; see also 132, his quotation from T. R. Glover who says of Tertullian that he was "the first man of genius of the Latin race to follow Jesus Christ and to re-set his ideas in the language native to that race" (*The Conflict of Religions in the Early Roman Empire* [London: Methuen, 1909], 307). The following comment on Cyprian by Peter Brown gives a feel for the context of violence between Roman culture and emerging Christianity: "He faced a deeply conservative Roman society, still tenaciously devoted to its ancient gods, behind whose brutal face he sensed the abiding presence of the Devil and his angels" (*The Body and Society, Men, Women and Sexual Renunciation in Early Christianity* [New York: Columbia University Press, 1988], 193).

35. *Early Christian Doctrines*, 176; cf. *The Dress of Virgins* in *Saint Cyprian: Treatises*, trans. and ed. Roy J. Deferrari, The Fathers of the Church, vol. 36 (New York: Fathers of the Church, Inc., 1958), 51; and ibid., *Works and Almsgiving*, 227.

36. Cf. *The Lapsed* in *Saint Cyprian: Treatises*: "prayers of satisfaction" (14); "They do not seek the patience [suffering?] important for health, nor the true medicine derived from satisfaction" (15); "Spurning and despising all these warnings, before their sins have been expiated, before confession of their crime has been made, before their conscience has been purged by the sacrifice and hand of the priest, before the offence of an angry and threatening Lord has been appeased, violence is done to His body and blood. . . ." (16); "The Lord must be implored; the Lord must be placated by our own satisfaction. . . ." (17); "Let each one confess his sin, I beseech you, brethren, while he who has sinned is still in this world, while his confession can be admitted, while the satisfaction and remission effected through the priest is pleasing with the Lord" (29). And *Works and Almsgiving*: "Divine goodness came to the rescue and by pointing out the works of justice and mercy opened a way to safeguard salvation, so that by almsgiving we may wash away whatever pollutions we later contract" (1); "The remedies for propitiating God have been given. . . . [D]ivine instructions have taught that God is satisfied by just works, that sins are cleansed by the merits of mercy" (5). It should be pointed out that in the context of the second half of the third century the emerging penitential system appeared as a less "rigorous" approach than the early refusal to readmit to communion those guilty of adultery, murder, or idolatry. Cf. *Early Christian Doctrines*, 217–18. We can observe here the process by which the ethos of eschatological transformation experienced in the New Testament is negotiated into cultural realities under the pressure of time and events. The pivotal point is the (culturally provided) mechanism of insitutionalized mimesis or deferral of violence, which in the course of time becomes a "theologoumenon" in relation to the God of the New Testament, the Father of Jesus.

Unity with the Church is the necessary condition of efficacy of the system: "He cannot have God as a father who does not have the Church as a mother."[37]

Ambrose gives pungent expression to mimetic transaction with the Devil, among other things calling it a "pious fraud" (see n. 74 below). Moreover, he presents the death of Christ decisively in terms of substitutionary punishment. "Since the divine decrees cannot be broken, the person rather than the sentence should be changed." This suggests that by the time of Ambrose the notion of a cosmic mechanism, of which God was simultaneously the broker and the creditor, was well enough established that the focus could begin to shift naturally to the individual who was its victim. Christ becomes the substitute for a condemned humanity.[38] Ambrose continues to strengthen the notion of primal guilt with his statement, "In that first Adam I was subject to guilt (*culpae obnoxium*) and destined to death."[39] An unknown contemporary of Ambrose, named Ambrosiaster by Eusebius, contributes to the gathering terminology of condemnation with his resounding, "All men sinned in Adam as in a lump (*quasi in massa*)."[40] An unnamed author of the period writes, "Assuredly we all sinned in the first man, and by the inheritance of his nature an inheritance of guilt (*culpae*) has been transmitted from one man to all . . . ."[41]

When we come to Augustine it is almost as if we should add a fourth element to the forces underlying atonement doctrine. The range of his work is so vast, his reflection developed over such a span of time, showing polyvalent on different occasions and issues, that it is impossible to give an entirely unitary account of his thinking. This of course is one of the reasons for his immense interest and influence. On the other hand, that influence would not add up to much if it had not provided a consistent force of construction to later Christian theology through the Middle Ages and beyond. It is the consistent way Augustine sculpted

---

37. *The Unity of the Church*, 6 (*Saint Cyprian:Treatises*).

38. Ambrose, *In Luc. Exp.* iv. 7, quoted in translation in *Idea*, with Latin original, "*Ut quia solvi non queunt divina decreta, persona magis quam sententia mutaretur*" (328). It seems Eusebius of Caesarea was the first to use the language of substitutionary punishment (see n. 74 below). The influence of formulae drawn from Christian Scripture must also be taken into account, particularly Isaiah 52–53. But as we will show, in chapter five, whatever punitive meaning there is in this passage, it was never appropriated in the New Testament. It needed establishment of a cosmic mechanism of reciprocity to give divine punishment of Jesus legitimacy in Christian tradition.

39. *De excess. Satur.* II. 6. This and the following two quotations are given in translation in *Early Christian Doctrines*, 354.

40. In Rom. 5:12. J.-P. Migne, *Patrologia Latina* (Paris, 1879), vol. 17.

41. Pseudo-Ambrose, *Apologia David Altera* 71, Migne, *Patrologia Latina*, vol. 14.

notions of God and man together, his symbiotic theology and anthropology, that built the powerful complex that continues to dominate
Christian thought.

Augustine progressively broke from the first Neoplatonic ambience of
his conversion to Christian faith. In his commentary on Genesis (*De
Genesi ad litteram*) he distinguishes between a natural divine providence
(*providentia naturalis*) that would correspond to the immanent reason of
Logos doctrine, and a "voluntary providence" (*providentia voluntaria*) by
which God orders the realm of human wills under the sovereignty of his
own.[42] According to R. A. Markus, Augustine had reached this point as a
terminus of reflection, finally separating completely the respective
spheres.[43] Under the heading of voluntary providence, God is seen as
actively using the severity of the civil powers to institute his will, to punish, correct, forbid, condemn.[44] On the human side, the development of
the doctrine of original sin had already reached its term in the idea not
only of the corruption of humanity but its primordial guilt. Augustine
expressed this graphically as humanity's essential participation in Adam's
sinful willing (babies are guilty of voluntary original sin for that reason).
He then went on to give the bleakest legal-disciplinary reading to the
notion of baptism: it frees from guilt (*reatus*) but not the actuality (*actus*)
of primordial sin in our members.[45] Alongside this, although Augustine
retains theoretically the principle of free will, nevertheless "a cruel necessity of sinning" rests upon the human race.[46] This "necessity" is a matter
of natural, historical, and cultural fact. It is existentially of a piece with
the necessity of the magistrate who finds himself obliged, in the given
sinful order, to torture and to kill,[47] which twin necessities God himself
sanctions and authorizes. Predestination and hell for babies are simply
logical entailments of this polarity of humanity as a lump of perdition

---

42. *De Genesi ad litteram,* Migne, *Patrologia Latina,* vol. 34; see, for example, III.x, 14;
V.xxi. 42; VIII.ix.17.

43. R. A. Markus, *Saeculum, History and Society in the Theology of St. Augustine,* 2nd edition (Cambridge and New York: Cambridge University Press, 1988 [hereafter *Saeculum*]),
86–91; see Introduction, x: "The cosmic and social order were prized apart."

44. *Saeculum,* 145, where Markus also quotes from a letter (*Ep.* 105.4.13) exhorting a
Donatist: "God himself is doing this [recalling you to the fold] through us—whether by
pleading, by threats, by rebukes, by punishment and by troubles; whether through his own
secret admonitions and visitation, or through the power of the temporal law." Cf. *City of
God* (trans. Henry Bettenson, intro. John O'Meara [London: Penguin Classics, 1984]), Bk.
1, 1: "God's providence constantly uses war to correct and chasten the corrupt morals of
mankind."

45. *Early Christian Doctrines,* 364–65; cf. *Retract.* I. xiii. 5, Migne, *Patrologia Latina,* vol.
32.

46. Ibid.; cf. *De perfect. iustit. hom.* IV.9, Migne, *Patrologia Latina,* vol. 44.

47. "Deliver me from my necessities!" (*City of God,* XIX, 6).

(*massa damnata*)[48] and God as a ruler of terminal violence bringing closure to a cosmic structure of mimesis.

Augustine is writing at a time when the experience of the church is separated by a qualitative shift from the embattled, persecuted church of Tertullian and Cyprian. As the church merged with the *saeculum*, the neutral space and time where in Augustine's view the earthly and heavenly cities could not be clearly distinguished,[49] the question began to form as to who could be sure of salvation.[50] What was to be the fixed point of security when the world had joined with the church, when the latter now consisted of time servers as much as disciples? The answer remained locked in the inscrutable divine will. Conversely, where the church had in fact joined the world, ecclesiastical leaders such as Augustine began to take an active part in choosing how and when to apply the terror of the empire. In particular, the circumstances of the coercion of the Donatists had brought Augustine explicitly to defend the advantages of force; and already in the decade and a half leading up to this he had entered readily into the theological euphoria over the shift of the might of empire to the cause of Christ.[51] The vision of a God

---

48. *Faith, Hope and Charity*, 8.27, in *Writings of St. Augustine*, trans. John Courtney Murray, S. J., The Fathers of the Church, vol. 4, (Washington, D. C.: Catholic University of America, 1947), 392. Also *Admonition and Grace*, 7. 12, ibid., 259–60: "Consequently, those who have not heard the Gospel; and those who, having heard it, and having been once changed for the better, did not receive perseverance; and those, who having heard the Gospel, were unwilling to come to Christ (that is, to believe in Him). . . ; and those who could not even believe because they were infants, needing to be absolved from original sin by the bath of regeneration, but dying without having received it—all those do not stand apart from that mass which, we know, was sentenced to the loss of God; all of them, by reason of one, fall under condemnation. And they are singled out not by their own merits, but by the grace of the Mediator; that is, they are justified in the blood of the second Adam as by a free favor. . . ; we ought to understand that no one can be singled out of that lost mass [*massa perditionis*] for which Adam was responsible, except one who has this gift; and he who has it, has it by the grace of the Savior." Cf. *Ad Simplic.* 1, 2, 16; 1, 2, 20, Migne, *Patrologia Latina*, vol. 40.

49. "The *saeculum* for Augustine was the sphere of temporal realities in which the two 'cities' share an interest. . . . [T]he saeculum is the whole stretch of time in which the two cities are 'inextricably intertwined.' . . . [I]n it the ultimate eschatological oppositions, though present, are not discernible"(*Saeculum*, 133).

50. The question came, circa 395, from Bishop Simplicianus, successor to Ambrose and a former mentor of Augustine, now addressing himself to his pupil: "Why did God say, 'I have hated Esau?'" (Peter Brown, *Augustine of Hippo: A Biography* [Berkeley and Los Angeles, Calif.: University of California Press, 1969], 153).

51. Edicts closing pagan temples and banning pagan sacrifices issued from the chancery of Theodosius I from 391 onwards. For Augustine's early attitude to a Christianized empire, see *Saeculum*, 29–39. "From the 390s for some ten or fifteen years, Augustine appears to have joined the chorus of his contemporaries in their triumphant jubilation over the victory of Christianity." The Imperial Edict of Unity against the Donatists in 405 is generally seen to mark Augustine's full and explicit conversion to the use of force. But see P. R. L. Brown, *St. Augustine's Attitude to Religious Coercion* (*JRS* 54, 1964), 110–11; here Brown argues this shift is rooted in Augustine's already established concepts of "divine violence" and "the invincible purposes of an omnipotent God."

untrammeled in violence reacting to a humanity unrelieved in sinfulness was to be symbolically and practically mediated by the ancient subjugator of peoples, the Roman Empire, now the ally of the church. It is as if the cultural logic of proximate violence assimilated into practical theology by Tertullian, Cyprian, and Ambrose moved now to penetrate the furthest metaphysics of heaven itself. And it was Augustine's relentless mind, his "ruthless dialectical technique," that helped drive it there, finally achieving in his understanding of God an imperial stasis of violence.[52]

Here, the mentality of lex Romanorum may be seen to reach a synthesis with the worldview of Gnosticism, especially given the possibility of permanent traces of Manichaeism in Augustine's thought.[53] Was the Deus Christianorum as constructed by Augustine infected with the "principle of evil" that Mani had hypostasized in separating it from the "principle of good?" We should remember Augustine was a "hearer" of the Manichees for nine years. Markus has a plausible answer; he believes metaphysical polarity assumed a psychological form in Augustine. "The tension that Manichaean teaching projected onto two separate natures in permanent conflict was now transposed into terms of conflict within the self. . . ."[54] Brown says much the same, suggesting Augustine was able to avoid direct association with Manichaeism by giving his assessments of sinful human nature a psychological rather than a mythological grounding.[55] Nevertheless, discernible lines of Gnostic cosmology remain. According to Rudolph, "He appropriated (its) heritage most clearly in the impressive historical review of the two 'realms' (*civitates*), the devil's or that of the wicked (*civitas diaboli* or *impiorum*), and God's (*civitas Dei*), and thus shaped the Christian historical metaphysics of the Middle Ages."[56] What before was a static panorama of separate realms was both hidden and confused, by

---

52. *Augustine of Hippo*, 154. In respect of the development of Augustine's thinking, both Brown and Markus see his reading of Paul, around the year 396, as determinative for the evolution of his theology of irresistible divine will. My argument here is that this reading cannot be taken as pure meditation divorced from sociocultural setting, in particular the iron violence of a Roman imperium newly converted to Christianity.

53. *Augustine of Hippo*, 370, 384.

54. Robert Markus, *The End of Ancient Christianity* (Cambridge: Cambridge University Press, 1990), 61. See also 47–48.

55. *Augustine of Hippo*, 389; see also 154–55. This ability to psychologically reconstruct mythological polarities is a major element in his genius, underlying its enduring modernity and influence.

56. *Gnosis*, 370. See also 371, his quotation from H. Blumenberg, *Säkularisierung und Selbstbehauptung*, 2 (Frankfurt: Suhrkamp, 1974), 155: "The gnostic dualism was set aside for the metaphysical principle of the world, but it continued to be alive within mankind and its history as absolute separation of the called and the rejected. This crudity thought up for God's justification has its hidden irony, in that in a roundabout way, through the idea of predestination, that very authorship of the absolute principle for the cosmic corruption was reintroduced, the elimination of which was the aim of the exercise."

overlaying one with the other indistinguishably, and then stretched forward in time to the point of scission at the eschatological judgment. In the meantime a true polarity of principles was maintained intact in God's will, very much as a judge of show-trial terror holds the possibilities of freedom and condemnation equally available to decision.

If separation of "Gods" is the true mark of Gnosticism, then Rudolph must be right; that we are dealing here with "translated Gnosis."[57] In this case a vigorous Roman legalism has become wedded to a metaphysical dualism and allows it expression without resorting expressly to dualist cosmology. It is this powerful combination that has provided the successful translation of Gnostic anxiety within orthodox Christianity. So, along with the figure of the Devil, the notion of a juridically absolute and punitive God has mediated substantively the Gnostic scheme, and in this way determined the production of traditional doctrines of atonement. However, I would also suggest that at a key point behind Gnosis lies the concrete image of the cross: the traumatic vision of the Son of God violently expelled from the world. On this basis we might then conclude that Augustine's thought was merely one other attempt, though singularly effective, to resolve tensions intrinsic to Christianity itself. The kerygma of the cross splits in two the psychological monad of the ancient cosmos, and systematic theologies from Gnosticism through Augustine and onward are successive attempts to heal on a metaphysical level an irreparable wound so created.

Elements of a cosmic vision of harmony, peace, and indeed nonviolence, together with a passionate desire for God, remain part of his provocative, paradoxical legacy. But it was the figure of divine terror he so relentlessly articulated that played a key role in the full-fledged Latin doctrine of atonement at the end of the eleventh century, and beyond that in Luther's attempt to break with all external mechanisms of negotiation—though, precisely, not with divine violence—at the beginning of the sixteenth. It is this core tradition of Western atonement theology that is at issue here.

THE THEOLOGICAL TRADITION OF ATONEMENT

On the basis of the three broad reflections I have presented—on Christian substitutionary metaphysics, Gnosticism, and the Roman legal mentality—I want now to follow a more detailed account of this core tradition. By means of successive examples a compelling picture will emerge of the way mimetic exchange has been the crucial vehicle of thought in this area of

---

57. *Gnosis*, 371, again quoting Blumenberg, op. cit., 157.

Western theology, and so provided a theological grounding for the Christian praxis of violence. We saw at the beginning of the chapter a passage where Tertullian depends on Irenaeus for his account of Christian redemption, drawing on Irenaeus for the idea of a mimetic transaction with the devil. Here again is the text from Irenaeus, a *locus classicus* for development of popular atonement theology.

> [T]he mighty Word, and very man . . . redeeming us by His own blood in a manner consonant to reason, gave Himself as a redemption for those who had been led into captivity. And since the apostasy tyrannized over us unjustly, and, though we were by nature the property of the omnipotent God, alienated us contrary to nature, rendering us its own disciples, the Word of God, powerful in all things, and not defective with regard to His own justice, did righteously turn against that apostasy, and redeem from it His own property, not by violent means, as the [apostasy] had obtained dominion over us at the beginning, when it insatiably snatched away what was not its own, but by means of persuasion, as becomes a God of counsel, who does not use violent means to obtain what he desires; so that neither should justice be infringed upon, nor the ancient handiwork of God go to destruction.[58]

It should at once be recognized that there is a struggle in the language, one that seeks a way to express the forcible removal of property from the hand of a rival, but without falling into the same type of practice as that rival. The crucial word perhaps is persuasion, *suadela* in the Latin, which connotes something sweet and pleasant, or advocacy before a court of law. It is behavior worthy of God (*decebat Deum*), to be like this, to be persuasive. The Marcionite background is corroborated by this insistence on the redemptive God's nonviolent character, as opposed, in Marcion's scheme, to the violence of the Creator God.[59] The advancing rhetoric palpably suffers a tension: on the one hand, God's character is marked by nonviolence, on the

---

58. *Against Heresies*, V.i.1. Irenaeus actually does not name the Devil but uses a circumlocution epitomizing the events of Genesis 3. Elsewhere the identification is made with the serpent of Eden, e.g., V.xxi.2–3; see also III.xxiii.1, where if anything the mimetic exchange is more clearly expressed: "He who had led man captive, was justly captured in his turn by God; but man, who had been led captive, was loosed from the bonds of condemnation."

59. "In its soteriological aspect the death of Christ was regarded by Marcion as in the nature of a purchase. Mankind belonged by right to the Creator, and therefore the Good God could justify himself in freeing mankind from allegiance to the Creator only if he had first purchased them in a lawful manner. (The method of wresting them away by superior force was, of course, alien to his nature!)" (E. C. Blackman, *Marcion and His Influence* [London: SPCK, 1948], 102).

other, some powerful means of regaining his property from the rival hypostasis had been found. Irenaeus does not elaborate, and one can sense his attempt to remain in proximity to a gospel sense of nonviolent redemption, but the Rubicon has been crossed. From now on the door is open to interpretations of a legal-mimetic transaction that dispossesses the personalized enemy of humankind, or some kind of trick with the same effect and the same rationality giving it justification.

Irenaeus' other noteworthy doctrine of redemption or atonement, known as "recapitulation," may also be understood as a mode of answering Marcion, this time by removing the ground on which he stood. The phrase we have seen is *"longam hominum expositionem in seipso recapitulavit, in compendio nobis salutem praestans,"*[60] meaning that the long career of humanity is repeated again in Christ who then offers salvation in a transformed summary version. He also says, "That which He appeared, that He also was: God recapitulating in Himself the ancient creation, in order that He might slay sin and destroy the power of death, and give life to men."[61] So rather than a revolution of gods as proposed by Marcion, or Gnostic dualism in general, we have a radical renewal of the whole of the human story. Irenaeus offers a figure of anthropological restoration *in radice* rather than mythological expulsion. This remarkable concept—a repetition of all human history in the key of life rather than death—is sympathetic to the notion of atonement as abyssal compassion, and in the sixth chapter I will look at how by this concept it might be given greater theological coherence. Yet, on another register, Irenaeus is sufficiently impressed by the Gnostic case to give the Devil a formal role, setting up a subtle exchange of cosmic powers, while seeking at the same time to subsume the change within a dominant key of nonviolence.

The attempt did not work. Tertullian's blunt rhetoric proved how swiftly mimetic polarity defined Irenaeus's concept. A fifth-century Armenian text from Eznik of Kolb gives us some idea of the powerful dynamics at work and, on this evidence, how deeply Marcion is influencing orthodox Christianity, including Irenaeus in the restrained form we have seen. Eznik is writing in fact to oppose Marcionite doctrine, and as he does so he gives an account of the graphic Marcionite theory of redemption. After his death Jesus confronts the Lord of Creation:

> And Jesus said this to him: "There is a case to be tried between me and you and there is no judge other than your own Laws, which you have written. . . ." Jesus said to him: "Have you not

60. *Against Heresies* III. xviii.1 1–2. For Latin text see n. 3 above.
61. Ibid., III.xviii.7.

written in this your Laws that whoever kills should die, whoever spills the blood of the just, his own blood must be spilt?" And he said: "That I have written." Jesus spoke to him: "Therefore surrender to me that I might kill you and spill your blood, just as you have killed me and spilt my blood. Because I am rightfully more just than you and have done great services for your creation. . ."

But when the Lord of Creation saw that he was defeated he still wished to say something. Since he had been accused by his own Laws he yet could give an answer. Since he would be guilty of murder on account of (Jesus') death he prayed beseechingly: "Because I honestly and unwittingly killed you, because I did not know that you were God, but took you for a man, so I give to you as satisfaction all those who will believe in you, to take wherever you want." Then Jesus left him and went away, and he took Paul and revealed to him the price and sent him to preach, that we might be bought with the price, and so that each one who believes in Jesus would be sold by [the God of] Justice to the [God who is] Good.

This is the beginning of the heresy of Marcion aside from many irrelevancies. Moreover not all among them know this, rather only a few do. And they do not say this teaching openly: the Stranger has bought us with the price from the Lord of Creation. Not all know how and by what means he made the purchase.[62]

---

62. Quoted by Adolf von Harnack, *Marcion: Das Evangelium Vom Fremden Gott*, 376–77 (German trans. from the Armenian by I. M. Schmid, *Des Wardapet Esnik v. Kolb, "Wider die Sekten"* [Vienna: Verlag der Mechitharisten Congregation, 1900], my translation into English). "Und es sprach zu ihm Jesus: 'Gericht is zwischen mir und dir und niemand sei Richter als deine eigenen Gesetze, die du geschrieben.' . . . Sprach Jesus zu ihm: 'Hast du nicht geschrieben in diesen deinen Gesetzen, dass, wer töte, sterben soll, wer Blut des Gerechten vergiesst, selbst sein Blut vergiessen müsse?' Und er sprach: 'Ich habe es geschrieben.' Jesus sprach zu ihm: 'Gib dich also in meine Hände, dass ich (dich) töte und dein Blut vergiesse, wie du mich getötet und mein Blut vergossen hast. Denn ich bin mit Recht gerechter als du und habe deinen Geschöpfen grosse Wohltaten erwiesen. . . .

"Als aber das Herr der Geschöpfe sah, dass er besiegt sei, noch etwas zu sagen wusste, weil er durch seine eigenen Gesetze beschuldigt wurde, noch eine Antwort geben konnte, weil er um seines (Jesu) Todes willen des Todes schuldig geworden, da hat er flehentlich: 'Dafür, dass ich gesündigt und dich unwissend getötet habe, weil ich nicht wusste, dass du Gott seiest, sondern dich für einen Menschen hielt; dafür gebe ich dir zur Genugtuung alle jene, welche an dich glauben wereden, sie zu führen, wohin du willst.' Da verliess ihn Jesus und entrückte und nahm den Paulus und offenbarte ihm den Preis und sandte ihn zu predigen, dass wir um den Preis erkauft seien, und ein jeder, welcher glaubt an Jesus, wurde verkauft von dem Gerechten dem Guten.

"Dies ist der Anfang der Irrlehre des Marcion ausser vielen Nebensachen; auch wissen dieses nicht alle unter ihnen, sondern nur wenige; und sie sagen nicht mündlich diese Lehre: der Fremde hat uns durch den Preis von dem Hern der Geschöpfe erkauft; wie und wodurch er aber erkauft habe, das wissen nicht alle."

The impression of this final paragraph is that the teaching reserved for the few is precisely the harsh mimetic exchange between Jesus and the Lord of Creation. Perhaps here was an element of scandal, inasmuch as there now appears a parity of violent justice between the two, something that the doctrine of the Stranger God of the New Testament was meant to exclude. So at the last moment the figure of the benevolent God is turned on its head in order to beat the Lord of Creation at his own game. The role of satisfaction in the account makes this conclusion unavoidable, and the concept here makes its appearance, as far as I know for the first time, as a pivot in the exchange between divinity and evil. Following the convolutions of this concept will lead us by a few short but powerful twists to Anselm of Canterbury, to his argument for the need now for Christ to satisfy God's offended honor, and then also to the notion of the merits of Christ by which, reciprocally, humanity is saved. The trail of this concept reveals how the force of proximate, then deferred violence has shifted finally to God the Father, having traveled from the Demiurge or Devil through the figure of Jesus. In this case Anselm would represent the orthodox assimilation of the Marcionite scheme; the benevolent God now assimilates all the violence of the inferior God. If there is truth in this archaeology it means once again that a prevailing account of redemption in the West is a transposition of Marcionite heresy. This time divine unity and sovereignty are saved but divine violence is established formally and metaphysically. The logos of sacred violence is identified with the God of the New Testament.

Meanwhile, as we know, the transaction with the Devil was to enjoy its own undisputed supremacy as the popular understanding of redemption for the first half of the Christian era. "This ransom theory of Irenaeus became, and for nearly a thousand years continued, the dominant orthodox traditional theory on the subject."[63] The writings of Origen in the first half of the third century were to give the theory further development and additional prestige in both East and West. Origen has a truly broad range of commentary concerning Christ's death, and essentially his stress is on the "philosophical" version we have already noted, the contemplative-transformative power of Christ's teaching and example. Yet he is also to be credited with an authoritative statement of Christ's death as a trick played to outwit and overpower the Devil, and it was this scenario more than anything else that was to determine popular imagery up to the time of the schoolmen. "But to whom did he give his soul as a ransom for many? Surely not to God? Could it be then to the evil one? For he had us in his power, until the ransom for us should be given to him, even the life of Jesus, since he [the evil one] had been deceived [*apatethenti*, tricked, out-

---

63. *Idea*, 247.

witted], and led to suppose that he was capable of mastering that soul, and he did not see that to hold him involved a trial of strength greater than he was equal to."[64]

A meticulous exegete, Origen is responding here to the "ransom" passage in Matthew's Gospel, and he is also very much aware of a germane passage such as 1 Corinthians 2:8.[65] However, although presented in fairly restrained form, the image of a trick needed to breach the Devil's sphere of security suggests again a concession of metaphysical status to this personalized force of evil. What I want to make specific is the cultural momentum of mimetic logic: it moves from a narrative-metaphorical language toward an articulated, "rational" language in which God overcomes a rival hypostasis by some form of violence. Without one or other really coming first, the hypostasis invokes the mimesis, and the mimesis reinforces the hypostasis. Subsequent writers were to continue heightening the mimetic content, but there were a few outraged objectors along the way.

A fourth-century writer by the name of Adamantius or Pseudo-Origen is one of these, and his remarks are also notable for appearing in an attack on Marcionites; parallel to Eznik of Kolb he treats the notion of transaction simply in terms of Marcionite doctrine. "The Devil then holds the blood of Christ as the price of man. What immense and blasphemous folly! . . . He laid down that which he took. What sort of sale was this, when the prophet says, 'Let God arise and let his enemies be scattered.'" Earlier in the same passage he observes, quoting, it seems, a proverbial saying, "He who sells and he who buys are brothers." This is a reductio ad absurdum of Marcionite dualism at the point of its doctrine of redemption, effected by means of a basic mimetic analysis.[66] Gregory of Nazianzen, one of the fourth-century "school of Cappadocia," is perhaps the best known protester against the notion of transaction with the Devil. "I inquire to whom was the blood of God poured out? If to the evil one—alas! that the blood of Christ should be offered to the wicked one!"[67] However, he goes on to suggest, the traditional language should be maintained and reexplained. The ransom perhaps should be seen in an allegorical fashion, as paid by the Son to God "to whom He is seen in all things to yield." This shift shows how easy it was to move the locus of exchange from the Devil to God, and the attempt to sanitize in this way is persuasive witness to its influence. "If

---

64. *In Matt.* xiv. 8, quoted and translated in *Idea*, 259, my brackets.

65. "None of the rulers of this age understood this; for if they had, they would not have crucified the Lord of glory" (*The New Oxford Annotated Bible, New Revised Standard Version* [New York: Oxford University Press, 1991]). Cf. Origen, inter alia, *In Rom.* iv. 11.

66. Background, quotation, and translation from *Idea*, 302.

67. *Poemata Dogmatica*, 1. viii. 65-69, Migne, *Patrologia Graeca*, vol. 37, 470; translation in *Idea*, 309.

it was absent from creeds and conciliar canons, it was the very pith and marrow of popular theology."[68]

Gregory of Nyssa, another Cappadocian, gave the imagery a full exposition, moving through a subtle progression of tropes and arguments in a struggle to justify an exchange with the Devil. Human beings are slaves who have sold themselves into slavery. It would be simply illegal to rescue them from their owner by an act of force.

> If any one out of regard for the person who has so sold himself should use violence against him who has bought him, he will clearly be acting unjustly in thus tyrannically rescuing one who has legally been purchased as a slave; whereas, if he wishes to pay a price to get such a one away, there is no law to prevent that—in the same way, now that we had voluntarily bartered away our freedom, it was requisite that not the tyrannical method of recovery, but the one consonant with justice should be adopted by Him who in His goodness had undertaken our emancipation.[69]

Consequently the Devil was persuaded to accept Christ by a process that was essentially one of commodity desire, but in this instance the contents were much more than what was evident from the packaging. Therefore, once the transaction was complete the Devil immediately became the debtor.

> It was out of [the devil's] power to look on the aspect of God, face to face, except by looking at some portion of that fleshly nature which through sin he had so long held in bondage. Therefore it is that the Deity invests himself with flesh, in order, that is, to secure that he, by looking upon something of like nature and akin to himself, might have no fears in approaching that supereminent power; and might yet by perceiving that power, exhibiting as it did, yet only by gradual stages, more and more splendor in the miracles, deem what was seen an object of desire rather than fear. Thus, you see how goodness was united with justice, and how wisdom was not divorced from them.

---

68. *Idea*, 309. Second quotation of Gregory of Nazianzen: *Oratio* xiv. 22, Migne, *Patrologia Graeca*, vol. 36.

69. This and the following three quotations are from *Oratio Catechetica Magna* 22, 23, 24, 26, translated by Rashdall, *Idea*, 305.

Gregory then changes the logic from that of exchange, to guile and subversion. He introduces the famous image of the fish hook, and with it the near-physical notion of overwhelming life injected into the realm of death.

> In order to secure that the thing offered in exchange on our behalf might be the more easily accepted by him who demanded it, the Deity was hidden under the veil of our nature, that so, as is done by greedy fish, the hook of Deity might be gulped down along with the bait of flesh, and thus, life being introduced into the house of death, and light shining in darkness, that which is the contradictory of light and life might vanish away; for it is not in the nature of darkness to remain when light is present, or of death to exist when life is active.

The description moves as an abyssal descent, "life . . . into the house of death," and it shows how the tradition in its imaginitive development does also employ the crucial metaphor used in this book. But it lacks a radical anthropological viewpoint and, as in the case here, still enshrines it within an overall mimetic field between God and his cosmic rival. A trick has been played and where there is deceit there is violence. Gregory seeks to vindicate this by appealing, inevitably, to the approach we saw in Tertullian: the logic of mimetic reciprocity. "By the reasonable rule of justice, he who practiced deception receives in return that very treatment, the seeds of which he had himself sown of his own free-will." At the final moment the structure of mimesis forces Gregory to involve God in an *imitatio diaboli* (imitation of the devil), at once liable to decoding as a God/Devil equivalence that Adamantius demonstrated against the Marcionites. It was this deep incongruity in the argument that led to the powerful twelfth-century reaction against "rights of the Devil" as the starting point in theology of redemption.

In the East, Athanasius is the author of the major early study explicitly on atonement, *De Incarnatione Verbi*. This work contains explanations that are clearly a matter of substitutionary sacrifice, even perhaps of substitutionary punishment. The significant shift again is carried through: it is now God who requires the death of Christ, not the Devil.

Athanasius argues that humanity is under a curse as a result of sin, the content of the curse is death, and it would be impossible for God to go back on his word and undo the curse merely because human beings repented.[70] As a result Christ's death becomes necessary as a fulfillment of

---

70. Athanasius, *Contra Gentes and De Incarnatione*, vi, vii.

God's truthful word. It is not hard to suggest here a sketch outline of the Anselmian doctrine of satisfaction, but Athanasius lacks all the obsessive dynamic of honor and mimetic exchange characteristic of the Abbot of Bec. His broad picture places much more stress on the remedial effect of substitution than its violent mechanics, on a quasiphysical incorruption communicated simultaneously by a surrogate death and the presence of the immortal Word in human flesh.[71]

> He [the Word] took to himself a body which could die, in order that, since this participated in the Word who is above all, it might suffice for death on behalf of all, and because of the Word who was dwelling in it, it might remain incorruptible, and so corruption might cease from all men by the grace of the resurrection. Therefore as an offering and sacrifice free of all spot, he offered to death the body which he had taken to himself, and immediately abolished death from all who were like him by the offering of a like. For since the Word is above all, consequently by offering his temple and the instrument of his body as a substitute for all men, he fulfilled the debt by his death. And as the incorruptible Son of God was united to all men by his body similar to theirs, consequently he endued all men with incorruption by the promise concerning the resurrection.[72]

Christ has made death disappear from his followers as thoroughly as straw from fire.[73] It is this dynamic, transformative impact of the eternal Logos, following in the Alexandrian philosophical tradition, that remains the dominant impression of *De Incarnatione*. Athanasius's work constitutes a point of terminus in the East, with a range of expressions, more or less refined, available in the tradition, but never straying far from the basic spectrum it represents. In the West, on the contrary, the twelfth century would provide two dramatic rereadings of atone-

---

71. Frances Young, in *Sacrifice and the Death of Christ* (London: SCM Press, 1975), believes the view of Athanasius to represent "a sort of 'self-propitiation' offered by God to God to make atonement for the existence of evil in the universe" (93). I would consider this understanding itself to be heavily dependent on the twelfth-century Anselmian scheme, and also later Reformation thought. The core issue in Athanasius is the problem of death itself and redemption from it, not the responsibility of evil and appeasement of wrath.

72. Athanasius, *De Incarnatione*, ix, 155. See also xx: "Through the coming of the Word into it [a human body], it was no longer corruptible according to its nature, but because of the Word who was dwelling in it, it became immune from corruption. And two things occurred simultaneously in a miraculous manner: the death of all was fulfilled in the Lord's body, and also death and corruption were destroyed because of the Word who was in it."

73. Ibid., viii, 153.

ment doctrine, one of which was itself to become another kind of terminus, rendering proximate and deferred violence absolute in the person of God. The other was entirely the reverse, but it was the first that
was to establish itself as the dominant Western account from then on.

As I have already emphasized, this reading was facilitated by the
background and perspective of Roman law in almost all the major
thinkers at the foundations of the tradition. Tertullian, Cyprian,
Ambrose all trained in Roman law. Augustine was a rhetorician prepared
for public office. Thus Ambrose develops the idea of a transaction with
the Devil in terms of civil justice, an exposition of mimetic exchange
consonant with a lawyer's imagination. The case of Adam is of an ances-
tor incurring a debt to the Devil that then descended like a burdened
estate, with ever accumulating interest, to his offspring. Christ by his
death wiped out the interest, then transferred the debt to himself: as
such he is "bonus creditor."[74]

With typical magisterial style Augustine further establishes the idea of
a debt paid to the Devil. "In this redemption the blood of Christ was as it
were the price given for us (but the devil on receiving it was not enriched
but bound), in order that we might be loosed from his chains . . . and that
he might not . . . draw with himself to the ruin of the second and eternal
death, anyone of those whom Christ, free from all debt, had redeemed by
pouring out his own blood without being obliged to do so."[75] The translation loses the force of Latin expressions and their echo of ancient
Roman law. Particularly noteworthy is the clause "*ut nos ab eius nexibus
solveremur,*" which is rendered by "in order that we might be loosed from
his chains." The *nexum* is a surety preliminary to, or accompanying, an

---

74. Ambrose, *In Ps.* xxxvi. 46. Quoted and translated in *Idea*, 328. At the same time he
understands the incarnation of Christ explicitly as a reciprocal fraud to the Devil's earlier
fraud; but the second fraud, of the Lord's, is holy: "*pia fraus est*" (from *In Luc. Exp.* iv. 12,
in *Idea*, 328). Ambrose was also able to see the death of Christ in terms of penal substitution. The concept implies that the debt to the Devil was also one of punishment adminis-
tered by the Devil, but that God was in fact the final arbiter of the sentence against humanity (see n. 38). In the East, as noted above, Eusebius of Caesarea was an exponent of penal
substitution (see *Demonstr. Evan.* X.1, Migne, *Patrologia Graeca*, vol. 22, 724). This theme
arises inevitably out of the logic of mimetic exchange: what is a deferral of violence in the
case of the Devil becomes appeasement or expiation when referred to the ultimate judge
of humanity, God. As I continue to point out, this shift occurs spontaneously in the matrix
of mimetic theology.

75. Augustine, *De Trin.* xiii. c.15, in *St. Augustine, The Trinity*, trans. Stephen McKenna,
The Fathers of the Church, vol. 45 (Washington, D. C.: Catholic University of America
Press, 1963), 397–98; Latin original in *Idea*, 331, n. 1: "*In hac redemptione tamquam
pretium pro nobis datus est sanguis Christi, quo accepto diabolus not ditatus est, sed ligatus:
ut nos ab eius nexibus salveremur, nec quenquam secum eorum quos Christi, ab omni debito
liber, indebite fuso suo sanguine redemisset, peccatorum retibus involutum traheret ad secun-
dae ac sempiternae mortis exitium.*"

actual object sold, and once handed over to the buyer he becomes himself "bought" (*emptus*) and "obligated" (*damnatus*).[76]

Augustine's *nexibus* functions in the context of debt and therefore
has the same meaning as the *nexum*.[77] In this light they are not to be
understood in any primary sense as chains, but as physical objects
charged with self-alienation, prior to the necessary *solutio* by handing
over the physical price, together with the terrible *nexum* itself. In this
connection we may perhaps understand that the Devil's binding
nexum, from which Christ looses humanity, has anthropological reference in an alienation experienced at a cosmic level. The Devil may be
interpreted as a kind of reservoir of all accumulated displacement of
human self-worth and power through history.[78] Then, in his turn, this
figure is bound (*ligatus*), or mimetically indebted and dispossessed, by
the unreturnable *nexum* of Christ's unindebted life (*ab omni debito
liber*). However, there can be little doubt that Augustine understood
nexibus as real, ontological indebtedness in respect of a personified
Devil.[79]

Elsewhere Augustine continues to unpack mimetic indebtedness,
describing sin as a kind of deed held by the Devil, entitling him to fix us in
death. This would be the alienation of the debtor from the side of the creditor. Into this situation Christ entered and was undeservedly put to death.
Because of this the creditor became himself the debtor, and as a result no
one who deserved death, but who was redeemed from debt by the coun-
tervailing credit of Christ's blood, deserved it any longer.[80] Again and again
he plays on these reversals of indebtedness and the scheme appears perfectly settled in his mind.[81] At the same time it is clear that the scheme is
transcended by the overarching judgment of God; thus ultimately the Devil

---

76. This etymology comes from Mauss, op. cit., 47 (and see his n. 8, 118–19). He comments: "[T]hese supplementary exchanges are fictitious expressions of the movement of
personalities and the objects confounded with them" (ibid.).

77. *Oxford Latin Dictionary*, nexus -us, 3. (leg.) = NEXUM.

78. This fits phenomenologically with the picture of the Satan (the Adversary) in the
book of Job, whose place and function is twice stated as "going to and fro on the earth, and
. . . walking up and down on it" (1:7, 2:2). Perhaps we can feel here the weight of the rent-
man's tread.

79. The *massa damnata* is an ontological reference. For the realism of his notion of the
Devil, see his image of the mousetrap with Christ as the bait, by which the Devil was
enticed to his ruin, *Serm.* cclxiii. 1, also *Serm.* cxxx.2, in Migne, *Patrologia Latina*, vol. 39.

80. *De Trin.* xiii. 16, in *St. Augustine, The Trinity*, 399–400: "The devil was holding fast
to our sins, and by means of them was deservedly fixing us in death. He, who had no sins
and was undeservedly led by him to death, released them. So great a price did that blood
have that he who slew Christ for a time by the death that was not due, should no longer
detain anyone who has put on Christ in the eternal death that was due."

81. Cf. *De. Trin.* xiii. c. 14.

is not an independent agent but acts as the executioner of God's supreme judicial decision. This is the point where a transaction with the Devil and penal substitution merge into one, but more significantly it is subordinated to Augustine's final view of God, as an arbitrary dispenser of mercy in a sea of condemnation. It does not cross his mind that the elaborate descriptions of mimetic set-off or exchange between Christ and the Devil lose all redemptive meaning if their positive effect is a foregone conclusion in the mind of God. Here the Crucified is a passive function of a remote and indifferent will, and ultimately no more than a kind of window-dressing of mercy while inside the house a throne of violence rules.

So, suddenly at a certain point in Augustine mimesis loses all its powerful economy and explanatory force. God's ultimate violence is what remains, and it is inscrutable, insuperable, irredeemable. Only for some is it allowed to be deflected by Christ. Here we have an ontological dualism in the heart of God, so absolute that it is beyond mimesis, and in comparison to which a mimetic rivalry between God and the Devil might seem positively healthy. On the other hand, it is the very insistence on the freedom of grace that brings this break in mimetic economy, and in its positive aspect—that some human persons are indeed brought to free-flowing charity beyond mimetic exchange—contains the genuine radicalism of Augustinian doctrine.[82] All that is necessary is to substitute abyssal love for transcendent will and that radicalism becomes an unconditional act of redemption.

After Augustine theology becomes either a repetition of, or an attempt to escape Augustine. Anselm of Canterbury may be counted the first real break in the Augustinian legacy, although he is also profoundly influenced by the Augustinian God. What I hope to show is that Anselm effectively reintroduced mimesis into the Augustinian non-economy, and so reaffirmed the historical-cultural worth of the Redeemer. Although this came with its own immense cost, it is a significant release from the Augustinian impasse. Meanwhile, there is a long lapse of time between Augustine and Anselm, a period in which cultural factors and processes may be counted generally much more determinative than reflective theology. In this connection the figure of Gregory the Great emerges as uniquely important. He is to be counted the primary popularizer of Augustine and chief mobilizer of the typical mindset of medieval faith. Both his position and prolific, accessible writing gained him enormous influence: "Gregory was in after time more read and lauded than Augustine. For nearly half a millennium he dominated

---

82. See, for example, *Enchiridion de fide, spe et caritate*, xxxi and cxviii, Migne, *Patrologia Latina*, vol. 40; and *De spiritu et littera*, 5, ibid., vol. 44.

without a rival the history of dogma in the Occident. . . ."[83] He was yet another figure trained to law and public office, and he handed on a now more or less standard form of the Roman legal model of relationships between God and humanity.

In relation to the Eucharist and penance this legacy is particularly striking. According to Gregory, the body and blood of Christ are really present in the elements, and this receives its phenomenological necessity from the cultic principle that each Eucharist performed by a priest is a real, discrete repetition of the sacrifice of Christ. This separate sacrifice "is not, as was the death upon the cross, for the sins of all men, or of all the elect, but only for the sins of the participants, or of those for whose benefit it may be specifically offered."[84] It achieves its beneficial effect by its value as *meritum*. The same effect is attained by penance, which was now explicitly a deferral or preemption of divine violence. "For either man himself by penance punishes sin in himself, or God taking vengeance on him smites him."[85] The scheme of divine violence is established to such a degree in the mind of the average Christian in the era after Augustine that it is now settled that there is another place of suffering, separate from hell, where those who are to be saved will complete after death whatever is outstanding to their required punishment. This is purgatory, taught emphatically by Gregory. Prior to this possibility postmortem, sources of deferral also include the intercession of the saints and angels. Again, Gregory played a crucial role in fixing this in the medieval mind's eye. The following perfectly captures the ambiguous medieval atmosphere of proximate divine violence and multiplied sources of mimetic deferral.

> If you had a case to be tried on the morrow before some great magistrate you would surely spend the whole of today planning for it; you would seek a patron and would beg him earnestly to become your defender. Behold the severe judge Jesus is about to come; the terror of that mighty council of angels and archangels is at hand. In that assembly our case will be tried and yet we are not seeking patrons who will then come to our defense. Our holy martyrs are ready to be your advocates; they desire to be asked, indeed if I may say so, they entreat that they may be entreated. Seek them as helpers of

---

83. Harnack, *Outlines of the History of Dogma*, 388.

84. Arthur Cushman McGiffert, *A History of Christian Thought*, vol. II (New York: Charles Scribner's Sons, 1933), 156.

85. Gregory, *Moralia*, IX, 54, trans. Arthur Cushman McGiffert, ibid., 152.

your prayer; turn to them that they may protect you in your
guilt; for the judge himself wishes to be importuned that he
may not be obliged to punish sinners.[86]

Gregory's cosmos was crowded with demons, angels, and saints, all
needing to be held at bay or recruited to one's aid, and presided over by
a Christ who was supreme judge, and who was also a warrior Savior
who had vanquished the Devil in a form of armed conflict.[87] At almost
every turn this universe was posited on institutionalized mimesis, a
constant daily practice that negotiated the possibility of human security in the face of eternal violence.[88] It is significant that Gregory personally instigated the missionary extension of Christendom to include the
Anglo-Saxons, and progressively through the eighth century, willing or
pressed, the continental Germans were incorporated. The shift to
Christianity was perhaps facilitated by a deliberate attempt at inculturation in Gregory's writings, and in the process the old Mediterranean
worldview suffused with a recognizable philosophical and "secular"
ambient was displaced.[89] As barbarians became Christian, Christianity
was itself reformulated within a warrior ethos, where personal honor,
fealty, and fierce folk religion extruded a vigorous new landscape over
older features of imperial order and intellectual faith. Anselm of
Canterbury is the pivotal figure who drew on this new cultural force to
produce, in turn, a dynamic new account of atonement.

86. *Homilia in evangelia*, xxxii. 8, trans. McGiffert, ibid., 158.
87. Cf. *Moralia* xxxii.12–xxxiii.6, which elaborates the encounter through a detailed
reading of the Leviathan passage in Job, including the use of the hook metaphor (citation
and summary in *Idea*, 316).
88. However, Gregory's monastic or contemplative teaching is on a different level and
moves to overcome conflictual mimesis through a profound phenomenology of human
transformation; see particularly his notion of *compunctio cordis*, the loving desire that is
both pain and delight, and where possession of God is characterized by God's absence.
This is a desire virtually without an object. Cf. Jean Leclercq, *The Love of Learning and the
Desire for God*, trans. Catharine Misrahi (New York: Fordham University Press, 1974),
31–44. This possibility of transcendence, but only through monastic dedication, is again
typical of the medieval construct.
89. Cf. Markus, *Saeculum*, which argues that Augustine ultimately endorsed the neu-
trality of the Roman state in relation to Christian faith and sacred history (although in
practice its forces could be deployed by the church). The state had a minimum beneficial
value that was to be neither despised nor triumphantly appropriated by Christianity.
Augustine's *City of God* includes a telling use of pagan sources that themselves debunked
all aspects of Greco-Roman religion, apart from the philosophical. Cf. Book iv.30, 31;
vi.5–10, particularly vi.10, which quotes at length from Seneca's *Against Superstitions*. In
the following chapter we will have the opportunity to note both Germanic religiosity and,
by way of contrast, the condition of "anomie" in the post-Augustinian Empire, understood
as loss of solidarity and consensus, and surely a primary marker in the experience of a "secularized" world.

A Master-Text of Divine Violence

It is time now finally to turn to this landmark work. Anselm's *Cur Deus Homo* is unquestionably the major single document in Western atonement doctrine. It occupies a commanding position, guarding the route back to the older popular consensus about the meaning of Christ's death, and pointing the way forward decisively to what was to become the subsequent common, reflex model. The intellectual concentration of its argument produces the appearance of seamless and irresistible logic, closely allied to the powerful, almost automatic response evoked by its key tropes. To study *Cur Deus Homo* is to be confronted with a reasoning that gives the impression of being cast in stone, of being a force almost of nature. One is left unsure of whether this is a result of the impact of the text itself, or of the cultural construct that it both invoked and promoted. Thus, although frequently contested and even more frequently unread, it maintains a privileged, even sacred status in the Western theological canon.[90] It

---

90. F. R. Barry concludes his examination of doctrines of atonement with the judgment that the Latin or Anselmian doctrine "is what Atonement means in popular orthodoxy" (*The Atonement*, 159). Colin Gunton, in *The Actuality of the Atonement* (Grand Rapids: Eerdmans, 1989; 94–96), stresses the necessity of an objective justice and applauds the *Cur Deus Homo* in its accent on the "cosmic disorder" of sin and the picture of God as taking responsibility for the restoration of true order. The Swiss theologian H. U. von Balthasar, developing a method of dramatic tension between the justice of God and the act of salvation in Christ, similarly situates the value of the *Cur Deus Homo* in its internal logic of God (*The Glory of the Lord: A Theological Aesthetics*, trans. Andrew Louth and others [Edinburgh: T. & T. Clark, 1984], 237 ff.). Raymund Schwager, a theologian with strong intellectual links to René Girard, follows von Balthasar in his method of "God-drama," and similarly vindicates the essential reasoning of the *Cur Deus Homo*. In *Jesus in the Drama of Salvation, Toward a Biblical Doctrine of Redemption*, trans. James G. Williams and Paul Haddon (New York: Crossroad Publishing, 1999), he posits an Anselmian method of achieving agreement between different qualities of God (justice and goodness), reached by taking them to a level "higher than which nothing greater can be thought." Thus Anselm's timebound "images" are not to be taken for his "true thought" but are simply "the starting point of a long process of purification of ideas" (6–15). In similar mode R.W. Southern, the premier British biographer of Anselm, has this to say about the *Cur Deus Homo*: "Everything of importance in Anselm's argument can survive the removal of every trace of feudal imagery. . . . The power of the *Cur Deus Homo* doesn't come from its feudal imagery, but from its combination of religious insight and logical force" (*Saint Anselm: A Portrait in a Landscape* [Cambridge: Cambridge University Press, 1990], 221). The problem with these approaches is threefold. 1) They seem to assume that there is a level of essential ideas independent of cultural, historical, and linguistic conditions, and therefore not open to "deconstruction" either anthropologically or epistemologically. 2) The history of the tradition, including its divine violence, is "saved" in a final ontology where all tensions are resolved. The level of anthropological crisis disclosed by the cross is thereby neutralized, at least on the theoretical level. 3) The rehabilitation of the *Cur Deus Homo* proves in fact a covert form of retaining its mimetic architecture, without which the putative level of pure ideation simply cannot be "read." Thus, the real consequence is to preserve the whole discourse of divine honor, justice, satisfaction, and violence. See the final chapter for an attempt to pursue some of these issues further, to a greater degree of consequence.

has established itself as the default logic of Christ's death in this tradition, and without needing to be referenced it has created a pervasive aura that in effect makes the argument without making it.

Against this near-geological character we need to remind ourselves of the particular and conditioned circumstance of its production. It arose at the threshold of the intellectual renaissance of the twelfth century and drew its stimulus from a flourishing feudal and monastic culture. In short it is a triumphant articulation of a defining cultural and historical moment. Moreover, we know that, as with most of his other writings, Anselm took considerable pains over its composition and the immense scope of its influence is testimony in part to the care and rigor with which he approached his task.[91] Finally, and most crucially in terms of our argument here, the *Cur Deus Homo* is from beginning to end predicated on intense mimetic sensibility. The way this sensibility serves step by step both to provoke and construct the argument is the case I now want to illustrate.

The document is constructed as a dialogue, which echoes not so much classical models as the spiritual colloquy of monks. In the final chapter, Anselm's discussion partner declares joyfully: "In proving that God became man by necessity [*ex necessitate*]. . . you convince both Jews and Pagans by the mere force of reason [*ratione*]."[92] This conclusive phrase makes precise the political and theological project behind the *Cur Deus Homo*. At the opposite end of the book, its very first chapter, Anselm makes a personal statement of why he engaged in it. He says that he had often been urged by many to set down in writing the rational answers (*rationes*) that he gave in conversation to questions raised on issues of faith. And the motive for which these had been sought was not to arrive at faith by reason, but that the things believed might become a delight "to intellect and contemplation."[93] He then brings up abruptly the question that moves this work, the one for which infidels ridicule the fatuous simplicity of Christians (*simplicitatem christianam quasi fatuam deridentes*), and which also perplexes ordinary believers: why did God become man? What was the necessity of this personal intervention by God, which could have been carried out "by means of some other being, angelic or human, or merely by his will?"[94] He

91. A relatively short work, it took three years to finish, 1095–1098 (*Saint Anselm: A Portrait in a Landscape*, xxviii; hereafter *Portrait*).

92. From *St. Anselm: Proslogium; Monologium, an Appendix in behalf of the fool by Guanilon; and Cur Deus Homo,* trans. Sidney Norton Deane (Chicago: Open Court Publishing, 1910; hereafter *St. Anselm CDH*), II, 22, 287; Latin text in *Pourquoi Dieu s'est fait homme*, intro., French trans., and notes, René Roques (Paris: Éditions Du Cerf, 1963); hereafter *Pourquoi*.

93. *Pourquoi*, I.1, 210, "intellectu et contemplatione" (my trans.).

94. *St. Anselm CDH*, I.1, 179.

then says he will conduct his argument by means of question and answer, and with another monk, Boso, whom he says is the most insistent among the many in seeking an answer to this question. We can catch here a glimpse of a vibrant monastic culture at a key juncture of time, and in this moment exercising itself against a perceived theological and cultural challenge. The threat is the more intensely felt because monks and monasteries were a self-conscious Praetorian Guard of the Christian faith: they renounced the world for its sake, and if only for that reason forces in the world could not be allowed to shake it from them.[95]

Anselm was foremost in championing this monastic ideology, seeing it as the only safe means of salvation in a dangerous world. His simile of the "town, castle and keep," given in live teaching to his monks, makes the point and vividly reflects the feudal scenery of the eleventh century. The town is prone to attack, and the faithful laity are those who dwell within its walls, but the enemy breaks in here easily, and ordinary believers will be fortunate if they escape. The monks are much more secure within the castle itself; they indeed have many alarms but they are safe so long as they remain inside and keep out of sight. However, only those in the keep, who are no less than the angels of heaven themselves, are totally immune from danger. Meanwhile, the enemy destroys without difficulty all those who live in the open countryside, that is the Jews and other unbelievers.[96]

This last point is also another important cross-reference for the circumstances of composition of the *Cur Deus Homo*, and gives itself a graphic picture of the perception from within the monastery walls of the situation of the Jews. From the parallelism of infidels and Jews, at the end of Anselm's book, we can infer both that the Jews were classed in one breath with Muslims, and that it was they who probably had the major role as critics of the Christian story of redemption. We know in fact that Anselm had at least indirect experience of the reasoned opinion of Jews from his visit to Westminster, London, between 1092 and 1093. During this time he lodged with the abbot, Gilbert Crispin, who was himself engaged in the final recension of a book, *Disputatio Judaei et Christiani*. This text, essentially respectful and tolerant in tone, presents the opinions of some learned Jews from Mainz, recently arrived in London. They

95. "From the sixth to the eleventh century, monasteries were not the only cultural centers since schools also existed in the towns. Yet, as a matter of fact, it is particularly the theology which flourished in monasteries which provided the substance for preaching and the religious instruction of the people. Many bishops were monks and it can be maintained that the spirituality of the Western Church, its 'piety,' in every domain of its activity, was completely impregnated with monastic doctrine" (*The Love of Learning and the Desire for God*, 236).

96. Summarized in *Portrait*, 223, from *Memorials of St. Anselm*, ed. R. W. Southern and F. S. Schmitt, *Auctores Britannicic Medii Aevi*, i, 1969, 66–67.

believed that the Christian doctrine of the God-man was both unnecessary and derogatory to God.[97] Gilbert's work answered the charge with the
traditional doctrine of the rights of the Devil, which is precisely what is
abandoned in Anselm's work. It seems reasonable to conclude that the
issue was discussed during the visit, and it may well have been the occa-
sion for Anselm's seminal thought on the matter.

Jews in this period were increasing in numbers throughout the towns
of northern Europe, including England, and learned rabbis provided the
only significant, formidable opposition to Christian doctrines. In addition
Christian thinkers were in the infancy of intellectual development, with
Anselm himself as a pioneer figure. Even in the thirteenth century as
Christian theology gained greater heights of sophistication, there
remained the feeling that the intelligent enemies of Christendom were still
somehow better prepared.[98] How much more was this the case in the
eleventh century and in the years 1095 to 1098, when Anselm wrestled
with the composition of the *Cur Deus Homo*? It was in 1096, in the course
of the mobilization of the First Crusade, that the first mass persecution
and murder of Jews in Christendom took place, including in Mainz from
where Crispin's disputants had migrated.[99] The complex of forces within
monasticism—its position in feudal society, its defense of the faith, its cultural and spiritual vigor, and yet its simultaneous lack of intellectual confidence—was anything but academic. The emotions that swept along a
gathering tide of pilgrims, adventurers, and killers cannot be divorced in
any simple way from the feelings of monks whose lives were also staked on
their faith, though with a very different set of proximate means and objec-
tives.[100] Anselm's *Cur Deus Homo* did not start life with an ideal intellectual birth, but in very real conditions of challenge and reply, touching the
very core of the parties involved.

The grounds on which the challenge itself was made could not indeed
have been more incendiary. The reiteration of the case at issue by Boso is
as follows. "Infidels ridiculing our simplicity charge upon us that we do

---

97. *Portrait*, 198.
98. Ibid., 199.
99. See Fred Gladstone Bratton, *The Crime of Christendom* (Boston: Beacon Press,
1969), 110: members of the synagogue in Mainz ritually slew each other rather than submit to the Crusaders.
100. See the remark of Peter the Venerable, abbot of Cluny, toward the middle of the following century. Jews, because they were "not far away from us, but in our very midst, are
much worse than the Saracens," from Jaroslav Pelikan, *The Christian Tradition*, 3, *The
Growth of Medieval Theology (600–1300)* (Chicago: University of Chicago Press, 1978),
245. Pelikan observes: "Presumably it was an expression of some such judgment when
Crusaders, on their way to make war with the Muslim infidel in the Holy Land, interrupted their journey to massacre Jews in Europe."

injustice and dishonor [*injuriam et contumeliam*] to God"; and he proceeds to recount the humiliating events of the gospel story as applied to
the Christian God, culminating in "crucifixion among thieves."[101]
Anselm's sense of feudal honor was deeply imbued, and most of all in relation to God. A childhood dream preserved by Eadmer is significant.
Anselm climbed the mountain above his home and came to the court of
God. On the mountain's lower slopes women were carelessly reaping the
corn, and Anselm resolved to accuse them to their Master. When he
arrived he found the great Lord alone with His steward, the rest of the
household being engaged with the harvest. Anselm sat down at the Lord's
feet and was brought white bread by the steward. In the morning, when he
awoke, he confidently asserted that he had been in heaven and had fed on
the bread of God.[102] We can almost breathe here the sharp, fierce air of feudal devotion rising as Christian spirituality. And for the rest of his life
Anselm's "favorite image of the relations between God and Man was that
of a lord and his vassals."[103] For a mentality that saw God as supreme feudal lord, any derogation of God's honor is an outrage of cosmic proportions. It literally threatened everything. Southern describes feudal honor
as having a "solidity": it pervades and links all gradations of society. It was
"essentially a social bond which held all ranks of society in their due
place."[104] To challenge the honor of the Christian God, the supreme Lord,
was to threaten the capstone and cement of the universe. To do so by
means of the doctrine of Christianity itself was to set fire in the family hall.

As Anselm says, in perhaps the key existential phrase of the whole argument of *Cur Deus*, "In the order of things, there is nothing less to be endured
[*nihil minus tolerandum*] than that the creature should take away the honor
of the Creator, and not restore what he has taken away."[105] We may interpret
this first of all as a direct felt response to the taunts of "infidels" heard by
Anselm. But then with a kind of forensic genius (and precisely because the
vital point was so unnegotiable), Anselm turns the logic round in his own
favor: he makes it the very basis of necessity of what had been challenged in
the first place. It is precisely to make "satisfaction" for God's offended honor
that the life and death of a God-man becomes inevitable.

At the same time, Anselm is not simply instituting a feudal image of
God. It is important also to recognize the intensely Platonic worldview in

---

101. *St. Anselm, CDH*, I.3, 182.
102. Anselm told this story fifty or sixty years later to Eadmer (*The Life of Anselm by Eadmer*, ed. and trans. R. W. Southern [London and New York: Thomas Nelson and Sons, 1962], I.ii); and *Portrait*, 6.
103. R. W. Southern, *Portrait*, 222.
104. Ibid., 225–26.
105. *St. Anselm CDH*, I.13, 206.

which he distilled his thinking. This is related to the wider philosophical range of Anselm's thought, and nowhere is its eidetic character more evident than in the famous "ontological argument" from the *Proslogion*. Anselm seeks to construct an argument for God's existence out of pure thought. In the course of this argument he shifts, almost imperceptibly, from what is in the mind to what *is* in itself. The characteristics, evidenced here, of immense confidence in the determinative reality of thought and a view of mental objects as continuous with real objects are also on display in the *Cur Deus Homo*. In this treatise Anselm presents ideas of the beauty and order of the universe virtually as real objects constitutive of its physical reality. United with these, God's will or justice also forms part of the essential continuum, so that Anselm seamlessly fits together a logos theology of an inherent intellectual order, with the Augustinian notion of voluntary providence that maintains its own justice. In this frame any dishonor to God sets the whole linked system of universal essence, order, right, and feudal relations, spinning madly out of control.

[A]s the individual creature preserves, naturally or by reason, the condition belonging, and, as it were, allotted to him, he is said to obey and honor God; and to this rational nature, which possesses intelligence, is especially bound. And when the being chooses what he ought, he honors God; not by bestowing anything upon him, but because he brings himself freely under God's will and disposal, and maintains his own condition in the universe, and the beauty of the universe itself, as far as in him lies. But when he does not choose what he ought, he dishonors God, as far as the being himself is concerned, because he does not freely submit himself to God's disposal. And he disturbs the order and beauty of the universe, as relates to himself, although he cannot injure nor tarnish the power and majesty of God.[106]

---

106. *St. Anselm CDH* I. 15, 208–9. Another governing concept that does not appear here but is very close to order and beauty is *rectitudo* or right. Through *rectitudo* Anselm combines truth and justice in the human individual, just as he combines them in the universe via order and beauty. "Truth is Rectitude as perceived by the mind; Justice is Rectitude as chosen for its own sake by the will" (*De Veritate*, cc. 11, 12; 191, 194 in F. S. Schmitt, ed. S. Anselmi Opera Omnia, vols. i–iv [Edinburgh: Thomas Nelson & Sons, 1946–1961], trans. in *Portrait*, 172). Roques observes in respect to *CDH* I.13 that order in the universe is in fact an expression of the rectitudo of God: "L'*ordo rerum* est l'expression de l'*ordo*, de la *rectitudo*, du *jussus* ou de la *justitia Dei*...." (*Pourquoi*, 272). For the link between God, justice, and honor, see *St. Anselm CDH* I.13, 206: "There is nothing more just than supreme justice, which maintains God's honor in the arrangement of things, and which is nothing else but God himself." In these texts we can see how Anselm constructs an indivisible universe of truth, order, beauty, honor, and justice.

Anselm is at pains to keep God's ultimate transcendence intact even as he lodges his personal honor squarely in the fabric of the universe. The resulting solidity of the scheme is not affected; it is of course strengthened. The key effect is to enshrine the notion of honor, a mimetic category par excellence, in an abstract setting of eternal essences, and conversely to make the essences solid by their connection with divine honor. This at-once heady and dangerous combination is perhaps what constitutes the triumph of the *Cur Deus Homo* as a piece of northern European or Romano-Germanic thinking. It embeds the iron of feudal honor in Platonic amber, and materializes Platonic ideality in terms of feudal law. It has remained an object of intense fascination ever since.

By means of this triumphant scheme Anselm is able finally to break from the tradition of the "rights of the Devil" without incurring censure. The argument against the traditional account is put in the mouth of Boso and it is allowed to stand there as conclusive for the whole of the debate. This is probably no accident. We know that Boso is the one who pressed Anselm more than any other for a solution to the central question of the *Cur Deus Homo*, and that in 1094 Anselm called Boso to Canterbury, probably to help him in preparing the book that was to provide an answer. Boso had originally come to study with Anselm at Bec about ten years before, because of some "difficult questions" (*perplexae questiones*) then preoccupying him.[107] We can construct here a picture of an acute and troubled mind wrestling with issues of faith and doctrine, and perhaps in an area where Anselm was himself to encounter a profound challenge. It is a glimpse almost of the clashing of eras, as one seeks to find a way past the other. The judicial ownership of man by the Devil was certainly an idea both men wanted to see over and done with.

Boso declares that it would be intelligible to grant the Devil some rights over man if either were in any way independent of God. "But since neither the devil nor man belong to any but God, and neither can exist without the exertion of divine power, what cause ought God to try with his own creature (*de suo, in suo*)."[108] This is the argument in a nutshell, and so easily it sweeps away a millennial tradition, the whole Marcionite-Irenaean idea of a rival hypostasis to God. Behind it stands the challenge of the infidels, again rehearsed by Boso shortly before these lines. It was in God's power to save humanity by a word; how unbelievable, therefore, by means so "unbe-coming" (*tam indecentia*)![109] Accordingly it is the supreme prestige of God that is at stake. Congruent with this, no other entity should be given nego-

---

107. *Portrait*, 202–3.
108. *St. Anselm CDH* I, 7, 187.
109. Ibid., I, 6, 185.

tiating power on a level with him, or be allowed to reduce him to such conditions. Anselm "had too uncompromising and too unitary a view of God's dominion over the whole Creation to accept any view which diminished God's majesty in the smallest way."[110] In other words, the concept of absolute feudal honor was the only acceptable starting point for a theory of atonement. Much more germane was the question of human beings' offense to God's honor, given by freely handing themselves into the power of the Devil. How were they to reverse this "calumnious reproach still heaped on God," by an existence that could "conquer the devil by the pain of death, while wholly avoiding sin?"[111] In other words, how were they to face the due punishment inflicted by the Devil, all the while maintaining a blameless life?

We can indeed hear the screeching of gears; it is human beings now who have the duty to compensate God, not God to bargain with the Devil. The weight of the universe falls on humanity, and it is an impossible weight, entailing a deferral of violence of unheralded immensity. The name of the deferral is satisfaction for sin.

In the central section of the dialogue, chapters eleven to twenty-four of the first book, Anselm lays out his relentless vision of divine honor. He begins by explaining the nature of satisfaction, and it is quite clear. "He who violates another's honor does not enough by merely rendering honor again, but must according to the extent of the injury done, make restoration in some way satisfactory to the person whom he has dishonored. . . . So then, everyone who sins ought to pay back the honor of which he has robbed God; and this is the satisfaction which every sinner owes to God."[112] So it is not simply the reinstitution of the denied service that is at stake; this is basic distributive justice. What is required is something extra in relation exclusively to the sense of offense. And, again, in the world inhabited by Anselm, the response to offense is not expressed in a sudden, passionate outburst of anger. The anger is real but is locked into the "objective" or hypostasized nature of honor mediated by the total system of relationships. As I suggested earlier, it is the system of regulated mimesis itself that produces the commodity of honor, which then acts as a spiritual quantum attaching itself to individuals. Its loss becomes a crisis of proximate violence, because the whole structure as such is a product of proximate, then deferred violence. The loss of honor opens a breach in the system, but so long as the system holds it is a very specific breach and may be repaired, its violent effect redeferred, by specific requirements. These constitute satisfaction.

---

110. R. W. Southern, *Portrait*, 209.
111. *St. Anselm CDH* I, 22, 231.
112. Ibid., 1.11, 202–3.

The proof of this is that if satisfaction is not given then, unchecked and extreme violence ensues. The *Cur Deus Homo* states this unambiguously.

> It is impossible for God to lose his honor; for either the sinner pays the debt of his own accord, or, if he refuse, God takes it from him. For either man renders due submission to God of his own will, by avoiding sin or making payment, or else God subjects him to himself by torments, even against man's will, and thus shows that he is the Lord of man, though man refuses to acknowledge it of his own accord. And here we must observe that as man in sinning takes away what belongs to God, so God in punishing gets in return what pertains to man.[113]

Anselm is not as afraid as many of his commentators to make plain the logic he is using. It is either satisfaction or torment, and this is by no means an arbitrary requirement by a vengeful God. It is inherent in institutional mimesis. Violence is its beating heart, and it either creates a sophisticated system of honor and satisfaction, within which individuals are socially secure (saved), or unleashes itself with unchecked fury.

What now remains for Anselm is to elaborate the specific mechanics of satisfaction for sin. He establishes with Boso that the least offense against God is of greater seriousness than the annihilation of the whole universe (and indeed all possible worlds), and this terrible alternative should be preferred to even the slightest glance contrary to God's will (I.21, 228–29). Having established this as a principle, he then infers that there is no satisfaction for sin unless it be to restore something greater than this immensity of value that should be lost in preference to a single sin (I.21, 230).[114] The figure of Christ is then introduced and, threading through a number of discussions relating to other aspects of Christian doctrine, the conclusion is reached: only someone who is "greater than all else but God himself," that is, someone who is in fact God, can make this satisfaction. But only a man ought to make this satisfaction (II.6, 245). God, therefore, must become man. Yet, one outstanding question remains: in what way is this satisfaction to be paid in the human condition, given that a life of obedience is no more than would be expected of any man? Anselm suggests that the extra on the part of this individual, which constituted satisfaction, was "to give up his life or to lay down his life, or to deliver himself up to death for God's honor" (II.11, 258).

---

113. Ibid., I.14, 207. Following references given in text.

114. At this point he also merges the argument with the necessity of conquering the Devil by pain of death, while avoiding sin—once again to restore God's honor.

The circle is nearly complete. The death of Christ is locked up in the code of satisfaction. It is encased in a splendid inevitability that at the same time is freely accepted by Christ. He becomes the perfect knight, whose death fills the land with the perfume of nobility and the legend of honor vindicated. There is, however, a further mimetic repercussion: the "merit" passed on from God that defers the violence accumulated this time by Christ. As a result of his death Christ now places the Father under obligation to repay. "You surely will not think that he deserves no reward [*retributione*], who freely gave so great a gift to God?" (II.19, 263). The Father cannot give his Son anything that he does not have already, so the fruit, retribution, and merits (*fructum et retributionem . . . meriti*) of his death are handed on fittingly to his family and brothers (*parentes et fratres*) who are wasting away in so much debt and misery (II.19, 284–85).

Ultimately it is the logic of mimesis that decides. On the one hand, such is the charged immensity of Christ's gift to the Father that humanity is assured salvation on the smallest of conditions. Boso concludes and Anselm does not demur: "[I]t seems to me that God can reject none who come to him in his name [Christ's]" (II.19, 285). On the other, it does not take much to see that overall we are dealing with a mimetic refinement of brutal vengeance: that indeed without this smallest of conditions, absolute revenge takes its place, and therefore Christ's death is a displacement or substitute for that revenge. It was immediately possible, therefore, that the idea of penal substitution would break out once more from the tight reciprocities of satisfaction; and indeed it did so, more vigorously than ever before because all alternative explanations had effectively been discounted. From Anslem onward penal substitution simply leaps the formal steps of satisfaction, moving at once to the point of wrath that lies behind the whole, and making Christ bear this passively rather than offer compensation actively. The Anselmian scheme opened the "opposition between the justice of the Father and the love or mercy of the Son, which was to become so prominent a feature in popular religious thought."[115] Penal substitution is the logical realization of this opposition. But it is also a terrifying sacrificial crisis in which the violence of both God and man against the innocent victim is fully exposed and never resolved. In its harsh light the need for a scapegoat, for a surrogate victim, would be pressing and permanent. The *Cur Deus Homo* does not pre-date the First Crusade but its genesis cannot be divorced from cultural conditions that mobilized the cross for war, with terrifying consequences for European Jews. This is a point I will continue to develop in the next chapter. But in its own historical career this document would carry within itself precisely those

---

115. *Idea*, 357.

conditions, even as it sealed them into a theological worldview and rose to become a master text of Christian thought. It would provide a permanent cultural vehicle, a culture medium in every sense, for the infection of sacrificial crisis in Western society and history.

For, in other words, we could say that the Demiurge of violence had found its character armor in feudal honor. The mimetic logic that had been established in relation to the Marcionite Creator, quickly reinterpreted by Irenaeus in terms of the Devil, now crept back into God the Father established in a relationship of opposition to Jesus. The hypostasis of violence had been melded with the Father, but in a way at once more unchallengeable and dangerous than before because it would always remain in vigor at a supreme level. Anselm's reasoning appears successful because it establishes an exact calculus of institutional mimesis that appears to resolve matters absolutely. However, this is not true sacrificial thinking, which always seeks to achieve some sort of unconscious identification between the violence of the group and the figure of the God. The problem with the Deus Christianorum presented by Anselm is that there is never this sort of closure. The relational mimesis is so thematic, alongside the narrative repetition of the actual violence of the cross, that there is always the barely suppressed awareness of massive violence that is deferred in fact only barely. The functioning of the deferral is simultaneously within a relationship of identification between the Father and the Son, and an attribution of continuing responsibility for the suffering of the Crucified on the part of the sinner who hears the message. At a certain level no one could believe that any true father would be "satisfied" by the execution of a beloved son, least of all when the preacher tells me that I brought about his death!

Peter Abelard, Anselm's astute contemporary, immediately drew this conclusion. He is quoted in the list of charges against his errors, drawn up by Bernard of Clairvaux, as stating that God should be much more angry with humankind for the crucifixion of his Son than for the transgression of eating an apple. He then makes the following comment that very probably has Anselm in its sights. "If Adam's sin was so great that it could be expiated only by the death of Christ, what expiation can there be for the very murder committed against Christ . . . ?"[116]

---

116. *Idea*, 362–63, from the *Capitula errorum*: "Quod si tantum fuerat Adae peccatum, ut expiari non posset nisi ex morte Christi; quam expiationeem habebit ipsum homicidium, quod in christo commissum est . . ?" See also *Commentary on Romans*, ed. E. M. Buytaert, *Corpus Christianorum Continuatio Medievalis*, II, 116, 210–14.

It is not accidental that Abelard is so forthright in his attack on the Anselmian scheme. He himself is famous for his development of an alternative idea of atonement, and generally it is remarkable that around the turn of the eleventh century there should have been such concentration on this issue, and such radical divergence of views. Where Anselm seeks to establish a doctrine by "absolute reasoning" (*necessaria ratione*),[117] the mind of Abelard goes in a very different direction. He presents Christ's death mainly in terms of its contingent affective impact on the individual. And yet, even more remarkably perhaps, these two accounts do have something in common. Where Anselm's reasoning, as we have seen, is predicated on systematic or institutionalized mimesis in the conflictual sense, Abelard turns to the same "faculty" but now presented in terms of an example of surrender, or a mimesis of open-ended giving that has forfeited all exchange. The suffering of Christ, rather than being translated into a calculus of proximate and deferred violence, is understood as effective precisely because it loses that necessary logic. It is the loss itself that seems to call forth the salvific experience.

> To us it appears that we are none the less justified in the blood of Christ and reconciled to God by this singular grace exhibited to us in that His Son took our nature, and in it took upon himself to instruct us alike by word and example even unto death [*usque ad mortem*], (and so) bound us to Himself by love [*amplius per amorem astrinxit*]; so that kindled [*accensi*] by so great a benefit of divine grace, charity should not be afraid to endure anything for his sake: which benefit indeed we do not doubt kindled the ancient fathers also, who expected this by faith, unto a supreme love of God no less than the men of (this) time.[118]

In his hymnography concerning the Passion of Christ, Abelard pushes the idea further, invoking "compassion" as effectively the principle of redemption. "Make us have compassion on thee, Lord/That we may sharers of thy glory be" (*Tu tibi compati sic fac nos, Domine/tuae participes ut simus gloriae*).[119] Thus at the very height of what might be

---

117. " For what is clearly made out by absolute reasoning ought by no means to be questioned, even though the method of it be not understood" (*CDH* 1. xxv).

118. *Idea*, 359; Latin text from *Capitula errorum*, ibid., 363.

119. Colin Morris remarks, "The stress on compassion here is enormous. It becomes almost the central point of the passion, as if man was justified by compassion, by pity for suffering humanity" (*The Discovery of the Individual*, 1050–1200 [New York: Harper & Row, 1972], 143).The verse of Abelard is from the *Oxford Book of Medieval Latin Verse*, ed. F. J. E. Raby (Oxford: Clarendon Press, 1959), no. 171.

called a solidification of theology in the frame of conflictual mimesis, a daring thinker turned the principle upside down. The very weakness that suffers from violence, and is usually "saved" by a mimetic doubling of that violence, becomes itself in its failure the point of significance and liberation. This is the movement of abyssal compassion, in terms of both the fathomless response of forgiveness on the part of the Crucified and the answering experience of transformation on the part of the believer. It is an extremely important testimony to the power of the core gospel tradition that a radical thinker moved to formulate this meaning of redemption already in the twelfth century.

However, the huge problem with Abelard's formulation, as seen from an objectivist or metaphysical standpoint, is that it contains no guarantees, no necessary reasoning that would compel intellectual assent, or at least provide a fixed universe in which atonement can be demonstrated. As Barry puts it: "What if Christ's example leaves the sinner unmoved? The purpose of God is then, it would seem, defeated."[120] From this viewpoint atonement must "work" regardless of the contingent response of the individual. But surely it is the very undecidability of mimesis that makes the figure of the cross simultaneously fragile and powerful, and so constitutes its very particular drama. Indeed, the anthropological methodology used here and its positing of a transformative mimesis requires that the Abelardian version of Christ's death be retained, with all its contingency. It is only the real possibility of failure that also constitutes the possibility of real change. If we start with a mimetic analytic, only the open (weak) possibility of Abelard's version offers a breakthrough. In a world of conflictual mimesis, compassion as an alternative must depend itself on "failure" that cannot command assent or predict success. Thus a mimetic anthropology can only offer a nonmetaphysical account of atonement.[121]

Meanwhile, it was of course the Anselmian formulation with all its metaphysical force that was destined for historical success. Thomas Aquinas avoided the argument of necessity but integrated the notion of satisfaction fully into the medieval doctrine of redemption. From this conservative theological basis it continues to remain in force in Roman

---

120. *The Atonement*, 147.

121. Or, if metaphysics is inescapable, we are dealing here with a metaphysics of loss, that which is "true," but *because it fails*. The message of the Resurrection vindicates this loss rather than contradicts it dialectically. Allied indivisibly to the cross it makes it thematic. Of course there is, as always, the opportunity for the reentry of a metaphysics of presence, but *remaining* metaphysics of loss it may always also be, or move closer and closer to being, the loss of metaphysics. See chapters five and six below for an account that situates the meaning of the cross in a refiguring of time, a "new time" that both is and is not present.

Catholic teaching and homiletics.[122] However, it was the Reformed tradition, I believe, that most deeply appropriated the crisis provoked by the Anselmian doctrine of atonement. Its radical solutions may be seen to drive the crisis to a further extreme. It is important to look at the way Martin Luther wrestled with the issue, to see how he both attempted to escape the Anselmian heritage and remained thoroughly in its thrall, serving to hand on a less differentiated and more overtly violent rendering of Anselm's formal mimetic logic.[123]

A GOD IN CRISIS

Luther wanted to be done with the notion of satisfaction, and from an assessment of its origins that had the ring of truth. "We . . . would send it back to the judges, advocates and hangmen from whom the Pope stole it."[124] At the same time his concept of the substitutionary nature of Christ's death is more extreme than anything envisaged before, and its very force dragged with it the traditional terminology. Christ was made a curse for us, was made "to become the greatest thief, murderer, adulterer, robber, desecrator, blasphemer, etc. . . . In short, He has and bears all the sins of all men in His body—not in the sense that He has committed them but in the sense that

---

122. See *Catechism of the Catholic Church* (Chicago: Loyola University Press, 1994), para. 615, quoting the Council of Trent: "Jesus atoned for our faults and made satisfaction for our sins to the Father." Aquinas believed there were other possible ways open to God to bring about salvation, however none were "more fitting" than Christ's death. So he goes on to say there was a "condign satisfaction" in the fact of the one atoning for infinite fault being of infinite worth. "Christ's passion, then, was not only sufficient but superabundant atonement [*satisfactio*] for the sins of mankind" (*Summa Theologiae*, vol. 48 [New York: McGraw-Hill; London: Blackfriars, 1963], 3a. 1, 2 ad 2. See also vol. 54, 3a. 48. 2. The idea of ransom or redemption is then wrapped with satisfaction as the notion of a debt of punishment (*reatus poenae*) which was paid by Christ. "As therefore Christ's passion provided adequate, and more than adequate satisfaction for humanity's sin and debt of punishment, his passion was as it were the price by which we are freed from both obligations. *Satisfaction offered for oneself or for another is called the price whereby one ransoms oneself or another from sin and from punishment*" (48.4, my italics). Thus satisfaction is equated with punishment perhaps even more clearly than in Anselm.

123. The following discussion focuses on the thought of Martin Luther and does not treat the theology of Calvin. On the one hand Calvin does not say anything essentially different from the doctrine of penal atonement; rather he energetically reinforces the image of God as judge to the point where God becomes "three angry letters in a book" (see Timothy Gorringe, *God's Just Vengeance*, 136–41). On the other, his gridlock concept of the divine decrees, either to salvation or perdition, seems to legalize and harden Luther's more existential and dramatic sense of conflict within God. In this light Calvin could be read as a further attempt to reestablish sacred order in God, and therefore of course in human experience. Luther's sense of order is perhaps at once both more romantic (discovered in individual sensibility) and pragmatic (enforced by the prince.)

124. *Works* (Weimar edition) xxxiv.i, 301 f., quoted in Gustaf Aulén, *Christus Victor*, trans. A. G. Herbert (London: SPCK, 1940), 134.

He took these sins, committed by us, upon His own body, in order to make satisfaction for them with His own blood."[125] In this vein, of identifying Christ physically with states of penal condemnation, he goes so far as saying that Christ "really and truly offered Himself to the Father for eternal punishment on our behalf. His human nature behaved as if He were a man to be eternally condemned to Hell."[126] The logical (mimetic) content of punishment within satisfaction reaches here full realization.

Such statements can also be read against a background complex of theology and anthropology characteristic of Augustine, the vision of an unconditionally violent God in opposition to an unrelievedly sinful humanity: salvation intervening in an entirely arbitrary manner.[127] But in the case of Luther we must also note a peculiar aggravation of the Augustinian heritage. The added element of Nominalist theology emphasized the utter freedom of the divine will beyond any notion of justice or punishment, or any reason whatsoever. Luther's personal experience was not just of personal crisis, but of a God in crisis too.[128] God was simultaneously vengeful toward human sin and yet so totally removed from ordinary concepts of goodness and justice as to be beyond any juridical scheme himself. To this extent the Anselmian calculus could be seen to be overcome. God was simultaneously just and merciful, not by turns, and not changed into one or the other by virtue of mimetic exchange. And yet conflictivity remains, now affecting the eternity or substance of God himself.

> The curse, which is the divine wrath against the whole world, has the same conflict with the blessing [as death does], that is, with the eternal grace and mercy of God in Christ. Therefore the curse clashes with the blessing, and wants to damn it and annihilate it. But it cannot. For the blessing is divine and eternal, and therefore the curse must yield to it. For if the blessing in Christ could be conquered, then God himself would be conquered. But that is impossible.[129]

---

125. *On Galatians*, iii.13, *Luther's Works*, ed. Jaroslav Pelikan, vol. 26 (St. Louis: Concordia, 1963), 277.

126. *Commentary on Romans*, ii. 218, quoted in *Idea*, 400.

127. The amount of direct influence of Augustine on Luther is a matter of scholarly debate, but generally the Wittenberg Reformers are seen as heirs of the broad Augustianian tradition, above all on the issue of grace. For example, Alister E. McGrath, *Reformation Thought, An Introduction*, (Oxford: Blackwell, 1988), 61.

128. William of Occam and his successors propagated the view that God could do anything he liked that did not imply logical contradiction, including commanding someone to hate him, or becoming incarnate in an ass or a stick; cf. *Centiloquium Theologicum* (conclusiones v, vi), quoted in *Idea*, 388. For Nominalism's influence on Luther, ibid., 397.

129. *On Galatians*, iii. 13, *Luther's Works*, vol. 26, 281–82.

It is almost impossible to sort out in rational categories what precisely is going on here: the shocking image of a God in conflict with himself. The following is helpful.

> Wrath and love fuse upon the cross. . . . It is not that the Son by his sacrifice has placated the irate Father; it is not primarily that the Master by his self-abandoning goodness has made up for our deficiency. It is that in some inexplicable way, in the utter desolation of the forsaken Christ, God was able to reconcile the world to himself. This does not mean that all the mystery is clear. God is still shrouded at times in thick darkness. There are almost two Gods, the inscrutable God whose ways are past finding out and the God made known to us in Christ.[130]

It is as if Marcionite dualism elaborately scaffolded and concealed in the doctrine of satisfaction is deliberately resolved into a kind of primary chaos, in and on the cross. In Girardian terms this could be understood as a full-blown sacrificial or mimetic crisis, but within the concept of God itself. Salvation emerges marginally the winner, and apparently only in those for whom an interior, subjective assurance guarantees a share. "Faith cannot be otherwise but a lively and unhesitating opinion by which a man is exceedingly certain he is pleasing to God."[131] The Augustinian God of predetermination is on this count bound positively to the salvific experience of the individual. At the same time the world remains bound to God's wrath. Luther's theology, therefore, is a successful resolution of a mimetic crisis on the level of the private conscience. But for the realm outside this internal zone of security the terror is objective and divinely impersonal. "When a magistrate condemns to death a man who has done him no harm, he is not his enemy. He does this at God's behest. There should be no anger or bitterness in the man's heart, but only the wrath and sword of God. Also in war, where in defense one has to hew, stab and burn, there is sheer wrath and vengeance, but it does not come from the heart of man but from the judgment and command of God."[132] The fact that this wrath may ultimately be an inscrutable doublet for God's mercy only serves to

---

130. Roland Bainton, *Here I Stand* (Nashville: Abingdon Press, 1978; paperback, Tring, England: Lion Publishing, 1987), 63.

131. From *Operationes in Psalmos*: "Fides autem esse nullo modo potest, nisi sit vivax quaedam et indubitata opinio qua homo certus est super omnem certitudinem sese placere Deum. . . ." (quoted in *Idea*, 409, my trans.).

132. *Weimar Ausgabe*, XLI, 746–47, quoted by Bainton, op. cit., 241.

displace the crisis of violence more effectively from the mind of the Christian.[133]

At all events the key to the peace of the believer remains the atoning death of Christ. Whatever the duality in God, the mechanism that turns the wrath of God to mercy for the individual is the substitutionary death of Christ. "The theology of Luther represents the most exaggerated expression of that substitutionary view of the atonement which, in less naked and exaggerated forms, was not originated by him."[134] Gustav Aulén strongly rebutted this view and insisted that Luther's statements must be read in terms of God's act of absolute victory over the evil powers or "tyrants" that hold humanity in thrall; thus to connect Luther's teaching to the Anselmian or "Latin" view of the atonement is a basic error.[135] Instead he relates Luther's view to what he terms the "Classic" idea, which is precisely the earlier church doctrine of victory over the Devil, but understood without any connotation of transaction or exchange. In fact it appears that what Aulén is doing is to read back into the church fathers Luther's very particular variety of dualism in the heart of God. "There should, then, be no doubt at all that in Luther we meet again the classic idea of the Atonement. It is the patristic view that has returned; but it has returned with greater depth and force than before. We may see this most clearly in his treatment of the enemies from which Christ delivers mankind."[136] To the regular trio of sin, death, and the Devil Luther adds two more, law and wrath, and these two are directly expressive of God's will and subjectivity. In other words God's victory becomes an internal victory over his own judgment exercised against sin, excluding any reciprocity between God and a rival power. Ultimately, therefore, it is the idea of wrath that "leads us to the very heart of Luther's theology,"[137] because it is here that the drama of redemption is most powerfully experienced.

---

133. The consequences for political theology are acute. "Luther's social ethic has been described as 'defeatist' and 'quietist', encouraging the Christian to tolerate (or at least fail to oppose) unjust social structures. . . . The failure of the German church to oppose Hitler in the 1930's is widely seen as reflecting the inadequacies of Luther's political thought. Even Hitler, it appeared to the German Christians, was an instrument of God" (*Reformation Thought, An Introduction*, 145). Writing directly to a political question, the crisis of the peasant's revolt, Luther condensed his political theology in the elemental dichotomy that seals the world's fate: "God's kingdom is a kingdom of grace and mercy, not wrath and severity, but the kingdom of the world is a kingdom of wrath and severity. . . . [N]ow he who would confuse these two kingdoms . . . as our fanatics do, would put wrath into God's kingdom and mercy into the world's kingdom" (*Works of Martin Luther* [Philadelphia: Muhlenberg Press, 1943], 5.39, quoted by Gorringe, op. cit., 135–36).

134. *Idea*, 420.

135. *Christus Victor*, 30.

136. Ibid., 124

137. Ibid., 129.

Wrath is overcome by an absolute act of mercy, but somehow also remains in the deep structure of God, almost the negative legitimation of the very act of salvation itself.

> It is God's act of victory, when Christ goes in under the Divine wrath, and bears the burden of the punishment which on account of that wrath impends upon men. Thus the Love of God breaks through the Wrath; in the vicarious act of redemption the Wrath is overcome by the Love which is ultimately, as Luther says, *die Natur Gottes*. But the fact that the Wrath is overcome means not at all that it is to be regarded as only a pretended wrath, or that it ceases to exist; rather, through the Atonement it is *aufgehoben*, transcended in the Hegelian sense—that is, it remains latent and behind the Divine Love, and forms the background of the work which the Love fulfills.[138]

It is disingenuous to suggest that this is not profoundly a result of the Anselmian scheme, that Luther somehow skipped four hundred years of medieval culture and arrived at this schism in the heart of God without the catastrophe of "satisfaction" working to precipitate it. Rather Luther provided its radicalization in an internal, "psychic" division of God, consolidated, even as it was repressed, on the cross. Again, the advantage is that God is made to bear the weight of the deferral of violence in an interior fashion, rather than in Anselm's insistence on the human, indeed historical, function of Christ's actions. So the individual who connects with Christ's salvation in Luther's version may indeed have a greater sense of closure and spiritual peace than in Anselm's. At the same time there is both a greater insistence in popular preaching on the punishment Christ endured for the individual, in order that the individual might appropriate a personal sense of substitution and, correlative to this, the enduring violence of God in and against a sinful world. As Aulén says, not it seems without relish, wrath remains latent behind divine love. What else is this than the explicit remainder of the violent Demiurge in the Lutheran figure of God? What else does it signify but the continuing validation of Christian violence at the eternal level, despite all the abyssal compassion of the Crucified?

So Luther in his own way repeats the intransigent force of the Anselmian formula, and if anything makes the doctrine of a God of violence yet more visceral and destructive. Through a long tradition of

---

138. Ibid., 131–32

mimetic reasoning the dark hypostasis of violence is fixed in the background of Christian imagination and, despite vigorous protest on any number of occasions, nothing has been able to dislodge it. Anselm's *Cur Deus Homo* is a pivotal document that at once brings substitutionary trends of thought in the early church to a refined level of expression and fixes in almost unshakable manner a dualist reference in the Western understanding of redemption. At root there is a logic of mimetic exchange used to explain the violence suffered by the Crucified. In the latter chapters of this book I will seek to develop an alternative approach to the redemptive meaning of this suffering, and on a variety of registers, including rhetoric, narrative, Scripture, and philosophy. At the heart of them all is the event of abyssal compassion, producing alteration in the self of the believer. This can be read and understood by and through all these methods of reflection. But perhaps most crucial will be the thought of the cross as an interruption of time itself, permitting an "anarchic" new beginning in the very meaning of God. With such an unanticipated beginning, at that singular point, it will perhaps be possible to break creatively in terms of discourse, if not finally in terms of culture, with a theological tradition enshrining a God of violence.

Chapter Three

THE WARRIOR CHRIST AND HIS PITY

While Anselm of Canterbury was still in process of finishing his seminal work, the *Cur Deus Homo*, he left England seeking refuge from the continual confrontation he was experiencing with the Norman king, William Rufus. The issues were essentially feudal dues and ecclesiastical policy, matters on which Anselm showed an independent spirit. After a series of bruising disagreements Anselm set out to consult with Pope Urban II whose claim to the pontificate he had defended against William. Six months of traveling brought him to Rome, where he met with the pope in the latter part of April, 1098. Details of their discussion do not concern us here. What is fascinating is a small episode in the immediate context of this visit in Italy. Anselm was lodged in a mountaintop village away from the heat and bad airs of Rome. It was here he concluded the *Cur Deus Homo*, and it was from here he was invited by a Norman knight, Roger of Apulia, to be present at the siege of Capua, which Roger was prosecuting on behalf of a fellow prince. The knight was "moved by the archbishop's fame" to make the invitation, and so Anselm and his companions spent several days at the siege in specially provided tents, at a tolerable distance from the sound and fury of military operations.[1] Urban II also came to attend the spectacle, and while Eadmer contrasts the relative demeanors in the camp of the worldly pope and the humble archbishop, he passes absolutely no remark on the general picture of these two eminent churchmen so much at ease with a warrior aristocracy and assisting at a cruel act of war almost as entertainment.[2]

---

1. *The Life of St. Anselm by Eadmer*, ed. R. W. Southern (London and New York: Thomas Nelson and Sons Ltd., 1962), 109 [hereafter *The Life*]. The description of the lodging echoes the sound of battle: "remoti in tentoriis a frequentia et tumultu perstrepentis exercitus."

2. Roger was the son and successor of Robert Guiscard, who had become a vassal of Pope Nicholas II in 1059 and had proved invaluable in rescuing the embattled Gregory VII from captivity in Rome at the hands of the Holy Roman Emperor, Henry IV, in 1084. Urban, who had been adviser to Gregory and was the heir of his ecclesiastical policy and struggle against the emperors, had every political reason to support the military campaigns of the Norman knights. See *The Life*, 109–11, and notes; also Hans Eberhard Mayer, *The Crusades*, 2nd ed. (Oxford: Oxford University Press, 1988), 17–18.

There is a further twist to the vignette. Roger's vassal, another Roger, count of Sicily and founder of the Norman-Sicilian state, came to help enforce the siege. He crossed over into Italy, including several thousand Muslim soldiers in his brigade, and took up position blockading Capua from the south.[3] Eadmer describes how Anselm gave gifts of food to these "pagan" troops and was enthusiastically venerated by them when he passed through their bivouac. He says many of them would have accepted conversion to Christian faith through Anselm's teaching, except that the count had forbidden it, probably as part of the understanding on which he had recruited them in the first place.[4] This was very likely the first time Anselm had encountered people of Islamic religion, certainly in any numbers. At the very end of the *Cur Deus Homo* he writes that "even the pagans" would be forced to accept the necessity of the Incarnation, given his argument, and it is not improbable that this added note of missionary zeal was prompted directly by Anselm's encounter before Capua. Two years earlier Urban II had energetically recruited the First Crusade, and in terms of holy war against Muslims. Once again, therefore, the cross-references between the genesis of Anselm's work and the context of a violent Christendom cannot be ignored. In this chapter I wish to develop a sense of this organic context, and in particular the way the figure of Christ was molded to fit a warrior mentality within an acculturated Christianity. Those who "took the cross" in the First Crusade participated in the symbolic world that also produced the *Cur Deus Homo,* and their action and mind-set provide an illustration of background dynamics at work in this document. In a word, my argument is that both the militarization of the cross and its interpretation as satisfaction arise via the figure of Christ as warrior-hero, which at root is a formulation out of mimetic violence. At the same time we will see that Anselm's spirituality, and that of others influenced by him, gave evidence of what seems a diametrically different register, which in fact suggests its own radical critique of the former. This paradoxical factor is also part of the medieval impact and legacy of the cross, and it allows us also to ask the more general question: how can the image of the cross, which must inevitably show itself as an icon of love, have been actively assimilated as a banner of war? How can the figure of the cross have functioned as generative violence? As is at once evident, I want to

---

3. See René Roques, *Pourquoi Dieu s'est fait homme,* Latin text, intro., trans., and notes, *Sources Chrétiennes,* vol. 91 (Paris: Éditions du Cerf, 1963), 34. Also *The Life,* 111, n. 2. Roger, count of Sicily, was the brother of Robert Guiscard.

4. *The Life,* 112.

ask this question within the frame of mimetic anthropology, and I turn
now to examine the phenomenon of the First Crusade with the intellectual tools that it gives us.

VIOLENCE IN SEARCH OF ITS OBJECT

It is impossible to propose one clear cause or even complex of causes for
the savage fervor of the First Crusade.[5] Reading the descriptions one is left
with the impression of a spontaneous, unprecedented outburst. It is as if
one of the amorphous, undefined movements of history, where masses of
people erupt from somewhere "beyond" and break across a self-identified
line of civilization, arises within the borders of a documented society and
culture itself. The image here is of a movement propelled out from the center toward a goal beyond the line, to seek to integrate it within the expanded borders of that selfsame culture. The fact that Jerusalem is the goal, with
its immense accumulated meaning as the center, the true spiritual pole of
the earth, serves to reinforce the irony, and yet credibility, of the model. It's
as if the struggling identity of Europe at this point pushed outward to
assimilate Jerusalem in a symbolic and conceptual order, rather than simply relocating its population toward a desirable focus of material wealth
and power elsewhere. The Europe of Franks, Germans, Saxons, and
Normans displaced itself in order to displace other places, rather than aim-
ing purely at the investing of territory. The self-identification of crusaders
by "taking the cross," literally by strips of cloth in the shape of the cross
sewn on the shoulder of their cloaks, displayed to all the world that before
they took a step they had already claimed the inheritance of Jerusalem. The
question is, what did the cross mean used in this way, and what significance
did Jerusalem have in relation to it? In terms of mimetic anthropology we
might ask, what foundational murder or murders were being invoked
and/or enacted in order to ground the uncertain soul of Christendom?

There were of course material conditions that prompted the east-
bound movement en masse. Primogeniture in France and Italy is often
cited as a problem that left younger sons of noble families without estates,
forced to choose either the monastery or a life of dissolution or banditry.
The proclamation of the Crusade offered them the chance for adventure,
lands, and titles in the east, backed by right of God and the church.[6]

---

5. "The success of the Clermont appeal has still not been fully explained and probably
never can be" (*The Crusades*, 9).

6. *The Crusades*, 21 ff. Mayer also gives the somewhat different custom of *frérêche* in
southern France as a cause. Property was held in common by the brothers, also uncles and
nephews, but marriage itself was controlled in order to restrict the numbers of shareholders.
The Crusade offered a chance to break free from constraints of a stringent family system.

Primogeniture in France seemed to have been established progressively after the year 1000. That period was marked by a severe agrarian crisis brought on by rising population and failure of production. The situation improved gradually when the church and nobility acted to prevent the breakup of estates into uneconomic units, but conditions of landlessness and acute poverty remained for many.

> Several years of drought had certainly led to poor harvests and shortages, and hence to . . . ergotism, a terrifying condition which could lead to insanity and death and was brought on by eating bread made from rye which had not had ergot removed from it. The poor were very numerous in all the armies of the First Crusade. . . . It is possible that between 1096 and 1101 many of them took advantage of the chance to seek a new life for themselves, but we actually know very little about them, let alone their ideas and aspirations. They appear often enough in the narrative accounts, but usually only as an amorphous mass causing problems for the leaders, particularly when it came to feeding them.[7]

This undefined or undifferentiated group was in fact essential to the relative success of the First Crusade. It was one of their numbers, a Provençal servant named Peter Bartholomew, who during a blockade of the Christian forces within Antioch had the dramatic revelation that the sacred lance that had pierced Christ's side was to be found in the cathedral of St. Peter.[8] Its successful discovery on 14 June 1098 rallied the throng of Franks and Normans who in an aggressive sortie routed the Turks. It was also the poor who in the winter following this victory forced the quarreling leaders to continue south and pursue the attack on Jerusalem.[9] All these crusaders had slipped into a kind of dream world even before they left Europe, an unreality consisting equally of unspeakable cruelty, visions, and the physical company of the saints and the dead to comfort and encourage them. From an anthropological perspective, their state of consciousness could be read as the kind of hallucinations associated with the moment of acute mimetic or sacrificial crisis.[10] This could also then explain why the drive to a violent conclusion in Jerusalem was so powerful.

---

7. Jonathan Riley-Smith, *The First Crusaders*, (Cambridge: Cambridge University Press, 1997), 16–17; hereafter *First Crusaders*. Evidence from an account written ten years after Urban's proclamation at Clermont: Robert of Rheims, "Historia Iherosolimitana," vol. 3, 728, of *Recueil des historiens des croisades; Historiens occidentaux*, 5 vols., ed. Académie des Inscriptions et Belles-Lettres (Paris, 1844-1995 [hereafter *RHC Oc*]).

8. *The Crusades*, 52.

9. *First Crusaders*, 13.

10. Ibid., 15; cf. *Violence and the Sacred*, 162–64.

The background of crisis was social as well as economic. William of Tyre, constructing a chronicle several decades after the events, but drawing on contemporary documents and reminiscences of survivors, described the general situation in Europe prior to the first crusade. "All things were in such disorder that the world appeared to be approaching to its end, and was ready to fall again into the confusion of chaos."[11] The sense of an end is regularly understood in terms of millennial preoccupations peaking around the beginning of the eleventh century, expressing the belief that the return of Christ and the appearance of the Antichrist would be revealed first in Jerusalem.[12] There can be little doubt that biblical literature provided much of the language and thought forms of the time; however, the sense of an end did not arise simply from biblical language. There were very concrete dysfunctions of European political society that along with economic stress provoked the free-floating, unresolved feeling of breakdown, which then could find a biblical construction. The tenth century was marked by the collapse of law. "The disintegration of the Carolingian Empire had brought with it a decline in the authority of the state and a general decline of public morals. Everywhere in the tenth century the warrior class, composed of men who were gradually coming to be called knights, was patently brutalized. Private property, especially church property, was attacked just as greedily as it ever had been by Vikings or Magyars. The state could do very little about this unhappy state of affairs and it became increasingly difficult to see any sign whatsoever of public order or security."[13] In response to chaos the church intervened progressively in the constitution of civil society, and thus provided another essential piece in the sociocultural jigsaw that produced the Crusades.

The church as an institution, with an inherited sense of authority and right (*ius*), was always capable of playing a default role in establishing civil order in some shape or form. Now it stepped boldly into the arena with an energetic attempt to bring the warlords under ideological control, and in effect to convert them to its service. The movement of the Peace of God, preached largely by the emerging Cluniac reform, sought to engage the nobles by oath to observe the immunity of clergy, unarmed persons, peasants, and ecclesiastical property. From about the middle of the eleventh century onwards the approach was widened, attempting to restrict the days and seasons on which raiding and feuding was permissible.[14] The impression is of a society in which

---

11. Quoted in *Michaud's History of the Crusades*, trans. W. Robson, vol. 1 (London: Routledge & Co., 1852), 54; hereafter *Michaud*.
12. *First Crusaders*, 26.
13. *The Crusades*, 15–16.
14. Ibid.

armed gangs, of greater or lesser size, with chiefs claiming noble title of greater or lesser pedigree, struggled for advantage upon the back of whatever peasant and monastic production existed. When the church sought to regularize this violence by administering oaths, establishing penalties, and seeking redress in the case of unrepentant disturbers of the peace, it was also inevitably drawn into a warrior ethos. Then, in the bitter disputes of the Investiture Contest, Gregory VII (1073–1085) sought to win the warrior classes explicitly to the cause of the church. He shifted the use of the ancient term, *militia Christi*, meaning the clergy, those who fought with the weapons of the spirit, to *militia sancti Petri*, the knights of Peter who were now the physically armed militia of the church.[15]

By means of a cumulative process the church had integrated a warrior culture into its own self-concept. Reciprocally the warriors appropriated an ideology of Christian calling and destiny.

> The knights, as a class, had acquired their own professional ethos—an ethos firmly rooted in the Church's conception of the world—with its visible liturgical expression in the ceremony of dubbing. It is important to realize that on the eve of the crusades there existed a fully developed class of knights, sharing a moral code which transcended political frontiers, and which enabled them to undertake common enterprises.[16]

So, by a mutually consistent double progression, both a sense of chaos and a developing militarization of Christianity prepared the moment of eruption. Connected to the latter a further key ingredient should be highlighted. The vital element in the full-term evolution of the crusader was the concept of penitential or meritorious violence. The idea of penitential pilgrimage to Jerusalem was already well established from the tenth century onward, building on a general tradition of devotional pilgrimage to the Holy City from the fourth century. Violent men like Fulk Nerra, count of Anjou, or Robert the Devil, Count of Normandy, went on pilgrimage to the Holy Sepulchre to seek forgiveness for crimes of rapine and blood-

---

15. Riley-Smith suggests that Gregory referred to the knights most commonly as *fideles beati Petri* (the faithful of blessed Peter), but the terms seem interchangeable, and he makes the same key point; see *First Crusaders*, 44–46. An example of the militarization of pastoral catechesis, almost at the same moment of composition as the *Cur Deus Homo*, is Bishop Bonizo of Sutri's *De vita christiana* (c. 1090–1095), which lists a catalogue of the virtues of a Christian knight (*The Crusades*, 19).

16. *The Crusades*, 19.

shed.[17] Sometimes these pilgrimages were voluntary expressions of penance, other times they were imposed by confessors. Now, the penitential value of a specifically military undertaking was secured because of its identification with pilgrimage to Jerusalem; the Council of Clermont that legislated for the First Crusade explicitly attached the crusade penance and its reward to the idea of pilgrimage.[18] At the same time the idea of war itself as a penitential exercise had already been broached by the pivotal figure, Gregory VII. In his exhortation to knights who took up the cause of reform against the emperor, he said they were engaged "in defending righteousness for the name of Christ and in order to win eternal recompense in a holy war so pleasing to God."[19] One of his imperial opponents, Sigebert of Gembloux, wrote that it had been Gregory who first put forward the idea of penitential warfare when "he had ordered the Marchioness Mathilda [a key partisan of Gregory's ideas] to fight the Emperor Henry for the remission of her sins."[20] Indeed, Mathildite priests recorded that in their blessings on her army in 1098, "We were to impose on the soldiers the danger of the coming battle for the remission of all their sins."[21] In other words the act of fighting in a just war was itself a penance precisely because of the danger of the violence involved.

In these statements the powerful confessional phrase of *remissio peccatorum*, employed in the Nicene Creed, is assimilated directly into a mimetic transaction, of violence endured for the sake of divine violence deferred. Technically this phrase should not have been used in connection to the remission of physical penalties imposed in confession, which was the normal objective of a penitential pilgrimage. In fact it appears not to have been mentioned in the decrees of Clermont; but Urban II used it in his recruitment of volunteers, and it was cer-

---

17. Ibid., 13. *First Crusaders*, 27–28.

18. *First Crusaders*, 66–67. See R. Somerville, *The Councils of Urban II. 1: Decreta Claromontensia* (1972), 74: "Whoever for devotion only, not to gain honor or money, goes to Jerusalem to liberate the Church of God can substitute *this journey* for all penance" (my italics; quoted in Jonathan Riley-Smith, *The First Crusade and the Idea of Crusading* [Philadelphia: University of Pennsylvania Press, 1986], 29; hereafter *Idea of Crusading*).

19. *First Crusaders*, 50–51; from *The Epistolae Vagantes of Pope Gregory VII*, ed. H. E. J. Cowdrey (Oxford: Clarendon Press, 1972), 54.

20. *First Crusaders*, 51; from "Leodicensium epistola adversus Paschalem Papam," *Monumenta Germaniae Historica* (hereafter *MGH*), *Libelli de Lite Imperatorum et Pontificum* 2 (Hannover: Impensir Bibliopolii Hahniani, 1960, 1969), 464. In 1089 Urban II used the same ideology—an act of war for the remission of sins—in recruiting knights for the occupation and defense of Tarragona against the Moors (*First Crusaders*, 66).

21. Ibid., 51; from Bardo, "Vita Anselmi episcopi Lucensis," *MGH* Scriptores in Folio et Quarto, ed. G. H. Pertz et al., 34 vols. (Hannover: Hahn,1826ff.; Nendeln: Kraus Reprint, 1963), 20.

tainly taken up enthusiastically by other propagandists of the First Crusade.[22] Used by the preachers in this way, it undoubtedly carried implications of remission of "penalties due to sin in the next world" as well. In other words, relief from the suffering due in purgatory was granted, and this effect was produced ultimately by the authority of the church ("power of the keys").[23] It is true that the fully developed concept of indulgence—an absolute waiver of all penalties granted by the transcendent power of the church out of the "Treasury of Merits" of Christ—was not present at this point. Rather a stress on the mimetic effect of violence endured (i.e., a deferred divine violence and a proximate human violence demanding compensation) remains the dominant rationale.

> Urban's crusade "indulgence" was not really an indulgence at all. It was the categorization of the crusade as a penitential war of the type established by Pope Gregory VII and it was an authoritative pastoral statement that the penance the crusaders were taking on themselves was going to be so severe that it would be fully "satisfactory," in the sense that God would be repaid not only the debts of punishment owed on account of their recent sins, for which penances had not yet been performed, but also any residue left over from earlier penances which had not been satisfactory enough. Urban, therefore, was not granting a spiritual privilege, which was what the developed indulgence would be in that it presupposed that God would treat a meritorious act as if it was "satisfactory" even though it was not; he was proclaiming a war in which the fighters would be imposing condign punishment on themselves by their own efforts.[24]

It would be difficult, I think, to overstate the significance in the conjuncture of these themes. Evidently we are fully in the regime of "satisfaction," the key trope of the *Cur Deus Homo*. The warrior holds an irrecusable claim on divine forgiveness, because his whole life has been thrown into the bargain, over an extended period involving extreme hardship and danger. However, from the side of church preaching, this may still be announced as a gift of divine grace communicated by the pope. For it was necessary that the pope first announce the war pilgrimage as *remissio pec-*

---

22. *First Crusaders*, 68.
23. *The Crusades*, 30–32, 293–94.
24. *First Crusaders*, 68–69.

catorum in order for the crusader then to claim it. In essence, therefore, the idea of plenary indulgence was first mooted by the popular movement of the First Crusade in which the papacy, assimilated to a warrior ethos and its mimetic logic, played an authoritative role.[25]

Now, if a powerful warrior mimesis before God—"I lay down my life, so instituting satisfaction for all my sins"—had been given credibility and prestige by papal thinking since Gregory VII, what indeed does that say about the contemporary ethos behind the ideas and composition of the *Cur Deus Homo*? Anselm had contact with the court of the Norman kings of England, both indirectly and directly during the 1080s onward, as well as being abbot of an important monastery that would certainly have experienced a trickle-down of news and attitudes working through Christendom. Would an intelligence as sharp and sensitive as Anselm's have missed the emergence of a pivotal idea like meritorious violence? Or, should we perhaps say that out of the permeating warrior ethos of the time Anselm distilled his own version, parallel to that of the pope? At all events we are in the context of a categorical shift in church thinking. "It is no exaggeration to say that the idea of penitential warfare was to be a revolutionary one, because it put the act of fighting on the same meritorious plane as prayer, works of mercy and fasting. . . ."[26] If we add Anselm's participation in this shift, at one level or another, to the other influences behind the *Cur Deus Homo*, and see the idea of Christ laying down his life for God's honor as the theological sophistication of a thought that was coalescing at that very moment in the preparation of

---

25. "We, acting as much on our own authority as on that of all the archbishops and bishops in Gaul, through the mercy of almighty God and the prayers of the catholic church, relieve them of all penance imposed for their sins." This, one of Urban's statements in relation to crusaders, makes explicit the function of church authority mediating the mercy of God; quoted by Jonathan Riley-Smith, *Idea of Crusading*, 29, from H. Hagenmeyer, *Die Kreuzzugsbriefe aus den Jahren 1088–1100* (Innsbruck: Wagner'sche universitäts-Buchhandlung, 1901), 137. For the viewpoint of the knight see the famous statement by the contemporary historian of the First Crusade, Guibert of Nogent: "God has instituted in our time holy wars, so that the order of knights and the crowd running in their wake . . . might find a new way of gaining salvation. And so they are not forced to abandon secular affairs completely by choosing the monastic life or any religious profession, as used to be the custom, but can attain in some measure God's grace while pursuing their own careers, with the liberty and in the dress to which they are accustomed" (*First Crusaders*, 69, from Guibert of Nogent, "Gesta Dei per Francos," 124, *RHC Oc* 4). It again becomes evident that an embryonic plenary indulgence is at work if you consider that penances, including pilgrimage, were imposed in confession in relation and equivalent to a specific sin or sins and absolution granted in view of this penance. To establish formally a meritorious penance without this specific reference, its merit attached to the fulfillment of a vow of pilgrimage, implied a nonspecific or general remission of sins. This was the burden of Abelard's fierce criticism of crusade penance. See Mayers, *The Crusades*, 32.

26. *First Crusaders*, 48–49.

the First Crusade, then we have yet another picture of the undertow of culturally mediated violence in this work. If alongside this we also place the role of mimetic violence in producing the developed medieval church practice of indulgences, we can begin to sense perhaps the broad infection of theology by generative violence underlying the reaction of the Reformation.[27] The violence of the crusades had literally stormed heaven and torn open its treasuries for venal distribution by Christendom. The possibilities of exploitation were infinite, and the necessity of reform to restore, as it were, heaven's integrity was, sooner or later, inevitable. Luther's instinct against Anselmian satisfaction was surely of the same ilk, but as I showed in the previous chapter the problem here was chronic, and could only be treated by a kind of pain medication, not resolved. Outside the relief of salvation, warrior violence if anything was even more terrifyingly unleashed in the doctrine of the wrath of God and the world as its realm.

Urban II's fateful speech at Clermont on 27 November 1095 is recorded in a number of versions, none of which is completely trustworthy. However, from other sources including his letters, the decrees of the Council of Clermont, and the charters made by knights responding to his call, a plausible reconstruction can be made. It is almost certain that Urban made some reference to a displacement of internecine violence among the Christian warriors outward onto the enemies of Christian faith.[28] Michaud's nineteenth-century account has a literary-romantic flavor, but it gives a clear impression of the received understanding of what

---

27. "Particularly momentous was the decree [Fourth Lateran Council, 1215], now approved for the first time by a council, though it had been proclaimed by the pope as early as 1198, that a man who equipped another man should receive the same plenary indulgence as a genuine crusader. In the interests of sound finance this decree was probably as unavoidable as the taxation of the clergy; nevertheless it was a distortion of the original crusading ideal. From here it was but a short step to the commutation of crusading vows in return for a straight money payment. Taken together with a development which was, in itself, admirable—the organization of the Apostolic Chamber and the collectorates into a model of bureaucratic efficiency—this meant that the door was wide open for all kinds of abuses in the financial administration of the curia and the Church—the abuses which were to culminate in the intolerable pre-Reformation traffic in indulgences" (*The Crusades*, 219).

28. *Idea of Crusading*, 26. There are four eyewitness accounts of Urban's speech but written in hindsight after 1099. Three of these report reference by the pope to the behavior of the warriors contrasted with that of the new Christian knights: Fulcher of Chartres, *Historia Hierosolymitana*, ed. H. Hagenmeyer (1913), 136–37; Robert the Monk, cf. n. 8 above; Baldric of Bourgueil, "Historia Jerosolimitana," *RHC Oc.* 4, 14–15; all cited by Riley-Smith, *Idea of Crusading*, 166, n. 5. One of the decrees of the Council of Clermont, extending the Peace of God to cover the property of crusaders, demonstrates that the mutual violence of the knights was a very live issue (ibid., 22). Furthermore, charter evidence from knights departing on crusade indicates that a number of them explicitly linked renunciation of violence against the church and peasantry to taking the "way of God" [the crusade] to Jerusalem (ibid., 37–38).

happened on that day, including its resonance up to the modern period, and as indicated it is very probably rooted in the pope's actual statements.

> Christian warriors, who seek without end for vain pretexts for war, rejoice, for you have today found true ones. You, who have been so often the terror of your fellow-citizens, go and fight against the barbarians, go and fight for the deliverance of the holy places; you who sell for vile pay the strength of your arms to the fury of others, armed with the sword of the Maccabees, go and merit an eternal reward. If you triumph over your enemies, the kingdoms of the East will be your heritage; if you are conquered, you will have the glory of dying in the very same place as Jesus Christ, and God will not forget that he shall have found you in his holy ranks.[29]

On this evidence it is unmistakable that Urban II provided a scapegoat in the technical sense, and the polarization of violence that he unleashed can be witnessed gathering force in the territories of Provence, Burgundy, Champagne, Lorraine, quickly spreading to Normandy and England, and also Swabia, the Rhineland, and Northern Italy. Its eddies and currents created a number of very large groups on the move, some of which set off almost at once, in the spring of 1096, before the pope's preferred date of August 15th.[30] But such was the crisis of collective violence produced that it did not wait to find its official surrogate victim but sought it out at once, and so precipitated a fateful moment in Europe's history. Many of the rolling armed bodies destined to fight Muslims in the East immediately turned their attention to attacking Jews in the heart of Europe.

The first outbreaks seem to have occurred in France directly after the Crusade was preached, indicated by letters from French Jews to Rhineland Jewish communities warning them of impending danger.[31] But the records of persecution in the Rhineland itself are much more extensive, and it is here that the storm of terror reached its flood. The figure of Emich of Leiningeneral, already notorious for tyrannical behavior, is indelibly associated with the most brutal slaughter of Jews.[32] With a force exceeding

---

29. *Michaud*, 50–51.

30. *Idea of Crusading*, 49–50.

31. There is some evidence of a massacre in Rouen, and other cities of Lorraine, affecting Jews refusing to be baptized. See Paul E. Grosser and Edwin G. Halperin, *Anti-Semitism: Causes and Effects. An Analysis and Chronology of 1900 Years of Anti-Semitic Attitudes and Practices* (New York: Philosophical Library, 1983), 104; hereafter *Anti-Semitism*.

32. *Idea of Crusading*, 35, 50–52.

10,000 men he set about killing Jews en masse. In Speir they killed twelve Jews, but the bishop of Speir protected the rest of the community and cut off the hands of some of the murderers. At Worms the bishop was unable to give protection and 500 Jews were massacred after they had paid Emich protection.[33] The worst horror occurred in Mainz, where between May 25 and 29 the Jewish community was annihilated. At first Archbishop Rothard offered effective resistance, closing the city gates before Emich. Many Jews sought refuge in the bishop's palace where they also brought their possessions for safekeeping. Then in disputed circumstances Rothard's opposition crumbled. Emich's followers forced entry to city and palace, and in two days of massacre over 1,000 Jews met their deaths.[34] Some crusaders turned north to Cologne, but their search was largely fruitless because Jews had dispersed into the surrounding countryside. It seems later they were discovered and killings continued there and in further towns along the Rhenish valley. Others of Emich's force, marching in entirely the wrong direction for Jerusalem, headed down the Moselle valley killing Jews in Tier and Metz. The persecutors' intention according to one account was to "wipe out or convert,"[35] and sometimes forcible conversion was accepted as the alternative to death by the Jewish communities. For example, at Regensburg the army of the legendary crusade preacher, Peter the Hermit, coerced almost the whole community to baptism. At other times Jews died at their own hands, or those of fellow Jews, rather than submit to defilement.[36] Estimates vary as to the total number of deaths, but it seems at least 10,000 Jews were murdered in northern France and Germany, one-quarter to one-third of the Jewish population there at that time.[37]

This quantum leap in the persecution of Jews, the birth of pogrom on a sudden, massive scale, manifests how completely Urban II's strategy constituted a moment of generative violence: the directing of destructive group differences outward on a third party that then serves to consolidate the cohesion and identity of the primary group. How otherwise can we explain the immediate turn to the annihilation of a body of people that had nothing to do with the formal strategy behind the crusade? It was of course relatively easy to associate Jews and

---

33. *Anti-Semitism*, 105.

34. Ibid. Also *Idea of Crusading*, 50, 54. See Ernest A. Rappaport, *Anti-Judaism, A Psychohistory* (Chicago: Perspective Press, 1975), 73, which suggests the bishop colluded with Emich for material gain.

35. *Idea of Crusading*, 53; quotation from a Christian writer, Ekkehard of Aura, "Hierosolymita," 20, *RHC Oc. 5*.

36. *Anti-Judaism, A Psychohistory*, 72.

37. *Anti-Semitism*, 104.

Muslims via the common *topoi* of Christ, the Sepulchre and Jerusalem, and the crusaders were quick to make these connections.[38] But the mental pathway of connection and substitution does not explain at all why they embarked on the pathway in the first place. The process becomes immediately intelligible once we recognize that the choice of a surrogate victim is inherently substitutionary anyway; undifferentiated group violence like a kind of chaotic element seeks the nearest polarizing attraction that presents itself. In the case of the Jews they were also clearly preselected through existent cultural hostility. They were subject to an embedded tradition of vitriolic condemnation by church fathers and leaders, and it seems that the eleventh century had already witnessed some outbursts of violence. However, it was never church policy to seek their elimination, rather the reverse.[39] And, crucially, they had never been attacked before on this scale and with this project, by rolling masses of people with the intention to annihilate. A threshold had been crossed, a beast had been let loose: it would never be completely caged

---

38. In Rouen it seems men who had come to take the cross began to say, "We wish to attack the enemies of God in the East, once we have crossed great tracts of territory, when before our eyes are the Jews, more hostile to God than any other race. The enterprise is absurd" (*Idea of Crusading*, 54; from Guibert of Nogent, *De vita sua*, ed. E.-R. Labande [1981], 246–48.)

39. Ambrose, Chrysostom, Augustine, and Jerome all may be quoted with terrifying statements against Jews; cf. *Anti-Semitism*, 78–80. Augustine gives the rationale for the strategic tolerance of their existence that expressed official church theology and policy. "They were dispersed all over the world—for indeed there is no part of the earth where they are not to be found—and thus by the evidence of their own Scriptures they bear witness for us that we have not fabricated the prophecies about Christ. . . . God has thus shown to the Church the grace of his mercy in the case of her enemies the Jews . . . forbearing to slay them—that is . . . not putting an end to their existence as Jews . . . for fear that they should forget the Law and thus fail to bear convincing witness. . . . Thus it was not enough for the psalmist to say, 'Do not slay them, lest at some time they forget your Law,' without adding, 'Scatter them' [Ps. 59:12]" (*City of God* [London and New York: Penguin, 1984], Bk. XVIII, ch. 46). Bernard of Clairvaux took up the same argument at the time of the Second Crusade, but with a slightly different edge reflecting—and giving it seems *post factum* justification to—recent events. The Jews witness to Christianity now not by their Law but through their suffering. "The Jews must not be persecuted, they must not be killed. . . . They are for us, so to speak, living documents representing the Lord's Passion. Wherefore they were scattered all over the world, so that while they suffer the just punishments for so great a crime, they may be witnesses of our redemption" (*Epistola CCCLXIII, 6*, Migne, *Patrologia Latina*, vol. 182, col. 567). For earlier eleventh-century persecutions see *Crusades*, 13, and *Anti-Semitism*, 103: in the year 1012 after the news of the desecration of the Holy Sepulchre by the deranged caliph, Hakim, retaliatory killings and forced baptisms of Jews are reported to have taken place in Rouen, Limoges, and Rome.

40. "The Crusades opened a new era of anti-Semitism. In the period up to the Crusades, anti-Semitism was for the most part an elitist phenomenon. Church Fathers, Doctors, Popes, Saints, Bishops and Council, secular rulers and noblemen were constantly repeating strictures against the Jews and exhorting the people to shun the Jews. This indicates the populace did not take the restrictions very seriously. The situation changed

again.[40] From 27 November 1095 onward it had become possible to persecute the Jews of Europe on a massive and intentionally terminal level. It was the birth of the Holocaust as a (de)structural potential of European culture, and simultaneously a significant moment in the generation of that culture itself. The fact that the Crusades subsequently effected the direct practical contact of Europe with Islamic culture, including benefits of rediscovery of Greek philosophy, the revitalization of math and science, and the expansion of mercantile capitalism, should not mask the first key moment of spiritual and mental organization witnessed in the assault on the Jews.

A standard cultural motif by which the attack on the Jews is sometimes understood is that of the vendetta. It was an unconditional obligation in the small societies constituted by petty castellans and their vassals, understood in terms of relationships within a family, to avenge injury done to any member of the group. The crusaders themselves seemed to have given this rationale for their murderous actions. They were kinsmen exacting vengeance for the death of Christ, and they could address their victims in these terms.

> You are the children of those who killed the object of our veneration, hanging him on a tree; and he himself had said: "There will yet come a day when my children will come and avenge my blood." We are his children and it is therefore obligatory for us to avenge him since you are the ones who rebel and disbelieve in him.[41]

As regards the Turks, when the crusaders had achieved the final catharsis of conquering Jerusalem one of their leaders wrote to Urban, informing him that "[t]he Turks, who inflicted much dishonor on Our Lord Jesus Christ, have been taken and killed and we Jerusalemites have avenged the

---

dramatically in the 11th century. The anti-Semitic and anti-Jewish doctrines and preaching had seeped down into the consciousness of the people and the atrocities committed against the Jews that followed sprang from the people. The Church and state elites in the 11th and 12th centuries frequently found themselves in the role of restraining this mass anti-Semitism and protecting the Jews from popular attack" (*Anti-Semitism*, 120). These lines show that what had "seeped" was much more than the elites envisioned, suggesting therefore a generative movement at the level of the people. Moreover, as Riley-Smith points out, the image of restrained elite and murderous common people is not itself completely warranted by the facts. Crusading groups that turned into persecuting mobs, including that of Emich, held distinguished lords and knights in their ranks (*Idea of Crusading*, 51–52).

41. Reported by a Jewish writer, Solomon Bar Simson, "Chronicle," trans. S. Eidelberg, *The Jews and the Crusaders* (1977), 25; quoted in *Idea of Crusading*, 56.

injury to the supreme God Jesus Christ."[42] What is immediately important
is the fact that the crusaders were able to see themselves somehow as a collective kinship avenging the death of Christ. On this reckoning it was the
cultural model of vendetta, and in respect of Christ, that focused the
disparate violences of the populations of western Europe into a mass
force of arms. Or, to put it the other way round, the common language
of Christ, particularly the dead Christ, allied to the theme of vendetta
produced the mobilized and directed violence of the Crusades.
Although this idea very well describes the symbolic form that helped
give shape to the ultimate ideology of the Crusades, it begs the question, similar to the one above, of why disparate violences can in fact be
made to coalesce into mobilized, mass violence. How can small scale,
local violences make symbolic links operative between them and cohere
into such terrifying proportions unless there is a polarizing tendency in
the first place? In mimetic theory it is the scapegoat or surrogate victim
that is the absolutely crucial element deciding what is otherwise undecidable. Only a common victim can act to systematize or polarize random violence. The fact that the Jews were preselected in church history
does not lessen the fact that there and then they provided an organiz-
ing principle for the collective violence of Christian warriors who pre-
viously had fought each other. The Jews, therefore, far from representing a second stage, derivative persecution, in a logical progression from
the first proclaimed enemy, the Turks, were in fact a primary structural
element in mobilizing the violence of western Europe, so that the Turks
could then be attacked and Jerusalem conquered. Whatever the crusaders may have said about the "logic" of first attacking Jews, this was
ultimately rationalization of the implacable necessity to organize at
once around a victim. The Jews acted as a first condenser and conduit
by which to channel the mass violence of Europe eastwards.

   So what is being argued here is that the symbolism of Christ and
Jerusalem acted as metonyms and cues for crusaders to find a common
victim in the Jews, but beneath these "cognitive" operations should be
seen the unstable plasma of violence itself always needing to be directed by means of the victim, and out of this producing a new force field
of purpose and meaning. Vendetta against Jews and Muslims depends
first on scapegoating. Or vendetta is a way of giving ideological shape
to scapegoating. On this basis we may now directly examine the ideology of vengeance for the death of Christ, as a more complex moment
of formulation that manifests the generative violence at work in

---

42. Raymond of Aguilers, *Liber*, ed. J. H. and L. L. Hill (1969), 134, quoted in *Idea of
Crusading*, 48.

Christendom. We will do so by working through a number of texts from the period that can give us a greater awareness of a peculiarly Christian violence. We may then look beyond these to other cultural expressions that perhaps suggest an authentic alternative that this whole book seeks to argue.

A TERRIBLE PITY IS BORN

There is a remarkable passage in the greatest vernacular epic to emerge from the First Crusade, one of the genre of *chansons de geste* that celebrated the heroic virtues of Christian knights, the *Chanson d'Antioche*. It is a twelfth-century composition that in the section quoted below seems to reflect an earlier eighth-century legend, that the destruction of Jerusalem by the Romans was an act of vengeance for the death of Christ. This idea was incorporated fully into the twelfth-century poem, *La Venjance Nostre Seigneur*, where Christ is seen prophesying that his crucifixion would be avenged by the events of C.E. 70.[43] Here, in the *Chanson d'Antioche*, the historical work of vengeance is transposed directly to the crusaders. First, the good thief comments:

> "It would be most just, moreover, if you should be avenged
> On these treacherous Jews by whom you are so tormented."

> When Our Lord heard him he turned towards him:
> "Friend," said he, "the people are not yet born
> Who will come to avenge me with their steel lances.
> So they will come to kill the faithless pagans
> Who have always refused my commandments.
> Holy Christianity will be honoured by them
> And my land conquered and my country freed.
> A thousand years from today they will be baptized and raised
> And will cause the Holy Sepulchre to be regained and adored. . . .

> "Know certainly
> That from over the seas will come a new race
> Which will take revenge on the death of its father."[44]

---

43. Ibid., 56.

44. *La Chanson d'Antioche, Édition du text d'après la version ancienne,* ed. S. Duparc-Quioc, 2 vols. (Paris: Librairie Orientaliste Paul Geuthner, 1977), viii–xi, also 68, 79, 223, 363, 383, related to vengeance for Christ; translation here from Riley-Smith, *Idea of Crusading,* 55–56.

A text like this is of capital importance in understanding the cultural models at work in the self-definition that crusaders proposed for themselves. It will also lead us further in appreciating what is at stake in a doctrine of atonement that uses the trope of honor as central to its argument. First, the relationship of kinship ("revenge the death of its father") echoes the Solomon Bar Simson quotation above from the crusaders, which describes the role of the "children," again using the ideology of prophesied revenge, and in that instance contrasts the faithful children to the "rebel" children. Depicting Christ as the father betrays the fact that it is not Christian doctrinal metaphors at work here; rather we are looking at images of feudal patriarchy, the warrior "father" around whom the kinship group finds its unity and protective rigor. Second, the progression from the crucified Christ to vengeance, to the regaining and adoration of the Sepulchre, is made without embarrassment or hesitation, and the sequence brings to mind the sacred (violent) emotions surrounding the epos and death site of a warrior-hero, rather than the deeply nonviolent atmosphere in the last pages of the canonical Gospels. Both these motifs, of kinship and sacred emotions, are present in a sermon preached under the walls of Jerusalem in 1099 by a bishop-monk, Baldric of Bourgueil, who gave the following version of his own words in the *Historia*, written in the first decade of the twelfth century:

> Rouse yourselves, members of Christ's household! Rouse yourselves, knights and foot soldiers, and seize firmly that city, our commonwealth! Give heed to Christ, who today is banished from that city and is crucified; and with Joseph of Arimathea take him down from the cross; and lay up in the sepulchre of your hearts an incomparable treasure, that desirable treasure; and forcefully take Christ away from these impious crucifiers. For every time those bad judges, confederates of Herod and Pilate, make sport of and enslave your brothers they crucify Christ. Every time they torment them and kill them they lance Christ's side with Longinus. . . . What are you doing about these things? Is it right for you to listen to these things, to see these things done and not lament them? I address fathers and sons and brothers and nephews. If an outsider were to strike any of your kin down would you not avenge your blood-relative? How much more ought you to avenge your God, your father, your brother, whom you see reproached, banished form his estates, crucified; whom you hear calling, desolate, and begging for aid.[45]

---

45. Baldric of Bourgueil, "Historia Jerosolimitana," *RHC Oc.* 4, 101, quoted by Riley-Smith, *Idea of Crusading*, 48–49.

The central image here is of taking Christ away by force from his tor-
mentors and restoring him to the place of honor at the core of his armed
kinship. It sharply evokes the cultural institution of the band of warriors, or
comitatus, gathered round its hero leader in which one of the greatest crimes
was the abandonment of the leader on a field of battle. This institution
brings us into the broader realm of sociocultural history, and in respect of
Germanic peoples among whom the *comitatus* was especially prominent.
The discussion here intersects with an important thesis on the transfoma-
tive effect of a "German" cultural ethos on European Christianity. Basically
the "Germanization" argument states that early Mediterranean Christianity
responded to a society marked by dislocation and anomie. World-rejecting
eschatology, personal soteriology, plus the revolutionary organization of the
ekklesia, an extended artificial kin group based on mutual love, all help
explain the startling success of Christianity in this context. However, when
Christian religion turned beyond its Mediterranean cradle it encountered
groups with a still vigorous traditional culture. Much of the old "Indo-
European" cultural system was preserved, if not enhanced, among the
Germanic peoples: strong family and kin relations, practice of religion
indistinguishable from the sense of the collective, a powerful warrior and
war-fighting ethic. It was very difficult to assimilate this to the ambient and
values of early Christianity; instead a considerable degree of accommodation to Germanic culture, particularly in cult and war, was indispensable in
order to effect a formal change in religious allegiance.[46]

---

46. James C. Russell, The *Germanization of Early Medieval Christianity* (New York and
Oxford: Oxford University Press, 1994); hereafter *Germanization*. Here is a summary statement. "The early medieval Germanization of Christianity, in most cases . . . was not the
result of organized Germanic resistance to Christianity, or of an attempt by the Germanic
people to transform Christianity into an acceptable form. Rather, it was primarily a consequence of the deliberate inculturation of Germanic religiocultural attitudes within
Christianity by Christian missionaries. The process of accommodation resulted in the
essential transformation of Christianity from a universal salvation religion to a Germanic,
and eventually European, folk religion. The sociopsychological response of the Germanic
people to this inculturated form of Christianity included the acceptance of those tradi-
tionally Christian elements which coincided with Germanic religiosity and the resolution
of dissonant elements by reinterpreting them in accordance with the Germanic ethos and
world-view" (39). The appropriateness of using the term "German" in respect of this
worldview may be questioned, given the fact that to designate an amorphous body of people beyond a certain border with a single name is often the act of a colonizing/metropolitan
power. It was indeed Julius Caesar who gave the continental tribes beyond the lands he had
conquered in Gaul the name of Germans (Malcolm Chapman, *The Celts: The Construction
of a Myth* [New York: St. Martin's Press, 1992], 39, and *The Conquest of Gaul,* trans. S.
Handford [Harmondsworth, UK: Penguin, 1951], vi. 21–24, i. 47). Chapman also points
out the Greeks called everyone to their north and west *keltoi*, Celts, including of course the
Germans! However, if we keep in mind that this is used here as a cultural designation to
cover a number of politically identifiable groups of the time, viz. Saxons, Franks, Normans,
Swabians, and Rhinelanders etc., it may be allowed to stand.

One of the key institutions that propagated the Germanic value scheme was indeed the *comitatus*. "The Indo-European warrior ethos . . . was preserved by the Germanic people throughout the periods of contact with Christianity in late antiquity and the early Middle Ages and perhaps beyond."[47] With this ethos in mind we can draw out further the image of Christ as abandoned chief of the warrior band. The *comitatus* consisted of young, fierce warriors exhibiting exceptional daring and unquestioned loyalty to their hero chief. Tacitus gives a famous description of the Germans, including this institution.

> Both prestige and power depend on being continually attend-ed by a large train of picked young warriors, which is a dis-tinction in peace and a protection in war. . . . On the field of battle it is a disgrace to a chief to be surpassed in courage by his followers, and to the followers not to be equal to the courage of their chief. And to leave that battle alive after their chief has fallen means lifelong infamy and shame. To defend him and protect him, and to let him get the credit for their own acts of heroism, are the most solemn obligations of their allegiance. The chiefs fight for victory, the followers for their chief.[48]

We can perhaps begin to sense what Baldric of Bourgueil was evoking in his speech before Jerusalem. This association is powerfully reinforced if we turn to further literary and iconographic evidence within newly Christianized Germanic culture. The ninth-century *Heliand*, the first work of epic German literature, predating the extant *Nibelungenlied* by some four hundred years, presents the figure of Christ as *drohtin* or lord in the midst of his thanes, his warrior companions. It is essentially the Gospel story based on a Latin and Old German version of Tatian's *Diatessaron*, and its net product is a "German Christ," or more accurate-ly a "Saxon Christ."[49] It seems to have been written in the aftermath of Charlemagne's thirty-five-year war of conquest and conversion of north German Saxons (772–807), during the continuing outbreaks of rebellion

---

47. *Germanization*, 118. See G. Ronald Murphy S.J., *The Saxon Savior*: "We know that the ideals of the *comitatus* (i.e., retinue, companions) were still greatly influencing the sec-ular and religious imagination of St. Ignatius Loyola in the sixteenth century" (*The Saxon Savior*, [New York and Oxford: Oxford University Press, 1989], 96; hereafter *Saxon Savior*).

48. Tacitus, *The Agricola and the Germania*, trans. and intro. H. Mattingly, rev. S. A. Handford (New York: Penguin, 1970), 112–13; original in Cornelius Tacitus, *De origine et situ Germanorum*, pars. 13–14.

49. *The Saxon Savior*, 3–4. Murphy argues that this fascinating composition represents a skillful strategic Christian accommodation to pagan German culture.

that occurred well into the middle of the ninth century. As such it continues the basic project of Christianization via a literary construct that makes the gospel sympathetic and responsive to a Saxon ethos. One of the key motifs by which this is achieved is in the image of the disciples in the company of their lord, especially in the circumstances immediately prior to Christ's arrest. Here the author turns "to the old epic stories of the warrior culture and depicts Christ and his disciples as embattled warrior group making their last brave stand against a superior enemy force."[50] The single verse in John's Gospel that tells of Thomas the Twin's rallying call, "Let us go, that we may die with him" (11.16), is expanded in the *Heliand* to ten verses.

> Then, one of the twelve,
> Thomas, did speak—he was truly an excellent man,
> a loyal thane of his lord. "Let us never reproach his deeds,"
> quoth he, "nor reproach his will. But we should remain with him,
> should suffer with our lord. For that is the choice of a thane:
> that he standeth steadfast with his liege together,
> doth die with him at his doom. Let us all do so therefore;
> let us follow his path, nor let our lives
> be worth aught against his, unless we may die
> in this host with our lord. So honor will live after us,
> a good word before the kinships of men."[51]

The "Battle of Maldon," a fragmentary poem composed at the threshold of the eleventh century, tells of a Viking attack on the coasts of England and in terms that repeat the same crucial image of fighting thanes in honor bound to their lord. An old warrior, Byrhtwold, reminds the younger men of the code of the hero gang.

> Byrhtwold encouraged them brandishing buckler,
> aged companion shaking ash-spear;
> Stout were the words he spoke to his men:
> "Heart must be braver, courage the bolder,
> mood the stouter as our strength grows less!
> Here on the ground my good lord lies
> gory with wounds. Always will he regret it

---

50. Ibid., 95.
51. *The Heliand, Translated from the Old Saxon,* trans. Mariana Scott (Chapel Hill, N.C.: University of North Carolina Press, 1966), song XLVIII, quoted in *Saxon Savior,* 97–98. All further quotations of the *Heliand* are from Scott's translation as reproduced in *Saxon Savior.*

who now from this battle thinks to turn back.
I am old in years; I will never yield
but here at the last beside my lord
by the leader I love I think to lie. [52]

So at the beginning of the century which, at the other end, would see the *Cur Deus Homo* and the First Crusade, there is evidence of the cultural vigor of the *Heliand* topos of the warrior band surrounding a "good lord . . . gory with wounds." A continuum of this powerful cultural emblem may surely be detected in the crusader knights with thoughts fixed on Jerusalem and the capture of the Holy Sepulchre. Neither is connection to the *Cur Deus Homo* purely contextual: at the moment of Christ's arrest when he surrenders to the forces that will bring about his death, the author of the *Heliand* has him say, "Fate *[wurd]* is at hand so that it will happen as God the Father powerfully planned it." [53] Earlier, in the prayer in the Garden of Gethsemane, the author changes Tatian's "Father, if this chalice cannot pass away unless I drink it, then your will be done." Instead Christ says, "If you want it to be this way, then I want to drink it: I take this chalice in my hand and drink it to your honor, my lord chieftain, powerful protector." [54] Here it seems Christ is acting, in his turn, as the warrior thane of his own *comitatus* lord, willing to die to protect his honor. How far away are we here with this "most profoundly pagan belief" in fate, and then the core warrior code of honor, from Anselm's "necessity" of the incarnation and death of Christ for the sake of God's honor?[55] It is of course not possible to suggest direct textual dependence, nevertheless at some level, explicit or implicit, partial or dominant, a cultural continuity of themes presses for recognition.

Following the arrest the *Heliand* subtly shades the picture of Christ from a persecuted prophet to that of a prisoner of war. "They locked his hands together with military / handcuffs and his arms with chain." According to Murphy he "is treated throughout the passion account as a handcuffed prisoner of war being subjected to torture."[56] But before this provocative image is established there is one final chance for the warrior companions to show their true mettle as knights, and in line

---

52. Charles W. Kennedy, *An Anthology of Old English Poetry* (New York: Oxford University Press, 1960), 169.

53. Song LVIII, *Saxon Savior,* 106.

54. *Tatian, Lateinisch und Altdeutsch mit ausführlichem Glossar,* ed. Eduard Sievers (Paderbörn, Germany: Ferdinand Schöningh, 1966), 182, 2, "Pater mi, si non potest calix hic transire / nisi bibam illum, fiat voluntas tua"; and *Heliand,* song LVII, in *Saxon Savior,* 104.

55. Ibid., 33–34.

56. *Heliand,* lines 4917–4918, *Saxon Savior,* 108–9.

with the account from John's Gospel the opportunity must fall to Peter. Here is perhaps the best known sequence from the *Heliand:*

> Then he got really angry,
> Simon Peter, the mighty, noble Swordsman,
> his mind was so upset that he couldn't speak a single word:
> his heart became bitter, because they wanted to tie up
> his lord there. So he moved angrily
> that determined noble warrior to stand in front of his liege lord,
> right in front of his lord. No doubting in his mind,
> no hesitation in his chest—he drew his steel blade,
> the sword at his side, and struck straight ahead
> at the first man of the enemy, with all his hand's strength,
> so that Malchus was cut and wounded on the right side by the
>   sword:
> his ear was chopped off, he was so badly wounded in the head
> that his cheek and ear
> burst open with a mortal wound; blood gushed out,
> pouring from the wound. The cheek of the enemy's first man
> had been cut open. The people around stood back—
> they were afraid of the slash of the sword.[57]

This is a graphic account of a warrior defense by Peter involving a fatal head wound to the front man of a charge, thereby checking the advance of the whole troop of Christ's enemies. The author returns then to a more recognizable version of the canonical Gospels (Christ uses the traditional words, "those who live by the sword . . ."), but the warrior image of Peter is secured. This text, or others cognate with it, may also provide a literary background for the use of the phrase we have already seen, *milites sancti Petri* (warriors of Saint Peter), from the mouth of the German monk, Hildebrand, Pope Gregory VII.[58] The theme of a body of knights scattered throughout Christendom, bound personally to him and the church after the pattern of the swordsman Peter, is borne out by a letter of his in 1079

---

57. Ibid., song *LVIII*, 106–7

58. *Idea of Crusading*, 6. Roland Murphy proposes in unambiguous terms a critical role for the *Heliand* in the development of the Christian warrior culture of Europe. Its "synthesis provided an evangelical basis for the imaging of Christian discipleship in soldierly terms and opened the imagination and conscience to create the ideal of the northern Christian soldier—the knight. This evangelical synthesis [*sic*] . . . facilitated, and was the embodiment of a founding element of the culture of Europe," (op. cit., viii). And, it "may indeed be *the* poetic source for the high culture of the Middle Ages which would eventually . . . march off in Christian warfare against stubborn nonbelievers in the East" (ibid., 121).

to a noble named Wezelin who had rebelled against one of Gregory's political allies. "Know," asserted the pope, "that we will unsheathe the sword of St. Peter against your presumption."[59]

Before we leave the *Heliand* it is valuable to place in relief one further reference to Germanic paganism, something of considerable significance. In Germanic mythology the god Woden/Odin possesses knowledge of the sacred runes that hold power over human life. He attained this knowledge in a horrifying moment when he is sacrificed to himself by hanging and stabbing.

I know that I hung
On the windswept tree
For nine whole nights
Pierced by the spear
And given to Odin—
Myself to myself
On that tree
Whose roots
No one knows.

They gave me not bread
Nor drink from the horn;
Into the depths I peered,
I grasped the runes,
Savouring I grasped them,
And fell back.[60]

In its retelling of the gospel the *Heliand* makes Christ, rather than Odin, the one who imparts the runes, and when it comes to depict the crucifixion it colors elements of this climactic pagan scene into the gospel account. Christ's cross is initially called a gallows from which he is hung,

---

59. *First Crusaders*, 51, from *Das Register Gregors VII* (ed. E. Caspar, 2nd ed. [*MGH Epistolae Selectae* 2, 2, Berlin, 1955], 463–64). According to Riley-Smith, this statement of the pope was given formal theological articulation a couple of years later by a group of theologians connected to the Gregorian reformer, Mathilda of Tuscany. They were elaborating on Augustinian ideas of justified warfare, including valid authority, and proposed that the papacy itself had the right to summon knights to fight in its defense. One of this group, a certain John of Mantua, maintained that although the successors of Peter should not personally wield the sword, they retained direct authority over it. He based his argument "on the incident in the Garden of Gethsemane when . . . Christ had told [Peter] to put [his sword] back into its scabbard rather than throw it away" (*First Crusaders*, 47–48). It seems Hildebrand's belligerent phrase already contained this idea.

60. From the Norse epic, the *Hávamál*, trans. Magnus Magnusson, *The Vikings* (New York: Elsevier-Dutton, 1980), 86.

and once erected it becomes a tree on a mountain evoking the cosmic tree of Odin's torture.

> There on the sandy gravel they erected the gallows
> up on the field, the Jewish people set it up,
> a tree on the mountain. [61]

So behind the gospel story of the Crucified we glimpse the shadowy outline of the sacrificial death of Odin. There is in fact a triple reference to the site of the crucifixion, the sandy gravel of the North Sea shore, a field, and a mountain, all open spaces where ritual hanging from a tree could have occurred in the experience of the people.[62] Certainly the *Heliand* author makes the gospel story replace the cult of the ancient gods, but as Murphy says, his intention is "to sing the song of the Savior to the melodies and refrains of the old music."[63] How much of that music, in particular its rhythm of sacred violence, was preserved in the Germanic image of the Crucified? We learn that the image of the Crucified began to appear in Western Christian art from the mid-ninth century onward, mainly in England and Germany. Progressively from the tenth century reliquary and altar crucifixes began to show the dead or dying Christ, head tilted down to the right and eyes cast down or closed, rather than the earlier image of the triumphant Christ, standing erect on the cross, open-eyed, regally crowned, serene in victory. The earliest surviving crucifix to represent the dead Christ seems to be the one given by Archbishop Gero (d. 976) to the cathedral in Cologne for an altar of the cross.[64] In understanding the cultural transition to this image the

---

61. *Heliand*, lines 5532–5534, *Saxon Savior*, 111. For Christ as "Lord of the Runes," ibid., ch. 5. It is worthwhile noting how the Christ figure is vividly sketched within an Odin template when at Christ's baptism the Holy Spirit did not simply descend upon him but "sat upon our Lord's shoulder," in the standard image of Odin's ravens (ibid., 79).

62. "Hanging was one way of disposing of the victim, particularly among the Germans, and in the Viking Age it was a method of sacrifice associated with the cult of Odin" (H. R. Ellis Davidson, *Myths and Symbols in Pagan Europe* [Syracuse, N.Y.: Syracuse University Press, 1988], 64). Also, "It seems likely that Germans and Scandinavians relied on information learned from their strangled victims . . . since in a verse of the poem *Hávamál* Odin claims that by his skill in runes and magic spells he could cause a hanged man to walk and talk with him. Valuable knowledge, it appears, could be acquired from a man who died a violent death" (ibid., 60).

63. *Saxon Christ*, 93.

64. Elizabeth C. Parker and Charles T. Little, *The Cloister Cross, Its Art and Meaning* (New York: The Metropolitan Museum of Art, Harry N. Abrams Inc., 1994), 146. See Gertrud Schiller, *Iconography of Christian Art*, 2 vols., trans. Janet Seligman (Greenwich, Connecticut: New York Graphic Society Ltd., 1971–1972), 141–42: "The Cross of Gero dates from the beginning of the development of the monumental crosses. . . . [I]ts historical significance lies in its representation of suffering in its extreme physical consequences. The Death of Christ is here an elemental occurrence. It was never presented thus in

famous Ragnarok Stone (c. 950) at Kirk Andreas on the Isle of Man may perhaps provide a key. On one side it depicts Odin, naked and with a raven on
his shoulder, gripped in the jaws of the wolf Fenrir. In Germanic mythology
Fenrir's cavernous mouth represents the emptiness of the abyss, destined to
devour Odin and bring about the Ragnarok, "the doom of the gods." On the
reverse side of the stone there is a belted figure (presumably an apostle) bearing aloft the cross and the Book, trampling on a serpent.[65] Clearly the juxta-
position of the two scenes represents the substitution of Odin by Christ. In
addition the devouring of Odin takes place under a large Celtic cross which,
according to Murphy, perhaps implies that the coming of (Celtic)
Christianity is itself the twilight of the gods. There is little doubt that the
whole complex celebrates the victory of the Christian religion, but why is the
scene with Odin represented anyway, as if in its own right, unless there is
some synthesis or sublation also intended? As a concrete display of signs we
might say that the unsuccessful or suppressed term of the pair actually sup-
plements for a presence that is not possible on its own, just as the successful
term seeks to make absent that on which itself depends. The sign of Odin
lingers on in the making of Christ present. The image of the Crucified
depends on the "lost" image of Odin for its emerging cultural vigor.

Developing the analysis, we could hazard that the Western production
of three-dimensional representations of the suffering Christ from the
tenth century onward is prompted by a dynamic interchange between the
sacrificial traditions related to Woden/Odin and the concrete narrative of
the gospel passion. Without the cultural power of the former, the latter
would have gained no purchase; without the reiterated historical narrative
of the latter, there would have been little impetus to reproduce the physical image of suffering.[66] In contrast to this it is sometimes suggested that

---

Byzantine art.... The hands follow Carolingian tradition and hang down, but they are
nailed to the Cross at different heights. This distorts the axis of the body and pushes it out
of the vertical. The body sags, the belly protrudes, one hip and the slightly bent knees are
pushed to the left; the feet, pointing in the opposite direction, stand side by side on the
suppedaneum. The fact that the figure is standing not only checks the downward movement but creates a slight upward movement that ends in the knot of the loin-cloth. Christ's
head has fallen forward on to his chest; the individual forms of the face, especially the
mouth, all have a descending movement and are thereby involved in the tilt of the head.
The eyes are closed; the hair spreads over the shoulders.... [I]n none of the earlier works
is personal and suprapersonal suffering represented as it is on the Cross of Gero. The
strong movements to either side, forwards and backwards, up and down, create an overwhelming sense of hanging on the cross."
    65. *Saxon Christ,* 76, 80.
    66. "During Holy Week a third kind of time becomes prominent in ninth-century forms
of worship. A cluster of ceremonies appears which cannot be explained in terms of
absolute or cyclical time. These ceremonies involve representation of events, figures, and
scenes from the Gospels. Their common element is their use of linear time. Past time is not
absolutely present, as during the Mass, nor is it eternally recurrent, as in the annual cycle.

it was the sacrificial concept of the Eucharist that shaped the image of the crucifixion as that of a dying or dead victim. Jaroslav Pelikan is more accurate when he describes a mutually reinforcing complex of motifs: "As the central act of Christian worship, the sacrifice of the Mass gave meaning to, and derived meaning from, the image of the suffering and death of Christ on the cross as atoning sacrifice."[67] However, we should also add behind this the type of the sacrificed Odin contributing precisely to the meaning of Christ's "atoning" death. Through the Middle Ages all the dimensions of Christian cult and expression were shifting to fit the new mind-set. The sacrificial understanding of the Eucharist, broadly rooted in Christian tradition in a simultaneously symbolic/real sense of sacrament, became progressively more materialist and "objective," demanding ultimately the concept of change of substance in the bread into the substance of the flesh of Christ.[68] Thus the elevation of the host at the Mass that emerged in the twelfth century became a true event of crucifixion; for it was itself "the body of the Saviour . . . visibly suspended on the cross."[69] Realist cult and symbol reinforce each other, because beneath the sacrificial interpretation of both Eucharist and the cross lie palimpsests of the prophet of the gospels and the tortured hero of German imagination.

"The Dream of the Rood," an Anglo-Saxon poem from the eighth century, bears impressive witness to the gospel in Germanic voice, but here a different, more complex tonality is heard. The poet has a vision of "heaven's tree."[70] He sees the tree "shift in robes and colors; now it was reddened with wet / drenched with the shedding of blood"(22–23) He gazes in sorrow until next he hears the tree speak to him personally:

Instead, each event is a unique point on a line constantly moving forward into the future. An event occurs once and is forever and irrevocably past. This is historical time, and the representational ceremonies that use it are germinal history plays" (O. B. Hardison, *Christian Rite and Christian Drama in the Middle Ages* [Baltimore: Johns Hopkins, 1965], 84; hereafter *Christian Rite and Christian Drama*). Cf. n. 73 below.

67. Jaroslav Pelikan, *The Christian Tradition 3, The Growth of Medieval Theology (600–1300)* (Chicago and London: University of Chicago Press, 1978), 137.

68. Ibid., 78–80, 188–203. For the broad interpretation see Augustine, for example: "the visible sacrifice is the sacrament, i.e. the sacred symbol (*sacrum signum*), of the invisible sacrifice;" from *The City of God*, X, 6, quoted in J. N. D. Kelly, *Early Christian Doctrines* (London: Adam & Charles Black, 1965), 454 ; cf. ibid., 449–55.

69. *Christian Rite and Christian Drama*, 64–66, See also *The Cloister Cross*, 147: "In the Gothic period, it was to be an image of the suffering Christ wearing his crown of thorns on an unadorned cross which visually expressed the meaning of that climactic moment in the Mass [i.e., the consecration and elevation]."

70. "The Dream of the Rood," line 14, in *The Web of Words*, text with translation and analysis by Bernard F. Huppé (Albany: University of New York, 1970), 65; hereafter *Web of Words*. Verse lines given after text.

It was many years ago—I yet remember—
that I was hewn down in a corner of the holt,
torn away from my roots. Then rough enemies took me afar,
made me an object of terror, and commanded me to hang their
    felons;
these men, these many foes bore me on their shoulders to a
    mount
where they set me and made me fast. (28–33)

The extraordinary first-person narrative displaces the focus from the Crucified to the cross, from the hero-victim to the instrument of torture. The cross complains about what the "rough enemies . . . these many foes" have done to it, and by its means. Clearly this is not yet the crucifixion of Christ, the central drama of the Christian religion, but is in fact the making from the tree "an object of terror," an instrument for the execution of outlaws. The Saxon is *waefersyn*, which can also mean "war-banner."[71] A moralizing reading could see all this as the sins of the world loaded upon the Christ, but the tone is vivid and experiential and the focus for the intended reader would surely have been the physical object of terror on the hillside where a doomed victim was hanged. By this bold stroke the writer brings to the foreground the supplement that had in its turn allowed Odin his sacred presence, the technique for execution of victims in his name. The cross is allowed to speak, and does so at once as a universal gallows where countless victims have died. The cross is referred to three times as a gallows in the 156-line poem, and twice as a means of torture or punishment, continuing the evocation of the Germanic mode of execution. It is hard to avoid the sense here of a disclosure of the sacred, of the violence of ritual killing.

In the paragraph following the one quoted, the cross declares that it was somehow obliged to go through with the execution of Christ and not defend him against his foes. The cross protests again and again that it did not retaliate, did not use counterviolence, but instead "endured many hateful misfortunes"(50–51). In fact the cross presents itself as the victim. "They pierced me with dark nails, the wounds are visible on me / the gaping blows of hate"(46–47). Meanwhile, the actual figure of Christ is kept free of all description of suffering, apart from a fatal wound in the side, which is presented as a voluntary surrendering to death (49), and a mention of "heavy torment" (61) from which he is lifted at the end. We find here the paradox of a clear heroization of Christ moving in parallel with, and almost separate from, the cruel pathos of the tree.

---

71. *Web of Words*, 85.

I saw mankind's protector
most manfully hasten to ascend me . . .
The young hero prepared himself —he who was God almighty—
great and gallant he ascended the gallows' abject height
magnanimous in the sight of many when mankind he wished to
    free. (39–41)

The figure of the warrior Christ is displayed in primary colors and we are
unambiguously back in the frame of Germanic religion. "Vigorous and single minded, [Christ] strips himself for battle and a kingly victory. The action
is entirely his, an eager sacrifice; there is no question at this point of his being
nailed to the cross. Instead he climbs to embrace it. It is pre-eminently an act
of dominant free will by a prince confident of victory. With the agony transferred to the cross, Christ can sensibly be seen to rule from the gallows."[72]
This reserving of the passion to the cross, leaving victory for the Christ,
unambiguously constructs the Christian Savior as a figure worthy of a warrior culture that honors acts of valor carried out in protection of the kinship.
The genius of the poem is this uncanny combination of intense compassion
aroused by the actual instrument of Christ's death, with rigid adherence to
an ideal warrior code by which Christ himself is presented. Arguably we see
here a functional separating out of the kerygmatic and the mythic: the former given expression in the historic Passion narrative, particularly associated
with Good Friday, the latter tending indistinguishably to Christian credal formulation and received, traditional images of heroes and gods.[73] On one hand
the poem discloses violence through compassion, on the other it celebrates it
in full dress of a warrior culture. Later, as we shall see, in the twelfth and thirteenth centuries the mood of compassion was discovered explicitly in relation to the person of Christ, and the displacement shown by "The Dream"
was no longer applied. Nevertheless, the focus of "The Dream" on the cross
is striking for its reference to a continuum of human violence and its victims.
It is almost as if the poet, caught halfway between the gospel narrative and
the Germanic ethos, intuits an irreconcilable tension between the two and
resolves it by means of poetic virtuosity alone. The Christian piety of com-

---

72. *The Dream of the Rood,* ed. and commentary by Michael Swanton, Old and Middle
English Texts, general editor G. L. Brook, (New York: Manchester University Press, Barnes
& Noble, 1970), 71.
    73. In regard to liturgy we are close here perhaps to the dramatic Easter deposition rit-
ual, in which a simple cross is used to impersonate the body of Christ in the representation of a tomb, first mentioned in the later tenth-century *Regularis Concordia* of
Aethelwold (*PL*, cxxxvii. 493–94), cited in Swanton, op. cit., 52. The Good Friday imprope-
rias, words of reproach spoken as by Christ while a cross is processed (*ecce lignum crucis*)
also came into general use between the ninth and tenth centuries; see *Christian Rite and
Christian Drama,* 131–32.

passion in later centuries never again seems to make this (dis)connection, and is able to coexist with warrior Christianity without apparent difficulty, most discordantly in the figure of Bernard of Clairvaux.

Meanwhile, "The Dream" itself, continuing the heroic motif in respect of the now dead Christ, evokes a pity that is thoroughly consistent with the warrior ethos. At this point, we are close again to the story of the Crusades. Christ is brought down from the cross. The poet lavishes seven long lines on the description of the deposition of the dead figure, compared to one alone on the event of his death on the cross. Again I reproduce the poetry to concretize the emotions at play.

> They laid him down weary to the bone stood at his body's head
> gazed at the Ruler of heaven. And there he rested himself awhile
> tired after the great conflict. They began to make a tomb for him
>> then
> the men in the sight of the murderers, hewed it from the marble
>> stone,
> therein did set the Ruler of victories; they began to sing the
>> mournful dirge
> bereaved in the evening time when tired they thought
> to depart from the great Lord. There he rested with a little com-
>> pany. (63–69)

The actual word for the "men" at verse 66 is *beornas*, meaning "warriors" or "heroes."[74] Christ's company of warriors, the *comitatus*, take him down from the cross, just as Joseph of Arimathea in the *Heliand* "took him into his arms, the precious body, as one should do with one's liege-lord."[75] They stand at the head of the body, and later raise a "mournful dirge," the same Saxon expression as used for the ritual lamentation of the hero Beowulf, abandoned by all his warriors, bar Wiglaf, in his hour of need.[76] Christ is referred to repeatedly as tired and resting, imaging the immortal sleep of the slain hero. His men dig an earth grave for him directly on the battlefield, but quickly it becomes a marble monument, a reference probably to the Constantinian shrine. Then they depart, leaving him with "little company," that is, alone.[77]

---

74. *Dream of the Rood*, 115. This term is used also for Christ at v. 42, and of the enemies at v. 32. In none of these instances does the translator give the meaning of "warrior," clearly wishing to "demilitarize" the text.

75. *Heliand* LXVIII, 5733–734, *Saxon Savior*, 113.

76. *Dream of the Rood*, 124. Cf. *Beowulf*, trans. and commentary by Marc Hudsaon (London and Toronto: Lewisburg Bucknell University Press, 1990), 169, line 3148.

77. *Web of Words*, 97.

Three lines later we are told, "The body grew cold / the fair corpse."
(72–73) The whole scene is heavy with the pathos of the young warrior
cut down and/or abandoned in action, his body the ambiguous locus of
horror, desire, regret, and loss. It is this complex of feeling that may
appositely be termed *warrior-pity*, the pity aroused by the fallen warrior, and it is one that easily translates into a project of further violence.
Desire of or for the dead is dangerous desire. Someone slain heroically
in battle has reached a perfection of group approval, often literally set
in stone, monumentalized, that may only be attained by following him
into death. The apotheosis of the warrior leader only serves to exacer-
bate the loyalty felt to him when alive, and there is also something erotic in the dead limbs of a hero with all their evidence of physical prowess
now more helpless than a child. At the same time a reciprocal sense of
shame, of loss of honor, may occur, if there is any implication that the
warrior companions did not match the courage of their lord. Within a
very different fabric of relationships this is indeed the nature of the
gospel story, and it seems moreover an experience not unknown in
Saxon culture if we are to judge by the *Beowulf* epic.[78] Here, I believe, is
the explosive core of the gospel story translated into a warrior ethos.
The more the passion of Christ was mentally and physically expressed
within the folk culture of the time, the more potential there was for a
project of open-ended violence. The overall eirenic spirit of "The
Dream" depended upon the rigorous separation of gospel suffering and
the hero Christ: once this polarity was resolved into unity, once the
hero-god was seen plainly to be a victim, an unbearable offense followed by a project of vengeance would always be a collective psychic
possibility. The terrible pity of Christ appropriated by a warrior people,
even at some vague, borderline level, only needed the prompting of
papal legitimation (a war pilgrimage as penance) to be turned into
exponential violence. In this sense the preparative work of the Christian
story within a Germanic warrior ethos did indeed provide the (de)sym-
bolization for massive violence against Jews and Turks. The disruption
of sacred symbolism produced by semi-evangelism should be counted
an integral factor, along with social and economic forces, in producing
the "sacrificial crisis" of the eleventh century in northern Europe.

The most evocative goal of the crusade was gaining possession of the
Holy Sepulchre, and it was there that the theme of the dead Christ was

---

78. "The epic tradition acknowledged both loyalty and flight from the lord in his time
of danger, something both the Anglo-Saxon tradition and the Gospel story agree on. . . ."
(*Saxon Savior*, 100).

most vivid and concrete. Recall the words of Baldric of Bourgueil, appealing to the image of the Sepulchre, while echoing the mood of both the *Heliand* and "The Dream."

> With Joseph of Arimathea take him down from the cross; and lay up in the sepulchre of your hearts an incomparable treasure, that desirable treasure. . . .

Directly following, Baldric says: "and forcefully take Christ away from these impious crucifiers." Here is the heroic project of the armed pilgrimage to Jerusalem, of the *miles Christi*: to rescue the dead Christ, or the place that represented this, from abandonment among his enemies. Frequently in the charters of the knights who went on crusade there is mention of desire to free Jerusalem or the Holy Sepulchre from "contamination," to "cleanse" it, "to wipe out the defilement of the pagans." It seems Urban II probably expressed this same sentiment in his recruitment speeches.[79] This language is more directly cultic than related to a warrior code, but given the fact that Christ and his story were experienced above all in the context of cult and worship, it is probable that there was a bundle of references in such statements.[80] In terms of mimetic anthropology the sense of contamination is linked to a crisis of violence, violence uncontained by sacred order. Both ritual defilement of a holy place and the dishonor of one's lord would contribute to this "contamination," and would indifferently tend toward the same generative violence. Around 1135 Bernard of Clairvaux penned "the apotheosis of the Christian assimilation of the Germanic warrior code:" his recruitment tract for the military order of the Knights Templar, the *De laude novae militiae* (Praise of the New Militia).[81] He also deploys the language of contamination; he says it would be intolerable to let "infidels pollute the holy place." But he does so precisely within the dominant scheme of "the warriors' Chief [who] inflamed with violent anger entered the temple holding, certainly not steel, but a whip of cords in his most holy hand, and drove out the merchants. . . ." He concludes that "the example of such a King galvanizes the army devoted to him, which judges it much more

---

79. See *First Crusaders*, 62, 67.

80. Amanieu of Loubens is reported to have wished to "fight and kill those opposed to the Christian religion, nay rather to cleanse the place in which the Lord Jesus Christ deigned to undergo death for the restoration of the human race" (*First Crusaders*, 62; from "Cartulaire du prieuré de Saint-Pierre de La Réole," ed. C. Grellet-Balguerie, *Archives historiques du département de la Gironde* 5 [1863], 140).

81. *Germanization*, 40.

unworthy and profoundly more intolerable to permit infidels to pollute
the holy place than to see it overrun by merchants."[82]

Bernard's pamphlet is simultaneously a handbook on crusading war
and a spiritual itinerary of the Holy Land. In both these frames it is the
Holy Sepulchre that represents the climax of the argument, and he
reserves for it by far the longest sequence. Toward the end of the relevant section he repeats the familiar figure of Christ resting and speaks
of the physical reminders of this for the pilgrim warriors. "It is no small
advantage to see with the eyes of the body the place where the Lord's
body rested. And even if this place is now empty of the sacred members
it is full of signs for us and happy ones too."[83] Earlier he had declared
that the Sepulchre was preeminent among the holy places, because "the
memory of death more so than life moves to piety" ("amplius movet ad
pietatem mortis quam vitae recordatio").[84] Bernard stylishly juxtapos-
es *pietas* and *mors* (piety and death); the root *pietas* of course contains
the connotation of "pity" and would forcefully suggest in this context
that the death that moves to piety is a matter of warrior emotions experienced in the presence of the slain chief. It is this violent religious mor-
bidity of piety/pity—warrior pity or the pity of death—that Bernard
understood in his knights; and it was within its cultural dynamic that
he was able to insist that warrior death, whether endured or inflicted,
was "for Christ," and that the death inflicted on the enemy was indeed
"gain for Christ."[85] By the same token he exhorts the knights to fall
harshly upon their opponents, viewing their ranks as so much sheep for
slaughter, while invoking the Scripture as a battle cry: "Do I not hate,
Lord, those who hate you . . . ?"[86]

---

82. ". . . militum Dux, vehementissime inflammatus, armata illa sanctissima manu, non
tamen ferro, sed flagello, quod fecerat de resticulis, introivit in templum, negotiantes
expulit. . . . Talis proinde sui Regis permotus exemplo devotus exercitus, multo sane indig-
nius longeque intolerabilius arbitrans sancta pollui ab infidelibus quam a mercatoribus
infestari. . . ." (*Éloge de la nouvelle chevalerie*, intro., trans., notes, and index by Pierre-Yves
Emery, Sources Chrétiennes, vol. 367 [Paris: Les Éditions Du Cerf, 1990], 74; hereafter
Éloge [my trans.]).

83. ". . . nec parum proficitur cernendo, etiam coporalibus oculis, corporalem locum
dominicae quietis. Etsi quippe iam vacuum sacris membris, plenum tamen nostris et
iucundis admodum sacramentis" (*Éloge*, 120, my trans.). Bernard is probably thinking of
the parade of relics, including a flat stone where Christ's body was said to have laid after
being taken from the cross, all included under the one roof of the crusader's church con-
secrated in 1149 (see *First Crusaders*, 23–24).

84. *Éloge*, 98.

85. ". . . mors pro Christo, vel ferenda, vel inferenda . . . ;" and later, "Mors ergo quam
irrogat, Christi est lucrum . . ." (*Éloge*, 58, 60).

86. "At vero ubi ventum fuerit ad certamen, tum pristina lenitate postposita, tamquam si
dicerunt: *Nonne qui oderunt te, Domine, oderam, et super inimicos tuos tabescebam?* Iruunt in
adversarios, hostes velut oves reputant. . . ." (*Éloge*, 70, quotation from Ps. 139:21).

The coexistence in Bernard of this crusade ideology and an intense Christ-centered mysticism would be incomprehensible, except perhaps there is the possibility of ambivalence in the very image of the Crucified itself. Bernard's contribution to mystical theology is considered one of its primary tributaries in Western Christianity. As one historian has it, for Bernard, "Man's aim, fulfillment and highest dignity lay in becoming absorbed into the Deity, being caught up wholly in the process of love in which God the Father embraced God the Son. . . . Bernard's mysticism, inspired by St. Augustine and the Song of Songs . . . set up currents of great spiritual power, which remained a force for several centuries; German mystics of the fourteenth century, Spanish mystics of the sixteenth century, French mystics of the seventeenth and eighteenth centuries all found inspiration in him."[87] What was the nature of such powerful spirituality if it could shape-shift with such ease into the ideology of holy war? In illustration of the dissonance we might highlight a key image, given currency by Bernard and which was also to become a standard of mystical language: the metaphor of a spiritually significant figure as a "mother" who nurtures her children. Bernard made prolific use of this image, applying it in apostrophes of Moses, Peter, Paul, prelates, abbots (including himself), and with great affective impact in relation to the crucified Christ. He exhorts his monks by a striking rhetorical inversion to "suck not so much the wounds as the breasts of the Crucified. He will be your mother, and you will be his son."[88]

It seems in fact to have been Anselm of Canterbury who introduced to the Middle Ages the figure of Jesus as mother, and the same sensed tension is apparent in him: a discordance between his *Cur Deus Homo*, so dependent on an ethos of mimetic revenge, and the tone of intense sensibility and compassion emerging in his *Prayers and Meditations*.[89] Anselm created a new kind of poetry with these prayers, more intimate, personal, emotional, and demanding than anything seen before. They were the first collection of devotional prayers to circulate under the name of their author, and they quickly became popular, attracting a number of imitations also attributed to him. As such Anselm must be considered a

---

87. Friedrich Heer, *The Medieval World, Europe from 1100–1350*, trans. Janet Sondheimer (London: Weidenfeld and Nicolson, 1990), 80.

88. Letter 322, Migne, *Patrologia Latina* 182: col. 527, trans. from Caroline Walker Bynum, *Jesus as Mother, Studies in the Spirituality of the High Middle Ages* (Berkeley: University of California Press), 117, hereafter *Jesus as Mother*.

89. Ibid., 112. "And you, Jesus, are you not also a mother? Are you not the mother who, like a hen, gathers her chickens under her wings? Truly, Lord you are a mother. . . . For, longing to bear sons into life, you tasted of death, and by dying you begot them" (*The Prayers and Meditations of Saint Anselm with the Proslogion*, trans. and intro. Sister Benedicta Ward, S. L. G., foreword by R. W. Southern [Harmondsworth, UK: Penguin Books, 1973], 153).

key protagonist of the emerging "individualism" of the epoch, with its accent on the inner self and the experience of "love."[90] But as the author of the *Cur Deus Homo,* Anselm also participates in an affective ambivalence that should also be seen as characteristic of the period. Bernard clearly represents and widens the polarity of emotions, promoting the ideology of war "for Christ" alongside an identificatory love of the Crucified. Bernard's religious order, the Cistercians, played a key role in promoting the spiritual importance of the Crucified. Aelred of Rievaulx allowed his monks only one image on the altar, the crucifix. It was to be "a representation of our Savior hanging on the cross; that will bring before your mind his Passion for you to imitate. His outspread arms will invite you to embrace him, his naked breasts will feed you with the milk of sweetness to console you."[91] Another key reference was the lance wound in Christ's side, which doubled as penetrative access to life-giving fluids and a womblike protection or stronghold. Again Aelred:

> Then one of the soldiers opened his side with a lance and there came forth blood and water. Hasten, linger not, eat the honeycomb with your honey, drink your wine with your milk. The blood is changed into wine to gladden you, the water into milk to nourish you. From the rock streams have flowed for you, wounds have been made in his limbs, holes in the wall of his body, in which, like a dove, you may hide while you kiss them one by one. Your lips stained with blood, will become like a scarlet ribbon and your word sweet.[92]

How is it possible to reconcile these tender aesthetics of maternal protection and nourishment with the cruel reciprocities that we see issuing elsewhere from the dead Christ? Are we forced to admit a certain essential undecidability, along the lines proposed by Borch-Jacobsen: that love and aggression are bound together undecidably, a "devouring identification," and that feeding on Christ is itself a form of violence? Caroline Bynum places the affective relation with the Crucified in the context of the twelfth-

---

90. Ibid., 9–10; and *Saint Anselm, A Portrait in a Landscape,* 91–112.

91. *De institutione,* ch. 26, trans. M. P. McPherson in *The Works of Aelred of Rievaulx* 1: *Treatises and Pastoral Prayer,* Cistercian Fathers Series 2 (Spencer, Mass.: Cistercian Publications, 1971), 73. Aelred makes the theme of identificatory imitation explicit in the following: "The Cross of Christ is, as it were, the mirror of the Christian" (*Sermo ix, in ramis Palmarum* [Migne, *Patrologia Latina* 195, col. 263 D], quoted by Colin Morris, *The Discovery of the Individual* [New York and London: Harper & Row, 1972], 116).

92. *De institutione,* McPherson, op. cit. 1, 90–91.

century emergence of the individual, signaled by thinkers like Colin Morris, but to be understood also in relation to new forms of community and the central category of likeness and imitation.[93] Le Goff believes that the centrality of the suffering of Christ also brought the humanity of Christ to the fore and contributed to a progressive change in the understanding of the human person.[94] These seem like positive humanizing developments, suggesting that the phenomena of the Crucified should not be reduced to an undecidability that is as violent as it is benign. On the other hand, Johan Huizinga has argued that the piety of the late Middle Ages centered almost exclusively on the humanity of Christ and brought with it a "strain of pathetic tenderness about the Passion of Christ."[95] The accent on Christ's suffering for sin and images of blood associated with it gathered force in the late thirteenth and fourteenth centuries, changing metaphors of suckling wine, water, and milk, to the direct drinking of blood, and producing graphic representations and descriptions of Christ's Passion, something that has been labeled a "gospel of gore."[96] The implication here may be that the later Middle Ages represent a pathology linked to the Crucified, and one that again cannot be far away from an ethos of violence.

CONFLICTED COMPASSION

A forceful reevaluation of the significance of such images has recently been made by Ellen M. Ross. She sees them in terms of a "rhetoric of transformation generated by the bleeding figure of Christ." The intention of the rhetoric is to evoke a response of love, and this was a central pastoral and homiletic strategy during the period 1250–1450 in England and, by extension, in other areas of medieval Europe, too.[97] "[T]he textual and artistic sources demonstrate the integral place of Jesus' pain and anguish in evoking both repentance and compassion in the process of persons' transformation. Compassion, the initial root of repentance, arises in the viewers and readers who witness the excruciating suffering of Jesus. Manuscript illumination, sermons, wall paintings, and devotional literature emphasize

---

93. *Jesus as Mother*, 82–90.

94. J. Le Goff, *Medieval Civilization*, trans. Julia Barrow (Oxford: Blackwell, 1988), 159.

95. Johan Huizinga, *The Waning of the Middle Ages: A Study of the Forms of Life, Thought and Art in France and the Netherlands in XIV and X Centuries* (first published in Dutch, 1919; London: Arnold, 1976), 173.

96. *Jesus as Mother*, 151–54,

97. Ellen M. Ross, The *Grief of God, Images of the Suffering Jesus in Late Medieval England,* (New York and Oxford: Oxford University Press, 1997), 6–8; hereafter *The Grief of God*.

the details of Jesus' suffering to foster empathy in the witnesses to this suffering."[98] The transformative process continues beyond initial repentance, leading to practical imitation of Jesus in works of mercy, and then "mimetic identification" with the Crucified, which then becomes an embodiment or revelation of the divine. The feminine persona given to the Crucified favored the role of medieval women as models of this transformational process, Julian of Norwich and Margery Kempe affording prime examples. "The doubly-gendered Jesus who lactates, bleeds, nurtures, heals and feeds the world with his body becomes the root metaphor for an entire epoch."[99]

This very positive assessment does not deny that alongside the invitation to compassion lay the inevitability of eternal damnation if the invitation is refused. The wounds of the victim that evoke a change of heart can also turn to condemnation if one should die having refused to change. Ambivalence remains: the victim is the source of judgment as well as transformation. At one level this is only to be expected given the apocalyptic terminus of judgment proclaimed by the Gospels. What Ross does not refer to is the possibility of ambivalence within the figure of the Crucified itself, the possibility of a rhetoric of violence arising from the wounded Christ as the converse of a rhetoric of transformation—precisely the polarity exemplified by "The Dream." This ambivalence seems classically presented in a medieval description of Christ the knight who goes battle-weary and wounded to the soul, his lady, seeking refreshment.

[A]s a most gracious and faithful knight he does not cease to knock and cry: "Behold my wounds," and so forth. "O, human soul, blush then, and . . . [open] the soul's affections for God and his favors, which are so firmly shut through sin, and do so with keys of contrition, confession, love and charity."[100]

This is a plausible cameo for the full emotional gamut of Germanic Christianity: a simultaneous sense of heroic appeal and gospel passion, based in the figure of the warrior chief subsumed into Christ but by no means erased. The wounds indeed call for transformative compassion, but the figure of the knight remains, always capable of turning a pitiless sword on the enemy, as Bernard taught. The profound question that we have reached is whether it is possible to indicate a transformative compassion

98. Ibid., 132.
99. Ibid., 134–35; cf. 31–40.
100. From Siegfried Wenzel, ed. and trans., *Fasciculus Morus: A Fourteenth-Century Preacher's Handbook* (University Park: Pennsylvania State University Press, 1989), 205, 207, quoted in *The Grief of God,* 64.

that might escape this ambivalence. Can the pity of Christ at any point be genuinely other than the pity of death that issues from a slain hero? Can that pity become, in Ross's phrase, an "aesthetics of response" that does not rebound back into violence, including also self-inflicted violence? Nietzsche said, "Almost everything we call 'higher culture' is based on the spiritualization of *cruelty*, on its becoming more profound."[101] That word *almost* leaves a certain gap in his question, and an interpretation of that gap, not in a Nietzschean way of course, but perhaps as the "unthought" possibility of transformation, may be left open—if only because medieval culture sought to attest to it so passionately.

Furthermore, we may perhaps state the issue the other way round. The pity of death must contain a profound element of identification with the victim, without which the desire for revenge would lack all mimetic force. As we have seen, according to Borch-Jacobsen the chief or leader is the object of narcissistic-libidinal identification by the crowd; the permanence of this identification in death must also be necessary to explain the urgency of vengeance. But should the individual sense within this identification a perfect absence of violent reciprocity, a renunciation of revenge (including against oneself), and find this in some way without measure—such that the victim is a kind of abyss of nonviolence, without the subject ever being able to reach a final point of reversion to violence— then would not genuine transformative compassion become an existential possibility? Merely by tracing within the identification a route of infinite nonretaliation would it not be possible to refigure the subject's mimesis into the opposite of revenge? Into forgiveness? This could well be called a limit possibility, but one precisely without limit. I believe that in its ultimate depths this is what the medieval rhetoric of the cross intended.

At the same time, if this is the case, if this is the anthropological core of transformation by the cross, we are at once confronted by a dramatic contradiction in respect of the dominant model of atonement of the later Middle Ages. "Again and again, the same Anselmian insight is generated on the basis of medieval narratives. Instead of abandoning human persons to the consequences of their misdeeds, God intercedes through the work of Christ and establishes a new order of mercy while satisfying the demands of justice."[102] The sting, as always, is in the word *satisfying*. If a radical experience of transformation is intended through compassion for the Crucified, and this "works" by means of an infinite

---

101. *Beyond Good and Evil*, section 229, in *Basic Writings of Nietzsche*, trans., ed., and commentaries by Walter Kaufmann (New York: The Modern Library, 1992), 348.
102. *The Grief Of God*, 16.

nonviolence within his wounded body, then the Anselmian scheme at once reinstitutes a profound content of violence in that same body. Christ goes to the cross because he identifies with God's offended honor and brings its satisfaction or revenge down upon himself. Once the language of satisfaction had become part of the stock-in-trade of medieval preachers and writers, so that it provided the meta-theory by which to interpret the cross, then the rhetoric of transformation generated by the wounded Christ would always meet a shocking dissonance at its core. The identification of nonviolence suddenly could become the identification of violence, and the irreconcilibility of the two would set up wider and wider eddies of guilt, pain, and doomed attempts at secondary compensation. At the level of abyssal compassion violence is dissipated; at the level of atonement doctrine it is essentialized. It is the classic mixed message, I forgive you/I cannot forgive you; and the child of such a conflicted parent must necessarily manifest acute anxiety and dysfunctional behavior. The medieval audience transfixed before the image of the Crucified would find itself pushed to further and further extremes of autoidentification with this figure in order simultaneously to underscore the human nonviolence of Christ and defer the divine violence of satisfaction, in their own bodies. This was "the mysticism of pain that promises redemption to those who pay in blood";[103] its standard-bearers were the flagellants, but it could just as easily turn outward against a third party, a scapegoat. The various libels against the Jews arising at this time, including the accusation that they kidnapped Christian children and/or eucharistic wafers to use in ritual repetitions of the crucifixion, should also be read in relation to this explosive religious construct.[104] The parity between these accusations and the complex of Christian anxiety provoked by the post-Anselmian Crucified is too close to be accidental.

In contrast to these anxieties, the shame of the Christian warrior for having abandoned his lord is a simple thing, and indeed this was probably already overlaid with cultic and sacrificial associations. Generally, however, we may be certain that from the thirteenth century onward, as the

---

103. Gorringe, *God's Just Vengeance*, 102.

104. The first accusation of ritual murder seems to have been in respect of a twelve-year-old skinner's apprentice named William, found dead in woods near Norwich, England, in 1144. See *Anti-Semitism*, 106–7, 121–22; and Joshua Trachtenburg, *The Devil and The Jews, The Medieval Conception of the Jew and Its Relation to Modern Anti-Semitism* (New Haven: Yale University Press, 1943), 109–39: "The earliest explanation of these alleged crimes . . . held that the Jews *crucified* Christian children, usually *during Passion week*, in order to reënact the crucifixion of Jesus and to mock and insult the Christian faith" (131, italics in original).

Anselmian account gained ascendancy, the image of the wounded Christ would be crossed by an irreducible layer of metaphysical violence. The multiple presence of the image of the Crucified would have served constantly to call this to mind, hand in hand with a rhetoric of transformation. Unlike the temporally uncertain prospect of a last judgment, this would have been a constant ingredient of daily life, injecting a continual religious and mimetic crisis at the level of folk religion, and very probably serving to foster in itself a feeling of imminent judgment. We may imagine in fact a systemic reversal to crisis, at levels that went progressively deeper than simple vengeance for a hero lord and in themselves substantially more complex and disturbing. At such a point overlapping and conflicting layers become impossible to track, and a new, cleaner paradigm of redemption seems desperately required.

These are speculative reconstructions, but we are evidently at the threshold of the Reformation, which broke decisively with a human-sided imitation or transformation, while retaining the centrality of the cross as the work of God alone. There must have been something profoundly out of kilter with the medieval appropriation of the Crucified to provoke such an acute reaction. The argument here in fact leads to the hypothesis that the whole dense and multilayered complex of Germanic warrior religion—vengeance, satisfaction, crusade, indulgence, cross, compassion, and identification—all this contained elements of anthropological contradiction that could not be sustained at a certain level of personal seriousness. Luther's intensified sensibility, his famous *Anfechtung*, was the lightning rod that served to break the storm. For Luther, man's condemnation and justification issued equally and solely from God and were made manifest in the cross. Humanity made absolutely no contribution. It might be said that Luther represents a radical break with the anthropology of the cross, carrying through instead a reactionary theologization of the cross. Here the revelation of God is a hidden revelation; God is hidden in and through the suffering of the Crucified, hidden to any schematism of the mind.[105] The categories of an *opus alienum* and

---

105. "Because men misused the knowledge of God through works, God wished again to be recognized in suffering, and to condemn wisdom concerning invisible things by means of the wisdom concerning visible things, so that those who did not honor God as manifested in his works should honor him as he is hidden in his suffering" (from Luther's proof of Thesis 20 of the Heidelberg Disputation, in Gerhard O. Forde, *On Being a Theologian of the Cross: Reflections on Luther's Heidelberg Disputation, 1518* [Grand Rapids: Eerdmans, 1997], 78–79).The heading of Thesis 20 states: "That person deserves to be called a theologian . . . who comprehends the visible and manifest things of God through suffering and the cross." The Latin text translated as "manifest" has *posteriora*, meaning also "back" or "hinder parts," and refers to Exod. 33:18–23, where Moses asks to see God's glory but is granted only to see his back. Thus the cross is God's "back parts" and it is only thus we are allowed to glimpse him (ibid., 77–78).

an *opus proprium* in the cross express the paradox from the side of the believer; before God can build he must first destroy, and the cross is first the revelation of his wrath before it can be God's mercy.[106] So, as we have suggested in the previous chapter, the violent tensions of the medieval figure of the Crucified are swept up into God *absconditus sub contrariis* (hidden under opposites), and Christian consciousness may in this way find peace. The lament of the tree in "The Dream" would not find a place in this *theologia crucis*, because it revealed the cross as gallows, as a product of human violence, and so in a way a work of men. However, between the two, between "The Dream" and the *theologia crucis* stands the Anselmian account. It was the medieval masterwork on atonement that made both the tree's lament and Luther's *Anfechtung* unsustainable, for one because God's honor hypostasized the violence, for the other because that hypostasis, answered only by human works of compensation, became unbearable.

CHRISTIANITY IN CRISIS

At this point we may refer again to the thought of René Girard. He argues that the Hebrew and Christian Scriptures move progressively to the unmasking of violence in its hidden cultural role, and in so doing they engender a cumulative historical crisis because the age-old mechanism of generative violence becomes more and more untenable. In regard to the gospel Passion he says: "In the long run, it is quite capable of undermining and overturning the whole cultural order and supplying the secret motive force of all subsequent history."[107] In his last book to treat this question, *The Scapegoat*, he underlines the trans-historical revolutionary force of the Gospel narratives. "The Passion reveals the scapegoat mechanism. . . . By revealing that mechanism and the surrounding mimeticism, the Gospels set in motion the only textual mechanism that can put an end to humanity's imprisonment in the system of mythological representation based on the false transcendence of a victim who is made sacred because of the unanimous verdict of guilt." And then later: "History need only progress some more and the Gospel will be verified."[108]

---

106. See Alister E. McGrath, *Luther's Theology of the Cross* (Oxford: Blackwell, 1985), 151–56.

107. *Things Hidden since the Foundation of the World* (Stanford, Calif.: Stanford University Press, 1987), 209, 144–79; hereafter *Things Hidden*.

108. *The Scapegoat* (Baltimore: Johns Hopkins University Press, 1986), 166, 207.

In Girard's opus these statements have the disturbing quality of mixing claims related to a "scientific" methodology of anthropology with a rhetoric of biblical faith. The approach taken in this present study is always to separate the two discourses, and to be aware at each point in which separate field of discourse we are operating. At this point, therefore, I choose to read these assertions clearly within the narrative discourse of biblical religion, with its central component of eschatology. That the methodological separation is not simply an intellectual discipline, but is directly related to the overall purpose of the study, must be evident from the following. Surely the first and most appropriate place of application of such statements is the sociological community most intimately affected by the destabilizing force of these Scriptures. The deconstruction set in train by the disclosure of the victim must chronically affect the community that chooses to bear its memory, the Christian church. As Girard himself makes clear, historical Christianity effectively reintegrated its own radical, desacralizing Scripture within traditional cultural solutions: this is what he calls the "sacrificial reading" of the Gospels.

> In a remarkable paradox, but one that accords well with the sacrificial course of mankind, the sacrificial reading (that is, the logic of violent *Logos*) refashions the mechanism that has been revealed and thus of necessity annihilated—if the revelation were genuinely accepted—into a kind of sacrificial cultural foundation. This is the foundation that both "Christianity" and the modern world have rested upon, right up to our own time.[109]

In other words, the institution of Christendom is a sophisticated reculturation of the gospel Passion within the forces of sacred violence. What this reflection does not bring out is the way in which cultural Christianity was unable to sustain its foundation thus constructed; precisely, and above all, because of its *own* central symbols and texts, its sacrificial reformulation was always undermined from within. In mimetic anthropology these are the formal conditions for "sacrificial crisis," the state in which any institution must turn to greater and greater paroxysms of violence within its own historical domain, seeking the ever elusive sacrificial solution. Girard hints at this in respect of Christianity but nowhere does he make it fully thematic. I include the following long quotation because I think it is the nearest Girard has got to such an analysis.

---

109. *Things Hidden*, 224.

I believe it is possible to demonstrate that historical Christianity took on a persecutory character as a result of the sacrificial reading of the Passion and the Redemption.

All the features of the sacrificial reading cohere. The very fact that the [Christian] deity is reinfused with violence has consequences for the entire system, since it partially absolves humankind from a responsibility that ought to be equal and identical for all.

Reducing the responsibility enables one to particularize the Christian event, to diminish its universality, and to search for the guilty men who would absolve humankind of guilt—the role the Jews fulfill. At the same time, violence continues to have repercussions, as we have seen, in the apocalyptic destruction that traditional readings still project upon the deity.

What turns Christianity in on itself, so that it presents a hostile face to all that is not Christian, is inextricably bound up with the sacrificial reading. That reading cannot possibly be *innocent*. It is not difficult to demonstrate the close connections between resacralization and the historical development of Christianity—which is structurally parallel to that of all cultures, being characterized, like them, by the gradual exhaustion of sacrificial resources, amid the increasing disintegration of all cultural formations. [110]

What Girard could immediately have added was that this "disintegration" was necessarily exacerbated in Christian culture because of the uniquely destabilizing power of its central topos of the cross. And that the apocalyptic "repercussions" of violence are intrinsically related to Christianity's resacralization, which works hand in hand with a specific, internal subversion of sacrificial resources. In fact one gets the impression that Girard went to the edge of a critical abyss in respect of historical Christianity, looked over, and turned back. This is certainly true of the later Girard who has gone some way to rehabilitating the traditional Christian reading of Christ's "sacrifice" and maintained almost a complete analytical silence on Christianity's violent history.[111] Moreover, Girard already expressed a trans-historical understanding of Christian history, which acted to defuse some of its scandal.

---

110. Ibid., 225, italics in original.
111. See, for example, *The Girard Reader*, ed. James G. Williams, "A Conversation With René Girard" (New York: Crossroad Publishing, 1996), 272–75, 280.

On the level of history, the sacrificial reading is not an "error," the result of accident or lack of insight. If we really understand the victimage mechanism and the role it has played for all humanity, we can see that the sacrificial reading of the Christian text—however baffling and paradoxical in principle—was inevitable. It had on its side all the weight of an age-old, uninterrupted religious history, which among the multitudes of pagans had never been challenged by anything resembling the Old Testament. . . . [T]he peoples who were evangelized had not been affected [i.e., prepared, as were Jews at the time of the Gospels] by the Old Testament. In these conditions, the role of historical Christianity becomes necessary within an eschatological process that is governed by the Gospels—a history directed towards revealing the universal truth of human violence. But the process requires an almost limitless patience: many centuries must elapse before the subversive and shattering truth contained in the Gospels can be understood worldwide.[112]

Here eschatology is really something else than its biblical variety; it is much closer to historical dialectic, giving the reader a "God's eye" view of things rather than placing him or her before a radical choice. Historical Christianity, although schematically accounted for, loses any sense of a radical contingency intimately allied to the moral drama of human affairs, something that Girard elsewhere vigorously asserts. No matter how locked into historical processes, human responsibility is always at issue. Second, Girard's use of the words "inevitable" and "necessary" brings reminders of Anselm's *ex necessitate,* the "fate" of Germanic paganism, and therefore seems to reintroduce an element of sacred violence as part of the apologetic. Again this might make sense in terms of a formal dialectic, but you cannot have your moral cake and eat it; you cannot, on the one hand, claim Christianity's specialness because of its disclosure of violence and, on the other, vindicate its historical actuality by reason of the inevitability of violence. Finally, the comparison with the experience of the Old Testament does not stand up on every side. Again and again the story of the Hebrew people is marked by the intervention of prophets who profoundly challenged their behaviors and projected severe historical consequences. The Hebrew Bible in its present form is a product of

---

112. *Things Hidden,* 252.

postexilic Judaism, and above all in the Deuteronomic history it reads the story of national collapse as a result of the people's failure to keep the covenant. Nothing resembling this permanent critical reckoning with itself, within its own sacred text, is the case in historical Christianity; unless, of course, the cross is taken with full seriousness. And in confirmation of this adventitious privilege, the phenomenon of historical Christianity presented by Girard is not controverted from within, rather it is vindicated.

In contrast, what I have attempted to show in this chapter is the way in which a central strand of historical Christianity has in itself been constituted by chronic mimetic crisis. Seeing the evidence within the full range of Girard's thought, we can say that the first and most obvious place in which the gospel's disruptive effect has been felt is in folk Christianity and in the church that sought to institutionalize it. This is not to blame Christianity vindictively, to create another scapegoat, neither is it to provide exoneration, a grand theoretical explaining away. It simply and clearly points out that the force of the hypothesis is to make the society most exposed to the gospel of the Passion to be the one that will be most prone to sacrificial crisis: i.e., the church. This crisis will have numerous manifestations, ranging from wholehearted transformation in compassion and nonviolence, to a long-term, systematic need to find surrogate victims; from renunciation of the world of desire prompted by Christ, to a bloody determination to control that world under the powerful symbol of Christ; from intense mystical devotion to the wounded humanity of Christ, to a Puritan expulsion of all human process in salvation; and all the variations among these points. In other words, the history of Christianity is a history of crisis, provoked by its own internal struggle and frequent failure before the figure of the Crucified. Thus it stands historically under judgment from its own central motif and message.

However, judgment in the light of abyssal compassion is something other than condemnation. It is a profound invitation to change. And as I will argue in the final chapter, there is also a sense in which the abyssal love of the Crucified offers the reconstitution of all history, not indeed by a reading of dialectical necessity, but by a transformed sense of time itself. Beginning from the cross all things are made new, certainly in the mind of the believer. Everything is given an anarchic new starting point, a kind of bottomless "future past" that presses on all known time in the manner of ultimate re-creation. If this is the true sense of time emerging from the cross, then the vindication of Christian history and its violence is redundant, if not plainly a negation of the cross itself. One has only to think of the Christian validation of warrior heroism in the West up until the contemporary period to get a sense of what is at stake here. The supreme honors granted to soldiers in countries like England and France—the Victoria Cross, the George Cross, and the Croix de Guerre—are a continued inversion of the figure of the Crucified in the culture of violence. Surely it is time indeed to let the cross speak for itself.

Chapter Four

Repetition, Rhetoric, and Compassion

How is it possible to move from a grammar of Christ's death built from mimetic violence to one that offers to transform the root of mimetic relationity itself? To be able to arrive at this question is in itself a revolutionary possibility, derived from mimetic anthropology and the analysis of tradition it makes available. But the search for an alternative takes us further, toward something new, toward the most radical possibilities disclosed in the existential event of Christ's death. It takes us in the direction of the abyss, toward the depths where humanity is discovered without foundations, that is, to the point where humanity is itself essentially the undecidability of mimesis. Christ's death reveals the foundational victim who stabilizes the chaos of mimetic desire; by implication, therefore, it also takes us to the place where humanity is in a way prehuman, sunk in uncontrollable mimesis. Here there is the experience of human nonbeing, of emptiness, chaos, and abandonment, and yet at the same time the possibility of an entirely new human formulation. Humanity may be constituted anew in and through the response of Christ in that place.

The content of the Christian proclamation is that this response is indeed singular and unparalleled in its formative power, and its moment, the moment in which it occurs, has for that reason been understood as eternal. However, the standard ideation of eternity is an eternity of ideation; and so the logos of Christ has been conceived in Platonic terms, identified with the eternal mind of God. Or, in the conflictual logic of mimesis, Christ's death has found its meaning in a court of divine judgment applying a timeless mimetic rationality. On the contrary, in the view I am proposing, the existential truth of Christ's death is a contingent moment of re-creativity in the midst of the bloodiness of human affairs, of human history itself. This then would produce a very different concept of "eternity," an eternity realized not in a motionless, atemporal ideality, but a singular movement within the contingent and particular, endlessly provoking a new, originary mimesis. Its eternity is its bottomless re-creativity in a place that has no end, no ground, no foundation, except the response of the Crucified in that nonplace. It is an "endless" dynamic in a place without end, the endlessness of the abyss evoking the response that has no end.

Here there is no *opus alienum*, no violence or wrath at the strict level of the theological, that is, in the moment of the Crucified, for violence is seen as specifically human-cultural, an anthropological phenomenon that Christ discloses and abyssally transforms. Rather, the identification of violence with the Christian concept of God derives from the primal construction of the sacred and its pervasive cultural force. In the light of this position all the lingering affection for the Anselmian scheme may be seen as an unwillingness at some level to let go of the metaphysical sanction of violence. This is the immensely powerful and formative grammar of violence; but I believe there has always been a subcurrent of tradition that works in a very different sense and whose language is so novel as to be barely formulable up to this point. It is above all the gospel narrative that has worked to produce this language, and so it is always realized in the practice of Christians who have radically appropriated its message. However, there are also vital hints and suggestions throughout the theological tradition where it has understood the work of the cross in terms of human solidarity and compassion. What is new here is the explanation of the cross made possible by mimetic anthropology, the way its logic allows us to articulate a grammar of the human abyss revealed and transformed by Christ.

George Lindbeck has developed the idea of religious doctrines as a type of grammar, seeing them as a set of rules or regulative principles that maintain the internal cohesion and truth of the overall narrative and worldview of that religion. These rules are thus comparable to the grammar of a language that tells us how to use that language meaningfully and correctly. However, some grammatical "rules" may in fact be false to the deep structure of the language. "Some rules may reflect temporary features of surface grammar or may even be arbitrary impositions (as in the day when attempts were made to force Latin patterns on modern languages). The deep grammar of the language may escape detection. It may be impossible to find rules that show why some crucial usages are beautifully right and other dangerously wrong."[1] Here precisely it is the question of crucial usages or grammar that lies at the

---

1. George A. Lindbeck, *The Nature of Doctrine* (Philadelphia: Westminster Press, 1984), 81–82.

heart of this study. Lindbeck is probably right also to indicate that it may be impossible to find a final "rule" to arbitrate these usages. It is only in the presentation of the alternatives, that is, by allowing first one and then the other to emerge in its own particular modality, that the expression that seems truest to the core Christian conversation may be found. In the present instance what we are seeking is an account that articulates "the cross to the cross," so to speak, most convincingly. For this purpose I will look now at a particular philosophical concept that helps illuminate the movement in the abyss, and with the impetus it provides continue to deepen our alternative thought of atonement. At the end I will turn to key instances of narrative literature that may be seen to carry through a kind of exemplary performance of the meaning of Christ's death, and so provide a privileged reiteration of this bottomless movement. In between there is a methodological interlude that will clarify the status of mimetic anthropology in relation to other non-foundationalist narrativist theologies, and then serve to locate it overall within the rhetorical genre of biblical faith. Thus an anthropological account of the cross will avoid a rationalist scientism, and remain rooted in the contingent and particular.

REPETITION BY VIRTUE OF THE ABYSS

Kierkegaard's notion of repetition is an absolutely key philosophical reference point for the meaning of an abyssal movement of redemption, of re-creativity in the abyss. It opens the possibility of a nonviolent articulation of the cross, because in the way Kierkegaard proposes it, it is by nature contingent, experimental, without the necessary end that metaphysics demands. A movement that lacks a necessary end or teleology brings us in a parallel relationship to the voluntarist, aphoristic thought of Nietzsche, but in contrast to the Kierkegaardian perspective that affirms the religious, Nietzsche celebrates an extramoral value in regard to violence. This difference will provide both the conceptual fork in the road past which a nonviolent grammar of atonement moves and help us understand more profoundly what is at stake in an abyssal account of Christ's death. It may seem that what lies before us in the chapter is a broad canvas of reflections and examples: and that very probably is the case! It demonstrates perhaps the character of the matter in hand. To arrive at some preferred language about the nature of Christ's death it is necessary to work our way through parts or *tessera* of a mosaic, dialectical, rhetorical, and illustrative. Only in this way will a portrait that is both sufficiently strong and yet non-essentialized have a chance to emerge.

Kierkegaard's work entitled *Repetition* is itself notable for the way it mixes themes of individual freedom with the problematics of mediated desire. Subtitled a "venture in experimenting psychology," it may at least partially be read as a novel; and indeed its characterization anticipates something of the Dostoyevskian world of exacerbated, despairing desire that so strongly informed Girard's literary criticism.[2] The pseudonymous author, Constantin Constantius, describes the passion of the young man who is the subject of his report in terms that unmistakably demonstrate the young man's beloved as the object of mediated desire. It is the conceit of a poet and, around that, the culture of the aesthetic in which the young man moved that models this desire and, in turn, spells its object's doom.

> [S]he was the beloved, the only one he had loved, the only one he would ever love. Nevertheless, he did not still love her, because he only longed for her. During all this, a remarkable change took place in him. A poetic creativity awakened in him on a scale I had never believed possible. Now I easily grasped the whole situation. The young girl was not his beloved: she was the occasion that awakened the poetic in him and made him a poet. That was why he could love only her, never forget her, never want to love another, and yet continually only long for her. She was drawn into his whole being; the memory of her was forever alive. She had meant much to him; she had made him a poet—and precisely thereby had signed her own death sentence.[3]

The figure of the poet is ironic here. On the one hand, it is linked to Kierkegaard's own self-assessment as a "poet," a creator of imaginative fictions that disclose a truth, evincing the universal in the particular. More dramatically, it refers to the crazed, dangerous existence of the young man in service of his desire.[4] This desire is first mediated to and then exacer-

---

2. Søren Kierkegaard, *Fear and Trembling, Repetition*, ed., trans., intro., and notes by Howard V. Hong and Edna H. Hong (Princeton: Princeton University Press, 1983), 125, xxvi . Hereafter *Repetition*.

3. Ibid., 137–38.

4. See Louis Mackey, *Kierkegaard: A Kind of Poet* (Philadelphia: University of Pennsylvania Press, 1971); and *Repetition*, xx–xxv. Ibid.,302: "[I]n *Repetition* . . . I wanted to depict and make visible psychologically and esthetically; in the Greek sense, I wanted to let the concept come into being in the individuality and the situation, working itself forward through all sorts of misunderstandings" (*Pap.* IV B 117, 281, 302, in Søren Kierkegaard's *Journals and Papers*, 7 vols., ed. and trans. Howard V. Hong and Edna H. Hong, with Gregor Malantschuk [Bloomington, Ind. and London: Indiana University Press, 1967–1978).

bated by Constantin Constantius, who had experienced an "alluring effect" from the young man; in return, as he says, "through casual coffee-shop associations, I . . . attracted him to me and taught him to regard me as a confidant."[5] Constantin gains a kind of control over the young man and urges him to disillusion the young woman with a pantomime of infidelity. The object is to break her free from him, and yet heroically bear the burden of the break. For his own part Constantin continually desires "repetition" of aesthetically pleasing experiences, and is constantly unsuccessful: for example, in his old lodgings in Berlin and then later at the Königstädter Theater, he seeks ecstatic sensations and in both instances there is the scarcely hidden gaze of the crowd that shapes his self-desire.[6] Finally, there is the admission that the young man's main object was "to redeem his honor and pride," while for Constantin it was "also a matter of honor and pride to keep at bay such childish, uneasy feelings!"[7]

However, Kierkegaard is still too much of a philosopher, too much in dispute with Hegel, to remain purely on a novelistic level of the manias of desire. He is not concerned to explore the abyssal phenomenon of the "underground man" as sheer epitome of the modern, though he comes close.[8] "Repetition" is the key question and it is essentially a philosophical category. It is finally illustrated in the event by which the young man overcomes his desire, and is pivotal to the resolution of the central "experimental" problem of the book.

---

5. *Repetition*, 133–34.

6. Constantin anticipates arrival in his room. "Sitting in a chair by the window, one looks out on the great square, sees the shadows of passersby hurrying along the walls; everything is transformed into a stage setting. A dream world glimmers in the background of the soul. One feels the desire to toss on a cape, to steal softly along the wall with a searching gaze, aware of every sound. One does not do this but merely sees a rejuvenated self doing it" (ibid., 151–52). Regarding the theater he says, "There is probably no young person with any imagination who has not at some time been enthralled by the magic of the theater and wished to be swept along into that artificial actuality in order like a double to see and hear himself and to split himself up into every possible variation of himself," (ibid., 154).

7. Ibid., 185.

8. For example, "The cryptic individual believes as little in noisy, powerful feelings as in the wily whispering of evil, believes as little in the ecstatic jubilation of joy as in the endless sighing of sorrow; the individual wants only to see and hear with pathos—please note, to see and hear himself. But the individual does not want actually to hear himself. That will not do. At the very same moment the cock crows and the twilight shapes vanish, the nocturnal voices fall silent. If they keep on, then we are in an altogether different realm where all this takes place under the disquieting supervision of responsibility, then we approach the demonic. Then, in order not to gain an impression of his actual self, the hidden individual needs an environment as superficial and transient as the shapes, as the frothing foam of words that sound without resonance" (ibid., 155–56).

The dialectic of repetition is easy, for that which is repeated has been—otherwise it could not be repeated—but the very fact that it has been makes the repetition into something new. When the Greeks said that all knowing is recollecting, they said that all existence, which is, has been; when one says that life is a repetition, one says, actuality, which has been, now comes into existence. If one does not have the category of recollection or of repetition, all life dissolves into an empty, meaningless noise. Recollection is the ethnical [*ethniske* (i.e., according to the Hong notes, "pagan")] view of life, repetition the modern; repetition is the *interest* [*Interesse*] of metaphysics, and also the interest upon which metaphysics comes to grief; repetition is the watchword in every ethical view, repetition is *conditio sine qua non* [the indispensable condition] for every issue of dogmatics.[9]

This is an extremely important synthetic statement, summing up in a few words the revolutionary category of repetition. On one side it locates repetition as the key concern of metaphysics, but differentiates it immediately from classical Platonic recollection as the locus of truth. The interest of metaphysics is the *inter esse* that is Being, the "in-the-midst-of-being" of human actuality and experience, the fact that there is something rather than nothing. But for Kierkegaard repetition finds no metaphysical self-identity, for it is a matter of what actually occurs, not what is gathered into a self-present concept. Therefore metaphysics founders in the enigma of repetition. As a concept it is suspended between the Eleatics, for whom all was one, and Heraclitus, for whom all is flux, and this suspension cannot be resolved on the level of the idea. It is an aporetic concept, that may be seen somehow as necessary and final but yet not intellectually sufficient to itself. As such it is set resolutely against Hegel's totalizing concept of mediation, his *Vermittelung* that functions by "sublation" or lifting up, and is the reconciliation of differences or opposites in a higher unity.[10] In this "systematic" concept one thing becomes another by a continuous movement that is, in fact, always the outworking of the ideal or the rational. Instead, for Kierkegaard, repetition is a discontinuous movement in actu-

---

9. Ibid., 149, brackets with original languages and English translation from Hongs.

10. For example: "For being which is the outcome of *mediation* we shall reserve the term: *Existence*" and "This immediacy that is mediated by ground and condition and is self-identical through the sublation of mediation, is *Existence*" (Hegel's *Science of Logic*, trans. A. V. Miller [New York: Humanities Press, 1969], 93, 478, quoted in *Philosophical Fragments, Johannes Climacus*, ed., trans., intro., and notes by Howard V. Hong and Edna H. Hong [Princeton: Princeton University Press, 1985], 279).

ality that nevertheless derives continuity. It is structurally intimate to the passion of existence that, Kierkegaard says elsewhere, produces movement. "This is the continual leap in existence that explains the movement, whereas mediation is a chimera, which in Hegel is supposed to explain everything and which is also the only thing he never has tried to explain."[11] Hegelian systematic continuity is locked in the silence of immanence, produced by thought. Its fundamental error is to introduce movement into intellectual logic, something that the latter cannot support. Its contrary effect is to make freedom illusory, and in order to rescue freedom Kierkegaard opposes repetition to mediation.[12]

So, on the other side, repetition is at the heart of the ethical life in the sense of a human work of self-repetition, but even more crucially for our purposes it is at the heart, too, of Christian dogmatics. The contrast with "pagan" recollection underlines this. Repetition "is actuality and the earnestness of existence"[13] that sustains both the ethical and religious life. But above all it is the religious that gives it meaning and it is this that pulls with it all the other senses, including the philosophical, not the other way round. "'Repetition' is and remains a religious category."[14] Kierkegaard certainly maintains the philosophical meaning, above all in contrast to Hegel, but it is precisely the religious meaning that gives it its dialectical vigor. For it is the religious movement in existence that is the paradigm instance of the task of human freedom, and so serves ultimately to demolish the Hegelian system, opening the abyss in philosophy itself. For what is the leap in existence but a leap in a void, which nevertheless is the place of human truth? So the category of repetition of itself precipitates the abyss in Western thought, and must be counted one of its principal dynamics in the contemporary intellectual landscape. And, again, it is the religious, and that means specifically Christian, force that it contains for Kierkegaard that provokes this crucial turn.

How much this is the case becomes clear in the narrative when the young man turns away from Constantin to the Book of Job, in order to find release from the impossibility of repetition, or movement, in relation to his obsessive desire for the beloved.[15] In *Fear and Trembling*

---

11. *Repetition*, 42.
12. *Pap.* IV B 117, 288–89; *Repetition*, 308.
13. *Repetition*, 133.
14. *Pap.* IV A 169; *Repetition*, 326. Constantin Constantius also goes as far as the apparently theological comment, "If God himself had not willed repetition, the world would not have come into existence. . . . Therefore, the world continues, and it continues because it is a repetition" (133).
15. *Repetition*, 214.

Kierkegaard made the figure Abraham the key to his argument; here it is Job. Unlike Abraham, the Job of *Repetition* does not proceed in paradoxical faith "by virtue of the absurd" but in terms of an unflinching assertion of his own righteousness before God. This is a decisively significant other half to the diptych of the two works that were finalized and published simultaneously on 16 October 1843.[16] What is at stake is the liberation of the young man from the stasis, or even death, of desire. In fact, in an earlier version the story had ended with the young man's suicide. In the later version he finds the book of Job and eulogizes Job's passionate defense on behalf of the afflicted.[17] He awaits in hope a comparable "thunderstorm" to the one that had marked the end of Job's torment, and a comparable event of repetition to the one by which Job had received his life back double; in other words, the repetition of his self, his self anew.[18]

Here is a story of redemption or vindication, built upon another story of redemption or vindication. The heart of Job's demand had been for a *go'el*, a vindicator on the earth, and in some measure his demand had been answered by his final restoration.[19] The same happens to the young man: his beloved marries someone else and immediately he is set free. To the extent that Job maintains his human innocence as a victim and awaits liberation his story is sheer anthropology. Kierkegaard's use of it is therefore very different from his unswerving accent on the inward virtue of absurdity in Abraham's faith, which of course is also meant as anti-Hegelian critique. What is absurd or incommensurable here, in the story of *Repetition*, is the actual event that brings the liberation and proves the individual right; and it this particular organization of contingency that leads the young man to the boundaries of the religious. In a later commentary on *Repetition*, Kierkegaard said of his characterization of the theme of repe-

---

16. Ibid., xxxiv.

17. See the letter of the young man to his "Silent Confidant": "Job! Job! O Job! ... [Y]ou who in your prime were the sword of the oppressed, the stave of the old, and the staff of the brokenhearted, you did not disappoint men when everything went to pieces—then you became the voice of the suffering, the cry of the grief-stricken, the shriek of the terrified, and a relief to all who bore their torment in silence, a faithful witness to all the affliction and laceration there can be in a heart, an unfailing spokesman who dared to lament 'in bitterness of soul' and to strive with God" (*Repetition*, 197).

18. "Job is blessed and has received everything *double*. —This is called a *repetition*" (ibid., 212).

19. Job 19:25–27. "But as for me, I know that my Vindicator [*go'el*] lives, and that he will at last stand forth upon the dust; Whom myself shall see: my own eyes, not another's, shall behold him, and from my flesh I shall see God; my inmost being is consumed with longing" (*New American Bible* [New York and Oxford: Oxford University Press, 1995]).

tition: "It is transcendent, religious, the movement of the absurd that commences when one has reached the border of the wondrous."[20] In other words, there is an actual movement that is absurd, not based on a rational scheme, in fact in defiance of the system, which is wonderful because it brings life where before it was impossible. It is radically interruptive in and at the same time that it is re-creative.

Thus the moment of the religious allows the young man to gain himself again as poet, by reason of a "religious primitivity," but then at that point for him "the religious founders . . . becomes a kind of inexpressible substratum."[21] In the words of another theologian he has experienced a kind of "cheap grace," a setting free that did not end in a true God-relationship; nevertheless there is irony here because the story parallels Kierkegaard's own liberation from relationship with Regine Olsen through her engagement to someone else, the resolution that was incorporated into the final version. Thus perhaps "one can learn very much from a young man."[22] My point is that although Job is not a hero of faith, and the young man less so, Kierkegaard in the twinning of *Repetition* with *Fear and Trembling* gives fair description of the necessity of some kind of external process, a transcendence of movement, that complements the incommensurable inwardness of faith in Abraham. This indeed is atonement, a movement produced in the actuality of existence bringing freedom.

> [F]reedom despairs of itself but still never forgets repetition. But in the moment of despair a change takes place with regard to repetition, and freedom takes on a religious expression, by which repetition appears as atonement, which is repetition *sensu eminentiori* [in the highest sense] and something different from mediation, which merely describes the nodal points of oscillation in the progress of immanence.[23]

Elsewhere he says that in his book he could "easily . . . have worked out how repetition progresses along this path until it signifies atonement, which is the most profound expression of repetition."[24] This indeed is a remarkable pathway, the progression of an idea that displaces the core Greek notion of recollection as the place of truth, toward the point where

---

20. *Pap.* IV B 117, 294; *Repetition*, 313.
21. *Pap.* IV B 117, 284; *Repetition*, 304; and 229.
22. *Pap.* IV B 117, 285; *Repetition*, 305.
23. *Pap.* IV B 117; *Repetition*, 320.
24. *Pap.* IV B 117, 293; *Repetition*, 313.

it reveals itself as the core concept of Christian proclamation, "Christ died for our sins." Except that in the actual existential experience that Kierkegaard writes from, it should probably be read in the other direction: from the religious event that gives movement in despair, to the selfsame abyssal movement as the paradigm of all human movement and its truth. When does repetition occur? "Well, that is hard to say in any human language. When did it occur for Job? When every *thinkable* human certainty and probability were impossible . . . the knot and the entanglement are tightened and can be untied only by a thunderstorm."[25] Precisely not a Greek deduction from a metaphysical principle, but an extrapolation from the impossibility of human existence discovered before God. This can be resolved into possibility only by Job's thunderstorm or, "in the highest sense," by Christian atonement.

Nowhere in Kierkegaard's writing does he pursue the nature of repetition in first-person terms of Christ on the cross. He does not move to analyze atonement itself as repetition, to show how Christ's abyssal death created the movement in the abyss upon which he bases his whole philosophy. Perhaps theologically he was still too determined by dogmatic considerations in the Lutheran tradition. It is true of course that he sees Christ's life as existential offense, as inserting contradiction into human culture, particularly as the essential offense of lowliness, poverty, suffering, and finally the powerlessness of the cross.[26] This is a significant reflection of the abyss opened on the cross but it is recounted in respect of the effect it produces on the believer, as the warrant in its offensiveness of the very truth of faith before which all human understanding comes to a halt. What it misses is the way the gospel figure of Christ himself entered into his own offense, that is, into the abyss, and thereby served to open it in his own person, and provide simultaneously an endless re-creativity in and from that endless place. This is the heart of repetition in the Christian kerygma, its foundationless, interruptive, nonsystematic power released by Christ. The lack of this aspect in Kierkegaard, I would suggest, is the reason why *Repetition,* while

25. *Repetition*, 212, original italics.
26. See Søren Kierkegaard, *Training in Christianity*, ed. and trans. with intro. and notes by Howard V. Hong and Edna H. Hong (Princeton: Princeton University Press, 1991), e.g., 102–5; also 133–38, for the suffering in Christ produced by the necessity of proceeding only by indirect communication and contradiction because of the essential offense of God as single human individual. This could be reexpressed as the abyss of compassion in contingency and particularity. For Kierkegaard the figure of Christ remains a dogmatic, and to some degree intellectual, consideration, in view of producing the offense of faith in the Christian believer. The particularism of the cross and its meaning in Jesus himself is largely lost in this scheme.

being philosophically provocative, fails to sustain the existential urgency of *Fear and Trembling*. It lacks the struggle and surrender of Christ himself. It is the reason why Job's defense of the victim, of the suffering, is somehow less imposing than the sacrifice of Isaac, and why Job's and the young man's experience of the thunderstorm is somehow less evocative than Abraham's unsurpassable faith. But when we introduce the abyssal dimensions of mimetic anthropology into the equation we suddenly enter into a new depth of understanding—but one that does not at all remove the offense. Repetition as the leap in existence that explains movement is first and foremost rooted in the Passion, the Passion of Christ, in the abyssal provocation of the gospel account of Jesus' judicial torture and murder responded to with a witness of truth and infinite giving. When we see it in these terms the category of repetition achieves its full religious impact, is given its full human and conceptual vigor. It is a movement that has no end, no ground, no foundation, beyond the response of the Crucified in the nonplace of the cross. It is the eternal dynamic in a place without end, the endlessness of the abyss evoking the response that has no end. Once we have brought it to this point, repetition both underpins the idea of abyssal compassion and suddenly receives there its most cohesive, provocative enactment.

A counterpoint to the abyss of compassion, and the setting of Kierkegaard's epoch-making category of repetition within it, must be Nietzsche's affirmation of cruelty and violence, and the will-to-power as including this affirmation, not indeed out of any kind of personal vindictiveness but because life itself includes it. There are countless examples of such an affirmation throughout Nietzsche's work; the following written in the final year of his productive career may stand as emblematic, particularly because of the explicit contrast it draws to the figure of the Crucified.

> Dionysus versus the "Crucified": there you have the anti-thesis. It is *not* a difference in regard to their martyrdom—it is a difference in the meaning of it. Life itself, its eternal fruitfulness and recurrence, creates torment, destruction, the will to annihilation. In the other case, suffering—the "Crucified as the innocent one"— counts as an objection to this life, as a formula for its condemnation.—One will see that the problem is that of the meaning of suffering: whether a Christian meaning or a tragic meaning. In the former case, it is supposed to be the path to a holy existence; in the latter case, being is counted as *holy enough* to justify even a monstrous amount of suffering. The tragic man affirms even the harshest suffering; he is sufficiently strong, rich, and capable of

deifying to do so. The Christian denies even the happiest lot on earth; he is sufficiently weak, poor, disinherited to suffer from life in whatever form he meets it. The god on the cross is a curse on life, a signpost to seek redemption from life; Dionysus cut to pieces is a *promise* of life: it will eternally be reborn and return again from destruction.[27]

In the assessment I have given, repetition is to be found in the highest (or indeed lowest) sense in the abyssal compassion of the cross, and the irreconcilable opposition Nietzsche sets up between the Dionysus and the Crucified testifies, in its way as powerfully as Kierkegaard's dialectic of repetition, to this place as the real crossroads in human life. If anything, Nietzsche was more clearly focused on the pivotal role of the cross than Kierkegaard. He descries the real, unnegotiable opposition to his philosophy in the meaning of the Crucified, and it is here too that this book wishes to touch, and perhaps at a deeper level than before, what is at stake in human existence. Where Nietzsche leaps from ancient cruelty to the *Übermensch*[28] by virtue of the will-to-power, Kierkegaard leaps to the religious, by virtue of repetition. It is in the distinction between these two approaches to essentially the same problem that the argument of this chapter has reached a pivotal point, and in a way that of the whole book. For Nietzsche "the philosophy of the sacrificial animal . . . is always sounded too late."[29] In other words, it seems, we kill first and ask questions later.

---

27. Friedrich Nietzsche, *Will to Power*, trans. Walter Kaufmann and R. J. Hollingdale, ed. with commentary Walter Kaufmann (New York: Vintage Books, 1968), 542–43

28. For example: "What is the supreme enjoyment for men who live in the state of war of those small, continually endangered communities which are characterized by the strictest mores? In other words, for vigorous, vindictive, vicious, suspicious souls who are prepared for what is most terrible and hardened by deprivations and mores. The enjoyment of *cruelty*; and in these circumstances it is even accounted among the *virtues* of such a soul if it is inventive and insatiable in cruelty. The community feels refreshed by cruel deeds, and casts off for once the gloom of continual anxiety and caution. Cruelty belongs to the most ancient festive joys of mankind" (*The Dawn*, 18, in *Basic Writings of Nietzsche*, trans., ed., and commentary by Walter Kaufmann [New York: The Modern Library, 1992], 166. See also *Genealogy of Morals*, II, 3, 6, 12 (ibid., 496–515). Then: "[T]o me justice speaks thus: 'Men are not equal.' Nor shall they become equal. What would my love of the overman be if I spoke otherwise? On a thousand bridges and paths they shall throng to the future, and ever more war and inequality shall divide them: thus does my great love make me speak. In their hostilities they shall become inventors of images and ghosts, and with their images and ghosts they shall yet fight the highest fight against one another. Good and evil, and rich and poor, and high and low, and all the names of values—arms shall they be and clattering signs that life must overcome itself again and again" (*Thus Spoke Zarathustra*, "On the Tarantulas," in *The Portable Nietzsche*, ed. and trans. Walter Kaufmann [New York and London: Penguin Books, 1982], 213).

29. *Mixed Opinions and Maxims*, no. 89, in *Basic Writings of Nietzsche*, 155.

For Kierkegaard Job "became . . . the cry of the grief-stricken . . . an unfailing spokesman who dared to lament . . . and to strive with God." In other words, someone who seeks to take the part of the victim *before* it's too late. The significance of the cross is a counterclaim to the lateness of the philosophy of the victim, and there is nothing commensurable between the two except the body of the victim. The lack of commensurability becomes an irreducible moment of passion, or the undecidable choice between two passions, for or against the victim, for or against *all* victims. It may perhaps be described as an inflexible aporetic doublet: because the mutual presence of each concept makes the other impossible, with no further point of negotiation between the two. As I have just suggested, it is not even fully a matter of choice. To resolve it, from the side of atonement, requires the "thunderstorm" in Kierkegaard's metaphor, a contingent set of events that becomes an encounter with the Crucified and thus attains the value of repetition in the awakening of compassion.

Contingency is crucial to the event of the cross, in its originary quality of response in the Christ, his foundationless free giving and bottomless forgiveness. For this event to be appropriated it must be met in its very contingency and particularity: the possibility that Christ is right here with me in this time and place, and did not have to be, yet was. In respect of my life there is nothing necessary about my life; its movement in existence is composed of innumerable factors that may or may not have been, and yet I must deal with them, and make a life from them, precisely because they *are* in their contingency. It is necessarily in these circumstances that the abyssal response of Christ comes to meet me and let me know that in the radical particularity of my life, of which I am the powerless sovereign, he yields himself to me without reserve. But how in fact does the message of such an abyssal yielding work? Here is an absolutely crucial moment for a human life; how does it become new life for me? Taking the gospel narrative as our cue, can we work our way deeper into its dynamic, from the anthropological point of view?

We see that after violence has accomplished its aim, once the Crucified is dead, it is then that the formal moment of the religious arrives. There is repetition of the life of the Crucified. Somehow the nonretaliatory victim is found to live again, and to live again in terms of nonretaliation. Like Job his life is given back double and more. However, this return to life is not at the cost of masking the original violence; on the contrary, it is doubly disclosed, first in its facticity and second, and primordially, by its undoing in compassion. The gospel name for this is resurrection. There is no getting to the bottom of resurrection; but that is the whole point! Resurrection is the eternal or bottomless affirmation of nonretaliation, or forgiveness, for all violence. It is the moment of the divine, but not a deus ex machina, rescuing Christ out of, away from, despite, the pit of death. The divine takes place in, we might say is constituted by and through, the whole anthropological reality of the Passion story. Resurrection is not a transcendent miracle vindicating Christ against his human history; rather it arises in and from that history, the precise, formal affirmation of the anthropological revolution of the cross. There is no limit to Christ's forgiveness, his gift of himself in the darkness of human violence and abandonment. And the very quality of this "no limit" resists, subverts, overturns the hitherto irresistible damnation of death. Where before a death inevitably ends in the rictus of the corpse, the sign of violence triumphant, in the cross, the event of the Crucified, it is changed endlessly into a glance of compassion and life begun over.

The fact that the gospel also clearly states this as personal, corporeal life gloriously regenerated should neither blind us to its essential anthropological constitution, and the discovery of the transcendent within that, nor should it be re-interpeted as myth seeking to construct this imaginitively. The proclamation of the new life of Christ is indivisible from the abyss of forgiveness, first because the effect of the latter in all those who have received it in their depths is of life reconstituted. But the possibility of biological life also reconstituted is an essential measure of the bottomless dynamism of the anthropological renewal *in radice* proclaimed in the cross. Death for human beings is not simply an organic event, it is significant, it has become significant; in fact it can fairly claim to be among the major significations or signs in human meaning, if not *the* major. This meaning has inevitably passed through the actual history of meaning and belongs therewith to its foundation in original mimesis and violence, in fact, in murder. Human organic death as having human meaning never escapes a connotation of murder; so the first human death in the Bible is indeed a murder. And, in broad cultural terms, what else are all the elaborate funeral rites of human societies but a way of coping with death's terrible mimetic content as violence to the other? Resurrection, therefore, reverses the human meaning of death as violence, constituting abyssal life in the place of death with all its deadly significance: abyssal, endless life in place of the abyss of violence. To say anything less is inevitably to fall back into the order of violence, in and through its warrant of death, no matter how well intentioned demythologizing Christians may be. What makes the resurrection of Christ credible, over against such demythologizing, and indeed over against all mythological attempts to cope with the violence of death, is precisely the abyssal love of Jesus in response to the acute crisis of violence that brought his end. It is the anthropological content of his death that provides the true content of gospel Resurrection, making it both different from every other mythological resurrection and possible to believe as a genuine, abyssal interruption of the order of violence. To experience the repetition of Christ is to be met in contingency by an infinite depth of life.

THE ANTHROPOLOGICAL HORIZON OF COMPASSION

We can continue to examine the anthropology of this experience by underlining the term that denotes a response of solidarity with the non-retaliatory victim, that is, compassion. This is not yet the same as faith, though it may well depend for its development, historically and culturally speaking, upon a kerygma that proclaims the life of the forgiving victim in and beyond death. In other words, the violence of the murder is not allowed to cover the phenomenality of the event, in the way that "successful" murder always seeks to do. On the contrary, life is reasserted, not as the possibility of revenge, but precisely in terms of a nonretaliation for the violence. Compassion is possible for all and is endless. On the other hand, perhaps we may speculate that the kerygma itself depends upon the theme of compassion to provide the anthropological ground for a faith in resurrection. The possibility of a profound sympathy with the victim that is not sadomasochistically complicit with the violence may surely be said to pre-exist the kerygma, and indeed to have found a first germinal realization in the mystery cults of classical antiquity.[30] Although the message of the risen Crucified acted to make abyssal the historical possibility of compassion, it did not invent it. As such, compassion can stand as a vital anthropological marker for a positive idiom of the cross, one that does not need to translate to the level of metaphysics for its significance.

However, once this is posited, we do then have to deal with an important objection that arises: is not compassion the "other side" of violence, an identification with suffering that depends first on an attack? Does it not, therefore, need violence in order to exist, does it not in some way become complicit with the violence it seeks to redeem? Nietzsche, who as we have seen asserts an inescapability of violence, also underscores the idea of this complicity. He launches a polemic against "pity" as intrinsically dependent on the phenomenon of violence. In contemporary terms he sees it as the product of the "religion of pity" that seeks a general reversal

---

30. See the Biblical hint of this in the remarkable passage at Zech. 12:10–11, discovering compassion in the "mourning for Hadad-rimmon."

of suffering among humanity, and under this he would certainly subsume any language and affect of "compassion." His argument is essentially the emotional complicity of pity with failure, with a putative self-contempt, self-pity, and then with generalized *ressentiment*. It is, therefore, a covert violence that mobilizes itself as desire to reverse failure.[31] He finds it impossible to conceive of a Christian pity freed of such convolutions of violence. A theme of free and nonviolent identification with the suffering of another, without some form of self-retrieval and dream of violent reciprocation, is inconceivable to him. Thus, a morality of pity is revealed as always a form of seduction wherein the one who registers the emotion of pity is brought under the power of the weak and suffering, and at the same time seeks secretly to establish his or her own power. The only version that is acceptable would be an "aristocratic" pity ultimately conditioned by the will and not by sensibility.[32] Any movement of surrender to compassion is always temptation of seduction, never transformation. Yet clearly that is not the New Testament idiom of compassion if we take the proclamation of unlimited forgiveness as its most essential mark.

---

31. See *Beyond Good and Evil*, 62, 82, 222, 260, and *Genealogy of Morals*, III, 14, in *Basic Writings of Nietzsche*. Nietzsche's common term translated as pity is *Mitleid*. A term used by the Synoptics frequently rendered in English as "moved by compassion" is *splangchnizomai*, derived from *splagchna*, meaning viscera or bowels, and implying a movement of sympathy at the most internal level of the human body. (See for example Mark 1:41, 6:34, and 8:2, and the parables of the Good Samaritan and the Two Sons, Lk. 10:33, 15:20.) This word is rendered in the German text of *Das Neue Testament griechisch und deutsch* (Herausgegeben von Eberhard Nestle, revised by Erwin Nestle and K. Aland. 17. Ausgabe. Stuttgart: Priviligierte Wuerttembergische Bibelanstalt, 1960), as an impersonal form of *jammern* (*es jammerte ihn*, he sorrowed), or *Barmherzigkeit* (tenderheartedness). It is interesting that *splagchna* refers originally to the visceratio of a sacrificial victim, and then, in a transferred sense, to the seat of powerful emotion or passions, such as anger or desire, in the human subject. Cf. *Liddell and Scott's Greek-English Lexicon* [Oxford and New York: Oxford University Press, 1994], and the article in Gerhard Kittel, *Theological Dictionary of the New Testament* (Grand Rapids: Eerdmans, c. 1985)]. It is New Testament usage, following late Wisdom and intertestamental writing, that seems most of all to turn a harsh visceral term connected to the violence of sacrifice into an expression of most tender mercy. That a "subjective" state of tender feeling should be articulated somehow in and from the ruined body of the victim speaks cogently to a progressive demystification and reinterpretation of ritual sacrifice in terms of compassion. What Nietzsche fails to see is the possibility of this sensation achieving progressive translation from its violent origins, so that culturally it may come to mean their opposite. There is a note of profound creativity here to which the New Testament is witness.

32. Cf. *Beyond Good and Evil*, 284. Nietzsche would perhaps have understood the pity for the dead hero that demanded revenge, such as we examined in the last chapter, as an example of heroic pity and morality (*Genealogy of Morals*, I.14, III.9). But perhaps also he would see its Christian manifestation as already fatally compromised by ressentiment—the revenge of the weak. Such is the labile and subtle nature of the emotions at play that both are possible.

Forgiveness so conceived is a compassion for the enemy even as the enemy displays only strength, cruelty, and oppression. It is a dream of the enemy as friend, an impossible identification with an as yet nonexistent "weakness" of the enemy whereby a true identification that is not rivalry or scapegoating might become possible. It is essential that at root it is indeed weakness that is imagined, because a moment simply of gentleness on the part of the enemy might still be the act of a violent will, whereas it is an incapacity to hurt that is the truly transformative or abyssal moment called into existence. Certainly for the one who forgives, all violent power is impossible. All that is possible is sheer prolepsis, a leap toward a nonexistent future, toward in fact the Kierkegaardian movement of repetition. The mimetic formulae of Borch-Jacobsen allowed us to understand theoretically the possibility of "repeating the other in oneself, dying to oneself—to be reborn, perhaps, *other*," of "primitive alteration" become transformative. The gospel figure of Christ proclaims an abyssal moment of such alteration, a dying to myself to the extent that the Christ dies and yet lives, and thereby the announcement of a totally improbable gift at the bottom of human alienation and abandonment. It is this proclamation that then becomes the basis of further, endlessly "alternating" replications of compassion, a Christlike yielding of myself, not to the violence of the other—that is only what appears to happen—but to his own abyssal possibility of transformation. It is this impossible yet proclaimed compassion that is the anthropological horizon of the cross, its promise of universal peace.

And it is this horizon that Nietzsche categorically denies. Yet Nietzsche's enduring importance is that in fact he identified the focus of the problem so precisely. It is Christianity's claim to posit a different anthropological starting point, and to reconstitute values on the scandalous basis of the cross, that he finds both actual and incredible. The New Testament tradition claims that what results from this basis is indeed infinitely greater than what up until that point would be regarded as a scene of unqualified disaster.[33] That here, with the full possible weight of gainsaying, of contradiction, an authentic transformation can take place. Nietzsche reasserts the judgment of a confident antiquity, that this is not simply absurd, it is perverse. It is the incommensurability of the two accounts at this point that remains the drama of atonement, after previous explanations invoking divine violence have been discounted.

---

33. See the next chapter for a hermeneutic of the New Testament tradition consistent with these themes.

In one of his aphorisms Nietzsche challenges any supposed human necessity of pity. "There are heights of the soul from which even tragedy ceases to look tragic; and rolling together all the woe of the world—who could dare to decide whether its sight would *necessarily* seduce and compel us to feel pity and thus double the woe."[34] By the same token of rhetoric, of course, all the violence of the world should not necessarily seduce us to reciprocate the aggressor, or not feel pity for the victim. Yet it is worth endorsing his point, because is it not the association of necessity with pity that lends it precisely its penumbra of violence? Only the absolute non-necessity of compassion in fact may save it from the charge of covert violence, and it is this absolute contingency of the event of the Crucified that makes it truly nonviolent and liberates it from Nietzsche's critique. Its truth is a completely free identification with the victim, without any implied metaphysics or deferred compensation. It is the gift without reserve, and the transformative experience of such a gift is its own vindication. The idea of this transformation is aided if we think that it may have the same primary structure as metaphysical desire: the loss of the "self" in favor of the "other." Except here the loss is thematic, surrendered to and embraced, not alienated and conflictual, and its movement is realized in the answering compassion of the "model," not in his oppressive excess. If we then provide in the body of disciples a communal or "circular" pattern of such compassionate loss, we may then have the possibility of the rediscovery or reinvention of the "self" even as it is abandoned. In this way we might construct the full image or mise-en-scène of transformation. It is the thought of a complete inversion or conversion of the structure of desire and, together with that, the birth of community, that warrants the eschatological name of "transformation." The limit awareness of a primary moment of compassionate loss in the Crucified may in turn be met by a responsive compassion or imitative transformation in the subject, an impossible liberation of the self from self. This, in a word, may be the content of a nonviolent account of atonement.[35]

Finally, if violence itself must be contingent because it comes from the undecidability of mimesis, the same should be true of compassion. In

---

34. *Beyond Good and Evil*, 30 (italics in original).

35. Here we are at a point that borders on a specific religiosity most often voiced in terms of *agape* (love) or the Holy Spirit. There is an incommensurability about this point that seems to demand a shift to traditional theological language, itself created because of the persistent claims of an experience of abyssal transformation. This shift is by no means improper, but my purpose here is to remain as much as possible on the level of the anthropological, and allow this to retain the word of the argument so that it may affect the meaning of the theological, rather than the other way round.

coherence with the anthropological frame of this study this underlines why compassion is or can be a secular reality. It does not depend upon a divine decree, upon an inscrutable act of God. It can be seen to arise undecidably or spontaneously within the world. To go beyond this point is perhaps even to lose the "free fall" both of violence and compassion, to prevent them in fact from existing. Thus violence is not really violence, compassion is not really compassion: rather they are manifestations of something beyond, an eternal destiny, the more unmovable the more inscrutable it becomes. On the contrary, it is only at the level of free concrete imitation—whether conscious or unconscious, externally mediated or transformative and conversionary—that any difference can be made. Only by the proximity of concrete exempla, either of violence or compassion, may human beings possibly be moved in one direction or another. To take this position is simultaneously to recognize a deep undecidability in human affairs and the extreme importance of cultural constructions of one sort or another. It is the tension and balance of these two factors that perhaps more than anything constitute the challenge of human history. Within this understanding the cross of Christ may be placed historically as an invitation to compassion, one that is exemplary in a normal sense, but also singular and epoch-making. The full range of the gospel proclamation, in its abyssal nature, including a sense of terminal historical crisis, makes it an instance unparalleled in its transformational challenge. It is perhaps worth emphasizing in this connection that Girard's biblical disclosure of violence cannot in fact take place, at least primordially, without the experience of compassion. It is only by identification with the Crucified in terms of a sense of limitless forgiveness (i.e., inherent nonviolence, nonretaliation) that a message of the innocence of the scapegoat can be validated in the first place.[36] In this sense Girard's thesis depends ultimately on a positive, conversionary idiom of Christ, although perhaps historically the image of the cross has indeed appeared much more as a negative disclosure of violence, including the long sacrificial crisis this has generated within an assimilated Christianity.

---

36. In Girardian analytic the event of "double-transference" is the way in which a mimetic crisis is resolved by finding the victim both guilty and then worthy of worship. For the transition to sacred peace to work the victim must at a certain final point—i.e., the point of death—be a locus of complete nonretaliation. But this moment is not separated out in the sacred: instead it is swallowed up in the dominant threat of violence, within a temporary, external, and ultimately false glow of peace. A kind of stasis of violence is achieved rather than a genuine unconditional nonviolence. What is suggested here is that the Crucified represents that moment separated out, existentially embraced and voluntarily nonviolent, and it is still in the process of being separated out. However, a critical awareness of that moment was always necessary in the tradition in order to generate the message of innocence.

A BIBLICAL TYPOLOGY OF VIOLENCE

The necessity of the cross is its contingency, nor more, nor less, and the essential contingency of an encounter with it is the reason why at the end of the chapter the thought of abyssal compassion is given final expression by particular examples, not dialectical argument. This will be itself a gesture of the nature of atonement developed here, but before we arrive at that point it is important now to clarify the methodological question itself, that is, the appropriate forms of discourse for an account that claims transformation in and through an anthropology of mimesis. Evidently narrative is a key starting point for discussion, but as we examine its relationship to the Bible we will see how it transcends its own boundaries and needs to be understood in a wider frame. Once again, by this examination we will come to a clearer understanding of the essential contingent nature of abyssal redemption.

To begin with, not all narratives are equal. A narrativist position that tends to claim that just because you narrate something it has equal title for its existence with everything else cannot be upheld. There are surely conflicting narratives. Nietzschean genealogy is the great example of a *counter*narrative, a reading backward that seeks to undo a prior, essentially Christian, narrative position. It is a narrative that exposes and deconstructs another narrative and forcefully denounces assumed narrative innocence. Alasdair MacIntyre sets out to rehearse a "classic" narrative of virtue rooted in Greek thought, one that asserts its priority over all others. His is a dialectical narrative, and ends up as a narrative of dialectics, specifically Aristotelian dialectics, as the most cogent form of moral thought. But narrative itself does not justify his position; it has to be evaluated finally by all the connections he makes, how they hold together, and how his final total picture persuades that it is indeed the best account of moral virtue.[37] On the other hand, the work of someone like Hans W. Frei suggests that narrative pattern is its own justification. He argues that with the emergence of biblical criticism and, under its impact, an extratextual "religious" interpretation, there was a loss of specific narrative understanding and thereby a primary internal logic was forfeited. Frei insists on a narrative thread with cumulative meaning, through which an individual may integrate the meaning of her own life, so that the narrative does not so much exist in the world as the world exists in the narrative.[38] Although this

---

37. Alasdair MacIntyre, *After Virtue* (Notre Dame, Ind.: University of Notre Dame Press, 1984); *Whose Justice? Whose Rationality* (Notre Dame, Ind.: University of Notre Dame Press, 1988).

38. Hans W. Frei, *The Eclipse of Biblical Narrative, a Study in Eighteenth and Nineteenth Century Hermeneutics* (New Haven and London: Yale University Press, 1974), 133–53; hereafter *Eclipse*.

certainly marks a welcome return to the integrity of the text, there is nevertheless the danger of a precritical enchantment that can, for example, judge equally "true" Moses' genocidal war against the Midianites and Job's human cry of the oppressed.

To propose a check on such enchantment I return to the question of mimetic anthropology and its specific method. This has the double advantage of allowing me to pose explicitly a related question of methodology that has always been in the background to my use of Girard's ideas but has so far not been addressed: what is the specific logic or set of logics by which Girard develops his argument? My argument will be that the full Girardian hypothesis, that is, of the biblical revelation of the victim, is a rhetorical claim in the best sense, which also belongs within the overall claim of biblical faith. In the last analysis, an anthropology of the cross bases itself in the proclamation of the cross, its kerygma, its announcement as redemptive word in the continuum of history. Its truth claim in terms of rhetoric consists in the simultaneous disclosure of violence and the internal, abyssal response of forgiveness, discovered always in the contingency of the event that is "Christ died for us." It is the powerful nexus of violence and nonretaliation presented here that constitutes the prima facie truth of the Christian message, conceived anthropologically. This nexus does not constitute proof of Christianity, which would in itself seem inimical to the abyssal response evoked, but it is nevertheless more than mere personal attachment to an idea. The rhetoric of Christianity is a distinguishable rhetoric; it proposes a content with a recognizable key image, impact, and dynamic. As such its "truth" contains a powerful consistency and resonance by which it may be vindicated, and vindicated in absolute personal terms in the response of faith.

Girard's work began with stories, above all the stories of nineteenth-century novels. The narrative intensity and critical force of these novels first alerted him to the principle of mimesis, and then reflectively to a moment of "novelistic conversion" internal to the writing of certain outstanding authors. The conversion consisted of a paradigm shift from romantic desire to a revolutionary understanding of imitated desire, and it is this conversion or shift that becomes his central critical tool. On the basis of what has been essentially a narrative disclosure, he then constructs a broader hypothesis of original or generative violence. We could say—using Aristotelian terminology—that this constitutes an *arche* or first principle at which he arrives by a kind of induction (*epagogé*), including evidence from literary, mythological, historical, psychological, ethnographical, and biblical texts. But in Aristotelian terms this multiplication of disciplines would signify a form of rhetoric that works by the accumulation of examples rather than a strict induction proper to a particular science.[39] However, once this *arche* is in place an "epistemic" deduction of mimesis and scapegoating becomes possible in a wide number of areas. We can see this process at work in the area of biblical narrative, where Girardian thought perhaps reaches its greatest intensity, because it immediately generates an internal relation to the biblical text by which this text then proceeds to explicate itself. It is this hermeneutical "lock" that is the most provocative and dramatic aspect of his intellectual pathway, and we should consider its structure with some precision.

In doing so it is useful to return briefly to the thought of Frei and Lindbeck, to test how a Girardian hermeneutic might register in their narratological schemes. As we have mentioned, Hans Frei describes how post-eighteenth-century biblical hermeneutics changed the older internal, typological method of interpretation. It did this by referring the text to wider frames of meaning (rational, supernatural, or historical) that were logically separable from it. Girard can be seen as reversing the direction, but in a way also congruent with modern critical rationality. By developing the hermeneutics of the scapegoat, or generative violence, as inherent to the biblical narrative, such that it is the narrative that is seen as first producing these hermeneutics, the anthropological, interpretative frame becomes itself the typology. Yet in this way biblical hermeneutics are also revolutionary: they are demonstrated as a world-subversive disclosure developing over a temporal sequence beginning with, sustained by, and promoted by the biblical narrative. Frei remarks on the Bible's realistic tone or verisimilitude as something provoking the inquiry into its factual or historical reference in the eighteenth and nineteenth centuries, as well as relativizing its interpretation as "myth."[40] His key question, however, is why the concurrent literary realism of the period was never applied as a technical model to the interpretation of the Bible. Why was the Bible never understood simply as narrative, with its own inner dynamic and meaningfulness? Why did novelistic realism, imposing itself more and more on the imagination of the time, never act as an interpretative model for understanding the Bible?

The Girardian response would very probably be to turn the question upside down: some of the great literary works of this period were in fact themselves barely concealed tradings on a biblical hermeneutic and there-

---

39. Aristotle, *Rhetoric*, I i, 1356a 36–1356b 4, in *On Rhetoric: A Theory of Civic Discourse*, trans., intro., notes, and appendixes by George A. Kennedy (New York: Oxford University Press, 1991).

40. Frei, *Eclipse*, 149, 274–75.

fore already a trace of its internal interpretative dynamic (i.e., the disclosure of mimetic desire, violence, and scapegoating).[41] Frei's position as
regards historical criticism of the New Testament might also then be challenged. It is not an empiricist distraction from narrative realism; rather, it
marches hand in hand with novelistic realism because both at root refer to
the same disturbing and yet deeply fascinating disclosure, or set of disclo-
sures, which as much as anything else contributed to modern historiogra-
phy and narrative sense. If we say that New Testament criticism has always
finally been the question of what was at stake in the life and death of the
prophet from Nazareth, then there is great cogency to this statement.[42] As
Walter Benjamin said, "Death is the sanction of everything the storyteller
can tell."[43] The narrative of Jesus' death underlines that manyfold, and at
the same time tirelessly raises to the surface the unasked question, how
and why should this be the case?

Therefore, if on this reading we can and do claim a biblical typology of
violence, this is also of a much more profound order than a simple literary figure or theme, and on two successive levels. As a key hermeneutical
frame of the text it surely qualifies, in Lindbeck's terms, as a regulative
principle in the religious meaning of the Bible. The disclosure of violence
can be seen as a deep "rule" of the biblical account that serves to define and
maintain the ultimate life-reference of the whole. He describes this
method of hermeneutics as the "intratextual reading," one that seeks "to
derive the interpretative framework which designates the theological controlling sense from the literary structure of the text itself."[44] This would
seem to fit the Girardian method well, except that the very concept of disclosure of violence is so actual that it at once breaks free from any tendency to make the text a hermetically sealed universe. It at once designates
theological meaning and then, at a second level, a profound (de)con-
struction of concrete human relations. This is what makes Girard's interpretative method striking, a *theologia crucis* of exceptional challenge and

41. See Girard, *Deceit, Desire and the Novel*, 294, 310. Also *Things Hidden*, 126-38, and
the discussion of Proust's conversion at 393–402; see specifically Jean-Michel
Oughourlian's iteration that great works of literature rehearse and reflect "the gospel revolution" (401).

42. The ultimate meaning of Christ's death is certainly the enigma with which Albert
Schweitzer concludes his enormously influential summary of the eighteenth- and nineteenth-
centuries' search for the historical Jesus, *The Quest for the Historical Jesus: A Critical Study
of Its Progress from Reimarus to Wrede*, rev. ed. (New York: Macmillan, 1968). See the next
chapter for an extended treatment of this central question of the New Testament.

43. Walter Benjamin, "The Storyteller," in *Illuminations*, ed. Hanna Arendt (New York:
Schocken Books, 1969), 94.

44. Lindbeck, *The Nature of Doctrine*, 120.

seriousness. It becomes itself a way of preaching the gospel in and to the contemporary world, one that is sharper than any two-edged sword, able to penetrate the secret places "between joint and marrow" where human violence resides. The synchronic tension of the text—what holds it together as a literary narrative—is simultaneously an unrelenting catalogue of the history of murder from Abel onwards.

The biblical typology of generative violence, articulated by anthropology, is at once a powerful hermeneutical, kerygmatic, and analytical insight, a kind of inverted logos theory, envisioning an antirationality at the root of culture laid bare by the cumulative biblical tradition. However, once this uncanny power or intensity is stated, it must also be recognized that the full Girardian argument is necessarily rhetorical. I do not want to underestimate its demonstrative force, its attention to data and to rigor in examining similarities and differences. Nevertheless, its final movement must come under the title of rhetoric, and at two levels. First, the key gap between violent origins and direct evidence can only be covered by multiplication of examples and structural convergences from a number of sources. This is partially what Girard is referring to when he describes his argument as hypothesis. Second, and more important, when it reaches the point of the biblical narrative it necessarily enters a realm where rhetoric or persuasion is the key mode of discourse, above all when Christianity puts forward the biblical text as universal proclamation. As John Milbank states, "Christianity . . . from the first took the side of rhetoric against philosophy and contended that the Good and the True are those things of which we 'have a persusasion,' *pistis* or 'faith.'"[45] Despite Girard's move to give anthropological underpinning to Christian doctrine it would be a serious mistake to consider this apodictic or, in his word, scientific. Biblical faith is almost as a matter of definition a pathway where at a certain moment all reference points disappear and the journeyer is asked to continue purely in trust. To resolve this journey into scientific objectivity would create a monstrous hybrid.[46]

---

45. John Milbank, *Theology and Social Theory, Beyond Secular Reason* (Oxford, UK and Cambridge, Mass.: Blackwell, 1993), 398.

46. Girard's own account of his methodology presents variant readings. He prefers to speak of it in categories drawn from physical science, rather than philosophy, arguing that its hypothetical nature would not count against it according to criteria used in this field. Here the crucial questions would be: Does the idea work? Does it succeed in the task of explanation? At the same time what he is advancing is a very particular science indeed, intimately linked to the Christian Scriptures. "I believe . . . that the end of philosophy brings with it a new possibility of scientific thinking within the human domain; at the same time, however strange this may seem, it brings with it a return to religious faith. The Christian text returns in a completely new light—not at all buttressed by some existing science that

For this reason the present study seeks clearly to distinguish two moments in the thought of mimetic anthropology, amounting to two separated discourses. On the one hand there is the rational or dialectical progression followed through in the first chapter, which can and should be assessed on its own merits. Then, there is the way in which this progression is read in and through the biblical narrative. This second moment must be held clearly distinct, and viewed in fact as only intelligible within an overall discourse determined by biblical faith. The first discourse may, with some reservation, be termed "scientific," i.e., based on observable evidence or data that is organized within a working hypothesis assessed in terms of probability. The second is very much the rhetorical presentation of a complex of meaning embraced, sometimes definitively, but without final foundations.

The genre of rhetoric conforms then to the contingency of compassion. If compassion is contingent in the moment when it occurs and compassion is the nature of the Crucified, then the message itself shares in the contingency of its anthropological realization. The *imitatio Christi* as the goal of the message arises not so much out of a matrix of eternal truth, fixed in doctrinal form, as out of diverse repetitions of a particular scenario with a profound anthropological resonance. In this light we may see the Christian message as a string of pearls proclaiming an anthropological possibility, where each pearl is recognizable as fitting with its companions, but none refers back to any kind of essential eidetic pearl beyond the continuum of those actually on the string. This image itself fits with the kerygmatic injunction of the Gospels that seems to expect neither more nor less than the repetition of its central scenario. On this basis, response to the Christian kerygma is a choice made out of undecidable powers, not necessary ones. It is a challenge to history from within history, a challenge because of the anthropological effect of the central scenario it proposes. It begins on an infinite plain of possibilities, which include undecidable violence and undecidable compassion, and yet it retains coherence as anthropological call; its call

would be exterior to it, *but as identical with the knowledge of man that is surfacing in the world today*" (*Things Hidden*, 438, my italics). Clearly there is a powerful feedback loop at work here, already suggested in respect of the typology of generative violence. However, to insist on the "scientific" nature of this typology is to make a maximal claim ultimately detrimental to biblical faith. Elsewhere Girard stresses the conversionary nature of such knowledge: "The knowledge of mimesis is really tied to conversion. That is why the matter of *fides quaerens intellectum* (faith seeking understanding) is so important. A personal knowledge, fully rational, and yet not always accessible to reason, is needed" ("A Conversation with René Girard," *The Girard Reader*, ed. James G. Williams [New York: Crossroad, 1996], 268).

has anthropological integrity. The cross has an internal logic that does not impose itself, but nevertheless always seeks to make crucial a choice between violence and compassion.

By this token, repetition or transformation through the cross does not seek as such to be in opposition, to create a dialectical contrast. This would be to reduce repetition to the realm of difference based in violence, and in a Girardian frame a repetition that establishes difference through polar opposition would be a return to sacred violence. Yet Christ on the cross is abandoned by the sacred, if by that we mean the world and a sense of God as securely linked to the world. The cry of dereliction by the Crucified signifies the opening of an abyss beneath the world of difference secured in being and meaning by sacred order. The Crucified expresses, cries out a place unsustained by any ultimate guarantee of order, any ontology. At the same time, on the cross Christ is seen as faithful to both the world and to God. This, as we have seen, becomes redemptive repetition, a faithfulness without external, visible, ritual continuity. It is the vindication of continuity by means other than the sacred, an astonishing "Yes" to human difference in the midst of a paroxysm of violent undifferentiation loosing itself on and through his body. The modality proper to its expression, therefore, is not philosophy but testimony, not the imperium of the systematic, but the deliberate echo of an unfathomable resonance. The repetition represented by the cross itself bears repetition. As the Psalmist put it: "Deep calls to deep in the roar of your torrents."[47]

Exemplary Fiction: Dostoyevsky and Wilde

A language of abyssal atonement is a series of experiments in repetition, each time anew, with no guarantee in a previous experiment. It expresses itself in a series of repeated glyphs or marks, where those marks begin each time again to (re)trace the scenario of the cross. Here precisely there is an attempt to evacuate systematic continuity, because such continuity is fatal to the "continuity" of compassion we have sought to describe. Two literary examples follow that perhaps will help illustrate what is at stake in this approach. These "experimental" examples are characterized by very different circumstances of origin, and yet each has powerful notes of compassion and a sense of repetition rather than mediation. They are from the writings of Fyodor Dostoyevsky and

---

47. Ps. 42:8, *New American Bible*.

Oscar Wilde. What is presented of these authors is not intended in any way as an exhaustive critical reading, rather it focuses deliberately on certain elements that serve simply to illustrate the themes of compassion and repetition. By the same token, again what is offered is not proof but reiteration, a going back over the impression of the cross imprinted so profoundly in certain places that it simply bears revisiting. What is revisited here is not a theme as such, certainly not an eternal idea, but a gesture that may in its very abyssal quality, its very lack of foundation, provoke the event of endless compassion. As always there is no guarantee, only the possibility of repetition in and through the abyss.

Dostoyevsky's *The Brothers Karamazov* is a doyen of literature in this sense. Its fraught relationships and their relentless display, the turning over and over again of a darkly flawed diamond, creates a narrative world always on the edge of disaster. Dostoyevsky refuses to bring any romantic salvation to his characters; to the last, erotic love between them is shot with lethal rivalry and betrayal. Such a world has always already lost any natural human innocence or good. Into this world the Christlike figures of Zossima and Alyosha emerge not so much as doctrinal truths, over against the demonstration of Karamazov fallenness, but as a kind of extreme solution born from within the chaos itself. They represent a complete, conversionary interruption of its themes, matching violence with love blow for blow. During Dmitry's trial, the public prosecutor describes the Karamazov condition in the following terms, while immediately expanding its application to cover everyone:

> [W]e possess broad, unrestrained natures, Karamazov natures . . . capable of accommodating all sorts of extremes and contemplating at one and the same time the two abysses—the abyss above us, the abyss of the highest ideals, and the abyss below us, the abyss of the lowest and most malodorous degradation. . . . Two abysses, gentlemen of the jury, two abysses at one and the same moment—without them we are unhappy and dissatisfied, without them our life is incomplete.[48]

This Dostoyevskian voice suggests an anthropology of twin abysses, abysses that are almost mirrors of each other in their depth and intensity, and which entail an inability, or unwillingness, to decide, an infinite inclusion of one abyss by the other. However, the final vector of the novel goes

---

48. Fyodor Dostoyevsky, *The Brothers Karamazov*, trans. and intro. David Magarshack (Harmondsworth, UK and New York: Penguin Books, 1984), 824.

beyond this; it attempts finally to undo the abyss of evil with the abyss of good, to make the latter endure and outlast the former and so to be conclusive. This has to be the sense at least of the final scene with Alyosha and the group of boys and their pledge to a life lived in memory of love. However, the point to underline here is that even as there is a struggle between abysses and a narrative teleology of one victorious over the other, the very doubling of abysses indicates that it is always at the selfsame level of depth that the issue is tried. The tension is therefore toward an immanent human solution in that the abyssal human condition can turn equally to evil or good, but only precisely as abyss. It is only a call at the level of human abyss that can seek to resolve the human dilemma. By the same token it is only the revelation of the depth of evil that provides the scenario of depth, and therefore to some degree the content, as abyss, of the possibility of good. This also may be true vice versa: the portrayal of the depth of good serves paradoxically to increase the sense of depth of evil and the possibilities of acting in contradiction of the good. Thus, for Dostoyevsky it appears that good and evil are outcomes of the same profound dynamic of the human condition and possess a cousinship where there is a very fine line between one and the other. Because one can easily slip over into the other, the resolution for good appears highly unstable, until perhaps certain exemplars become the objects of a deliberate and unconditional imitation.

Zossima and Alyosha are the narrative figures that represent this transformation. In constructing them Dostoyevsky seems almost to have gone to another extreme, composing, it seems, from hagiographic and iconographic conventions, and to such an extent that he has been accused of a lack of shading and tension in the portraits, especially of Zossima.[49] What is further striking is the degree to which these conventions are observed at the same time as Dostoyevsky reduces almost every doctrinal and ecclesiastical aspect to dramatic insignificance. It is as if he has produced a stiff liqueur of anthropological tenor while letting other intellectual, institutional, and even supernatural matter evaporate off. But what is one to say to the charge that, after all, this still amounts to a kind of sentimentality? Such a charge, it would seem, ignores the powerful realization of the human abyss achieved by a whole narrative in which good and bad echo

---

49. Sven Linnér, "Portrait of a Saint: Moral Ideal and/or Psychological Truth," in *Critical Essays on Dostoevsky*, ed. Robin Feuer Miller; vol. 6 of Critical Essays on World Literature, ed. Robert Lecker (G. K. Hall & Co.: Boston, Mass., 1986), 196, 203. And Jostein Børtnes, "The Function of Hagiography in Dostoevskij's Novels," in *Critical Essays on Dostoevsky*, 188–92.

each other in a kind of intimate oscillation, and where in the end it is always the abyss itself that is at stake.

The apparent lack of complexity in the portraits of Zossima and Alyosha is itself a function of the chaos of Karamazov passion and violence that has penetrated to the far side of all restraint, and may only be answered by an absolute, unrestrained goodness. The phrase "Everything is permitted" sounds like a death knell throughout the novel. It is not only the philosophical term and banner of Ivan's atheism, it is the tawdry slogan that binds Ivan, Dmitry, and Smerdyakov in complicity in their father's death. As such it comes to represent much more an ideology of the abyss than the product of dialectical argument. Within a situation of intense mimetic crisis where the desires of fathers and sons, lovers and rivals flow in and out of each other uncontrollably and where the horrors of cruelty and violence are always just round the corner, the only way out is the "conversion" of the abyss itself, and in fact, by virtue of the abyss. The abyss must surrender to its own emptiness, undergo a collapse of its own perennially self-defeating attempts to found and undergird itself in the overcoming of others; become, in other words, unconditionally abandoned to itself in self-giving. But if desire is the very soul and dark wind of the abyss, then this can only happen by the imitationary love of someone who has been able, in turn, to demonstrate the abyss as love. This is displayed most clearly of course in Alyosha's intense love for and personal imitation of the elder; but Zossima himself looks back to his brother, Markel. The latter died in adolescence, but during the brief illness before his death underwent a profound, exemplary conversion. During its course he makes the remark on which Zossima's own eventual conversion turns: "Every one of us is responsible for everyone else in every way, and I most of all." Shortly before his death he tells the young Zossima, "Live for me!"[50] Markel's conversion has an extrareligious sense, marked by intense joy, desire to serve all, and a declaration of paradise in the here and now. It is deeply anthropological, and yet at the same time takes place over the period of Easter. The religious message of Easter is, therefore, both invoked behind Markel's own transformation and translated immediately as anthropological truth. Zossima inherits this profound human change and continues to exemplify it over his own, much longer lifetime.

In the novel the key motif of transformation is forgiveness. By forgiving someone's offense the abyss uses its very depth to plumb beyond reciprocity, to an utterly unexpected level where something new can take place, including the transformation of the forgiven. However, in order for

---

50. *The Brothers Karamazov*, 339, 340.

this to be the case the act of forgiveness cannot be sheer loss and defeat. For in this case the original offense triumphs in its brute facticity. The act of forgiveness must somehow be eternalized, rendered everlasting, so that it continues to counter the historical permanence of the offense. Perhaps this is part of Zossima's thought when he teaches, "Whatever is true and beautiful is always full of forgiveness."[51] Yet beneath and beyond such hints at universal categories it is clearly the Gospel account of Christ that is repeated in the Karamazov narrative. This is paradoxically the more so when the christological pattern is described almost exclusively in terms of Zossima and Alyosha rather than by reference to the Gospels, and much less by reference to doctrine. As such the purported two-dimensional nature of these portraits is directly a function of their abyssal nature, echoing the abyss of the cross; on the surface they may appear bland but, precisely, they are an anthropology of endless forgiveness. They are there to cast into depths of incommensurable love all the Karamazov frenzy, hatred, and murder. Their effect of peace and forgiveness must be virtually unbroken, if the palpable effect of chaos is truly to be redeemed in the narrative. The missing third dimension may in fact be read as the quality of undergoing, of abyssal compassion, that is unfounded in its moment of enactment even as it repeats the pattern of Christ. As such it remains only a trace and unseen in the violent foundationalism of human affairs, very much an interior moment that leaves only a ripple on the surface of the text and must be taken very much on trust. The credal pattern itself is only properly accessed in this quality of the moment of compassion. Any dogmatic representation would at once betray the abyssal nature of forgiveness, and there can be little doubt that Dostoyevsky structured his narrative according to this insight. He repeats the abyssal ripple again and again, in order to plunge the terminal chaos of the Karamazovs into the hint of something paradoxically stronger, deeper, more endless than violence.

For example, the silence of Christ in Ivan's poem of the Grand Inquisitor is a landmark absence of dogmatic assertion. "The old man would have liked him to say something, however bitter and terrible. But he suddenly approached the old man and kissed him gently on his bloodless, aged lips. That was all his answer."[52] Very quickly after this Alyosha repeats the gesture of Christ in kissing his brother Ivan, at which Ivan cries "'plagiarism!' . . . looking very delighted." The plagiarism is both of Ivan's poem and a plagiarism by Alyosha of the person of Christ, one that seeks a repetition in the sense of atonement developed above: the making pres-

---

51. Ibid., 424.
52. Ibid., 308.

ent again of the sense of life through the movement of compassion. Yet, it is clear at once how lightly the text adheres to any formal statement of this; it much prefers to rehearse the abyssal movement itself rather than a credal formulation. The movement is also present in the story of Zossima's duel as a young man, in his refusal to shoot at his adversary, and in the story of the mysterious visitor who is influenced by this event to confess publicly his own crime of the murder. Strangely, no one believes his confession, but he dies a number of days later in a physical sign of the abyss of repentance to which he has surrendered. This strange ambiguity is displayed also in the fact that up to the last it was possible that the visitor could have repeated the murder, this time of the young Zossima. Just as there are twin abysses, therefore, there is always a double chain of repetition, both actual and possible, running through the novel, capping evil with evil and good with good.

So, very clearly, destructive passion is repeated from father to son, from son to lover-rival, and ever onward in an endless pattern of hostile desire. On the other hand, the chain of forgiving love runs from Markel to Zossima, to Alyosha, to Ilyusha, the persecuted youth befriended by Alyosha, and thence to Kolya. We could even claim that the novel is constituted by chains of imitational repetition emerging from the same abyss but generating very different worlds. Perhaps most significantly in terms of overall structure, we might indicate a succession of doubled scenes of death. We have already noted the murder victim of Zossima's visitor matched by the visitor's own death. Behind this there is the original Easter death of Markel, and more or less at the opposite end of the spectrum is the unhallowed death of "Stinking Lizaveta," which seems to fulfill a contrasting generative role. But, crucially, there are the doublets of Zossima and Fyodor Karamazov's deaths, and those of Smerdyakov and Ilyusha. It is as if throughout the novel a key character is very soon to die, whether by natural or violent causes, and the text is always in tension toward that point. The imminence of Zossima's death as an aged and revered monk provides much of the dramatic tension of the first half of the book. Parallel to this is the ever growing possibility of the elder Karamazov's violent end, and indeed soon after Zossima's exequies the pivotal murder takes place. The circumstances of Zossima's funeral rites include the fact that his corpse began quickly to stink during the readings and prayers, reversing the expectations of some miraculous sign, at the very least an "odor of sanctity." Thus the abyssal movement of Zossima's death scandalizes the popular desire for "miracle, mystery and authority" and sows confusion and doubt even among his most ardent followers, including Alyosha. Yet this moment also provides a crisis and turning point in the life of Alyosha, "finally strengthening his mind for the rest of his life."[53] At this point the future hero of the book appears to make a definitive surrender to the abyss of love, in imitation of the abyssal death of his mentor.

Almost simultaneously Fyodor Karamazov is assassinated and the rest of the book plays out in the arrest and trial of the accused, Dmitry. Simultaneously two more deaths are being prepared. There is the suicide of Smerdyakov, the actual murderer, though in his own mind he was Ivan's accomplice. It is as if the taciturn servant acts as a sinkhole for all the metaphysical evil of the Karamazovs, and his self-destruction following parricide signals its own movement toward an abyss of extinction. The final death, however, repeats the motifs of Markel's death, of reconciliation, love, and transformative memory. It should be remembered that Ilyusha was the victim of a collective stoning by the group of boys, and it is from that event that he takes to his bed and does not recover. Parallels with the gospel story seem unmistakable, and yet they do not make of Ilyusha a saint; rather they seek to reconstruct without doctrinal overtones the outline of a death that provokes life-transforming memory, or the possibility of a repetition throughout life.

Here, finally, the radicalism of Dostoyevsky's project is revealed. He repeats the story of Christ without invoking Christ, at least in any formal way, and thereby seeks above all to affirm the abyssal movement of love rather than an abstract doctrine of salvation. There are twelve boys who gather for Ilyusha's interment and they hear Alyosha's farewell discourse in which he repeats that they are united in a "good and kind" feeling, a loving compassion for the little boy. They gather round a stone or rock, which is where Ilyusha wanted to be buried, but he was not in fact buried there. They all together invoke, "May his memory live in our hearts for ever and ever!" The boy is absent but his memory lives. And it is here at last that the physical "miracle" or transformation so much desired for Zossima is revealed: "[S]trange to say, there was almost no smell of decay from the corpse."[54] It is only when all aspect of competition or rivalry is removed from the scene that the hint of resurrection, of the permeation of the abyss by life, is allowed. By this progression Dostoyevsky has stripped the possibility of abyssal love of almost all supernatural and institutional features, moving from Zossima to Ilyusha, from the monastery to the world, from heaven to earth.

Perhaps Dostoyevsky has gone further than any other narrative writer in translating Christian theology into anthropology, without at the same

---

53. Ibid., 386.
54. Ibid., 903–12.

time too glibly forsaking theology. It may be appropriate, therefore, to conclude our brief commentary on *The Brothers Karamzov* with one of the places where the novel makes reference to formal religious practice. When Zossima lies in his coffin he bears an icon on his chest and an eight-cornered cross on the cowl upon his head. Eight deaths may be read as framing the work. We could perhaps imagine the eight-cornered Russian cross as the shape of the novel itself. If this were so, then the Dostoyevskian reading of the cross would be all those eight deaths, which interpenetrate and interpret each other. The two abysses cannot be understood without each other, and similarly no Karamazov death can be read apart from the continuum of all the contrasting deaths. Thus, without the abyss of Smerdyakov's despair, the importance of engagement in the covenantal memory of Ilyusha may not be grasped. And without the joyful love surrounding Ilyusha's deathbed, there can be no offer of hope for all the Smerdyakovs who inherit the evil of their lives. Ivan renounced his membership of any theological version of the human story if it made the torture of one innocent child necessary. Dostoyevsky's cross cannot answer such a problem dialectically; what it can do is relate the contingency of one corner to another, of one abyss to the other, of violence to forgiveness, of forgiveness to violence, and thereby affirm that even as the scandal of cruelty exists, so does the scandal of love.

To speak of scandal enables us to move with some aptness to our second illustration, the work of Oscar Wilde, although the true nature of the scandal here is perhaps hard to identify. It may be felt immediately that Wilde's aestheticism and romanticism put him about as far away as it is possible to get from the harsh realism of mimetic anthropology. Indeed his thought runs on a plane where the production of ideal beauty is the absolute, if not exclusive, goal of human life. So desire itself is not problematic for him; on the contrary, it is only questioned inasmuch as it is considered derivative and false, rather than true romantic spirit, the soul's desire for beauty. On such formal lines Wilde can be seen plainly on the wrong side of Girard's critical cut between "romantic lie" and novelistic truth, between the myth of essentialized desire and the disclosure of mimetic relationality. Nevertheless, such is Wilde's passion for authentic desire that it seems inevitably led somewhere else, in fact to the figure of Christ as true exemplar. And because of his preoccupation with Christ in this sense he perhaps ends by saying something of considerable importance about *imitatio Christi*. Throughout his literary career Wilde continually returned to the figure of Christ, but outside any formal religious or doctrinal meaning. In this way, although he terms Christ the greatest of the romantics, we may also say that he appropriates him anthropological-

ly rather than theologically. On this basis, Wilde's Christ strongly confirms
the thesis argued here, that an abyss of human transformation is demonstrated in the figure of Christ, and is of course available to artists at least
as much as anybody else. In particular Wilde's repetition of this abyss in
his life's work represents another "experiment" of that abyss; it is available
to us precisely as and for the purposes of example.

The figure of Wilde has received progressive recognition as someone
on the spiritual and institutional margins of the nineteenth century who
in fact did much to expand those margins through his writings and life. In
the Moises Kaufman play on the three trials of Oscar Wilde, the post-
structuralist stage professor, Marvin Taylor, reflects, "[T]here is a real
nexus of issues that are on trial with Oscar Wilde and they have to do with
the role of art, with effeminacy, with homosexuality, with the Irish in
England, with class. . . . So it's not just the fact that Wilde was being tried
for sodomy . . . that's not the . . . major part of what's going on. I truly
believe that the sodomy charges are really the less important. Wilde was
being tried for his subversive beliefs about art, about morality . . . about
Victorian Society."[55] These subversive beliefs extended significantly to the
figure of Christ and the sclerosis it experienced at the hands of official
Christianity. Wilde was a raconteur who told most of his stories before
writing them and, according to Yeats, when he wrote down his stories they
always lost some of their first oral verve.[56] Among the stories he told were
striking reworkings of the biblical text sometimes known as poems in
prose. In these poems he used the text against itself, returning it to a fresh
echo of its original oral source, and somehow suggesting depths to the
received text that the received text had covered over. Wilde also had an
ambition to rewrite the story of Christ on a grand scale, and the ambition
speaks both to the fascination that the Gospels held for him and his desire
to reachieve them artistically. He wished

> not to be remembered hereafter as an artist, poet, thinker, or
> playwright, but as the man who reclothed the sublimest concep-
> tion which the world has ever known—the Salvation of
> Humanity, the Sacrifice of Himself upon the Cross by Christ—
> with new and burning words, with new and illuminating sym-

55. Moises Kaufman, *Gross Indecency: The Three Trials of Oscar Wilde* (New York: Vintage Books, Random House, 1998), 75.

56. W. B. Yeats, "Introduction" to vol. III, *The Complete Works of Oscar Wilde*, reprinted in *Oscar Wilde: The Critical Heritage*, ed. Karl Beckson (London: Routledge and Kegan Paul, 1970), 396–97.

bols, with new and divine vision, free from the accretions of cant which the centuries have gathered around it. . . . Yes, I hope before I die to write the Epic of the Cross, the Iliad of Christianity, which shall live for all time.[57]

The Greek reference displays of course the classical ethos in which Wilde self-consciously stood and which helped shape his aesthetic vision. At the same time the only writing in which he managed a sketch of this Iliad, his prison-written *De Profundis*, presents Christ, on the contrary, as the headwaters of all that may be termed romantic. The distinctive mark of romanticism is the union of personality with artistic perfection, and it is Christ who begets this possibility. "[W]herever there is a romantic movement in Art, there somehow, and under some form, is Christ, or the soul of Christ."[58] So for Wilde Christ is seen as the source of a distinctive aesthetic sense, rather than a figure to be subsumed in a received classical culture. Much of this shows the influences of various nineteenth-century thinkers like Arnold, Ruskin, and Renan, but Wilde's insistence on an aesthetic Christ, on Christ as artist, is exceptional and develops a particular intensity in his own creative work.

For Wilde aesthetics meant the search for perfection of form and with that a theoretical understanding of the priority of art over nature, of concept over reality, and imagination over everything.[59] All this stood in and on the autonomous soul or personality, and Wilde deliberately made his own life an attempt to fulfill the ideal. His self-description in *De Profundis* is well known and recognized as containing more than a germ of truth: "I was a man who stood in symbolic relations to the art and culture of my age."[60] He

57. Oscar Wilde in *Oscar Wilde: Interviews and Recollections*, ed. E. H. Mikhail, vol. II (London: Macmillan, 1979), 316, quoted by Jerusha McCormack, "Wilde's fiction(s)" in *The Cambridge Companion to Oscar Wilde*, ed. Peter Raby (Cambridge, UK and New York: Cambridge University Press, 1997), 100–1.

58. Oscar Wilde, *The Letters of Oscar Wilde*, ed. Rupert Hart-Davis (New York: Harcourt, Brace & World, Inc., 1962), 482. The complete version of *De Profundis* is in fact contained in a letter to Lord Alfred Douglas and made available in this edition of his letters; subsequent references to *De Profundis* are to the text of this edition.

59. For Wilde as artist and critic see: Norbert Kohl, *Oscar Wilde, The Works of a Conformist Rebel*, trans. David Henry Wilson, European Studies in English Literature (Cambridge, UK and New York: Cambridge University Press, 1989), 83–104; *The Cambridge Companion to Oscar Wilde*, ed. Peter Raby (Cambridge: Cambridge University Press, 1997), particularly Lawrence Danson's "Wilde as Critic and Theorist," 80–95; Julia Prewitt Brown, *Oscar Wilde's Philosophy of Art* (Charlottesville, Va. and London: University Press of Virginia, 1997); Michael Patrick Gillespie, *Oscar Wilde and the Poetics of Ambiguity* (Gainesville, Fla.: University Press of Florida, 1996); Guy Willoughby, *Art and Christhood: The Aesthetics of Oscar Wilde* (London and Toronto: Associated University Presses, 1993).

60. *De Profundis*, in *The Letters of Oscar Wilde*, 466.

saw himself personally as a symbol of art that is self-generating and revelatory, and this is because all human beings are really such "symbols." As we have suggested, this thinking puts Wilde at a diametric remove from Girard, who regards ideal subjective autonomy as pure conceit in every sense. It is certainly provocative to bring into a Girardian conversation someone who observes unabashedly that "all imitation in morals and in life is wrong,"[61] and we shall return again to this divergence. For the moment our interest is with the aesthetics that renders such a statement possible. Wilde's philosophical position has much in common with a postmodern sensibility that understands truth as an effect of artistic or linguistic production rather than a flat congruence with given external reality.[62] Nevertheless, Wilde never remained simply on the level of epistemological idealism, but constantly sought within aesthetics a perspective of progressive liberation and realization of the individual.

The inescapable challenge of time is evident in a number of Wilde's stories and prose poems—the way its contingency or materiality confuses and reverses the best gestures of humanity. But time's obstruction of aesthetic realization threatens to become personally catastrophic during Wilde's imprisonment in Reading Gaol and it is this event that truly radicalizes his thought. In Wilde's case it is as if forces of the state constituted the obstacle to aesthetic repetition, setting its machinery in motion to prevent his aesthetic discourse from determining the nature of reality.[63] Needless to say, the state's victory was inevitable. Yet it is at this point that Wilde develops the aesthetic of Christ as Man of Sorrows, formulating the belief that suffering is the ultimate realization of the artistic life. Kierkegaard might perhaps say that for Wilde repetition had reached the level of the religious but, as with the young man, so enabling him to continue his existence as poet. Because for Wilde it remained resolutely a matter of the aesthetic; sorrow is the dimension of beauty that Christ imagined uniquely, and Wilde embraces this imagination in the figure of Christ as he finds realization through it. Christ "is just like a work of art himself. He does not really teach one anything, but by being brought into his presence one becomes some-

---

61. *The Soul of Man under Socialism* in *The First Collected Edition of the Works of Oscar Wilde*, ed. Robert Ross, vol. 8 (London: Methuen & Co., 1908; Reprint, 1969), 293.

62. See particularly Wilde's "The Decay of Lying" in *Complete Works*: "[Nature] is no great mother who has borne us. She is our creation" (1086). Cf. Danson's article cited in n. 87.

63. "You see, Wilde is an aesthete, that is, an artist who argues strenuously for an aesthetic approach. . . . His project is about art, about the power of art to transform man. Now as long as he is able to maintain control of the discourse, then he is incredibly . . . successful. . . . [W]hat happens in the trial is he comes head on up against legal discourse, and perhaps I would even say legal-medical discourse. And he begins to lose to this sort of patriarchal medical discourse. . . ." (*Gross Indecency: The Three Trials of Oscar Wilde*, 75–76).

vibrant surface of the text as it carries us along through the Prince's acts of mercy assisted by the swallow. Similarly in "The Nightingale and the Rose," the nightingale's gesture of supreme sacrifice in providing a red rose fails totally in terms of the story's human protagonists, the student and the professor's daughter. Yet in the movement of the text the image is immortalized and the strange dialectic of "Love that dies not in the tomb" is given its sotto voce in the final dismissive words of the student:

> "What a silly thing Love is," said the Student as he walked away. "It is not half as useful as Logic, for it does not prove anything, and it is always telling one of things that are not going to happen, and making one believe things that are not true. In fact, it is quite unpractical, and, as in this age to be practical is everything, I shall go back to Philosophy and study Metaphysics."[70]

This type of foregrounded commentary that makes a point by stating its reverse is a favorite device of the tales. It is the linchpin of "The Devoted Friend," where the Miller relentlessly exploits the naively generous Hans and yet retains control of the discourse so as always to appear vindicated. Pointedly, for established Christianity, the Miller's wife comments to her husband: "How well you talk! . . . [R]eally I feel quite drowsy. It is just like being in church." In this way the ethic of self-sacrifice becomes problematic when used to prop up an order of abuse and ideological screening. Here, not surprisingly, telling any story with a moral becomes "a very dangerous thing to do."[71] The irony multiplies when we see, of course, the real danger is precisely the moral of this tale, is the moral or sting in the tail, so to speak. A tale with a moral may work against a successful aesthetic, or be used to oppress the weak, or alternatively will it not perhaps eventually get the teller into serious trouble?

"The Young King" is a reprise of "The Happy Prince," but more elaborate and with a view to the danger that comes, this time explicitly, from taking the suffering of others seriously. The king lives in the palace Joyeuse surrounded by beautiful things for which he has a near religious reverence. The night before his coronation he experiences three dreams in which he is shown the cost in human life at which this beauty is bought. Awaking, he rejects his fine robe and ornaments, and at the cathedral tells the bishop of his dreams. The bishop, in Grand Inquisitorial style, advises him to ignore them. "The burden of this world is too great for one man to bear,

---

70. Ibid., 109.
71. Ibid., 117, 125.

and the world's sorrow too heavy for one heart to suffer." The church's abandonment of its founding exemplar is bluntly exposed. Then, in a simultaneous echo and reversal of the biblical Joseph and the Thomas à Becket stories, the nobles who enter with drawn swords, demanding the whereabouts of "this dreamer of dreams," are held back by a vision of the king transfigured by light. Although the danger is present, a triumphant epiphany of this Man of Sorrows secures the king's safety for the moment. However, "no man dared look upon his face," suggesting that the king alone is transformed and the world remains as it was.[72] Also perhaps there is a gospel echo of the transfiguration of the Son of Man, one who must indeed become the Man of Sorrows.

The recalcitrance of the world and its medium of time becomes a recurrent counterpoint to the tales' aesthetic of compassion. "The Star Child" learns solidarity with suffering by severe trials and so regains an original beauty he had lost. He is made king and institutes a reign of "love and loving-kindness." Yet he rules for three years only, then dies. "And he who came after him ruled evilly."[73] However, if political lack of compassion arises in the defective aesthetic of present time, it is also at the intimate level of imitation that the image of Christ is fatally marred in his followers. A true aesthetic is born out of the artistic soul, out of creative imagination, rather than external imitation. Nowhere is this clearer than in the Prose Poems. In "The House of Judgment," the evil man cannot be sent to hell because he has always dwelt there: but no more can he be sent to heaven and the reason, as he gives it, is: "Because never, and in no place, have I been able to imagine it."[74] In the poem provocatively named "The Disciple," the pool that mirrors Narcissus's beauty in fact only "loves" Narcissus because "in the mirror of his eyes I ever saw my own beauty mirrored."[75] Thus the disciple may ever be seeking himself as he appears to mirror his lord. This narcissism becomes a matter of bitter envy in "The Master." A young man appears to be weeping for the dead Christ in "the Valley of Desolation" but is in fact weeping for himself in mimetic rivalry with Christ. "All things that this man has done I have done also. And yet they have not crucified me."[76]

A Girardian reference seems to be vindicated by Guy Willoughby when he describes the young man as engaging in "unimaginative mimicry"

---

72. Ibid., 183–84.
73. Ibid., 252.
74. *Complete Shorter Fiction*, 258; the "Poems in Prose," reprinted in *Complete Shorter Fiction*, were first published in the *Fortnightly Review*, LIV, 301 (31 July 1894).
75. Ibid., 255.
76. Ibid., 256.

focused by "self-desire."[77] Girard might very probably call this a form of "internal mediation," and yet external mediation would also seem to lie on the same spectrum, i.e., the application of an external model without genuine "imaginative" sympathy. What is the solution? What is the way to avoid slavish imitation and its quick, modern inversion into mimetic rivalry? The question is crucial precisely when one comes to the figure of Christ, and Wilde was surely not inventing simple *jeux d'esprit* in his parables on the theme. The problem of transformation or conversion under mimetic influence is so intense that it seems only when the model of the Master is actually *lost* that an authentic personal imitation can take place. This indeed is the pattern of the gospel narrative of the road to Emmaus where the two disciples had lost their model, and then find him without knowing it, and immediately on seeing him for who he is lose him once more, but this time plunging with him into his re-creative abyss.[78] In *De Profundis* Wilde says, not without poignance, "Once at least in his life each man walks with Christ to Emmaus,"[79] and this pattern of loss and recuperation through loss is strikingly validated in his prose poem "The Teacher of Wisdom." It is the longest narrative in the genre, for it attempts to deal with the problem of discipleship or imitation over the span of time and the difficulty this presents.

From childhood the Teacher of the story has been filled with "the perfect knowledge of God," and when he comes to manhood he sets out to share his knowledge with the world. The gospel narrative of Christ is clearly reworked in the text; a great multitude follows the Teacher and he gathers eleven disciples in the cities he passes through, finally gaining one more, the Robber. But intervening is a profound crisis of soul for the Teacher; he has discovered by heavy experience that "He who giveth away wisdom robbeth himself." He becomes a hermit in order to preserve the knowledge he has left. The Robber passes his cave and is stung by the look of pity in the hermit's eyes. Then he too desires the knowledge of God, and seeks to extort it from him, threatening to "go to the City of the Seven Sins." The Teacher follows him for three days, entreating him to return, and at the last moment surrenders his remaining knowledge to the Robber. At once the Hermit is plunged into a great darkness in which the city and the Robber are seen no more.

> And as he lay there weeping he was ware of One who was standing beside him; and He who was standing beside him had feet of

77. *Art and Christhood: The Aesthetics of Oscar Wilde*, 96–97.
78. Lk. 24:13–35.
79. *De Profundis*, in *The Letters of Oscar Wilde*, 487.

brass and hair like fine wool. And He raised the Hermit up, and said to him: "Before this time thou hadst the perfect knowledge of God. Now thou shalt have the perfect love of God. Wherefore art thou weeping?" And He kissed him.[80]

The gospel and apocalyptic imagery shape the hermit's experience of loss on lines of Christ's death and three days in the tomb, followed by the abyssal new beginning, the resurrection of the Crucified, and with that the reconstruction of time itself. The intercalation of the figures of the Hermit and Christ, and also of the Robber, provokes a subtle loss of the ideal pattern, in which paradoxically the "pattern" more truthfully may appear. Thus apocalyptic reversal comes where it is most appropriate, where all is lost and, above all, all is lost by and in sorrowing compassion. It might be said that Wilde simultaneously deconstructs and constructs the *imitatio Christi*. Real imitation requires an imaginative leap that takes one out of imitation of the real, into darkness, into repetition without precedent. And at this point Wilde invokes apocalyptic time, the eschaton that undoes and transforms the troubled, conflicted time of his other stories. Perhaps we might say that here Wilde is able to let "theology" begin, for art to become theology in some coherent way, because the depth of loss and compassion in loss he has described meets the radical interruption of time proposed in the pages of the New Testament.

So much orthodox theology starts the other way round, erecting its conceptual scheme by which everything is prevalidated and secure. An aesthetic of Christ, on the contrary, is led to the point where everything is lost, and it is on this basis that reality may be transformed, that something new may occur. Such a theology of the aesthetic (or perhaps a postaesthetic movement of theology) seems demanded by the abyss of compassion. Without a time that changes time, compassion is the most foolish form of loss and must surely revert to further rivalry and mimetic challenge. For an aesthetic of sorrow to claim genuine beauty, a transformation of the actual must somehow be predicated; compassion itself implies or creates eschatology. We might say that compassion is, in the fullest and most profound sense, creative. And for that very reason this moment of theology cannot be rendered as metaphysics in the Wildean trajectory: it is the prolepsis of an utterly new, almost unnameable aesthetic, not its eternal origin.

At this final point, therefore, we might frame some key questions. Does not a Girardian antiromantic critique necessarily rejoin Wildean romanti-

---

80. *Complete Shorter Fiction*, 258–63.

cism at the moment when imitation falls into an abyss? From the Girardian side, is it not the case that both internal and external imitation fail at the point of the cross, where the imitation of loss is required? From the Wildean side, does not the ideal of beauty becoming the Man of Sorrows testify to the anthropological inventiveness of the cross? And does not this "invention" correspond closely to Borch-Jacobsen's "primitive alteration" of "self" with "other" but now transposed in the key of redemptive anthropology, rather than aboriginal chaos and war?[81]

In other words the imaginative or creative factor produced by Christ, on a fully anthropological register, is the abyss of nonretaliation and its appropriation by and as compassion. Girard has never taken up the task of a mimetic analysis of conversion such as we have broached here. He seems to apportion such a thought to the strict domain of theology, and this despite his programmatic statement that "as far as incarnation is concerned, anthropology and theology amount to one and the same."[82] Would not this statement clearly imply that an analysis of this kind be both possible and appropriate, that mimetic anthropology tracing the story of Christ necessarily ends in the abyss? At all events the pathway we have pursued here has attempted to display, in both Dostoyevskian and Wildean worlds, the abyssal nature of Christian imitation. Dostoyevsky contructs a chain of significant deaths, developing by repetition an anthropology of the double abyss and its future transformation by love. Wilde uses the genres of fairy tale and rereading of the biblical text to posit both the loss entailed by compassion and the creativity of such loss. In mimetic terms we might say that just as imitation of violence brings destruction and loss, so the imitation of love brings loss and creativity.

Atonement, therefore, is the possibility of nonviolence via the repetition of a rhetoric of anthropology, a rhetoric with the anthropological referent of the abyss as love. Violence itself is not a truth in an intellectual sense, a valid object of intellect. Rather it is a point of ultimate breakdown or collapse, the abyss and the blindness of the abyss. Mimesis, on the contrary, is the true *arche* of the argument, in the sense of a positive structural principle, and this is the starting point of a biblical anthropology of atonement. Mimesis is in itself the discovery of the abyss and culturally does everything it can to avoid it, but the nonretaliatory victim transforms imitation by virtue of the abyss, and so overcomes the cultural inevitability of violence.

---

81. Wilde also notes that "while Christ did not say to men, 'Live for others,' he pointed out that there was no difference at all between the lives of others and one's own life" (*De Profundis, The Letters of Oscar Wilde*, 480).

82. Unpublished manuscript of conversation with René Girard, ed. Giuseppe Fornari, 1997.

The kerygma of the cross is the constant repetition of this anthropological scene. It seeks to bring about "lived" repetitions of a new sense of life in those who find themselves overwhelmed by violence. Repetition bears repetition and brings it about, because it is repetition. Those who then assume this pattern pursue an imitation of loss that is compassion and, thereby, a loss of conflictual imitation. The alteration offered by Christ welcomes the other into a life alternative to that of violence. This is an account of atonement with strong anthropological coherence, but without metaphysical necessity. In the abyss of compassion there is surely no other way.

Chapter Five

CROSS TALK: HERMENEUTICS OF THE
DEATH OF JESUS OF NAZARETH

Why did Jesus die? The question may be considered the key question of the Christian religion, its *crux interpretum*, second to none. Systematic answers, of a second order to the New Testament itself, have been evolved in Christian thought from the postapostolic age onward. The most natural sense of the question, however, refers to the concrete episodes of the Gospels themselves, to the accounts of the career of the prophet from Nazareth, and thence to the hotly disputed quests for the historical Jesus that have been going on in New Testament criticism since the end of the eighteenth century.[1] In this reference the question comes to mean both what were the actual historical, social, and cultural forces that brought about this man's death and, along with these, what did this man himself intend by going to his death willingly, if not willfully. As the biblical historian N. T. Wright says, the death of this man is "one of the most secure facts in the history of the world," and under that strong rubric it is impossible to resist a close inquiry as to what precise factors conditioned it.

There is at once a further aspect to the rubric. "On the other hand, we know that literally thousands of other Jews were crucified within fifty years either side of Jesus. There were two others crucified the very same day, right beside him. What made Jesus special?"[2] The question broadens

---

1. See Albert Schweitzer's classic *The Quest for the Historical Jesus: A Critical Study of its Progress from Reimarus to Wrede* (London: A. & C. Black, 1954 [1906]). For the "second" and "third" quests see Marcus Borg, *Jesus in Contemporary Scholarship* (Valley Forge, Pa.: Trinity Press, 1994); and Ben Witherington III, *The Jesus Quest: The Third Search for the Jew of Nazareth* (Downers Grove, Ill.: InterVarsity Press, 1995; 2nd ed. 1997).

2. N. T. Wright, *The Original Jesus* (Grand Rapids: Eerdmans, 1996), 18. N. T. Wright's scholarship is set out in detail in *The New Testament and the People of God*, Christian Origins and the Question of God, vol. 1 (London: SPCK; Minneapolis: Fortress, 1992); and *Jesus and the Victory of God*, Christian Origins and the Question of God, vol. 2 (London: SPCK; Minneapolis: Fortress, 1996).

the "fact" into interpretation, to the level of response to the death of Jesus in the minds of those who witnessed it at first hand and through its impact on them were drawn to believe in him as Messiah. There is no escaping the problem that the concrete story of Jesus is mediated to us through the reports of those who did believe, who in the very telling of the story are also communicating a faith. Yet, there are biblical experts confident that it is possible to unearth from the pages of the Gospels themselves the conscious career and intentionality of its protagonist, and therewith the sense of a possible personal and primary interpretation of his death— indeed because of, and not despite, the enormous, multilayered impact this man and his death had. The theme of "theological politics" indicates for Wright the context in which this primary interpretation is to be sought. "It must be emphasized that here more than anywhere it is worse than futile to try to separate theology from politics. The tired old split between the Jesus of history and the Christ of faith was never more misleading at this point. Generations of Gospel readers in search of atonement theology, or at least atonement homiletics, ignored the actual story the evangelists were telling, with all its rough political edges, in favor of the theological scheme the story was deemed to be inculcating, or at least illustrating."[3] Wright is suggesting that church-historical atonement theology is a subsidiary and even distorting scheme imposed upon the primary traditions. Thus the metaphysical level of the question, the level engaged by these theologies beyond the personal and the historical, is undercut by remaining as much as possible in the concrete environment of the gospel narratives.

ESCHATOLOGY AND ATONEMENT

In this context Wright is very much asserting a valid continuity between the Jesus of history and the primitive faith of the Christian religion, and this is borne out by the paradigm case of Paul when Wright makes the claim of substantial continuity between Paul and the vision and praxis of Jesus. The shared element giving sufficient reason for this continuity is eschatology, the first-century Jewish context of belief in God's final judgment of the nations and restoration of the cosmos under a redeemed

---

3. *Jesus and the Victory of God* (hereafter, *Victory*), 541. A key force in maintaining a split was R. Bultmann, perhaps the century's most influential New Testament scholar. The methodological dogmatism is clearly on display in his remark: "The great difficulty for the attempt to reconstruct a character sketch of Jesus, is the fact that we do not know how Jesus understood his end, his death" (quoted in translation by Ben Witherington III, *The Christology of Jesus* [Minneapolis, Fortress: 1990], 250; from R. Bultmann, *Das Verhältnis der urchristlichen Christenbotschaft zum historischen Jesus* [Heidelberg: Kerle, 1960], 11–12).

Israel.[4] Here, for Wright, eschatology is the Rosetta Stone for understanding the function of Jesus' death in the New Testament, both in the
subsequent proclamation about him and then in terms of his own person and career. And furthermore it serves to mark the difference
between an absolute centrality of the death of Jesus in the New
Testament and another, parallel centrality in church history, but now
characterized by a static cosmic framework.

Invoking an author like N. T. Wright clearly weights the discussion
toward a "realist" assessment of the gospel narratives, implying, in other
words, that these accounts, while in many respects editorially structured
and elaborated, nevertheless convey a broadly accurate impression of the
life and times of Jesus of Nazareth. In particular the early Christian community did not invent but faithfully reported many of the eschatological
sayings in which Jesus is shown to articulate and understand his own reality and mission.[5] Bracing the discussion this way forces a hermeneutical

---

4. The following quotation from Wright carries a pungent flavor of first-century Judaic
eschatology, as well as Paul's appropriation of a special eschatology connected to the figure of Jesus. "The significance of Jesus' resurrection, for Saul of Tarsus as he lay blinded
and perhaps bruised on the road to Damascus, was this. *The one true God had done for Jesus
of Nazareth, in the middle of time, what Saul had thought he was going to do for Israel at the
end of time.* Saul had imagined that YHWH would vindicate *Israel* after her suffering at the
hand of the pagans. Instead, he had vindicated *Jesus* after his suffering at the hand of the
pagans. Saul had imagined that the great reversal, the great apocalyptic event, would take
place all at once. . . . Instead the great reversal, the great resurrection, had happened to one
man, all by himself. What could this possibly mean? Quite simply, it meant this: Jesus of
Nazareth, whose followers had regarded him as the Messiah, the one who would bear the
destiny of Israel, had seemed to Saul rather to be an anti-Messiah, someone who had failed
to defeat the pagans, and had succeeded only in generating a group of people who were sitting loose to the Torah and critical of the Temple, two of the great symbols of Jewish identity. But the resurrection demonstrated that Jesus' followers were right" (N. T. Wright,
What Saint Paul Really Said: Was Paul of Tarsus the Real Founder of Christianity? [Grand
Rapids: Eerdmans, 1997], 36; italics original). See the latter part of this chapter for a sketch
of the way in which Wright depicts Jesus' self-understanding, such that it can be seen largely on a continuum with, and generative of the views of, his followers and particularly, in
this case, Paul. On this basis he argues for an "*appropriate continuity* between two people
living, and conscious of living, at different points in the eschatological timetable" (ibid.,
181). Generally speaking, the term *eschatology* ranges in meaning from a cataclysmic end
to the space-time continuum, through future this-worldly events in which God directly
precipitates an end to the evil age and simultaneously the vindication of his people, to an
existentialist or linguistic-subversive sense in which we may speak of the world brought to
an end for an individual. See Borg, op. cit., 70–74, for a review of the field. The sense being
pursued here is clearly the middle one, generally understood to be the common first-century Jewish and Christian perception (Borg, 70; cf. *Victory*, 95–97).

5. Realist here does not mean naively positivist. Wright sites his work within the constant interplay of critical reconstruction and, agreeing with John Dominic Crossan, does
not seek an "unattainable objectivity." At the same time he considers "critical realism" to be
a valid approach to data that is at some point objective. See *Victory*, 54–55; and *The New
Testament and the People of God*, part II.

and existential break between the New Testament witness of Jesus' death and later church rationalizations about it. The central importance of eschatology drives a broad wedge between the world of the New Testament and later popular church formulations. On the other hand, generally and negatively speaking, historical criticism of the life and career of Jesus of Nazareth will always be open to revision, including the question of a death that is proclaimed as pivotal, and yet is nowhere linked in the texts to a systematic account of how and why. Many other historical-critical readings of the Gospels are possible, up to the one that suggests his death had no real significance for Jesus himself and was little more than an accident.[6] Thus critical perspective in itself simply brings to an explicit level the impossibility of deriving any one theory of atonement conclusively from a critical reading of Scripture.

At the same time, however, a serious historical-critical reading that adumbrates the dimension of eschatology in the life of Jesus may not be lightly dismissed. It has major defenders and exponents. With the work of Wright it has been given new impetus, shifting the dimensions of the debate significantly.[7] Furthermore, an overall eschatological reading of the New Testament coheres thematically with the anthropological thesis of the disclosure of the sacred by the event of the cross, and the subversive effect this has on subsequent human history. New Testament writers, particularly Paul, looked toward an imminent and definitive

---

6. See Crossan, *The Historical Jesus: The Life of a Mediterranean Jewish Peasant* (San Francisco: Harper Collins, 1991), 372–75 (hereafter *The Historical Jesus*), where he argues that the canonical Passion narrative is a scribal invention and suggests, by default at least, there is no redemptive coherence between Jesus' ministry and death. The same strong impression is left by the work of the Jesus Seminar, where none of the canonical material related to the Passion is traced back to Jesus; see Robert W. Funk and Roy W. Hoover, *The Five Gospels: The Search for the Authentic Words of Jesus* (New York: Macmillan, 1993).

7. "Wright has made it quite clear that anyone who still wants to argue for a rather non-Jewish, noneschatological, nonprophetic and nonmessianic Jesus will have to be prepared to argue long into the night. Even where Wright may be wrong, it will take much to show this is so, and I would suggest that he has managed to shift the burden of proof on those who want to argue for a nonmessianic Jesus" (Ben Witherington III, *The Jesus Quest*, 280). As well as Witherington himself, other major scholars who hold a position requiring in one way or another an eschatological Jesus include Raymond Brown (*The Death of the Messiah: From Gethsemane to the Grave. A Commentary on the Passion Narratives in the Four Gospels*, Anchor Bible Reference Library [New York: Doubleday; London: Geoffrey Chapman, 1994]); E. P. Sanders (*Jesus and Judaism* [Philadelphia: Fortress Press; London: SCM Press, 1985]); Martin Hengel (*The Atonement: The Origins of the Doctrine in the New Testament* (Philadelphia: Fortress, 1981), and *Studies in Early Christology* [Edinburgh: T. & T. Clark, 1995]); Markus Bockmuehl (*This Jesus: Martyr, Lord, Messiah* [Edinburgh: T. & T. Clark, 1994]); and Peter Stuhlmacher (*Jesus of Nazareth—Christ of Faith* [Peabody, Mass.: Hendrickson, 1993]).

rupture in time, and even though a later writer like the author of Luke/Acts may be seen as dampening eschatological expectations, these writings are still working in reference to a radical turning point introduced into the sequence of human affairs.[8] Critically deepening this hermeneutic to the level of Jesus himself brings to singular focus the existential source for a cultural theory of profound transformative effects. Mimetic anthropology both makes available conceptual tools describing such effects and refers to the New Testament itself as their key dynamic source.[9] A "thoroughgoing eschatology" is, therefore, the most apt New Testament hermeneutic cousin to give to a mimetic critique of atonement theology. More essentially, a description given of Jesus' personal, historical, and contingent assumption of Israel's destiny, bringing him to the agony of the cross, may be seen as the phenomenological and anthropological underpinning to a proclamation of abyssal compassion.

The purpose of this excursus, therefore, is not to provide an exhaustive review of Scripture relating to atonement, or a thorough exegesis of all passages that could be connected to the theme. Rather, it implies first and foremost that differing interpretations are possible, yet by this very token exchangist notions of atonement based in violent mimesis can by no means be taken as the natural meaning of the text. Such "received" beliefs about the significance of Christ's death in the New Testament are themselves highly prejudicial and derive much more from a cultural history that erected a superstructure of violent logic over its text than from a reading attentive to the actual historical crisis from which it arose. Simultaneously elements of such a reading combine much more sympathetically with the insights of mimetic anthropology at the root of this study. A historical Jesus who consciously and deliberately takes upon himself the profound crisis of his people and their time, in order to bring all things to a redemptive term, is a figure who can justly be considered to have entered the human abyss in order to transform it abysally.

---

8. See Hans Conzelmann's classic study *Theology of St. Luke* (London: Faber & Faber, 1960). Also Robert Sloan, *The Favorable Year of the Lord: A Study of Jubilary Theology in the Gospel of Luke* (Austin: Schola, 1977). The Lukan account of eschatology may in fact resonate more intimately with mimetic anthropology, describing a cultural interruption within history, rather than a catastrophic interruption of history.

9. The question of a precise theological and methodological connection between a critical reading of New Testament eschatology and the eschatological dimensions of mimetic anthropology is a task awaiting a much more profound study. The intention here is simply to point out a basic sympathy of themes and motifs, such as might provide a basis for such a study.

EARLIEST CHRISTIANITY

However, although the person of Jesus and the Gospels that narrate his story are seen at the heart of New Testament meaning, this is not in fact the place to begin our investigation. This is primarily the case because the Gospels are themselves late New Testament writings, and to attain to a first level in the history of Jesus means paradoxically digging back through oral and written traditions accumulated within them. The Gospels are in principle a subsequent stage of inquiry and the logical place to begin is at the earliest level of post-Pentecost Christianity, if only because it would be here that the impetus to proclaim Christ's death, plus to explain its function, appears at its most primitive and unadorned.

According to Vincent Taylor a variety of ideas characterized the earliest preaching and belief, but the belief that lay deepest included an understanding of Christ's death and resurrection as deliverance from sin, and as sacrifice.[10] Martin Hengel understands from Paul's frequent use of the "dying for" formula, and from the *paradosis* (community tradition) that includes it, and which in turn he handed on to the Corinthians around C.E. 49/50 (1 Cor. 13:3–5), that this is a formula of earliest Christianity, reaching back to the primitive Jerusalem community itself.[11] He traces the circumstances of the production of this formula to the conviction, first clearly articulated by the "Hellenist" or Greek-speaking Jews in Jerusalem, that the Messiah indeed had died, but his "accursed" death followed by resurrection had rendered the Temple redundant, replacing all its functions. In Acts 6:13, Stephen, the leader of this group, is accused of having made attacks "against this holy place [the Temple] and the law."[12] Hengel asks: "But what was the basis of these attacks on the sanctuary and the Torah? Presumably the certainty that the death of the crucified Messiah, who had vicariously taken upon himself the curse of the Law, had made the Temple obsolete as a place of everlasting atonement for the sins of Israel, and therefore the ritual Law had lost its significance as a necessary institution for salvation."[13]

The death of Jesus, therefore, very quickly took on a sacrificial, and even cultic significance. At the same time these incendiary ideas, adding

---

10. Vincent Taylor, *The Atonement in New Testament Teaching* (London and New York: Epworth Press, 1950), 50–52.

11. Martin Hengel, *The Atonement: The Origins of the Doctrine in the New Testament* (Philadelphia: Fortress Press, 1981), 36–38; hereafter *The Atonement*.

12. From *The New Oxford Annotated Bible, New Revised Standard Version*, ed. Bruce M. Metzger and Roland E. Murphy (New York: Oxford University Press, 1991).

13. *The Atonement*, 44, 49.

blasphemy to national and cultural betrayal, could not have been announced lightly in the Jewish context. Nor subsequently would they have been uncontroversial in a gentile one. Although earlier in this book Hengel convincingly situates the idea of vicarious death within the Greek and Roman background, demonstrating a *preparatio evangelii* of the central gospel motif, he is also at pains to point out the scandal of the cross: the outlandishly offensive *logos staurou* (word of the cross, 1 Cor. 1:18) so boldly trumpeted by Paul, and before him by Greek-speaking Christian Jews in Jerusalem.[14] "The new doctrine of salvation had not only barbarian, but also irrational and excessive features. It appeared to contemporaries as a dark or even mad superstition. For this was not the death of a hero from ancient times, suffused in the glow of religion, but that of a Jewish craftsman of the most recent past, executed as a criminal, with whom the whole present and future salvation of all men was linked."[15]

The traditions represented by the Gospels do nothing to soften this effect. Mark underlines Jesus' complete human failure with the cry of abandonment on the cross (15:34), taken from Psalm 22. Earlier the twofold invitation to come down from the cross is a pointed invitation to transform this scandalous death into apotheosis and triumph (Mark 15:30, 32). As Hengel points out, "[T]here is no hagiographical transformation of the scandal." Yet it is precisely the Gospels' unrepentant insistence on the cross that was to continue to provide material for anti-Christian polemic well into the future.[16] The final explanation that Hengel suggests for this blunt element of disgrace within the kerygma is always its transcendent effect as "atonement": one that overwhelmed and replaced the role of the Temple. He emphasizes its threefold revolutionary character: its effect was applicable to all humanity; it was God's own initiative; it had been achieved once and for all.[17] Nevertheless, he also recognizes it was set very much within the exceptional personal

---

14. For Saul/Paul's resistance precisely to this concept and sudden conversion between 32 and 34 C.E., see *The Atonement*, 44. E. P. Sanders gives the date as about 33 (E. P. Sanders, *Paul* [Oxford: Oxford University Press, 1991], 9). For the scandal of a crucified Messiah see also James D. G. Dunn, *The Theology of Paul the Apostle* (Grand Rapids and Cambridge, U.K.: Eerdmans, 1998), 209 (hereafter *Theology of Paul*); and ibid., 179–81 for Paul's experience of the "revelation" that was "a breakthrough from one age to another." For New Testament Greek here and below, see Nestle-Aland's *Novum Testamentum Graece* (Stuttgart: Deutsche Bibelstiftung, 1981).

15. *The Atonement*, 31.

16. Ibid., 43, with references to the arguments of the pagan Celsus; cf. Origen, *Contra Celsum* 2.33–37. See also Hengel, *Crucifixion* (London and Philadelphia: Fortress Press, 1977) 1–10.

17. *The Atonement*, 31, 47, 65–66.

experiences of the first group of disciples caught up in a potent reversal of themes following hard on their Master's horrendous death.

> We can hardly envisage these first days, weeks and months of the disciples after Easter as the meditative assembly of a quietistic group with esoteric mystical experiences; rather, what they experienced ought to be compared with the violent force of an explosion which broke up all traditional conventions and bourgeois assurances. Here something new and unheard-of emerged, a new experience which radically transcended the everyday life of Palestinian fishermen, peasants and craftsmen. To some degree people lived with an enthusiastic assurance that the heavens would open and the kingdom would dawn. It was no accident that the appearances of the risen Jesus were connected with the eschatological experience of the Spirit which was compared with the force of heavenly fire. At the same time that means that the Jesus community which first took shape after Easter understood these events as the beginning of the end of the world and the dawn of the rule of God. The resurrection marked the beginning of the general resurrection of the dead; in Paul Jesus still appears as the "first fruits of those who have fallen asleep" (1 Cor. 15:20). . . . It was hoped that believers would be made like him when he appeared. . . .[18]

The reality of some such experience seems undeniable. The alternative to experienced transition from abject failure to confident eschatology has to be some sort of conspiracy, in which there is a qualitative disjunction between the actual story of the original disciples and the textual layer of scribal imposition in which resurrection and Pentecost are successfully embedded.[19] The problem is that adequate trace evidence of such a seismic disjunction is very hard to come by in New Testament texts. What one might expect, for example, would be polemics against "bad" disciples who denied the experience, insisted on the purely "wisdom" nature of Jesus' teaching without eschatological interruption, proclaimed the continuing death of Jesus, and continued to see Temple sacrifice as necessary. That some such polemics would emerge would surely be the case if the Gospels were written within the lifetime of surviving "real" disciples of Jesus, or even those who remembered their tes-

---

18. Ibid., 66.
19. Cf. Crossan, n. 6 above.

timony, especially given the fact that on other issues polemics never fail to surface.[20]

The source of the experience is not immediately at issue, simply that its phenomenality—and on a significant scale—is the necessary condition for the emergence of the primitive kerygma. If this is true, then Hengel does not stress it enough; he does not link the experience in any constitutive way with the claim that the death of Jesus made obsolete the atonement function of the Temple. Yet ultimately it is only by virtue of such an experience that such an astonishing claim could be made. So many features of Jesus' death are noncultic, extracultic, and plainly unsympathetic to cult. Jesus' death on the cross does not have the serene transcendence of cult, its aura of calm and divine inevitability; it takes place in threatening dark, with swords, clubs, and flickering lights, among disagreement, failure, betrayal, fear, futile resistance, lies, conspiracy, an inflamed mob, an unclean imperial power, and above all and everywhere, brutal violence. Nor does it possess cult's essential repeatability and manageability.[21] Rather, as Hengel points out, it was proclaimed as a definitive event in effect brought about the terminus of cult. It is logical, therefore, that such an event could only be obtained existentially by means of a "cosmic revolution" that somehow was seen to swing the power of the universe in favor of this disgraced, humiliated man. What before had been precisely the item of elimination now became the keystone of meaning, and with that the very process of condemnation and elimination was brought into

---

20. The nearest evidence of such an alternative tradition is the putative Q document of Jesus' sayings and, outside the New Testament, an even more speculative very early Gospel of Thomas. There can be no proof that Q, if it circulated at all, did so without connection to a Passion narrative, and in particular to the words of the Lord's Supper, which also appear as part of Paul's primitive *paradosis* (1 Cor. 11:23). The version of Thomas that we have is from around the beginning of the third century, and it takes some audacity to force a proto-version back to the middle of the first. Wright in reference to the Jesus Seminar calls it "highly contentious" (*Victory*, 33), and in the case of Crossan "bravado" (ibid., 48). Perhaps even more crucial than the inadequate textual evidence there is the question of how the new religion in Jerusalem would have agreed to go beyond Temple and Law, against the resistance of traditional Jewish thought, if the radical element was based on the myth-making of ambitious and heterodox scribes, who had an incredibly short period of time in which to force people to accept their stories. (For example, if Saul/Paul is converted to the new, radical concept of redemption within two to four years of Jesus' death; see n. 14, above.)

21. See, for example, Emile Durkheim: cult "is a system of diverse rites, festivals and ceremonies which *all have this characteristic, that they reappear periodically.* They fulfil the need which the believer feels of strengthening and reaffirming, at regular intervals of time, the bond which unites him to the sacred beings upon which he depends" (*The Elementary Forms of the Religious Life* [New York: The Free Press, 1965; copyright 1915, George Allen & Unwin], 80, italics in original).

question. Only by means of such a definitive reversal of terms would a sense of transcendent "atonement" or, much better perhaps, "justification," be achieved. Ultimately the only reason the cross could displace the Temple was that it was already a qualitatively new experience of divine validation that rendered cult redundant, rather than retranslated it.

However, if this is the case, why is the New Testament so full of sacrificial language in respect of Christ's death, especially, as it seems, in Paul? It is to this question in general, and in particular relation to this formidable New Testament author, that we must now turn. Paul's letters are generally understood to be the earliest extant stratum of writing in the New Testament, and are therefore both an invaluable link to the primitive period and, of course, a testimony in their own right to a remarkable religious experience and its powerful articulation—so powerful, indeed, that Saul/Paul has more than once been indicted as the first Christian who in one way or another hijacked the gentler, less dogmatic, religious vision of Jesus. A scholarly presentation of this viewpoint in recent years has come from Hyam Maccoby, in his unambiguously titled *The Mythmaker: Paul and the Invention of Christianity*.[22] One of the key inventions of Paul is precisely Jesus' sacrificial death, influenced as he was—according to Maccoby—by the pattern of Greek mystery religions, of the dying and immortalized hero. However, as we have just seen, this kind of large-scale secondary imposition on the original Jesus traditions has serious evidential gaps in the texts; but, more crucially, it leaves unexplained the aboriginal testimony of faith in a crucified man that so unmistakably moved Saul both to fury and then subsequently to surrender. The problem is that the internal evidence of Paul's writings is consistent with someone who is first a zealous persecutor of emergent Christianity and then an ardent exponent of precisely those elements of the new faith most discordant with traditional Judaism.[23] Paul's experience has all the hallmarks of explosive conversion, rather than abstract innovation.[24] It must be reasonable then to posit an experiential dimension shared among

---

22. Hyam Maccoby, *The Mythmaker: Paul and the Invention of Christianity* (London: SCM, 1970). Maccoby's position can be traced in the nineteenth century to the views on Paul of the Tübingen scholar, F. C. Baur, who saw a deep divergence between Paul and the Jerusalem apostles; cited by David Wenham, *Paul: Follower of Jesus or Founder of Christianity* (Grand Rapids: Eerdmans, 1995), 2. Nietzsche's hand can also be discerned here: "[Paul] is the first Christian, the inventor of Christianity. Until then there were only a few Jewish sectarians" ("The First Christian," in *The Dawn*, no. 68, in *The Portable Nietzsche*, 79).

23. See Gal. 1:13: "You have heard, no doubt, of my earlier life in Judaism. I was violently persecuting the church of God and was trying to destroy it." Cf. 1 Cor. 15:9; Phil. 3:6.

24. See Dunn, *Theology of Paul*, 179, and 353: "The psychology of the conversion experience is easily recognizable and cannot be easily discounted."

the first Christians and capable of turning this man around. In precise terms we can conclude that some dynamic, first-hand version of the crucified and exalted Jesus was in effect among the first Christians and capable of bringing this man to his knees some time around 33 C.E.[25] As appropriated by the opponent turned neophyte it meant:

> The death and resurrection of Jesus were themselves the great eschatological event, revealing God's covenant faithfulness, his way of putting the world to rights. . . . Saul [because of this experience] was already living in the time of the end, even though the previous dimension of time was still carrying on all around him. The Present Age and the Age to Come overlapped, and he was caught in the middle, or rather, liberated in the middle. . . .[26]

Paul's manifold and generally unexplained language about the death of Jesus must be gauged against this background of a dramatically changed way of being in the world. His standard usage of "surrender" and "dying for" formulae, without further comment, seems to regard such statements as self-explanatory for the audiences addressed.[27] How could this be the case unless he shared some common assumption of the proven efficacy of this death that did not have to be argued through, for example, as did the role of the Law? The very lack of a coherent theory of atonement in the New Testament, compared to burgeoning development of such theory from the second century onward, testifies to a vigorous atmosphere of personal and cosmic reversal, brought about by this death, that in itself had no further need of conceptual validation.[28] J. Christiaan Becker

---

25. For this date see also *Theology of Paul*, 209–10.

26. N. T. Wright, *What Saint Paul Really Said*, 37. For a full exposition of counter-arguments to Maccoby and of continuity between Jesus and Paul, see David Wenham, *Paul: Follower of Jesus or Founder of Christianity* (n. 22, above).

27. For "surrender" see, for example, Gal. 1:4, 2:20; Rom. 4:25, 8:32; and Deutero-Pauline texts, Eph. 5:2, 25; Titus 2:14; and 1 Tim. 2:6. The "dying for" formula is almost exclusively limited to Paul; see 1 Cor. 8:11, 15:3; Rom. 5:6, 5:8, 14:9; 2 Cor. 5:14, 15 twice; Gal. 2:21; 1 Thess. 5:10. "How can Paul—with relatively few exceptions—content himself with formulae and not explain in detail the atoning death of the Messiah 'for us'? The reason is probably that the 'that' in this formula was in no way controversial, even in Galatia and the Roman church that was unknown to him" (Hengel, *The Atonement*, 54). See also *Theology of Paul*, 211–12, for the "enigmatic," formulaic nature of Paul's theology of the cross.

28. "The variety of metaphors [explaining Christ's death] also attests the impact of the proclamation of the cross on Paul and through his gospel. They would hardly have been living and fruitful metaphors had they not corresponded to experiences of conscience set at rest, of release and liberation, of reconciliation, and so on. From the beginning, we may well infer, the [Pauline] doctrine of atonement was not independent of the experience of atonement. From the first Christ was known by his benefits" (*Theology of Paul*, 232).

argues that the coherent center of Paul's thought is a Jewish apocalyptic worldview concretized in the death and resurrection of Jesus.[29]
Rather than apocalyptic atmosphere, he talks in terms of a dynamic
field of meaning. "We must . . . become aware of this coherent center
[to Paul's thought] as *a field* of meaning, a network composed of
parts that interlock in a symbolic relationship. The makeup of this
field as a whole is determined by the apocalyptic act of God in the
death and resurrection of Christ."[30] The specifically intensified quality brought to apocalyptic thought by the gospel of Paul is expressed
in the following:

> The imminence motif is much more intense in Paul's letters than
> in Jewish apocalyptic, since the death and resurrection of Christ
> already heralds the incursion of the future into the present.
> Christ who has come "in the fullness of time" (Galatians 4:4), has
> inaugurated the end of time so that after his death and resurrec-
> tion no eschatological timetable needs to be established, and in
> principle no other conditions need to be met before his glorious
> return in the triumph of God.[31]

The present running of the eschatological clock, wound and set
abruptly forward by the death and resurrection of Jesus, is no facile
expectation of a Second Coming. Rather, it is the present reconstitution of time and its world so that each moment loses its boundary in

---

29. J. Christiaan Becker, *The Triumph of God: The Essence of Paul's Thought*, trans. Loren
T. Stuckenbruck (Minneapolis: Fortress Press, 1990), hereafter *The Triumph of God*.
"Apocalyptic" may be considered a subset of eschatology; see for example Crossan, *The
Historical Jesus*, 238. Becker distinguishes four marks of apocalyptic thought: vindication
by God, universal salvation, dualistic structure of world, and imminence of God's action
(*The Triumph of God*, 21–33). This obviously overlaps with what I have referred to so far
as "eschatology." However, the term *apocalyptic*, as defined by reference to works of the
genre of "apocalyptic," may be understood as conveying a heightened sense of dualism and
imminence. A working definition of apocalyptic literature was given by *Semeia* 14: "A
genre of revelatory literature with a narrative framework, in which a revelation is mediated by an otherworldly being to a human recipient, disclosing a transcendent reality which
is both temporal, insofar as it envisages eschatological salvation, and spatial insofar as it
involves another, supernatural world" (J. J. Collins, ed. *Apocalypse: The Morphology of a
Genre. Semeia* 14; [Missoula, Mont.: Scholars Press, 1979]). The effective content of the
revelation is this combination of temporal and spatial difference, and in the New
Testament it is the death and resurrection of Christ that provides the breakpoint of change
on both counts of time and space—while remaining simultaneously and paradoxically
within the continuum of history.
30. Becker, *The Triumph of God*, 19; italics in original.
31. Ibid., 33.

the strict chronological succession of moments, and experiences instead a radical opening into a future of God already in the here and now. Because this altered sense of time and reality was dominant among the churches addressed by Paul, they were, in Becker's words, "apocalyptic movements"; they subsisted within the collapsing present of active Christian apocalyptic.[32] Ernst Käsemann's account of Pauline anthropology is also called in aid by Becker to explicate further the apocalyptic worldview. For Käsemann, Pauline "man is always himself in his particular world; his being is open towards all sides and is always set in a structure of solidarity." Thus, there is no final division between self and others, or ultimately between the cosmos and the self. "Anthropology is cosmology *in concreto*."[33] Accordingly, a constitutive change in one human corner of the cosmos implied a possible change in the structure of human being everywhere else, and will in principle be manifest in the reality of each human person. "For the love of Christ impels us, once we have come to the conviction that one died for all; therefore, all have died. He indeed died for all, so that those who live might no longer live for themselves but for him who for their sake died and was raised. . . . So whoever is in Christ is a new creation: the old things have passed away; behold new things have come" (1 Cor. 5:14–17).[34] Reading this passage in the light of the above, it is very difficult to misconstrue "dying for" as a form of exchange between Christ and some other, hostile force; rather it appears a determinative act of eschatological crisis by which time and space have been essentially reconstituted.

---

32. Ibid., 64. Compare Wayne Meeks's description of Pauline churches as constituted by individuals suffering "status inconsistency" within Greco-Roman society and finding new meaning in the "millennialist" groupings of primitive Christianity (Wayne A. Meeks, *The First Urban Christians: The Social World of the Apostle Paul* [New Haven: Yale University Press, 1983], 173–74).

33. Ernst Käsemann, *Perspectives on Paul* (Philadelphia: Fortress Press, 1971), 21, 22, 27; quoted in Becker, op. cit., 26. It is worth recalling here Käsemann's famous dictum: "Apocalyptic was the mother of all Christian theology" (E. Käsemann, "The Beginnings of Christian Theology," *Journal for Theology and the Church* 6 (1969), 40).

34. *New American Bible*, (New York and Oxford: Oxford University Press, 1995 [all subsequent New and Old Testament quotations are from this version unless otherwise stated]). Of course, this "real change" in the order of the universe still remains relational, as the phrase "in Christ" implies. There is a dialectic between an eschatological reversal and the need to appropriate it personally by faith. This points in fact to a deeply personal reference (and responsibility) for a changed cosmos; however, our purpose here is not to pursue a more subtle analysis, but simply to insist on the overall vibrancy and urgency of the Christian apocalyptic sense as the correct starting point for understanding the New Testament meaning of the death of Christ.

"Sacrificial Language" in Paul

A transformed anthropocosmology may, therefore, be considered the fabric of atonement in Paul, and presumably was so for the Jerusalem Christians who provoked his conversion, and was so subsequently for the gentile communities to which he ministered. There remains, however, one figure that still seems to exceed this picture of constitutive cosmic change; it is *orge* or the wrath (of God). This predominantly Pauline term is a favored trope by which to return Christ's death to some form of mimetic exchange. In responding to this it is useful first to point out that when it comes to available language in which to express a process of cosmic change, the most powerful must surely be the sacrificial metaphor, wherein the reconstitution of the world is always somehow implied and rehearsed as an authentic cultural event. Secondly, there cannot be a strict or simple sacrificial meaning in Paul, or anywhere else in the New Testament, precisely because of the apocalyptic context. On the contrary, sacrifice itself is undermined in the New Testament, and the way that Paul in particular uses sacrificial and exchangist terminology is self-demolishing. The continual attempt to return New Testament language to a "basic" sacrificial sense is in this light a failure to grasp the existential force of the original New Testament experience or to see how its significance continues to reverberate in the dynamic of the text itself, subverting traditional meanings.[35]

Romans 3:21–26, which Dunn calls "the core of [Paul's] own as well as of his shared Gospel,"[36] is the classic text to give in example:

21 But now the righteousness of God has been manifested apart from the law, though testified to by the law and the prophets,

---

35. At the same time it must be stressed that in the New Testament apocalyptic change is always mediated by the message of the cross and resurrection; it is never a work of prejudicial force. As such the enduring figure of the cross, around which pivots this seemingly impalpable change, is very easily misread as the figure of a mimetic exchange that takes place and is appropriated in a disjunctive way within history (staging) and yet outside of history (essence). What is being argued here is that the New Testament is a much more dynamic text, proclaiming apocalyptic change within history's continuum, and the change and the continuum are rendered, both at once, contingent and powerfully effective. See Becker, op. cit.: "Paul tempers the dualism between this and the coming age . . . by emphasizing continuity in the midst of discontinuity. . . . Furthermore, the proleptic experience of the new age is manifest in the new life in the Spirit made possible for Christians through the death and resurrection of Jesus Christ" (28–29).

36. *Theology of Paul*, 213. Dunn also expresses the natural reaction at the compression of this passage: "It really is astonishing that, after such an elaborate and extensive indictment (Rom. 1:18–3:20), Paul could be content to give the heart of his response to it in a mere six verses" (ibid., 176).

22 the righteousness of God through faith in Jesus Christ for all who believe. For there is no distinction;

23 all have sinned and are deprived of the glory of God.

24 They are justified freely by his grace through the redemption in Christ Jesus,

25 whom God set forth as an expiation [*hilasterion*], through faith, by his blood, to prove his righteousness because of the forgiveness of sins previously committed,

26 through the forbearance of God—to prove his righteousness in the present time, that he might be righteous and justify the one who has faith in Jesus.

The cardinal verse is 25, where a sacrificial logic seems on the surface to be at work; the terms *expiation* and *blood* have a tenor of self-evidence in the sense of some exchange by means of violence. There has been considerable discussion on the language of "expiation" in relation to "propitiation" and the appropriateness of the former rather than the latter in biblical usage. In his influential study, C. H. Dodd argued that the word group around *hilaskesthai* regularly implied "propitiation" in classical and popular Greek; however, it never held this meaning in the Septuagint or the New Testament. He sums up the point: "Hellenistic Judaism, as represented by the LXX, does not regard the cultus as a means of pacifying the displeasure of the Deity, but as a means of delivering man from sin."[37] An important factor in the argument is the fact that the Old Testament Hebrew verb *kipper*, regularly translated by *exhilaskomai* (expiate/atone) in Greek, never has God as its object; rather, it is always the sin that is acted upon.[38] There are a few instances, however, in which this Greek verb translates the Hebrew *chalah* (entreat/appease), and is then used with God as its object. A broader textual relation of *kipper* and "wrath" is also sometimes invoked, suggesting that this Hebrew word does sometimes imply the turning away of God's anger.[39] Generally speaking, there can be no absolute separation between propitiation and expiation when theology in any way embraces the violent mechanisms of the sacred. In the meantime the restraint of Old Testament language must surely be recognized, as well as the attempt to separate the figure of the covenant God from any direct relationship with sacrificial appeasement.

---

37. C. H. Dodd, *The Bible and the Greeks* (London: Hodder & Stoughton, 1935), 93.
38. *Theology of Paul*, 214.
39. Ibid., 214, n. 30 and n. 33.

In somewhat the same vein, the crucial aspect of the Romans passage is the direction of the text as a whole, but this in fact carries with it a much more radical transformation of terms. First of all, Paul begins with "But now," that is, the eschatological moment of change brought by Christ.[40] Whatever Paul is describing has to be assessed within the new dimensions of time produced by Christ's death and resurrection, the "now" of apocalyptic upheaval. Paul reemphasizes this at verse 26, where God's righteousness is demonstrated in the "now time" (*en to nun kairo*). Consistent with this, it is God who "presents" or sets forth the "expiation," so that the movement is from God, a divine interruption of the continuum of sin.[41] The importance of this eschatological movement cannot be overstated, and its retranslation back into some form of self-appeasement by God completely misses the point, abrogating the movement. Moreover, the word used here is not the actual Greek word for propitiation/expiation, *hilasmos*, but a much more elusive term, *hilasterion*, employed in the LXX nearly exclusively for the *kapporeth*, the lid of the ark, the "mercy seat," where the rite of atonement was carried out for the holy place and the whole assembly of Israel on the Day of Atonement. That this is primarily a place rather than a sacrificial object or action must lead us to infer a concrete existential reference to Christ's death on the cross, rather than a rereading of that death within a necessary sacrificial order. The note of "by his blood" seems again to oblige us to a sacrificial reference, but there is no reason why this may not also primarily refer us to the concrete details of Jesus' death as phenomenality of redemption. "By his blood" is the physical pouring out of a life without limit, not in the trick of sacrifice inflicting this on another, and in which always lurks the ghost of violence, but by the infinite act of self-giving in the Christ. The appropriation by faith guarantees the "subjective" level of the event. What is faith but subjective appropriation of the abyssal self-

---

40. "The same sense of eschatological transformation is expressed in the 'But now' with which Paul begins his exposition of the core of the gospel in Rom. 3:21" (ibid., 180). Dunn also notes the use of "revelation" terminology in verse 21, "manifested"/*pephanerotai*, comparable with use of *apokalyptetai* at Rom. 1:17, 18; cognate with the latter is "revelation"/*apokalupsis*, a word used by Paul to describe the Damascus experience, and it forms the basis of his gospel (Gal. 1:16).

41. See R. G. Hamerton-Kelly, "Sacred Violence and the Curse of the Law (Galatians 3.13): The Death of Christ as Sacrificial Travesty," in *New Testament Studies* 36 (1990): 98–118. He argues that the reversed direction—from God to humanity—should be read as a formal travesty, or parody, of sacrificial action, and thereby a disclosure of its status as human violence. "A sacrifice in which the god appeases humanity is a parody" (116). He suggests also that Rom. 3:21–26 manifests a preexisting Jewish-Christian idea of Christ's death that may have been already "anti-sacrificial." Paul further radicalized the Jewish-Christian direction.

giving of Christ, an appropriation that not only takes place "in" the subject but at a much more radical level that in fact creates the subject?

The challenge to understanding is to hold together two hermeneutics, sacrificial and apocalyptic, which for Paul worked together in practice, but for us, because of apocalyptic's greatly diminished intensity, tend to fold over into the more traditional, sacrificial half. Paul appears to be willing to turn to sacrificial terms as the most suitable language by which to enshrine or encode the anthropocosmic shift brought by Christ's death; but at the same time the sovereign dynamic of this change (its *dunamis*, Rom. 1:4)[42] cannot be neglected as its ultimate source of meaning. If nothing else the concrete shift from cult to a focus on Christ's death by crucifixion entails a reverse-flow effect by which the language itself suffers change of meaning. That which before meant both the transference of violence onto the victim and the cultural absorption of this process into the "sacred," becomes now a revelation of the innocence of a victim when he is manifestly vindicated by God. The precise apocalyptic and redemptive meaning of the crucifixion is the point of human abjection at which God's eschatological intervention is witnessed. Sacrificial logic is turned on its head, but such is the fixity of the lens by which we view and understand that logic that the overturning is not immediately clear or systemic. A first conceptual moment may be to say that here is in fact a "perfect sacrifice" that renders all others redundant, but if this is the case it can only be by virtue of the eschatological removal of the very grounds for sacrifice itself.

Or, if we put the removal in terms of abyssal compassion, then the transformative alteration offered by Christ is of such profound quality that it at once appears within a preapocalyptic language as the most effective sacrifice of all time, but simultaneously empties the very notion of sacrifice of all its structural sense. In other words, Jesus in the abyss of the cross, and recognized there in the proclamation, renders the exchange of violent mimesis meaningless, and replaces it instead with the bottomless gift of compassion.

Paul himself was not at all concerned to render his terms systematically, but this may surely be explained both by lack of adequate conceptualization and, more importantly, the dominance of the apocalyptic motif that provided the vital experiential-hermeneutic key for everything

---

42. Jesus Christ descended from David according to the flesh, was "established as Son of God in power [*dunamei*] according to the spirit of holiness through resurrection from the dead." The Greek has *ex anastaseos nekron*, which is literally translated as "by a resurrection of dead persons" (Nestle and Alfred Marshall, *RSV Interlinear Greek-English New Testament with Literal English Translation* [London: Samuel Bagster and Sons Limited, 1968]; hereafter *Interlinear*), implying again the universal apocalyptic of Christ's resurrection.

he said. Paul's use of compressed and allusive sacrificial formulae within a framework of the eschatological "now" must suggest both a recognition of the received signifying power of these formulae and a lively consciousness of their transformed meaning. If sacrifice is a primordial human mechanism by which the cosmos is instituted as meaningful and its power given and regulated, then as a first apocalyptic moment that reorders the cosmos, the death of Christ may well be expressed in a kind of residual sacrificial terminology. By the very same token, however, that terminology will already be seriously twisted from its natural alignment: God is very clearly the source of the process, and what God provides is much more a crucified and risen figure as phenomenality, as personal event and disclosure of redemption, rather than any traditional sacrifice as such. As a result the terminology may be seen always to unravel from its original weave, and it is the text itself that produces this unraveling. From a superficially symbolic reading of Christ's death to the apocalyptic abyss of Christ's suffering and resurrection, the reader is carried back to a *dunamis* that interrupts the sacrificial, a power that renders the sacrificial solution redundant. Deep vindication of all humanity, rather than confirmation of the role of the victim, is the apocalyptic end of the world as envisioned by Paul.

Romans 8:3 is another text with a phrase that carries cultic overtones: God sent "his own Son in the likeness of sinful flesh, and for the sake of sin [*peri hamartias*], he condemned sin in the flesh." Dunn thinks the phrase means "as a sin offering." He comments: "The phrase is used quite often in the LXX to translate the Hebrew *(lᵉ) chatta'th* ("as a sin offering"). Given the centrality of cultic imagery in the key gospel statement of 3:21–26, it must be judged highly likely that Paul intended a similar allusion here."[43] This is a good example of how commentators construct a catena of supposedly sacrificial texts, and then conclude that the sacrificial mechanism is both central and free-standing in Paul. At the same time, Dunn had commented earlier on the meaning of "likeness of sinful flesh," seeing here a statement of "complete solidarity and identity with humankind in its existence under the powers of sin and death."[44] This is a statement of abyssal redemption by Christ. Thus, even if there is a cultic meaning the concrete existential, and indeed apocalyptic, reference would seem to precede and predetermine it. Once more the cultic may be seen to unravel back to its hidden depths, and the sacrificial may be deciphered effectively by the apocalyptic.

43. *Theology of Paul*, 216.
44. Ibid., 203.

The same observations may be made in respect of 2 Cor. 5:21: "For our sake he [God] made him to be sin who did not know sin, so that we might become the righteousness of God in him." Robert Daly considers the "made to be sin" yet another reference to the sin offering, the Hebrew *chatta'th*, while Dunn sees a more specific reference to the scapegoat of the Day of Atonement.[45] But such insistence on a primary reference in the cultus swallows up the very obvious context of anthropocosmic transformation; immediately before at 5:14 we have "one died for all; therefore, all have died," and at 5:17, "whoever is in Christ is a new creation." At 5:21 there is the possibility of an alternative interpretation, "of Christ's Adamic solidarity/identification with sinful humanity," but while this does seem indeed a more plausible reading, there is no reason why they need in fact to be alternatives.[46] If Paul makes use of the sacrificial as perhaps the most powerful image available for the cosmic reordering in justice brought by Christ, this does not mean that the former defines the latter. Rather, a God-originated and definitive redemption, even while expressed in sacrificial terms, must be seen to work against sacrificial logic. To whom is God offering this sacrifice, and what can make it definitive if in fact it leaves the sacrificial system in place? No, sacrificial terms must surely be read in the light of cosmic transformation, and therefore also of their ultimate obsolescence, even while they enable us to have some reasonable cultural grasp of the power of the processes at work. At the same time, if the mode of transformation is the Adamic solidarity of Christ, then it is the very suffering of the victim, engineered by the sacred but responded to with infinite nonviolence (without sin), that is the nuclear point at which the cosmos finds re-creation.

But what of wrath! Bluntly formulated by a traditional theology of atonement, "the reason why a propitiation is necessary is that sin arouses the wrath of God" and, therefore, the death of Christ is God's "initiative to avert his own anger."[47] In many ways this is a rationale with a scent of the overripe, but the presence in Paul of the term *wrath* ensures that the notion of violent exchange in the divine economy will always be detectable in the New Testament for those impelled to seek it out. There is, however, another possible account, one that plunges a theology of wrath into depths of the violent sacred. It can at once be stated in three main points.

45. Robert J. Daly, *Christian Sacrifice*, Studies in Christian Antiquity, ed. Johannes Quasten, vol. 18 (Washington, D.C.: Catholic University of America Press, 1978), 239 (hereafter *Christian Sacrifice*). *Theology of Paul*, 217.

46. Ibid., 222, n. 82.

47. John R. W. Stott, *The Cross of Christ* (Downers Grove, Ill.: InterVarsity Press, 1986), 173, 169.

First, Paul's usage is broadly impersonal; of the eleven references to wrath in Romans and three in 1 Thessalonians, only one has the direct expression of a subjective genitive: "the wrath of God from heaven" (*orge theou*, Rom. 1:18). For the rest, we are dealing with expressions like "wrath in a day of wrath" (Rom. 2:5), "the law works wrath" (Rom. 4:15), and "never avenge yourselves, beloved, but give place to [the] wrath" (Rom. 12:19).[48] The use of the definite article is repeated elsewhere and conditions one instance where God is seen as agent, "inflicting the wrath" (Rom. 3:5), suggesting some form of objective realization, not a personal emotion. Translations frequently insert the denominator *God's* in place of the article, seriously over-determining the sense. Second, the etymology of the Greek is revealing. According to Bullinger, it is "anger together with the desire for revenge . . . to kill, and all the tumults of passion which terminate in killing." Its Indo-European cousinship can be traced in the German *krieg*, the French *orgueil*, and the English *rage*.[49] Of course, any term may be redefined by its use in a context, including a theological context, but these family resemblances are too urgently suggestive of anthropology, of precisely all-too-human phenomena arising from mimetic desire and rivalry. In this case "wrath" may be seen simply as a "theology" of mimesis run riot, a situation where the sacred is no longer able to restrain violence and so is manifesting its other "divine" aspect, that of sacrificial crisis or unlimited violence. Paul's uneasy combination of a subjective attribute and a much greater frequency of something like an impersonal force would be once again the unraveling of traditional language from its sacrificial fabric through the revelation of the cross—in particular that of the basically human origin of the violence against the Crucified, and so perhaps of all eschatological violence.

Third, nowhere in the New Testament is the crucified Christ said to suffer God's wrath. Where Christ is mentioned in connection with wrath he is said to deliver believers "from the wrath to come" (1 Thess. 1:10; cf. Rom. 5:9). Of course, this could be twisted around in forensic fashion to suggest the death of Christ as some sort of proleptic substitution; but a much less forced reading results if it refers to a final crisis of historical violence. In this connection it is almost axiomatic that the biblical tradition reads historical events in terms of divine judgment, which also therefore gives some sense

---

48. These and following New Testament translations related to "wrath" are taken from literal translation in *Interlinear*.

49. Ethelbert W. Bullinger, *A Critical Lexicon and Concordance to the English and Greek New Testament* (London: Samuel Bagster and Sons Ltd., 1974), 905.

50. See particularly the "day of Yahweh" with its many references to an outpouring of wrath/vengeance in specific historical connections: e.g., Amos 5:18-20; Zeph. 1:1–2:3; Isa.

to a divine volition behind catastrophic human acts of violence.[50] Paul is unequivocally in this tradition and clearly connects wrath and judgment.[51] But the key point to bear in mind is precisely that this is a reading of historical events that are seen as ultimately fulfilling God's purpose. We are not dealing with an abstract, atemporal staging of God's judgment that simply for the sake of human recognition takes place in a temporal frame. Much the reverse: it is history itself that is at stake in the prophetic and apocalyptic frames; and the apocalyptic differs from the prophetic probably most in its achieved sense of foreshortened time bringing nearer the moment of reckoning. Violence itself, in all its treacherous turns, provides its own terrible nemesis, and will do so in the imminent future. A long way removed from this are feudal concepts of honor, right, and law, which have the effect of making God's judgment an intensely personal matter of generative violence while setting it on a stage superficially internal to history. Wrath, rather than a theological reading of human-originated catastrophe, becomes a disembodied divine attribute hanging over all humankind without regard to historical situation, cause, or crisis.

Many commentators certainly prefer to go with a reading of judgment as internal to history. Dunn in respect of Romans says: "God's wrath, we might say, is his handing over of his human creation to themselves. Hence the threefold repeated judgment, 'wherefore God handed them over'—'in the desires of their hearts' (1:24), 'to disgraceful passions' (1:26), 'to a disqualified mind' (1:28). Evidently for Paul this is the same divine wrath that will be manifest in the day of judgment: we know the character of God's final judgment from the moral constitution of the world he has created."[52] However, it is from the perspective of mimetic anthropology that the nature of such a "moral constitution" becomes intelligible. Rather than some kind of gratuitous, mechanical system of reciprocity, it is much more the specific results of human violence in the state of mimetic indeterminacy. It is the way human beings turn on each other and themselves in the absence of sacred order that constitutes the reality of apocalyptic

---

2:1–22, 13:1–22, 24:1–26, 34:1–17, 61:1–3, 63:1–6; Jer. 46:1–12; Joel 2:1–3:5; Obad. 10–21. A passage like Isa. 26:20–21 may be taken as representative of key motifs: the divine origin of wrath, the possibility of being protected from it, and yet its ultimate character as disclosure of violence. "Go my people . . . hide yourselves for a brief moment until the wrath is passed. See, the Lord goes forth from his place to punish the wickedness of the earth's inhabitants; the earth will reveal the blood upon her, and no longer conceal her slain."

51. Cf. Rom. 1:18, 2:5–8, 3:5.

52. *Theology of Paul*, 42–43. See also C. H. Dodd: wrath in Paul is used "not to describe the attitude of God to man, but to describe an inevitable process of cause and effect in a moral universe" (*The Epistle of Paul to the Romans* [London: Hodder & Stoughton, 1932], 23); and A. T. Hanson, *The Wrath of the Lamb* (London: SPCK, 1957), 21, 37.

judgment: very much a product of the terrifying freedom and open-end-
edness of human consciousness once disconnected from the restraints of
the sacred. In this light wrath is even more deeply rooted in the human
process, but it is an anthropologeme of such potency that in fact it can
only be adequately stated theologically or, at least, in a theological connection. The absence of sacred order may always be read as a negative
effect of the sacred itself, a punishment of the god, and this plays some
part in the meaning of Paul's statements. Yet, at the same time, the apocalyptic matrix of Paul's thought pushes beyond this, simultaneously
describing God's wrath as revealed from heaven and as an objective,
impersonal phenomenon of the end from which Christ saves us.[53] In this
latter frame the choice presented by the kerygma is essentially between the
old human praxis of violence, now in definitive crisis, and a new, liberating praxis made possible in Christ.[54] Luther's error then becomes clear; in
making wrath a conflictual quality within God he lacked biblical-anthro-
pological radicalism and so produced a theological grotesque.

The error is perpetuated in the view that Jesus could only forgive sin
during his life in view of his forthcoming death, because God's holiness
and wrath ineluctably demanded the latter. Jesus' "right to forgive . . .
rests finally on the divine service which he renders in his death. Without
this it would not be possible."[55] Thus the God of the temple cult does not
grant forgiveness in response to animal sacrifice, and yet does so at the
death of the Son of God. The New Testament then becomes a maximal
version of exchange, much "higher" or more terrible than the Old. Dunn
at one point appears to fall into these dark regions, elaborating a theory
of "sacrificial chiasmus" or "interchange" in respect of Paul, which seems

---

53. Robert Hamerton-Kelly interprets "the wrath of God revealed from heaven" with an
accent on the *revelation* rather than any subjective quality of God; this revelation of wrath
"is the divine non-resistance to human evil. It is God's unwillingness to intervene in the
process of action and consequence in the human world by which we set up and operate
the system of sacred violence, and so paradoxically a sign of love as the refusal to abridge
our freedom and a respect for our choices even when they are catastrophic. . . . The Cross
reveals this paradoxical wrath as God's acceptance of our free choice to destroy ourselves
and each other, inasmuch as it is the supreme instance of this human rage against the
good" (Robert Hamerton-Kelly, *Sacred Violence, Paul's Hermeneutic of the Cross*
[Minneapolis: Augsburg Fortress, 1992], 102).

54. "[T]he death of Christ is the proleptic division between this age of judgment and
death and the new age of life; it is an abyss that no one can escape and before which all
humankind comes to naught" (J. Christiaan Becker, *The Triumph of God*, 83). A thought
of apocalyptic abyss is very much the key image of atonement adopted in this study.

55. See Büchsel in *Theological Dictionary of the New Testament*, eds. G. Kittel and G.
Friedrich (English Translation, 10 vols.; Grand Rapids: Eerdmans, 1964–1976), *lutron*, in
vol. 4, 347.

little different. Despite the fact that "there is no clear rationale in scripture or in Second Temple Judaism concerning sacrifice," he believes "it may be possible . . . to correlate Paul's language with what we know of the sin offering ritual in particular, and thereby to deduce at least Paul's own theology of atonement." In the sin offering, Dunn argues, sin is transferred one way, bringing death to the sacrificial animal, and its purity and life are transferred in reverse; and so Jesus' death is supposedly interpreted by Paul. Dunn admits this is not itself an evident Old Testament rationale, and applying it to Paul is also a speculative exercise.[56] The scholarly caveats demonstrate a house that Jack built, in effect crystallizing an Old Testament theory of sacrifice by means of putative sacrificial patterns from the New, and then using the theory to corroborate the patterns!

Methodologically this cannot be a more valid process than using mimetic anthropological theory to illuminate Pauline teaching. It is therefore less than consistent for Dunn to dismiss Robert Hamerton-Kelly because he "reads Paul through spectacles provided by René Girard."[57] Undoubtedly one may find considerable difficulty in accepting the particular accent in Hamerton-Kelly's application to Paul of mimetic anthropology. Nevertheless, his overall approach hews closer to the grain of an apocalyptic crisis bringing the end of an old order, rather than a sacrificial reading that essentially reaffirms a traditional Temple order on a cosmic scale.[58] If there is any interchange going on it is abyssal, within humanity; in other words Christ's non-retaliatory forgiveness enters the furthermost depths of human violence, without reserve, and this is proclaimed in and by the cross and resurrection

---

56. *Theology of Paul*, 218–22.

57. Ibid., 213, n. 22.

58. In fact in his Girardian thesis, *Sacred Violence: Paul's Hermeneutic of the Cross*, Hamerton-Kelly makes very little of Pauline apocalyptic. Nevertheless his general hermeneutic seems inescapably to sound the note of rupture in the present age: "For Paul the primary saving effect of the Cross is as a disclosure of Sacred violence," hence he (Paul) is telling us that "chaos reigns in the sacred precinct" (78–79). The real problem is that Hamerton-Kelly makes almost all the weight of this disclosure fall on Jewish Law and Jewish religious existence. "[T]he structure of Judaism . . . is Paul's exemplary instance of religion as violence. . . . Paul indicts the whole world but singles out the Jews as an acute example of sacred violence" (102–3, and throughout, 68, 76, 147ff.). Thus Paul's apocalyptic challenge to the whole world is severely muted, and the impression is that Jewish religion is being unfairly targeted by mimetic theory. Paul's polemic against the Law is more nuanced than Hamerton-Kelly allows, and it is clearly more contextual; it belongs to the historical circumstances of a split between two movements of first-century Judaism. Failure to stress these contingent circumstances makes "exemplary instance" appear like yet another instance of scapegoating.

together. In response to the proclamation, human beings may find a new experience of peace in the very space where they are most cruel. Here the mimetic transition from violence to peace can in fact appear as an "interchange," but it is best described in terms of Borch-Jacobsen's primary openness to the other that permits a free flow of the sense of self, of one as the other: of violence and victimization on the part of humanity, and then the response of bottomless compassion on the part of Christ. Essentially there is no exchange because Christ's abyssal forgiveness is always excessive, always beyond whatever violence is offered. If the mechanism of exchange were introduced here, then a quotient of violence would be restored to Christ's role, and the essential problem would begin all over again. On the contrary, the abyss of forgiveness is without bottom.

This abyssal reading can then be the matrix for understanding other Pauline "exchange" passages so consistently misread by sacrificial models. For example:

> For our sake [God] made him to be sin who did not know sin,
> so that we might become the righteousness of God in him.
> (2 Cor. 5:21)

Within this schema the appeal is to deep and transformative human experience that cannot be reciprocated, rather than to negotiation within a sacrificial system that is hypostasized to the point of being independent of God, and so can always reinstitute exchange. Traditional exegesis has always tended to the latter because it always ends up making sacrifice interpret Jesus' death, rather than the other way round.[59] Ultimately it is an issue of unmasking violence: if we accept that there is a mystique of violence lurking in sacrifice, then we can leave sacrifice behind and see a transformative encounter with violence as the final nature of the cross. If, on the other hand, we retain sac-

---

59. See, for example, Daly, who also renders the "sin" at 2 Cor. 5:21 as "sin offering," and links it in a chain of interpretation with Rom. 8:3 and 3:24 . He concludes: "[N]ot only is Christ's redemptive activity, especially his death, seen as a sacrificial action, it is also seen under the aspect of two particular sacrifices: the passover and the sin offering. No contradiction or confusion is implied by this two-fold aspect; it merely illustrated the conviction of the Early Church that the OT, *especially its soteriological institutions*, was both fulfilled and superseded in the person of Jesus Christ. For the Passover and the sin offering were the two rites which the Jews of NT times associated most closely with redemption and forgiveness of sins" (Robert J. Daly, *Christian Sacrifice*, Studies in Christian Antiquity, ed. Johannes Quasten, vol. 18 [Washington, D.C.: Catholic University of America Press, 1978], 237–40, my italics).

rifice as an impenetrable surd of human behavior, then the cross will always be refashioned in its terms.[60]

JESUS AND HIS STORY

When we now turn to the canonical Gospels it is possible to move further in projecting an eschatological background to mimetic anthropology, or alternatively an anthropological background to eschatology. What follows, then, is a critical glance at essentially two texts that are crucial for a sacrificial interpretation of Christ's death. My discussion is always informed by the attempt to give an eschatological account to the overall Jesus story, and this will bring us back to the search for a historical reading of the Nazarene that can form a radical unity with the perspective of abyssal compassion. This is not purely for symmetry's sake. Abyssal transformation is an account of the person of Jesus in the existential experience of the cross; it does not refer to an objective transaction in relation to his body, as sacrifice always does. It is essentially and profoundly a matter of his response, and a reading that somehow made the cross to be something extrinsic to his life would always undermine this positive thesis.

The ransom saying from Mark 10:45 (par. Matt. 20:28) is a paradigm case for interpretation: "The Son of Man did not come to be served but to serve and to give his life as a ransom for many." Along with the eucharistic words of institution, it is one of "the two great sacrificial sayings of Jesus."[61] The circles of debate surrounding this logion are deep and wide, first in respect to the overall issue of Son of Man sayings and then, as indicated, in regard to this saying's primary importance for sacrificial theology. The Son of Man problem should briefly be described as it touches centrally on the larger question of the eschatological perspective running like

---

60. Space does not permit, but a similar interpretation to the one given of these texts could be made of other key New Testament letters and passages. For example, 1 Pet. 1:18–21, 2:21–25; or Hebrews, so manifestly a "sacrificial" letter. The apocalyptic dimension is always present—marked in 1 Peter, not absent in Hebrews (9:26); sacrificial metaphors can be read precisely as that; and the radical reading would always be abyssal human transformation. Hebrews may even be understood as well within the apocalyptic genre—in the sense of describing a sacrifice taking place on a heavenly plane. Generally Temple restoration, including by heavenly intervention, is a feature of Jewish apocalyptic (J. J. Collins, *The Apocalyptic Imagination* [Grand Rapids: Eerdmans, 1998], 70, 76, 215). As such the sacrificial imagery may be seen as an elaborate statement in cultic-apocalyptic language of an event that renders cult obsolescent—even as it seeks a profound eschatological tension in human behavior (ch. 11, 12).

61. C. F. D. Moule, *The Sacrifice of Christ* (Philadelphia: Fortress Press, 1964), 11, quoted by Daly, *Christian Sacrifice*, 217, n. 11. See Stott, *The Cross of Christ*: the saying "is foundational to the New Testament doctrine of redemption" (177).

a core seam through the Gospels. The positions taken in relation to its meaning on the lips of Jesus are manifold and at opposite extremes. At one end is the view that the appellation is simply indefinite, meaning only "someone." Further on the continuum is the claim that it has broad, generic meaning, "human beings as such."[62] Somewhere in the middle is the position that the saying is essentially a circumlocution for the self, a verbose or indirect way of saying "I."[63] Some would drastically reduce the number of authentic instances; John Dominic Crossan unconditionally accepts only Luke 9:57–58 (because it is independently attested in the Gospel of Thomas), and for the Jesus Seminar only this and Mark 2:27 were graded as authentic (the latter because it is aphoristic and radical). Mark 2:27, for the Jesus Seminar, and Luke 9:57–58, for Crossan, are regarded as generic in meaning; but the latter for the Jesus Seminar is circumlocutory.[64]

The minutiae of the arguments are only saved from tedium by the drama of what is at stake. This emerges as we shift to the other end of the spectrum. There is a titular sense to the phrase in the New Testament (*ho huios tou anthropou*, the Son of Man) that has the apocalyptic visions of Daniel 7 as their very likely background. In this late Old Testament writing, a figure "like the Son of Man" is seen coming on the clouds of heaven. He is presented before the throne of God and everlasting dominion and authority are conferred on him (Dan. 7:13–14). The meaning of this figure is also disputed, falling into three possibilities. It is seen as referring to one or more angels. It may be a symbol for Israel. It is possibly an individual representative of and for Israel.[65] The question is whether Jesus spoke of a future Son of Man, in a sense related to the Daniel figure, and if he did, whether in any way he identified himself with this figure.[66] Somewhere in between this titular sense and the circumlocutory are references in the Gospels to the suffering, death, and resurrection of the Son of Man, as a prediction by Jesus of his own passion. Taken together, the titular future sense and the references to suffering, death, and resurrection of the Son of Man constitute the axis about which a redemptive program of the Jesus of the Gospels turns. To reduce Jesus to

---

62. *The Five Gospels*, 76–77.

63. For example, G. Vermes, *Jesus and the World of Judaism* (Philadelphia: Fortress Press, 1983), 89–95.

64. John Dominic Crossan, *Jesus: A Revolutionary Biography* (San Francisco: HarperCollins, 1995), 50. *The Five Gospels*, 49, 316–17.

65. Witherington, *The Christology of Jesus*, 238.

66. G. Bornkamm believes that Jesus referred to a figure apart from himself (*Jesus of Nazareth* [New York: Harper & Row, 1960], 228ff.).

a Jewish Cynic or a subversive sage is to disembowel the program, making it essentially the apocalyptic fiction of the primitive church. However, an apocalyptic fiction, divorced from the praxis and intention of Jesus, would seem inherently likely to self-decay into a purely sacrificial and mythical version of his death where biographical features, particularly those that reveal internal suffering and weakness, would be minimized if not erased. It is very difficult to see how an apocalyptic imposed on the "true" story of Jesus would not have accented the imminence of revenge at the moment of his death, rather than the bottomless surrender and nonretaliation reported by the four Gospels. Presumably what stands in the way is the actual witness of the Crucified, and within that a personal eschatological integrity and hope. An eschatology rooted in the mind and attitude of Jesus would likely be self-consistent and self-sustaining in this way. Furthermore, from the point of view of mimetic anthropology it is redundant to invent an apocalyptic Jesus, once the opportunity to "translate" him sacrificially had arrived. Looked at in this manner, the relatively minimal traces of sacrificial thought in the New Testament become simultaneous evidence of the transformative power of Jesus' death and of the overwhelming memory of Jesus' personal apocalyptic viewpoint, now vindicated.

Such a concept of Jesus allows us to open up a version of redemption that is abyssal, founded in the depth of the redeemer as subjectivity, *un fondo senza fondo*. The frame of our study then is intrinsically more sympathetic to the scholarship of someone like Witherington. He concludes that it is the Danielic figure that is the principal meaning of the Gospels sayings and within them of the self-understanding of Jesus: "The proper matrix in which to interpret the Son of Man material, that which provides the clue as to how Jesus himself viewed the material, is Dan. 7:13–14 and probably also the *Similtudes of Enoch*."[67]

We can now turn again to Mark 10:45, the doyen of sacrificial sayings. The Greek word used here meaning ransom (*lutron*) is itself the subject of considerable debate, in terms of both New and Old Testament backgrounds and how one or both inform the logion. Bultmann argued that

---

67. *The Christology of Jesus*, 261. In this viewpoint Witherington follows people like J. H. Charlesworth, *Jesus within Judaism: New Light from Exciting Archaeological Discoveries* (New York: Doubleday, 1983–1985); C. F. D. Moule, *The Origins of Christology* (Cambridge: Cambridge University Press, 1977), 15–16; and F. F. Bruce: "Jesus' special use of the expression . . . was derived from the 'one like a son of man' who is divinely invested with authority in Daniel 7:13f. Because it was not a current title, it was not liable to be misunderstood, as current titles were, and Jesus was free to take up the expression and give it what meaning he chose" (from "The Background to the Son of Man Sayings" in *Christ the Lord: Studies in Christology Presented to D. Guthrie* [London: InterVarsity Press, 1982], 70). For *Similtudes of Enoch* see Witherington, *The Christology of Jesus*, 234–48.

the Lukan parallel that omits the "ransom" reference is the more primitive form, and the Markan-Matthean version shows the influence of a Hellenistic-Christian doctrine of redemption.[68] Witherington points out that Bultmann and others who are normally in favor of Markan priority choose to make an exception here. He also demonstrates that the whole of Mark 10:45 may be translated back into Aramaic, and argues that the suggestion of Pauline influence (cf. 1 Tim. 2:6) is weak and should probably be read the other way around: an original Semitic concept being given a Greek form.[69] Perhaps most important, he indicates that the whole saying makes perfect sense as a Son of Man statement in which Jesus recasts the concept away from popular triumphant Messianism toward servant-hood.[70] This indeed is the sort of understanding of a creative yet deeply responsive role of Jesus in respect to the biblical tradition that Wright forcefully takes up.

The Lukan version, highlighting an anthropology of service and avoiding possibly the cultic implications of "ransom," could then be seen as giving an essentially correct reading of the primitive Jesus tradition. Luke places the logion with its context (a battle for prestige among the disciples) in a very different position from Mark. Where Mark locates it on the journey to Jerusalem, Luke sites it directly after the institution of the Eucharist. Thus the eucharistic institution is interpreted in terms of abyssal service rather than cultic sacrifice, and precisely over against an anthropology modeled in the image of kings, lords, great ones, and mimetic desire in relation to their power (Luke 22:25, par. Mark 10:42). However, as we saw above, it is precisely the eucharistic institution that is regarded as the other key sacrificial text of the Gospels. Reflecting on the Matthean version of the institution and its words of "blood shed for many" (26:28), Daly concludes: "This phrase . . . and its variants clearly characterizes Jesus' death as a bloody sacrificial death."[71] Daly, as many others, also links the institution formulae with the theme of the Suffering Servant, associated with the so-called Servant Songs in Second Isaiah, particularly the fourth, 52:13–53:12.[72]

---

68. Rudolf Bultmann, *The History of the Synoptic Tradition*, trans. J. Marsh (Oxford: B. Blackwell, 1963), 154; and *Jesus and the Word* (New York: Scribner's, 1958 [1926]), 196.

69. *The Christology of Jesus*, 252–53.

70. Ibid. And more dramatically, "The passion of the Son of Man was announced by Jesus himself" (Pesch, "Die Passion des Menschensohnes: Eine Studie zu den Menschensohnworten der vormarkinischen Passiongeschichte," in *Jesus und der Menschensohn* [Freiburg: Herder, 1975], 195, quoted by Witherington, op. cit., 256).

71. *Christian Sacrifice*, 221.

72. Ibid., 222.

The textual connections between the eucharistic narratives and the LXX of Isaiah 53 are the participles *peri* (in Matthew) and *hyper* (the other Synoptics and 1 Corinthians), meaning "for," and governing either "you" or "many" (*pollon*). The participles are heard as an echo of the Isaian *peri* at 53:4, 10; while the term *polloi* occurs in Isaiah 53 no less than five times. Because this text is widely assumed to have sacrificial connotations, the Eucharist is then conceptualized sacrificially through this lens.[73] However, in regard to the sources for a sacrificial interpretation available to the first Christians, it is Daly who comments tellingly: "The Jewish tradition, even when developing the idea of a vicarious atoning death, hardly ever mentions Isa. 53. Even the pre-Christian Jewish tradition is silent on this point; the glorious aspects of Isa. 53 are developed in the Jewish writings, but the suffering aspects are ignored."[74] It could hardly be clearer that whatever meaning Isaiah 53 had for the Gospels, it arose out of the matrix of the Jesus event and Christian experience, not from the background in Judaism. Is it not circular, therefore, to describe this text as sacrificial in its New Testament usage on the grounds of its original sacrificial meaning? In fact is it not necessary first to assume a sacrificial meaning of the New Testament passages where it is employed, and then to extrapolate a sacrificial content back to the Isaianic prophecy?[75]

The same logic is applied to Mark 10:45 too.[76] But others argue strongly that this verse should not be linked with Isaiah 53, certainly not in isolation from the whole Deutero-Isaiah meditation on redemption. Witherington, for example, contends that it more evidently parallels

---

73. The New Testament Scriptures make extensive use of Isa. 52–53. Major New Testament contributors like Paul, Peter, Matthew, Luke, and John allude to at least eight of the chapter's twelve verses. But perhaps the key verse suggesting divine punishment, 6b, is very noticeable by its absence in the New Testament: "But the Lord laid upon him the guilt of us all."

74. *Christian Sacrifice*, 123–24.

75. But see Wright, *Victory*, where he argues the following in respect of Isa. 53:10, "When you make his life an offering for sin he shall see his offspring, and shall prolong his days," which contains the Hebrew word *asam*, translated in the LXX with the regular phrase for "sin offering," *peri hamartias*. He says that "by the first century . . . the Levitical, i.e. sacrificial, meaning [of this word] would have been the first, and probably the only, meaning to be 'heard' " (605, n. 227). However, this must also be read in the context of Wright's broader dynamic; cf. n. 77 below. Whatever sacrificial connotations the passage had, they still belonged within a much deeper and wider set of references, beyond the institutional cult. Once again the sacrificial metaphor cannot be allowed to subsume the eschatological event: in the New Testament it works the other way round.

76. For example, *Christian Sacrifice*, 217.

Isaiah 43:3–4; the Hebrew text contains the word *kofer,* which exegetes believe stands behind the ransom phrase, while the Hebrew of Isaiah 53 does not. Linked to this is the argument that the verses at 43:3–4 were not used in the development of primitive Christian theology, unlike Isaiah 53, thus corroborating the claim that Mark 10:45 originates at the primary level of the tradition.[77]

The substantive *kofer* is part of the constellation of Hebrew words represented by *lutron,* and these carry a further set of implications. There are three Hebrew Bible terms that the Greek word is used to translate: *kofer, ga' al,* and *pidyon.* Without going into unnecessary detail we can point out that taken together the terms apply at least as much to civil as to sacral law. In respect of the key term *kofer,* five out of the six instances where it is the original of *lutron* refer to compensation between humans, always for a human life; the implication is that the offended parties may demand the life of the offender (see, for example, Exod. 21:30, where an ox has gored and killed a kinsperson). The *kofer* is a monetary sum in lieu of the demanded life. Against this background it is certainly possible to conclude that what is at stake is the mimetic structures of human anger. Similarly, the second word (*ga' al*) is fully dependent on the institution of the *go'el,* the avenger of blood; this person, normally the closest family relative, has the duty of vindicating or restoring, either by violence, purchase, or marriage, the alienated life, property, or possible offspring of a relative. It is precisely this name and role that is applied to the Hebrew God, in relation to Israel, ten times in Isaiah 41–60; clearly, therefore, it should be used to contextualize any use of *kofer* in Deutero-Isaiah.[78] Within this anthropotheological

---

77. Isa. 43:3–4: "For I am the LORD, your God. . . . I give Egypt as your ransom, Ethiopia and Seba in return for you. . . . I give men in return for you and peoples in exchange for your life." For the connection with Mark 10:45 see Witherington, *The Christology of Jesus,* 254; he also cites P. Stuhlmacher: "The connection between Isa. 43:3f. and Mark 10:45 is fundamental" ("Existenzstellvertretung für die Vielen: Mark 10.45 [Mt. 20.28]," in *Werden und Wirken des AT. Claus Westermann Festschrift* [Göttingen: Vandenhoeck und Ruprecht, 1980], n. 322). For *kofer* behind Mark 10:45 see Daly, 217; also Procksch, *Theological Dictionary of the New Testament,* eds. G. Kittel and G. Friedrich, vol. 4. 330. See also, Hengel: "[T]he *lutron anti* corresponds with the Hebrew *kofer tahat,* which probably goes back to Isaiah 43:3" (*The Atonement,* 50). Wright insists that "the picture of the 'servant,' whether in Isaiah 52:13–53:12 or in the other so-called 'servant songs,' was only in very modern times abstracted from the message of Isaiah 40–55 as a whole. If we are to stand any chance of understanding how a first-century Jew might have made sense of these passages, one of our first moves must be to read the surrounding contexts. And there we find, not a detached atonement-theology, but the prophecy . . . that YHWH would comfort and restore his people after their exile, would pour out his wrath upon the pagans who held them captive, and would return in person to Zion to reign as king" (*Victory,* 588).

78. For this and the following background on *lutron,* see Procksch, op. cit., 329–31.

frame, the sense of *kofer/lutron* becomes a statement of divine solidarity working a redemption from the consequences of human violence and death rather than of a divine anger from which God also strangely redeems.

It is, therefore, difficult to understand when Daly states in regard to *lutron* in the LXX, "the cultic predominates and sets the tone."[79] The evidence for this would be the cognate verb *kipper*, which means "to atone" and is used overwhelmingly in the priestly legislation of Leviticus and only once in Deutero-Isaiah, at 47:11. Obviously we are also dealing with a verb here, not the substantive in question; moreover, it is translated in the LXX by *exilaskomai*, and this word does not appear in Isaiah at all. So it would be very hard to see how the cultic sense could be textually related to Isaiah 53 or any other chapter in the Isaianic tradition.

Finally, it is true that the third word, *pidyon*, has a sacral meaning, often referring to an animal or human life that has fallen forfeit to God and which therefore must be redeemed (e.g., Exod. 13:13, 15). However, in Deuteronomy it is God who is regularly called the redeemer of Israel from the house of bondage in Egypt. Here God acts sovereignly, in complete freedom from exchange: "God does not pay a ransom, He acts in his own power." This also coheres with the theology of the redemption in Deutero-Isaiah. "In both cases there is liberation from bondage, and in neither is there a ransom, since Yahweh, as God of the world (cf. Deut. 4: 32ff.), owns both Israel and the nations. Thus the terms *ga'al* and *padah* approximate closely in post-exilic theology, which is very largely controlled by Deutero-Isaiah and Deuteronomy."[80] We should conclude from this that the word *lutron* as used in Mark 10:45 pushes us toward an understanding of Jesus in which he sees himself as an agent of God's transcendent redemption in the face of the structures of

---

79. *Christian Sacrifice*, 217.

80. Procksch, op. cit., 333. See also: "[T]here is a clear distinction between 'atonement' and 'redemption.' Atonement is a sacral act in which sacrifice is the means of expiation. Almost always, except in a few secondary instances, it is accomplished by blood sacrifice. But the cultic element does not belong originally to the idea of redemption" (ibid., 332). The question ultimately is whether the New Testament reverts to the cultic or is somehow a progression of the redemptive. In this connection we should note the so-called martyr theology that is also claimed for a role in New Testament thought about the death of Christ. (See, for example, *Victory*, 582, 605.) It is given its most forceful expression at 4 Maccabees 6:26–29 where one of the martyrs, Eleazar, prays: "Be merciful unto thy people, and let our punishment be a satisfaction in their behalf (arkestheis te hemetera huper auton dike). Make my blood their purification, and take my soul to ransom (*antipsuchon*) their souls" (R. H. Charles, *The Apocrypha and Pseudepigrapha of the Old Testament in English*, 2 vols. [Oxford: Clarendon, 1973], II, 674; Greek in A. Rahlfs, *Septuaginta*, 2 vols. [Stuttgart: Privilegierte wurttembergische Bibelanstalt, 1935], I, 1166). As Daly suggests, this has a ring of penal substitution about it (op. cit., 127). The ransom saying is astringent and allusive by comparison, hence its openness to a radical interpretation.

human violence, rather than presenting him as a passive self-offering in a cultic scheme hypostasized before God. The latter of, course, would most easily be understood as early church theology, working out of a sacrificial reading of Isaiah 53. But we have seen the difficulties with this. The former appears the more valid as both the attitude of Jesus himself and the original matrix of New Testament atonement theology. It attributes to Jesus a profoundly creative role, charting the dynamic yet inchoate meaning of his life and destiny in conversation with biblical tradition and through intimate dialogue with its God.

This is very much the territory of Jesus study presented in different modes by the New Testament scholars I have accented, particularly Witherington and N. T. Wright. It is impossible to do justice to the many aspects of their work in the space allowed here, to the many questions and problems to be dealt with, to the agreement and areas of divergence between these two and other scholars of the stripe.[81] However, my purpose has always been simply to suggest, both negatively and positively, the possibility of New Testament criticism that converges with the overall thesis of this book. An anthropological theory of generative violence linked to an understanding of the New Testament as culturally subversive and therefore provocative of crisis, all this demands a thoroughgoing apocalyptic criticism.[82] Then at a level of greater coherence still, the concepts of mimetic anthropology I have developed have provided, pari passu, the language for a nonsacrificial hermeneutic of abyssal redemption. The excursus has been in the way of a sketch whose overall pattern is in harmony with a wider stream of thought, although ultimately the latter depends, I believe, on the proclamation of the historical person of Christ essentially in the pattern I have presented. Historical criticism has served here to endorse that

---

81. In this category we could also include the work of Raymund Schwager, especially his recent *Jesus in the Drama of Salvation: Toward a Biblical Doctrine of Redemption*, trans. James G. Williams and Paul Haddon (New York: Crossroad Publishing, 1999). But there is sufficient difference of method—specifically his "dramatic" reading of Christ's career followed by a turn toward systematic theology—that warrants seeing Schwager in a somewhat different perspective. Accordingly we shall refer to this work in the concluding chapter.

82. See René Girard, *Things Hidden since the Foundation of the World*: "The confidence that all sacrificial religions show in the *ultimately positive* nature of violence rests inevitably upon the founding mechanism that has not yet really been revealed. This positive aspect of violence is absent from the Gospels. If the threat continues to be truly frightening, this is because it brings with it no remedy: it offers no recourse of any sort; it has ceased to be 'divine.' With the founding mechanism absent, the principle of violence that rules humanity will experience a terrifying recrudescence at the point when it enters its agony" (195, italics original).This is an apocalyptic picture providing a powerful re-reading of New Testament apocalyptic.

pattern of abyssal redemption. I want now to draw the sketch to a close by returning once more to the second key sacrificial text, the account of the eucharistic institution. Examining this in the light of Wright's over-arching account of the figure of Jesus can help us draw together a final picture of what this extraordinary man might have intended by his death and how it may be viewed in deep tones of nonviolence.

Jesus consistently told a story in his words and actions, and that story can be grasped as the story of Israel that was at the same time his own story. By means of it we come to see that he claims to represent Israel and acts in the belief that Israel's destiny was somehow reaching its climax in his own person.[83] The absolutely vital part of the Israel story was that given in Isaiah 40–55, telling of YHWH's return to redeem his people, implying a new exodus and an end to exile in a real sense, and necessarily involving the defeat of the forces of evil that occupied the land.[84] Two powerful symbols at the end of Jesus' ministry crystallized this praxis-story: the action in the Temple and the Passover meal.[85] These two symbols can be seen to interpret each other, and together make a prophetic bid actually to produce the reality envisioned.

Following Jacob Neusner and Bruce Chilton, Wright argues that "taken together [these two events] indicated that Jesus was in effect intending to replace the Temple, as the symbolic focus of Judaism, with his own newly instituted quasi-cultic meal." But unlike Neusner and Chilton, Wright does not consider the meal to be purely self-referential. Instead, "the symbols ordering Israel's life and hope were redrawn, focusing now upon Jesus himself."[86] Jesus' action in the Temple was both a kingly, messianic act and a judgment upon the Temple itself. As a focus of militant nationalism,

---

83. Wright follows a methodology of "praxis, story, and symbol," meaning that a coherent narrative of an historical figure can be made up by attention to characteristic words and actions that together tell a story and generate symbols (*Victory*, 139–43). For Jesus' story telling and actions as recapitulation of Israel's story, ibid., 130–31, 470, 517, 592–93. I focus on Wright's work partly because of the verve and yet scholarly rigor with which he carries it out. Like Schweitzer, with whom he frequently aligns himself (though with significant differences), he sounds a trumpet blast fully consonant with the world-shattering notes of first-century apocalypticism. But while Schweitzer's blast seemed to make Jesus somehow alien to the early twentieth century, Wright's has a resonance fitting the crisis of the early twenty-first. Wright's influences also include E. P. Sanders, M. Borg, R. A. Horsley, M. Hengel, C. K. Barrett.

84. Ibid., 470, 576–77.

85. Of course the version at John 2:13 places the Temple incident at the beginning of Jesus' ministry, but as Witherington observes, "most scholars are convinced that the Johannine placement of the story is likely to be secondary" (*The Christology of Jesus*, 110).

86. *Victory*, 558. Jacob Neusner, "Money-Changers in the Temple: The Mishnah's Explanation," *New Testament Studies* 35:287–90, 1989. Bruce D. Chilton, *The Temple of Jesus: His Sacrificial Program Within a Cultural History of Sacrifice* (University Park, Pa.: Pennsylvania State University Press, 1992).

albeit in a suppressed form, this institution of Israel, or rather the forces in and around it, would bring ultimate destruction down upon the nation.[87] In its place Jesus would offer a new construction of the central rite of the Jewish people, the Passover, together with its governing story, the Exodus. This construction took the old symbols and recast them around his own anticipated death. But perhaps because the looked-for result was not simply another religious ritual (and a religion with it), but a new human reality, YHWH's Kingdom, Wright is careful to specify that the Eucharist is a "quasi-cultic meal." In other words, the eschatological reality it looks toward comes close to overwhelming the cultic aspects, while still allowing them enough purchase to act as metaphors for this radically new event. In respect of the debate on the timing of the Eucharist meal, and the scholarly probability of the Johannine version that places it on the day before the feast, he comments:

> If [Jesus] believed that the kingdom was about to dawn, in other words that YHWH was about to inaugurate the new covenant, the end of exile, the forgiveness of sins, it becomes very likely that he would distinguish this meal from the ordinary Passover meal, while retaining enough of its form for the symbolism to be effective. If he believed that the kingdom was not merely a future event, waiting around some corner yet to be negotiated, but was actually bursting in upon the present moment, it would make sense to anticipate Passover night, celebrating a strange new Passover that would carry a kingdom-in-the-present meaning.[88]

Referring to Matthew's phrase on the blood of Jesus shed "for the forgiveness of sins," he pursues the same concrete, apocalyptic meaning. "Matthew is not suggesting that Jesus' death will accomplish an abstract atonement, but that it will be the means of rescuing YHWH's people from their exilic plight. These words make explicit the symbolic meaning of the meal."[89] But then how would Jesus' death rescue the people? The historical reconstruction of Jesus' central scriptural canon, uniquely formative for his personally chosen destiny, helps provide an answer. Jesus applied a creative exegesis of four main scriptural areas to his own life and coming death: Daniel, particularly chapter 7; Zechariah; the Psalter; and Isaiah 40–55, with 52:13–53:12 the focal point. This complex of readings is con-

---

87. Ibid. 413–28, 490–93.
88. Ibid., 557.
89. Ibid., 561.

strued as the matrix of his thought and together they contained the promise that ultimately the servant of God would be vindicated, including
beyond the experience of death. But there is no dogmatic formula. As
Wright puts it succinctly: "Why did Jesus die? Ultimately, because he
believed it was his vocation."[90] Even the crucial text, Isaiah 53, provided no
necessary reason. "[T]he allusions to Isaiah 53 should not be regarded as
the *basis* of a theory about Jesus' self-understanding in relation to his
death; they may be, rather, the tell-tale signs of a vocation he could hardly put into words. . . ."[91] Against this backdrop the Passover meal that
became the Eucharist is a profoundly daring manipulation of symbols,
pointing forward and back always to an immeasurable act of surrender by
which Jesus assumes the role of the victim in order to make it speak transformatively from its depth, but in a language of which he was yet unsure.

It is difficult to exaggerate the value of this approach for a view of
Christian redemption that is contingent, abyssal, open to failure, even as it
is proclaimed as gospel, vindication, and resurrection. Only such a Jesus
could be existentially shared as the source of forgiveness, which as we have
argued in regard to Pauline churches, must have been the character and
method of primitive Christian kerygma. Furthermore, it fits fully with a
tradition of Jesus teaching nonviolence and compassion toward the
enemy: the implicit risk in loving someone who may kill you is carried
through into a redemption that undergoes precisely that fate. If this were
not so, the climactic act of Jesus' life would have demanded less surrender
and faith than the ordinary behavior he required of his followers. Jesus'
personal final battle with evil was a battle totally consistent with the
Sermon on the Mount. As every other would-be messiah, he confronted
the might of Rome, the pagan blasphemers in the land regarded by the
Essenes as sons of darkness, but he did so by a pathway that confronted
the darkness itself. Hence Gethsemane, prior to the cross, and the remarkable witness of the New Testament to this event. The scene is of Jesus precipitated in a bottomless moment of weakness, fear, and sense of impossibility for all that was asked of him, and it is simply incredible as Christian
invention. "It is entirely comprehensible as biography"; in other words,
essentially historical.[92] Similarly, on the cross itself all violent martyr heroism, any verbal resistance to the tyrant bolstered by threats of divine
revenge, is plunged in a witness of nonretaliation and yielding of spirit

---

90. Ibid., 593, and 597–98 for the core Scriptures he appropriated.
91. Ibid., 604, italics in original.
92. Ibid., 606

carried to term in the final breath of death. Is this not the concrete praxis of Jesus in the human abyss that lies at the heart of the whole subsequent message of forgiveness of sins? What else could provide the basis for this proclamation, and the substantive early Christian practice, over three centuries, of nonresistance to violence, but the vast existential echo of this witness? Here is the singular and abyssal point from which the New Testament arises. It is an irreducible moment of salvation that is the necessary condition for this Scripture, and the basis for the entire argument of this book.

Chapter Six

JESUS, TIME AND AGAIN

The cross has always been proclaimed as sheer invitation, unconditional commitment, the "weakness" of compassion: and yet indissociably, at the very same moment, a formidable mimetic power of identification and transformation. As Peter Lombard, a twelfth-century theologian, wrote:

> So great a pledge of love having been given us we too are moved and kindled to love God who did such great things for us; and by this we are justified, that is, being loosened from our sins we are made just. The death of Christ therefore justifies us, inasmuch as through it charity is excited in our hearts.[1]

Throughout this book we have been in the orbit of this "charity . . . excited." I have put forward the idea of abyssal compassion in an attempt to explain the dynamic of this extraordinary internal movement. There is the abyss and the double-sided movement; on the one hand the compassion of the Crucified is a self-handing-over in favor of the abject, the condemned, the alienated; simultaneously, in the primitive mutuality of that moment, there is the possibility of alteration, in the spirit of the Crucified, on the part of the one who is met in suffering, including also the violent perpetrator who always "risks" mimetic identification with the forgiving victim. Then there are stories that recount, repeat, revisit this scene, the kind of stories that were told in the fourth chapter. Nowhere is there a guarantee. The moment of compassion and alteration can never be predicted, systematized, rendered anything but contingent: it may or may not happen. . . . This is the very passion in the story of the Passion, where its power and weakness are inextricably linked, where it is weakness that is power, that calls to us so powerfully in weakness. I have tried in this book

---

1. Peter the Lombard, *Sententiae* iii. Dist. xix.1, quoted by Hastings Rashdall, *The Idea of Atonement in Christian Theology* (London: Macmillan & Co., 1920), 371.

to be faithful to this paradox, this paradox of the Passion, of gospel passion in itself. It evokes "fear and trembling" because in it appears the immense drama of human existence, not simply in a paradigmatic form of human emotions provoked to the very limits of life and death—although it is very much that—but also in terms of the present moment, this moment of time, with a planet more and more densely occupied by human structures where violence rises to the surface, yearning fearfully for resolution.

If the Girardian hypothesis explains truthfully a biblical truth—that human culture is born out of original violence, that humanity has a cultural genetics in and through violence—then the world stands at a point of unconditional crisis. All restraining mechanisms are loosening their grip; the containing forces of traditional religion and the sacred are progressively abolished. There are no limits, no boundaries. This is true in terms of the ideology of liberal democracy, in respect of sexual, familial, and social identities and behaviors. But it is in fact most profoundly and systematically true in the relentless global procession of objects of desire; in the media, in information technology, in the superstores of the rich. This is where the crisis most properly manifests itself. The huge discrepancy between the rich and the poor, both on national and international levels, in one way belies the vaunted absence of boundaries, and does so in the most brutal form. And yet at the same time the omnipresence of telecommunication daily taunts every member of the species with an immediate sensation of things to be desired, things that are in fact possible only for the privileged few. The world begins to spin uncontrollably on a carousel of desire. And its spinning faster and faster becomes a vortex in which those thrown to the bottom for whatever reason must inevitably retort through violence, seeking to reverse their destiny. One can imagine scenarios in which such violence is harnessed by reactionary movements, seeking to control the vortex, to slow it, to give it a superficial sense of rhythm, order, and right. This is a solution that can arise itself out of disaster (economic, ecological, or cumulative right-wing frustration), and in turn create catastrophe on a scale that would dwarf all previous exercises in scapegoating and the making of victims. But such a response would never itself be able to dispense with hyper-market organization, i.e., a global economy based on intensified commodity exchange. Once human history has produced the planetary home as a supermarket of desire, and the supermarket as planetary home to billions, it is very difficult to see it leaving it by means of a rationally willed, disciplinary political program.

Am I wrong? What is the point of raising such impressionistic visions, particularly as they may seem tangential to the main content and method of the book? For voices like this we have to turn to the prophetic and the apocalyptic traditions of the Bible; but then immediately do we not have to recognize that the message of the cross belongs inherently in this prophetic and apocalyptic context? And especially if we pursue its meaning in terms of mimesis and violence, we see how the cross of itself demonstrates, displays, discloses the abyss in human affairs. So I do want to argue that the meaning of the cross as abyssal compassion takes its place redemptively in the contemporary vortex of human desire. The vortex itself points up the abyssal meaning of the cross and, at the same time, and always before, the cross reflects back the condition of the abyss that we are in and offers a redemption in and through this place. It is the purpose of the present chapter to take a further step in this trajectory. It intends to examine how the abyssal compassion of the Crucified acts to transform out of recognition the meaning of lived human time, to open a way forward unimaginable in terms of the constitution of present time, and so perhaps to show a way through the point of crisis to which we are now so relentlessly pushed. As the chapter unfolds it will engage in a conversation between the gospel message and some perspectives engaged in deconstructive philosophy. These have a startling, if adversarial, closeness to the understanding I am proposing, and therefore constitute a primary point of dialogue for its development in the contemporary context. There is a remarkable family likeness between an impossible "ethics" of deconstruction and the abyssal transformation hazarded by the cross. The question then arises, what comes first, the cross or philosophical ethics? And the question can be asked both historically and ontologically. Even as we pursue the discussion we will see how the notion of abyssal compassion and its transformation of time becomes itself ever more urgent and compelling.

THE CROSS THAT BREAKS THE SYSTEM

I have shown that the disclosure of a logic of violence (of the ability in fact for violent mimesis to produce a cognate metaphysics) has rendered prevailing Western accounts of the meaning of Christ's death untenable. The critique permits the so-called "moral influence" theory to come to the fore with new, contemporary urgency. The anthropology of an alternative effect of mimesis, via abyssal compassion, completes the rehabilitation of the Cinderella of atonement doctrines. We are left also with a radicalization of theology, an approach that discovers theology's vocation more and more on the level of the anthropological, understanding itself from that perspective rather than one of eternal or necessary ideas. Such an approach conforms to a "profound this-worldliness" of Christianity, and seeks to realize this intuition as its most proper principle of self-understanding.[2] Beginning from the cross, a theology of this character will take as its watchword the radical human contingency in the event of the cross; only the completely contingent inner movement of Christ can open the possibility of mimetic alteration, and so warrant a truly human character to redemption. Only a free, unfounded act of compassion may evoke a genuine human transformation, and therewith a transformation in the meaning of time itself. Once it is locked into an overarching necessity, we are back in the realm of sacred order, of violent necessity, and of the inevitability of sacrificial crisis when violent desire one more time seeks the same time as before, the time of the same, the time of violence. Articulating a language consistent with this contingency and its transformed time is the task of the emerging doctrine of atonement approached here.

The problematic disclosed by the cross is human violence. Anything that subsumes this violence into God obscures and negates this disclosure. Is it not, therefore, a matter precisely of a break with a dogmatic tradition that lifts up violence into God as it seeks conceptual integration for a God of vertical transcendence, of visible formal power? This is a tradition exemplified by Augustine, whose dialectic drives him into the unconditioned violence of predestination. The violence also infects Luther, and to a greater degree of spiritual crisis; and then continuing on through the Protestant tradition, up to and including the dialectical theology of Barth's *Church Dogmatics*.[3] A recent, Roman Catholic type of systematic theology has integrated the Barthian doctrine of election in Christ, but at the same time sought to overcome the notion of an eternal judgment of sin enacted in Christ. It wants to understand God's anger more concretely by reading human history as drama, where God is seen as reactive to human sin, rather than eternally characterized by violent judgment. Raymund Schwager works in this direction. He traces *Theodramatik* or God-drama through Christ's personal attitude, arguing that Christ's unconditional response of love "infiltrated sin-entrapped creaturely freedom," bringing with it "the well-founded hope . . . that not one will be lost." He pays close attention to the narrative of the New Testament, reading there the concrete history of Jesus' engagement with "the laws of this world," which

---

2. See Introduction, n. 21.

3. The concept of predestination is preserved "positively" as the eternal negative judgment of God against sin inflicted on his Son, the "the judge judged in our place." Karl Barth, *Church Dogmatics* (Edinburgh: T. & T. Clark, 1936–1977), 2/2, 161–67; and 4/1, 211f.

inevitably bring about his rejection and crucifixion.[4] But in the end Schwager, and *Theodramatik* in general, still seek a theological solution involving the cultural residue of a God characterized by violence. By reading the New Testament simultaneously as human drama and as response in the eternal mind of God, they inevitably tell a story of anthropological violence lifted up into the figure of the absolute Good. And then, necessarily, we are back with Luther's *opus proprium* and *opus alienum* in the formal theology of God. Does not a Girardian reading of drama tell us that the movement of the plot is itself sacrificial, depending on some final expulsion by which the whole violent structure, and structure of violence itself, continues to stand? The methodological victory is therefore hollow, and behind the cross, always ready to reinfect the whole, remains the shadowy structure of sacred violence.

If the intention is to break with divine violence, why not start with the cross rather than seek to end with it? This is the approach taken here; that in the concrete figure of the Crucified we are dealing only with human violence, and with an abyssal response of love that once and for all transfigures the notion of the divine. The problem is not a problem of dogmatics per se, for the greatest dogmatic definitions are full of paradox, of mutually exclusive propositions held together virtually by their own inner tension, and finally sustained only by the proclamation. The real problem is the attempt at full conceptual coherence attempted by the tradition around the dogmatic legacy, in a word by classical metaphysical theology. While such a coherence is attempted, above all in a doctrine of redemption, the anthropological legacy of the cross takes effect only by default, by its own internal dynamism. The issue here is surely never so much "God" as human beings. Should not the final purpose of redemption theology be that the alteration of compassion become infectious, much more than that the logic of the godhead be infallibly constituted, particularly if it be a logic internally in conflict, and ultimately one of conflict? Again, has not the religion of Christianity proceeded by breaks as much as by continuity? Perhaps Christianity by its own central motif, the cross, always seeks to escape from the density of any sacred order residual within it. Is not, therefore, the possibility of another radical break signaled by mimetic anthropology—the break of divine compassion with the human order of violence, including also the density of a systematic concept of God?

4. Raymund Schwager, *Jesus in the Drama of Salvation*, trans. James G. Williams and Paul Haddon (New York: Crossroad Publishing Company, 1999), 9, 111, 200–1. See Hans Urs von Balthasar, *Theo-Drama*, 4 vols. (San Francisco: Ignatius, 1988–1994).

Inevitably the question this kind of systematic theology is dealing with is the problem of evil, the perennial issue voiced by Ivan in his central dialogue with Alyosha. If God could not have made this universe without suffering, including so much of it generated by human beings, then he shouldn't have done so at all. This is a potent question, and Ivan was neither the first nor the last to hand in his ticket of participation in creation out of scandal at the wounding of a single child. However, the Augustinian-style solution, that human suffering, including that of children, is just punishment or correction by God in response to sin, is itself undermined by the teaching and praxis of the Gospel Christ. "Love your enemies . . . so that you may be children of your Father in heaven; for he makes his sun rise on the evil and on the good, and sends rain on the righteous and on the unrighteous."[5] Jesus cannot demand a deeper degree of love from his human audience than that which he predicates of the Father, and so love for enemies, taught unconditionally by Jesus, becomes an unconditional quality of God. And then it is surely the case that Ivan could not have made his complaint with any conviction were it not for the standard of compassion pervading his own cultural background by means of reiterated stories of the Gospels.[6] Certainly in his

---

5. Matt. 5:44–45 (*The New Oxford Annotated Bible, New Revised Standard Version*. All other New Testament quotations are from this version unless otherwise stated). Of course, it is also possible to make the counter point with the (equally) Gospel picture of an "eternal fire" of punishment (e.g., Matt. 25:41–46), and the Christian doctrine of hell associated with it. Schwager sees such doctrine as essential to establishing the reality and seriousness of human freedom over against God's demand for human conversion (op. cit., 198–201). Exegetically such passages may be understood as apocalyptic imagery at the crisis of the age rather than a literal definition of eternal torment; see John L. McKenzie, "Gehenna," *Dictionary of the Bible* (New York: Collier Books, 1965). Along these lines a radical analytic out of mimetic anthropology suggests such imagery is a prophecy of purely human and historical crisis, resulting from a rejection of the gospel proclamation. If men and women turn down the offer of (abyssal) peace, "the effect of the gospel revelation will be made manifest through violence, through a sacrificial and cultural crisis whose radical effect must be unprecedented since there is no longer any sacralized victim to stand in the way of its consequences. . . . *[T]he violence has become its own enemy and will end by destroying itself*" (René Girard, *Things Hidden since the Foundation of the World*, trans. Stephen Bann and Michael Metteer [Stanford, Calif.: Stanford University Press, 1987], 203, italics in original).

6. For simultaneous expression of bleak cynicism regarding the cultural plausibility of compassion and recognition of the key role it plays in Christianity's self-concept, as well as assertion of its being a historical phenomenon prior to Christianity, see Freud's *Civilization and Its Discontents*. Referring to the precept, "Thou shalt love thy neighbour as thyself," he says: "It is known throughout the world and is undoubtedly older than Christianity, which puts it forward as its proudest claim. Yet it is certainly not very old; even in historical times it was still strange to mankind. . . . If I love someone, he must deserve it in some way. . . . But if he is a stranger to me and he cannot attract me by any worth of his own or any significance that he may already have acquired for my emotional

argument with Alyosha, Ivan depends on the very sensibility to suffering that makes his brother a Christlike figure, to be able to convince him of the formal incredibility of his Christian faith.

Thus, the problem of evil is itself exacerbated by the Gospels, and indeed according to mimetic anthropology, finds both its human explanation and compassionate subversion in the narrative of the cross. This itself must serve to warn us that that an attempt to resolve the question of the cross systematically is disturbed from within, and perhaps in a certain critical way doomed in principle. Any final account of the logos of the cross *sub specie aeternitatis* will be undermined by its power to return the issue, again and again, simultaneously to human responsibility and the undecidable event of abyssal compassion. Or, put another way, the more the cross challenges human violence, the more it also challenges any inherited rationale of divine violence, no matter how abstract or clothed in traditional authority. Even a scriptural statement such as Paul's, "God has imprisoned all in disobedience so that he may be merciful to all" (Rom. 11:32), provokes questions if one takes from it a divine orchestrator of chronological history. What was God thinking of when he subjected so many, for so long, to so much torment, for the sake of demonstrating his love? So, from the systematic point of view the cross may always be found to become a problem to itself. Anthropologically, however, its dynamic is released with uninhibited power once the abyssal Christ is discovered in and through the figure and proclamation of the cross alone. Only from this side and in this setting, only by cleaving strictly to the anthropological reading of the cross announced in and as gospel, can we then also announce a God utterly of nonviolence. Once the rigor of this position is established, then perhaps, possibly, other questions may begin to fall into place, but not quite in the way we are used to expecting.

For do we not also have to say that when Christ yielded up his spirit on the cross, it was this that made God who he is in the Christian message? That Christ's final surrender had a determinative effect on the history of

---

life, it will be hard for me to love him. Indeed, I should be wrong to do so, for my love is valued by all my own people as sign of my preferring them, and it is an injustice to them if I put a stranger on a par with them. . . . [M]en are not gentle creatures who want to be loved, and who at the most can defend themselves if they are attacked; they are, on the contrary, creatures among whose instinctual endowments is to be reckoned a powerful share of aggressiveness. As a result, their neighbour is for them not only a potential helper or sexual object, but also someone who tempts them to satisfy their aggressiveness on him, to exploit his capacity for work without compensation, to use him sexually without his consent, to seize his possessions, to humiliate him, to cause him pain, to torture and to kill him. *Homo homini lupus* [man is a wolf to man]" (Sigmund Freud, *Civilization and Its Discontents*, trans. and ed. James Strachey, intro. Peter Gay [New York and London: W. W. Norton & Co., 1961], 68–69). Latin quotation from Plautus, *Asinaria*, II, iv, 88.

God, of the identity of God in history? This is not to say that Christ, from his side, was not himself responding to his vocation, that he had not indeed appropriated a deep logic of Hebrew faith and revelation, one that he also concretized in his own life. But what it does say is that historically and anthropologically at that moment, Jesus of Nazareth subversively changed the meaning of God, above all in regard to violence. It was his work, in the depth of his own human existence, and by a radical communication with and through his own tradition. The rest is history, or rather indeed the possibility of a completely new history. If the issue then must needs be developed "systematically," it will be by a language that is much more subtle and challenging than any theology of the cross that has so far been developed. It would involve a disruption to the very notion of time that controls the usual account of the biblical God. What follows now, therefore, is a sketch and a struggle to express what may in a certain way be inexpressible, if indeed we are tempted to seek a language of chronology, of presence in normal time, regarding a nonviolent God. What is perhaps possible is a language that speaks of an absolute contingency, one in the middle of time, if that were possible, and thereby offering an "impossible" reconstitution of all time.

The plan of a linear diachronic progression, from Genesis to Jesus, can be read as a structuring element in some passages of the New Testament, and it clearly appears in the later Christian tradition.[7] Extrapolated eternally, the cross becomes the single stroke of the pendulum between an eternal-chronological past in which God had no cause to forgive humanity its offense, and an eternal-chronological future in which grace and mercy are found. Rather than this impossible intellectual conundrum, surely it is better to understand the temporality of the cross as a profound synchrony that both accompanies and defies every formation of normal time. It is de facto a very concrete and specific historical memory announced in the kerygma, and yet is it not also a kind of an-archical moment of the abyss that can never be recuperated or assimilated by chronology?[8] There is an initial resonance here with the philosophy of Emmanuel Levinas, which seeks to name a similar strangeness or aberration of time in respect of the ethical phenomenon of responsibility.

---

7. For example, Rom. 3:21–26 and Heb. 1:1–2. See Jaroslav Pelikan, *The Christian Tradition*, 5 vols. (Chicago and London: University of Chicago Press, 1978), vol. 1, 58–62; vol. 3, 34–38. For Augustine's *plena narratio* (complete history of salvation), see Robert A. Markus, *Saeculum, History and Society in the Theology of St. Augustine* (Cambridge: Cambridge University Press, 1970, paperback 1988), 8–20.

8. The expanded spelling of *an-archical* (and *an-archic*, below) accents the root meaning of something without beginning or cause within the present order, or beyond itself, rather than the more usual sense of something provocative of disorder or chaos.

The relationship with a past that is on the hither side of every present and every re-presentable, for not belonging to the order of presence, is included in the extraordinary and everyday event of my responsibility for the faults or the misfortune of others, in my responsibility that answers for the freedom of another, in the astonishing human fraternity in which fraternity, conceived with Cain's sober coldness, would not by itself explain the responsibility between separated beings it calls for. The freedom of another could never begin in my freedom, that is, abide in the same present, be contemporary, be representable to me. The responsibility for the other cannot have begun in my commitment, in my decision. The unlimited responsibility in which I find myself comes from the hither side of my freedom, from a "prior to every memory," an "ulterior to every accomplishment," from the non-present par excellence, the non-original, the an-archical, prior to or beyond essence . . . .[9]

Levinas is arguing a phenomenology of moral responsibility whose deep order he seeks to evoke almost in defiance of language itself; language fails because it belongs to presence and theme, and in this capacity mediates the classical idea of conventional, self-present time.[10] In contrast his reflections relate to the phenomenon of the other understood in terms of an incommensurable time, an immemorial past in which I am answerable to the other before any possible order of being and beings takes place. But at once the homology between this and the time of the cross breaks down. First of all, as just stated, the event of the cross occurs in normal history, in a remembered linear past. The memory is carried by the kerygma, a strange and striking message but one that arises with unmistakable specificity, in concrete, recognizable circumstances in Roman-controlled Palestine. Jesus "suffered under Pontius Pilate." In this reference it is anything but primordial. It is thematic and historical. Second, within this

---

9. Emmanuel Levinas, *Otherwise than Being or Beyond Essence*, trans. Alphonso Lingis (The Hague: Martinus Nijhoff Publishers, 1981), 10–11.

10. See his remarks on language, where the issue is not language itself, as in so much deconstructive pyrotechnics, but something in the roots of language that language must distort in order to present. "In language qua said everything is conveyed before us, be it at the price of betrayal. Language is ancillary and thus indispensable. At this moment language is serving a research conducted in view of disengaging the *otherwise than being* or *being's other* outside of the themes in which they already show themselves, unfaithfully, as *being's essence*—but in which they do show themselves. Language permits us to utter, be it by betrayal, this *outside of being*, this *ex-ception* to being, as though being's other were an event of being" (ibid., 6, italics original).

specificity, the incommensurable time of the cross bends toward an unanticipated and unanticipatable future rather than an immemorial past. I shall comment on this at once, but first it is worth pointing out that Levinas himself suggests other patterns of the "pre-original" that lie closer perhaps to the time generated by the cross. Just before the above quotation Levinas had noted the cases of gratitude and prayer as other examples of the "intrigues of time," wherein something has to happen before it happens; we must be moved by gratitude before we can give thanks, we must be praying before we lift up a prayer. To use the term perhaps familiar here, we must already be altered before we can authentically express gratitude or prayer. But this indeed is not so much a forfeiture or sacrifice of self in an-archic responsibility, but more a response to something in the other that might be already an advent and a gift. And thus at once it seems the meaning of an-archic time exceeds absolute passive responsibility before the face of the other, and moves in the experience of positive alteration through the gracious self-giving of the other.

In this light the figure of the Crucified may be understood as one who "grants" responsibility abyssally, that is, gives himself without remainder and without end; and it is this granting that an-archically transforms the meaning of time as the time of absolute gift by and from another. The linear past of the gospel properly comes to me as an-archic because it has the power to reconstitute the moment absolutely, as forgiveness or fore-giveness. This is a kind of past that is also an absolute future, because it comes to me in a strange "before," facing or in front of my whole life, to begin it again absolutely and proleptically. It awaits my life as well as precedes it. All those who have been touched by Christ in whatever way always "remember" the moment of that touch as possessing futural vigor—one that is always there as possibility, that "comes" to me again and again as the incommensurable, as the eschatological "now" that reorganizes my time absolutely, ever anew. A pre-original "for-another" in the cross becomes the event and possibility of repetition, an experience on the part of the "self" of gratuitous solidarity with his or her suffering, provoking the open-ended alteration of compassion and newness of life. The abyss of the cross draws violent chronology into itself, to abolish it and there make time utterly anew. Thus the cross proclaims itself, presents itself, as a profound synchrony with every given moment, past or future, that at the same time disturbs each moment with and as the radically new. The gospel brings its an-archic past-future into human experience, a new arc of time not at all identical with chronological past or future. It is not the extension of chronology, but its unheralded interruption, though indeed historically heralded in the kerygma. It is announced while never being anticipatable; rather it is the cross that anticipates, comes before, and awaits. Its past-future arises again and again in Christian memory, in the word and the story of Jesus. The living "future memory" thus gives rise to the Christian virtue of hope, the sense that its an-archic past-future will continue to arise in personal and collective history, that the ever-renewed moment of absolute giving will ultimately lead to the radical reinterpretation of all ordinary time.

BETWEEN EMMAUS AND ATHENS

In the trembling of this thought it is apposite to turn to a reflection on the meaning of gift carried through by deconstructionist thinkers. It is no accident that Levinas's thought intersects at key points with that of Jacques Derrida,[11] and it is to this author, and to John D. Caputo, that I now turn to continue the exploration of a new language of the cross. Their work in the area of the gift brings them formally into the theme and manner of this discussion, for they advance the idea of nonexchangist giving to the other at the very edges of human possibility, constituting a different meaning of time and one tensed toward an ethical human future. Moreover, this idea is eventually taken up directly in relation to the Christian gospel tradition, and so becomes necessarily a conversation partner. The meaning of Christ's death that I have presented is found to become directly involved in a very contemporary conversation broached from a very different direction, and the effect is both challenging and exciting. It is as if the two disciples on the road back from Emmaus to tell the good news to the rest of Jesus' followers suddenly bump into a couple of Greek philosophers energetically using a language similar to the disciples', and referencing the actual story of Jesus into the bargain. Except perhaps the Greeks are in Jewish clothing, or are they Jews and Christians in Greek tunics? At all events in the context of this book it is impossible not to pursue this strange encounter. It is not possible to allow the parties to pass each other obliquely, as if each were seeing ghosts, and refuse them the opportunity to take up a collective conversation that somehow spans the ages. Indeed, to change the scene and its historical frame, it's as if the shadowy antagonists of

---

11. See, for example, "Différance" in *Margins of Philosophy*, trans. Alan Bass (Chicago: University of Chicago Press, 1982); "At this very moment in this work here I am," in *Re-Reading Levinas*, ed. Robert Bernasconi and Simon Critchley (Bloomington and Indianapolis: Indiana University Press, 1991). See also *Derrida and différance*, ed. David Wood and Robert Bernasconi (Evanston. Ill.: Northwestern University Press, 1988), where Bernasconi traces shifts in Derrida's thought under influence of Levinas.

Anselm's *Cur Deus Homo*, the Jews and pagans, were now brought
directly into the discussion, and in a language that, I think, is much
more appropriate to the actual gospel. Perhaps they are in this discussion because in some manner they have never really been apart.

The later writing of Derrida has moved beyond the elaboration of
strategies and styles of deconstructing texts to a more vital concern
with the question of the other (*l'autre*), and in the process makes a
subtle but real break with the Heideggerian background of a self-clos-
ing circle of Being. I believe it is important to pursue the progression
of this thought in order to arrive with a full script to the scene just
imagined, to be able to hear the confusion of voices suddenly focused
in the clarity of a shared thought, or at least a highly provocative question. In a series of reflections Derrida instances a much more Hebraic,
"personal" concept of what it means to think the Heideggerian event
(*Ereignis*) of Being. Drawing from a work by Maurice Blanchot,
Derrida makes use of the imperative of the verb *to come*, (*Viens!*) to
disturb the order of thought that is closed to the other. *Viens!* is an
invitation that refers undecidably both to the other in the ordinary
sense of the other person, and what is utterly other, that which cannot
be known, what he calls the absolute surprise, or absolute future.[12] I
should be careful to underline that although Derrida makes his language open or fractured to the coming of the other, he still continues
to operate within the philosophical tradition of the transcendental and
so preserves the accent on the impersonal. At the same time, although
the Heideggerian event still conditions the philosophical meaning of
the invocation of "Come!", it does not determine it and the "Come!"
retains a certain priority.

> The event of this "Come" precedes and calls the event. It would
> be that starting from which there is any event, the *venir*, the *à-*

---

12. Jacques Derrida, *Psyche: Inventions of the Other*, trans. Catherine Porter, in *Reading
de Man Reading*, ed. Lindsay Waters and Wlad Godzich (Minneapolis: University of
Minnesota Press, 1989), 25–65. For absolute surprise and future, see Jacques Derrida,
Specters of Marx: The State of the Debt, the Work of Mourning, and the New International,
trans. Peggy Kamuf (New York: Routledge, 1994), 65, 90. Among the most significant of
Maurice Blanchot's works for Derrida is *The Step Not Beyond*, trans. Ann Smock (Lincoln:
University of Nebraska Press, 1986); see Jacques Derrida, *Parages*, English trans. in "Living
On/Border Lines," trans. James Hulbert, in Harold Bloom et al., *Deconstruction and
Criticism* (New York: Continuum, 1979), 118–218. Both Blanchot and Derrida play on the
ambivalence in French of *le pas au-delà*, suggesting both "the step beyond" and "the not
beyond." Thus built into an approach to the other is the prohibition against any foreclo-
sure of her/its alterity.

venir of the event that cannot be thought under the given category of the event.[13]

The invocation, therefore, is essentially a disturbance in the pagan
indifference of *Ereignis*. "Come!" suggests more a call for Jewish and
prophetic justice than Hellenic-German concern for the philosophical
transcendental, and so Derrida himself comments: "Heidegger would
not have liked this apparently personal conjugation or declension of
coming."[14] To readers of the New Testament it will at once be evident
that the invocation is a textual echo of almost the last words of the
Christian Scripture, in its major work of Christian apocalyptic, the
Book of Revelation. Revelation 22:17 says: "The Spirit and the bride say,
'Come!' And let everyone who hears say, 'Come!'" It is undeniable, most
of all for deconstructionists, that this text supplies some of the sense
and vibrancy of the word "Come!" taken over from Blanchot by
Derrida. This is not the last time in the conversation between disciples
and deconstructionists that the words of the former may be seen to
provide seminal urgency for the metadiscourse of the latter. So that the
philosophers interrupting the talk of the disciples may be heard to say:
"Yes, yes, but in fact the truth of what you are saying is as follows!" We
will hear this interjection more than once in the conversation.

Derrida indeed "becomes aware" of the apocalyptic background to
the *Viens!*, and moves directly to control (by placing beyond control)
the meaning of such a powerful textual reference. "On a Newly Arisen
Apocalyptic Tone in Philosophy" recruits apocalyptic to the cause of
deconstruction first by scrambling up or making unstable the destination to whom the "Come!" is addressed. In the Book of Revelation it is,
of course, Jesus, "who is and who was and who is to come" (1:8), but
this is dependent on the words of a writer, and the deconstructive question is, as always, who is speaking, who is authorizing these words. Can
we ever know, and therefore can we ever be sure of a destination?[15] On

---

13. Jacques Derrida, *Raising the Tone of Philosophy: Late Essays by Immanuel Kant,
Transformation Critique by Jacques Derrida*, ed. Peter Fenves (Baltimore: Johns Hopkins
University Press, 1993), 164; hereafter this work cited as *Raising the Tone*. For the full
impersonality of Derrida's philosophical "ground," in fact even more impersonal than
Heidegger's Being, see the idea of *Khôra*; in "*Khôra*," trans. Ian McLeod, in *On the Name*,
ed. Thomas Dutoit (Stanford, Calif.: Stanford University Press, 1995) 87–127. However,
this impersonality is the very structure of openness that allows, paradoxically, for the coming of the other.

14. *Raising the Tone*, 166.

15. "On a Newly Arisen Apocalyptic Tone in Philosophy," trans. John Leavey, Jr., in
Raising the Tone, 154–56.

the basis of this uncertainty he then announces the deconstructive radicalization of apocalyptic. The very loss of knowledge about who speaks or writes, and their destination, makes the text apocalyptic; its "Come!" is one of absolute "tonal" openness to the indeterminate other.

> An apocalypse without apocalypse, an apocalypse without vision, without truth, without revelation, *envois* [sendings of the message] . . . addresses without message and without destination, without sender or decidable addressee, without last judgment, without any other eschatology than the tone of the "*Viens.*"[16]

The rejection of the Christian destination could not be more explicit, but the appropriation of the apocalyptic experience and movement of the "Come!" continues to be developed on other fronts. In a nuanced rehabilitation of Marx and Marxism, Derrida moves to co-opt another key theme of Judaic and Christian belief, that of the Messiah. He does this in order first to recuperate Marxism within a scheme that retains something of its historical challenge and call for justice, but without its historical rationalism and determinism. Marxism may be read as an example of a "messianic" without messianism, a passion for the coming of something nonpredetermined, because to determine it is in fact to prevent its coming. It is a "hospitality without reserve" that is formally impossible, but "without this experience of the impossible, one might as well give up on both justice and the event."[17] Second, as is evident, he is elaborating a specifically deconstructive language of the messianic, of the in-breaking of the other, that repeats and yet empties out the concrete figure of the one who is to come. This desconstructive messianism is abstract, nonidentifiable, desertlike, an "atheological" desert without the meditating and fasting figure of the Christ.[18] By means of this abstract movement he vindicates the gesture of Marxism that seeks a "non-contemporaneity with itself of the living present,"[19] very much the effect that we had posited of the cross, produced by

16. Ibid., 167.
17. *Specters of Marx: The State of the Debt, the Work of Mourning, and the New International*, 65.
18. It is "the movement of an experience open to the absolute future of what is coming, that is to say, a necessarily indeterminate, abstract, desert-like experience that is confided, exposed, given up to waiting for the other and for the event. In its pure formality, in the indetermination that it requires, one may find yet another essential affinity between it and a certain messianic spirit" (ibid., 90).
19. Ibid., xix.

its "now" of abyssal giving. But instead of the provocation of the cross he invokes "a universal structure . . . [an] irreducible movement of the historical opening to the future;" in short, "the formality of a structural messianism."[20] Such a surprise that the man in postmodern philosopher's robes, all patches and motley, should be tempted to take a disciple's cloak of one piece and spread it for his bed! Or, put another way, how astonishing that the philosopher, retreating from Jerusalem, also wants to drive philosophy into the desert, to find there manifested the messiah who is not there, only the yearning of sand in a fragmented landscape.

And yet even as he assimilates messianic motifs to a deconstructive master-reading, a disciple's question, of the priority of real events, rises to disturb him. What truthfully comes first, concrete biblical traditions or a universal formal possibility that structures them in actual history?

The problem remains—and this is really a problem for me, an enigma—whether the religions, say, for instance, the religions of the Book, are but specific examples of this general structure, of messianicity. There is the general structure of messianicity, as a structure of experience, and on this groundless ground there have been revelations, a history which one calls Judaism or Christianity and so on. This is one possibility, and then you would have a Heideggerian gesture, in style. You would have to go back from these religions to the fundamental ontological conditions of possibility of religions, to describe the structure of messianicity on the ground of groundless ground on which religions have been made possible.

That is one hypothesis. The other hypothesis—and I confess that I hesitate between these two possibilities—is that the events of revelation, the biblical traditions, the Jewish, Christian and Islamic traditions, have been absolute events, irreducible events which have unveiled this messianicity. We would not know what messianicity is without messianism, without these events which were Abraham, Moses, and Jesus Christ, and so on. In that case singular events would have unveiled or revealed these universal possibilities and it is only on that condition that we can describe messianicity.[21]

---

20. Ibid., 167, 59.
21. These remarks were delivered at a public roundtable, inaugurating the doctoral program in philosophy at Villanova University, 3 October 1994; quoted by John D. Caputo in *The Prayers and Tears of Jacques Derrida, Religion without Religion* (Bloomington and Indianapolis: Indiana University Press, 1997), 136–37; hereafter *Prayers and Tears*.

It seems to me that the philosopher is caught here, even as he typically hesitates. If he posits an originary structure, a messianic ontology, an ontological messianicity, he undermines the whole thesis of deconstruction—the absence of origins that could be brought to true presence in language, the lack of the proper, of original exemplars, the never knowing what is an example of what. On the other hand, if he accepts genuine singularities, on the sole basis of which it is possible to know messianicity at all, there then occurs a basic historical-critical priority for the Jewish-Christian experience in the centuries either side of the beginning of the Common Era. In this frame the only reason he can think the messianic is simply because he stands in the irreducible stream of two and a half millennia of traditions. They happened! And within this stream of traditions, surely, the most emblematically visible messianic tradition is that of Christianity—the figure of the crucified and risen Jesus who will return. Furthermore, this figure—despite the rational formulations of the tradition—remains the most deeply paradoxical and world-interruptive. Which other messianism dared base its transformation of history in a narrative of abysmal suffering and death? Against the backdrop of this figure we might also then ask how the presumed messianic singularity of deconstruction—its contemporary "Come!"—arrives without historical and spiritual dependence on the singularity of gospel tradition, and precisely including that tradition's creative tensions with the singular Jewish tradition and the singular Islamic tradition. In this case there appears more and more clearly something singularly at stake between the quasi-singularity of deconstruction and the eruptive singularity of first-century Christianity. Our animated discussion on the road outside Jerusalem becomes more clearly a matter of ultimate concern.

For in this discussion—which is now more like a contest—deconstructive philosophy seeks to outdo the cross in its abyssal scene, its desertedness, and on paper it may seem to do so. Its ascesis in regard to predictive knowledge, and with that its tone of absolute hospitality, its nonprejudicial openness to the *tout autre* (wholly other), at once abolish the cultural exclusivism connected to determinate religious traditions, along with the implication of violence so remorselessly validated by history. There is a feeling that deconstruction offers a more authentic "self-denial" and absolute gift, because it anticipates and demands nothing from the other even as it awaits its coming without reserve. But generally speaking this is angelic virtue, proper only to academics whose souls are self-illumining like Socrates', independent of concrete cultural traditions and models the rest of us appear to need. Indeed because it is a messianism without a messiah, and therefore without mimesis, because it lacks the redemptive-compassionate figures of Scripture, most profoundly that of Jesus, it may inevitably be seen to slip back into the culture of violence, into the sacred. What is the semigesture that Derrida makes, to claim ontological priority over the religions of the Book, but the hint of a massive expulsion? However, immediately having said this, it is also inescapable that deconstruction is vindicated precisely because the specific scriptural traditions, and perhaps most scandalously that bearing the name of Christ, have so consistently negated compassion in acts of cruel and massive violence. There is no moral high ground, only the challenge of the abyss.

This should be underlined. For even as I claim a priority for Christian messianism, in terms both of its historical tradition and the abyssal content of the cross, it is vital to point out that this latter can never be tied up in church membership, doctrinal formulae, or even the text of the gospel itself. If the Crucified is truly an abyssal figure, that he takes his place at the bottom of human culture and history (which is really no recognizable place and no ordinary time), then in some sense his abyssal gesture of love must be available to everyone who suffers or feels compassion for suffering. Clearly this is so in relation to the historical-kerygmatic figure of the Crucified, and to anyone who has ever glanced obliquely and without prejudice at the image of the cross, or witnessed an act or heard a story of self-abandoning compassion inspired by the cross. But there is also the extreme possibility that abyssal love is traced in the deep structure of culture itself, of human relationships, of mimesis, and indeed of violence visited on the victim but somehow also "imitated" in the strange mimesis of compassion. This is where, partly in contrast to the position I have just taken, the discourse of the cross rejoins Derrida's semigesture, not indeed of a Greek-style fundamental ontology, but more in terms of a "structure of experience" and "groundless ground" that would be explicated primarily in terms of anthropology, particularly the undecidability of mimesis. Yet any such deep structure must surely remain ineffectual, culturally compromised, and intellectually negligible without the specific revelation of the gospel. Only the absolute singularity of the gospel event is able to make the human trace of compassion both truly abyssal and historically dynamic. To go further on this question would carry us far from the discussion of the cross in its specific place in history and the interruptive anarchic moment of time that it introduces into chronological time. It is important at least to make the point, for in any encounter between disciples and philosophers the broaching of universal questions becomes inevitable. But now, at this moment, the disciples are sticking to their testimony, if only because the vigor and challenge of the singular kerygma arising in a specific historical setting is precisely what they have to offer, and they have no desire to see it dissipated. Very much affirming the vigor of this kerygma is the evidence of the language in which this encounter is in fact engaged: it appears, on both sides, to be itself provoked by an abyssal dynamic emerging from the cross.

Here at once is a key illustation of this claim in relation to the language of philosophy. The Heideggerian parentage of the term *deconstruction* is often noted, but behind this there is a startling further derivation—startling at least for philosophers who do not acknowledge the paths from Jerusalem they pursue. Heidegger's concept of *Destruktion* provides the filiation of *deconstruction* and signifies a breaking through to the primary, factical experiences that underlie a text. But as John D. Caputo points out, this was in turn suggested to Heidegger by Luther's *destructio*, which was the latter's word for the demolition of the crust of scholastic abstraction in an effort to get back to the original life of the New Testament. As a young man, lecturing on phenomenology of religion, Heidegger adopted this approach in relation to the text of Paul's letters to the Thessalonians, seeking the factical experience of the early Christian community, in particular that of temporality. According to Heidegger the authentic time of the *parousia*, the second coming of Christ, was not a matter of a "when," but a "how" of existential transformation, a radical openness to a possibility whose very indefiniteness was part of the transformative experience itself. Heidegger was by no means thinking simply as a professor of New Testament religion; his breakthrough to the an-archic temporality of the first Christian movement provided the blueprint for his authentic temporality of *Dasein*, where *Dasein* is pitched toward the certain yet indefinite possibility of its own death. His analysis of Thessalonians "recast in terms of a relationship to one's own death . . . became a centerpiece of *Being and Time*."[22]

This remarkable piece of intellectual history provides strict confirmation for the way in which both the discipline of theology and, more profoundly, the an-archic futurity produced by the message of the cross have served to shape the method and language of contemporary philosophy. However, John Caputo chooses to take this evidence in a very different direction, making it serve his own theme of a "religion" of deconstruction, a new "religion without religion." Here Christianity, along with the other religions of the Book, are subsumed in a "quasi-transcendental" absolute

---

22. *Prayers and Tears*, 139, 83. See Heidegger, *Phänomenologie des religiösen Lebens*, ed. Matthias Jung and Thomas Regehly, Gesamtausgabe, B. 60 (Frankfurt: Klostermann, 1995), 87–115.

openness to the other, but minus the dogmatic particularism and attendant violence of these traditions. Again we are made aware of the excite-
ment of voices halfway between Jerusalem and Emmaus, and of the key
question: which has intellectual priority, a specific tradition and kerygma,
or a universal ground?

Caputo's voice is higher-pitched than Derrida's and displays its own
brand of evangelistic fervor, repeating Derrida's lines for him and more
than once, and only half-jokingly, covering Derrida's shoulders in the
mantle of the historical Jesus.[23] In *The Prayers and Tears of Jacques
Derrida*, Caputo is an apostle himself, preaching a Derridean desire for
God that fluctuates "undecidably with atheism."[24] Here prayer is offered
without destination, faith affirms without kerygma, prophecy speaks
without authority, testimony makes no martyrs, tradition abandons
doctrine, inspiration forgoes the Spirit. Yet again and again, to make the
point of this deconstructive religion, John the (non)evangelist has
recourse to gospel images and stories; for in these, so often, are classically inscribed the radicalism of what he seeks to institute. Ultimately,
Caputo says, he does not care whether you can tell the difference
between a biblical prophetic passion and a prophetic deconstructive
passion, in other words between biblical and deconstructive religion.
Because "in the final account there is no final account."[25] And this is
both the strength and weakness of deconstructive religion. At one point
it is all abyssal commitment, and the themes and postulates of radical
openness toward the other seem so deeply layered and genuinely
unselfish that the disciple wants to throw his arms around the philosopher, exclaiming at last, "Brother!" But apart from the fact that it is
probably presumptuous in terms of deconstruction to name the other
"brother," Caputo's text reminds one of what Sartre said about reading
Hegel. While you are in the library and covered in the abstract wonder
of the historical dialectic of the Absolute, you are totally convinced. The
moment you step out on a city street under leaden skies, it all falls away
irretrievably, like a house of cards. Radical openness to the other
remains words on a page, inscribed by and in the words themselves, and
nothing more.

---

23. Caputo uses the image of the Jesus Seminar method of colored beads, by which the
New Testament scholars vote on whether purported sayings are historically from Jesus, as
a parable for the problem in interpreting Derrida's words, for the difficulty in getting to the
real Derrida himself! *Prayers and Tears*, 110, 115.
24. Ibid., 62.
25. Ibid., 114, 116. This of course is a final statement of account, marking a metaphysical doctrine.

In contrast, the two disciples on the road from Emmaus brought with them a concrete memory of the breaking of the bread, Jesus' proleptic symbol of his surrender in death that had vitally returned to them. It had borne testimony that this death broke the bonds of violent mimesis, of all culture based in its mechanisms, its crises and their solution by murder. The burning hearts of the disciples, which are nothing but the burning heart of the whole New Testament, are the irreducible, second-moment testimony of that triumphant death. It is the testimony to the testimony of Jesus that brings unity to the collection of texts that make the New Testament Scripture. But much more than a simple record, a recollection of something past, these texts also carry in them the interruption to chronological time, the an-archical future initiated by the Crucified. The central role of the breaking of the bread in the early Christian community (a practice passed on from the very first years of the movement) itself suggests disruption of time, because something Jesus did before and in view of his death had irrepressible meaning afterward, to such an extent that it signified that this death itself was overcome. Thus it was to be repeated continually in order to "declare the death of the Lord until he comes":[26] a concrete paradox sustained by the an-archical future of the signified Crucified. In this tradition we are dealing inescapably with a cultural institution that challenges given time, and one that continues to be practiced day by day. For all its vast failures, Christian praxis still harbors the potential to refigure time in love, and its deconstructive rereading seems to me more a contemporary judgment of its failures than a serious possibility of substituting the radicalism of its concrete forms.

If we return once more to the voices of the philosophers we can hear the graver voice of the duo speak critically of the Heideggerian circle of Being and time, approximating it to the economic circle of the gift. Derrida uses Marcel Mauss's "monumental" work in a somewhat different way from the way I used it in this book to illustrate mimesis. He refuses to rely on Mauss's anthropological data but sees that the very signification of "gift" implies its return, implies exchange. In its very phenomenality, its appearance as symbol, and its symbolic appearance, the gift at once "gives back" to the giver. "By its very appearance, the simple phenomenon of the gift annuls it as gift. . . ."[27] For there to be a true gift it must not appear as gift at all, either to the one giving or to the one receiving, because in either

---

26. From *Interlinear*.

27. Jacques Derrida, *Given Time: I. Counterfeit Money* (Chicago and London: University of Chicago Press, 1992), 24, 14; hereafter *Given Time*.

case repayment is immediately demanded by its presence, by its being a "present" in circular time, and indeed providing the formation of time as circular. The Heidegerrian analysis of time says that, along with being, time is "given" (*Es gibt Zeit*—"there is time" or "time is given"), and the *Es*, the It, assumes an "ownership" of the gift by giving Being and time into its "own" (*eigen*).[28] Derrida suggests that so long as this It is in play, giving to its own, (to "its self"), then the idea of time is coincident with Mauss's "selfish" circulation of the gift. If time always returns to the It that gives, it is in an everlasting closed circle of reappropriation, always returning to its own "present."[29] This leads to the conclusion (and a conclusion that is more and more clearly motivated by a certain interpretation of the Hebrew Bible) that a "true gift" will break the circle of time.

> [W]herever there is time, wherever time predominates or conditions experience in general, wherever *time as circle* is predominant, the gift is impossible. A gift could be possible, there could be a gift only at the instant an effraction in the circle will have taken place, at the instant all circulation will have been interrupted and *on the condition* of this instant. What is more, this instant of effraction (of the temporal circle) must no longer be part of time. That is why we said "on the condition of this instant." This condition concerns time but does not *belong* to it, does not pertain to it without being, for all that, more logical than chronological. There would be a gift only at the instant when the *paradoxical* instant (in the sense in which Kierkegaard says of the paradoxical instant of decision that it is a madness) tears time apart.[30]

The mention of Kierkegaard refers of course to his treatment of the sacrifice of Abraham in *Fear and Trembling*, and Derrida's own response to this classical exercise in philosophical and theological thought brings our imagined conversation to a new point of intensity. Kierkegaard rehearses the story from Genesis as a demolition of the Hegelian system of the Absolute from within. What is required by God from Abraham makes no sense, it is absurd, and so Abraham is required to believe "by virtue of the absurd," not by virtue of self-manifesting reason. Abraham suspends

28. Heidegger, *On Time and Being*, trans. Joan Stambaugh (New York: Harper and Row, 1972), 5; quoted in *Given Time*, 20–21.
29. Ibid., 21–22.
30. Ibid., 9.

his relation to the ethical universal that requires him not to kill his son, and does so because he has entered an "absolute relation to the absolute."[31] He is under an unnegotiable obligation in relation to God, but is completely unable to explain himself to anyone. This paradox is taken up by Derrida as the irreducible paradigm of deconstructive ethics. We are always in relation to the absolutely other, for which God is a name, and here the absolutely other refers also to the absence of systematic knowledge of the other. "Every other is totally other" (*tout autre est tout autre*)[32] because there is no final basis from which to anticipate it, predict it, structure it in advance. And so philosophical truth paradoxically underpins the ethical: we have no choice but to relate in absolute debt or duty to the *tout autre* if we are to be true to this truth.

> The account of Isaac's sacrifice can be read as a narrative development of the paradox constituting the concept of duty and absolute responsibility. The concept puts us into relation (but without relating to it, in a double secret) with the absolute other, with the absolute singularity of the other, whose name here is God.[33]

. The double secret consists of (1) the fact that, like Abraham, I am unable to explain myself to all others in my absolute duty to *the* other, and (2) the fact that there is no given relation, conceptual or structural, with the absolute other, who holds here the name of God. If we reconnect now with the concept of time, we can see that any true ethical act will only occur in the instant without foundation in any given, economic circle of being or time. It happens in the incommensurate instant, which is the only time in which a true gift, an absolute response to the other, can be said to take place. This true gift is for Derrida "the gift of death," for it always slays what it loves most and so also slays itself in the an-archic instant that "it gives." It is pure paradox and this paradox "like the gift and 'the gift of death' . . . remains irreducible to presence or presentation, it demands a temporality of the instant without ever constituting a present. If it can be said, it belongs to an atemporal temporality. . . ."[34]

---

31. Søren Kierkegaard, *Fear and Trembling, Repetition*, ed. and trans. Howard V. Hong and Edna H. Hong (Princeton, N.J.: Princeton University Press, 1983), 56.
32. Jacques Derrida, *The Gift of Death*, trans. David Wills (Chicago and London: The University of Chicago Press, 1995), 68. This quotes the original French; my translation given here.
33. Ibid., 66.
34. Ibid., 65.

There is something very close here to the temporality of the cross that I have been describing, of an absolute gift of self that breaks apart the frame of chronology. But Derrida is in fact talking about something that occurs in "me," in my atemporal act of absolute responsibility, not of the rupture of time by the abyssal gift of another. A question then arises whether the "gift of death" in fact escapes the circle of time constituted by reciprocity. When it slays the other (meaning in fact all the others, bar one, the *tout autre*) and even, included in this, as it slays itself, is there not a redistribution of the economy of sacrificial mimesis? Does not this new, atemporal time constitute perhaps a new, private or secret economy between me and the absolutely other? So that by sacrificing absolutely all present being and time, a new sacred order is born, a massive deferred and proximate violence and, through and in that, a transcendent circle of exchange? Is not a new exchangist temporality set up between me and the Absolute? This would be an extremely private order of potlach, an extremity of economic individualism between me and the other. If, however, the argument is that existential or symbolic slaying of the self in the instant of true gift saves it from exchange, then surely the death itself abolishes the gift, for nothing can be expected from the *tout autre* in terms of further life. If my death is my gift, without expectation of life, then there is no longer gift in any personal sense, indeed no more time, and all that remains is fate, annihilation, entropy. And so the other as Absolute may gather all into itself as absolute, terminal, sacrificial violence.

This question directed against the philosopher is warranted, not simply by the value of the question itself, but because its first part, that of a residual exchange, is precisely the charge made against Christianity by Derrida, as he moves finally to vindicate his atheological ethics against the New Testament. Now our conversation on the road is truly serious, a matter of life and death. In a harsh reading of Matthew's Gospel, Derrida accuses Jesus' teaching of instituting a secret exchange, a new circle of the economic gift, between the disciple and the heavenly Father. He concentrates on three verses in chapter six (4, 6, and 18), which repeat the injunction to do good (to give) in secrecy, so that "your Father who sees in secret will reward you." The reward, or reciprocal giving, is in relation to the three standard works of piety, of almsgiving, prayer and fasting, which are to be practiced by Christians in a manner different from the "hypocrites," the scribes and Pharisees. In this way, a new "secret" circular economy is established between the praxis of earthly renunciation, an absolute loss of all that would reciprocate the "sensible body," and a future, heavenly, "spiritual" reward from an all-seeing Father, the keeper of "celestial coffers."[35] This secret economy would seek to "exceed an economy of retribution and exchange only to capitalize on it by gaining a profit or surplus value that was infinite, heavenly, incalculable, interior, and secret." Or, paraphrasing Nietzsche, Christian economy "remains what it ceases to be, a cruel economy, a commerce, a contract involving debt and credit, sacrifice and vengeance."[36] In one sense this is little different from what has been claimed throughout this book in respect of key aspects of the Christian tradition. But Derrida is on the road outside Jerusalem and responding to words from the first generation of Christian testimony. This requires that we reiterate those words with considerable care, seeking to sense the full range of tones with which they were spoken.

First, Derrida elides a key phrase that precedes "the Father who sees in secret." At 6 and 18 these words are prefaced by the qualification of "the Father who is in secret" (*to patri sou to en to krupto*). What does it mean to say the Father is the one in the secret, the one in the hidden place, in the crypt?[37] He does not see from beyond, celestially above, the hidden place, as Derrida suggests; far from it, he is *in* it! This is a cryptology of the Father, not in terms of some hidden code as that word might suggest, unless the code is that of the whole gospel and its key is the cross. The phrase should be understood in the context of the whole Kingdom noneconomy, of its absolute gift, and its an-archic time, on the part of the Father as much as the disciple. If the disciple is required to practice such giving in the new time when the Kingdom is "at hand," then it is because the Father also does, in an-archic solidarity with her. Because the Father is in the abyss, gives abyssally, from the hidden place obscured to normal, economic-ontological sight and time, so does the disciple. This is the sense of the earlier injunction "Love your enemies and pray for those who persecute you, so that you may be sons of your Father is in heaven; for he makes his sun rise on the evil and on the good, and sends rain on the just and the unjust" (5:44–45). And it also works the other way. There is no temporal priority in the abyss, in the abyssal an-archic moment of love. Disciples are told to pray to the Father: "Forgive us our debts, *as indeed we forgave* our debtors."[38] Father forgive us in the same way, just as, rein-

---

35. Ibid., 98–101.
36. Ibid., 109, 114.
37. See E. W. Bullinger, *Critical Lexicon and Concordance to the English and Greek New Testament*, 11th ed. (London: Samuel Bagster and Sons Limited, 1974), note on *kruptos*. For Greek text see *Interlinear*.
38. Matt. 6:12, *Interlinear*.

stancing the moment, in which we have already forgiven. Forgive us, Father, in abyssal repetition of human forgiveness!

How could the gospel suggest this abyssal, undetermined circle between God and humanity, a circle without priority at the point of forgiveness? One direction on which to pursue an answer is another word and its textual thread, which Derrida again avoids. There is no doubt that the verb *apodidomi* as used in the three verses of Matthew 6: 4, 6, and 18 contains the sense of "reward." Another term in the context of the discourse supports it: *misthos*, meaning wages or payment, a word that plays out in an exact counterbalance between the payment or reward expected by disciples (5:12, 46; 6:1) and the one already garnered by the hypocrites (6:2, 5, 16). Clearly Matthew is structuring a polemical opposition between Kingdom economy and that of hypocritical righteousness based in triangular mimesis: you see my righteousness and it makes me desirable, and this is my reward. In terms of argument the former is seen as displacing or even "buying out" the latter. Thus, on the surface, this element of the text may indeed make Christian practice appear as simply a superior or eschatological form of the circle of the gift. However, we are not dealing with dualist categories here: the circle of the gift is a cultural theme of immense power, and its abyssal interruption, plus the full realization of the interruption, cannot be simply signaled by pointing to something different, over there, as it were. It must be undone and transformed from within, even as verbally it may continue to resonate with its old, violence-charged reciprocity. For this is the point. The Christian gospel does indeed talk of an eschatological reformulation of the gift, not as death but absolute life, overflowing without remainder or recuperation. But what would have the power to carry out this reformulation, to plunge the circle in the abyss to reconstitute it there as the possibility of overflowing, an-archic love?

Another word in close relation to *apodidomi* is one we have already cited in English, and it is one with a more final significance in the Gospel structure; it is the verb *aphimi*, which means variously to forgive, let go, suffer, yield. It is the word used in the Lord's prayer for the forgiveness of the one in debt, in an-archic symmetry between disciples and the Father. It is used of the complete foregoing of possession and reciprocity in respect of someone wishing to sue you for the shirt on your back (!): let him have, yield to him (*aphes*) your most vital covering also, your bedroll or cloak (5:40). But two particular instances of this verb provide an arc of significance that conditions all the others, together with the *kruptos*, and the nature of the reward, the rendering, the giving back or away, *apodidomi*, performed by the Father.

At 3:15 Jesus enters into the public view, seeking baptism from John who protests that the roles should be reversed and he should be baptized by Jesus. The latter replies *aphes arti*, "suffer [it] now," for it fits, it is called for, at this moment and in this way to fulfill all justice/righteousness. Jesus comes to the water of the river, an abyssal scene in the Hebrew mind, and an-archically fills it with justice, telling John to let go, let it happen, let me go down, suffer *now*. Again the instant in time that tears time open, that brings the absolute gift to reconstitute given economic time. The solid earth falls away in the waters of the Jordan, and time begins to flow in an impossible, abyssal, unanticipated, and unanticipatable arc. But what gives this scene its consistency and power, along with every other scene in the Gospel, is the reach of the same verb to the instant of Jesus' death.

At 27:50 the Crucified cries out with a "great voice" (*phone megale*) and "yields the spirit" (*apheken to pneuma*). Jesus' death cry is an inarticulate shout from the abyss, which reverberates and carries the moment through all given time. Its content and what gives it its power is not defiance or despair, but the yielding up, the letting go, the fore-giving and release of the spirit, his breath, at that nadir of human history into which all life plunges without reserve—until that moment. The absolute giving of the cross is shouted out from the hidden place, the crypt, the place of death, not in any sense of an Abrahamic secret of absolute responsibility that Derrida claims cannot be shared, but precisely to be shared, to be passed on in further great shouts of witness. It is proactive, not merely responsive, it is an affirmation of life in death, not death in life, "good news" rather than "the gift of death."

Four verses before the shout, Jesus had already cried out with the same "great voice," but this time with articulation, asking: "My God, my God, why have you deserted me?" This is a parallel shout, marking the moment of the abyss and its significance as absolute loss. For Jesus at that moment, the presence of the Father was also plunged in darkness, lost to inner sight, and surely lost, as far as he was concerned, to the sacred order that was putting him to death. This, therefore, must also be part of the great shout of witness, the shout from the abyss: that the Father is hidden there, *is there* in the hidden place, in the mode of abandonment, an abandonment of Jesus that is also an abandonment of himself. This can be read from the biblical relationship of father and son, of course figured paradigmatically in Abraham, where the father gives absolutely his beloved son. But this time it is God himself doing the giving, and the movement "by virtue of the absurd" is surely taken by God himself.

The point, however, is not just this biblical paradigm but the whole New Testament narrative, where in effect Jesus is redefining the meaning of God through his own teaching and praxis. The New Testament throughout its composition opens up the abyss in the concept of God; and most critically in his own abyssal moment Jesus plunges God into the abyss. For if the abyssal death of Jesus an-archically reconstitutes time, then the very concept of transcendence, of the divine, must be reshaped in that movement. In a word, no longer will God belong to the circle of time, of reciprocity, exchange and violence, but will be discovered in the an-archic moment that produces the unconditionally new, the unheralded, an absolute future in the "now." "Father, why have you abandoned me?" means ultimately that abandonment is self-abandonment, abyssal self-giving on the part of God. This then should be the reference for the Father who sees in the hidden place. It demonstrates the Father *of* the hidden place, precipitated in, through, and with Jesus into fathomless depths of fore-giving. The verses of Matthew 6 that say the Father is in the hidden place could not have been written without the horizon of the cross, either in Jesus' own words or in the editorial theology of Matthew. There is no secret economy here, no ultimate, celestial reward based on exchange, only a proclaimed abyssal giving that issues from the soul of Jesus at that moment, and which an-archically refigures every other moment of given time and the constitution of God with them. From that moment all divine giving is abyssal, and so also all human giving is imitation of the divine.

How is it that our grave philosopher standing within sight of Jerusalem is able to dismiss completely this world-shattering time of giving? What enables him to ignore its inscription in the chain of signs, through *kruptos*, *apodidomi*, and *aphimi*, culminating in the cries of abandonment and yielding on the cross? The method by which he carries this off appears at the end of *The Gift of Death*. It is the gesture of Nietzsche before him, which is called in aid to perform the dismissal, and to absolve Derrida from the task himself. Derrida quotes Nietzsche almost at the end of the text, and then simply goes on to suggest obliquely a recruitment of Nietzsche's own thought to the secret of infinite responsibility. The question of Jesus' death itself is completely subsumed. Here is the relevant quotation, from *The Genealogy of Morals*. The context is a description of the genesis of the human sense of guilt and debt as the turning of cruelty against oneself, and out of this comes the idea of debt toward the deity, one on an infinite scale; or, in other words, irredeemable debt. Nietzsche then says this:

> [S]uddenly we stand before the paradoxical and horrifying expedient that afforded temporary relief for tormented humanity, that

stroke of genius on the part of Christianity: God himself sacrifices himself for the guilt of mankind, God himself makes payment to himself, God as the only being who can redeem man from what has become unredeemable for man himself—the creditor sacrifices himself for his debtor, out of *love* (can one credit that?), out of love for his debtor![39]

At once we are back in the medieval court of Anselm of Canterbury, which Nietzsche fully authenticates in terms of genealogy, and in doing so dismisses the Gospel's absurd word of love. By simply quoting this passage, Derrida is able to erase the death of Jesus in one stroke, covering it in the cruelty of economic exchange. How much are both he and Nietzsche justified in terms of traditional doctrine of atonement! But Nietzsche in his own way, and of course our philosopher, Derrida, are arguing with disciples on a road outside of Jerusalem, and neither of them does justice to the latters' testimony by meeting the text of the Gospel in the full depth of its crucial moment, the cross.

For this text is of course not simply a chain of verbal signs, despite what may be gleaned of real importance from them. It is also a story, a narrative, with the final events of Jesus' life taking up at least a quarter of the four canonical accounts. John's Gospel, in particular, has been called a passion narrative with an extended introduction. Why this enormous focus on the end of Jesus' career, on its factical detail in all its profoundly disturbing dimensions? We have already at numerous points evoked a sense of this narrative, but I think it is possible to drive our awareness of its power and effect even deeper. First, I would like to summarize three key elements in its overall structure. Most immediately, there is the very grossness of Jesus' death, the assault on the soft tissue of a life, on its inherent corporeal fragility, and of course therefore on a human being brought to essential vulnerability and abjection. What is presented here is the relentless evidencing of a bodily human passivity. Then, intrinsically related to this is the mobilization of structural forces and murderous human dynamic against Jesus, the way in which virtually every sector of the historical, sociopolitical, cultural, and relational context combine to make this passivity a fatality, a terminal disaster and the disaster of a person. Third, and most profound, there is the quality of the person himself, the narrative of a deliberation, a decision, a controlled series of

---

39. Nietzsche, *Genealogy of Morals*, 2.21, from *Basic Writings of Nietzsche*, trans. and ed. with commentaries by Walter Kaufmann (New York: The Modern Library, 1992), 528; quoted in *The Gift of Death*, 114, from Dr. Oscar Levy translation.

words and actions, together with a bottomless fear, a void and anguish of soul, and yet also somehow a final calm, a confirmation of decision and, ultimately, a fathomless yielding of spirit. It is this specific combination of elements, the gospel narrative and kerygma, that constitutes the singularity, the absolute event, of New Testament messianism, even as Derrida formally suggests. No other narrative—mythological, historical, or literary—comes close to reproducing the nexus of intimately recognizable violence and reachless responsive forgiveness at the heart of the gospel. This, in a word, is the abyssal Christ, the Christ of the abyss, the passion of this book, a reflection of the Passion of Christ.

PHENOMENOLOGY OF THE CRUCIFIED

Is it possible perhaps to move further in reflection of this Passion, to enter still more significantly into its abyss? I would like to try, and what follows is in the nature of a thought experiment or meditation on the existential death of Christ, always within the frame of an an-archical interruption of time. Should we not say that the abyssal moment has a thisness that is its absolute singularity, and its singularity is its absolute thisness? Specifically, should not everything be understood to occur in the terrible particularity of Christ's final breath, in its extreme banality and isolation, with the soldiery casting lots for his clothes? The finitude of existence, and in a terminal sense, is here the necessary locus for the abyss of compassion and of the redefinition of God that we are positing. It is in the near infinite loss of excruciation, in a leaden Palestinian afternoon, the degree point immediately prior to annihilation, that it becomes possible to fathom the depths of human impossibility, and there, in the passion of Jesus, affirm human possibility to a most passionate degree.

In the radical aporia of time and space, immediately prior to the final necessity of death, we might imagine that there is one moment of absolute possibility.[40] On one side of death—the side of receding life—all human

---

40. Heidegger considers death as the most proper, unconditional (human) possibility. "So enthüllt sich der Tod als die eigenste, unbezügliche, unüberholbare Möglichkeit" ("Thus death unveils itself as the most proper, absolute, unsurpassable possibility," [*Sein und Zeit*, 16th ed. (Tübingen: Max Niemeyer, 1986), 250–51, my translation]). At the same time this most proper possibility of death is the *possibility* of the *impossibility* of any existence at all (die der Unmöglichkeit der Existenz überhaupt [ibid., 262). This strange, aporetic disclosure of possibility *as* impossibility may set the scene for the kerygmatic reversal of death's impossibility *as* possibility. Thus the most proper human possibility of impossibility is transformed by compassion into an-archic, eschatological possibility. Is this not the most proper account of atonement we can give?

actuality is disappearing, all connection both with the possibilities of freedom and the reign of the world.[41] From this side life may be seen as receding into a kind of extreme of impossibility, the end of all social integration
and a point of sensed isolation as near absolute imaginable. On the other
side, there is also the drawing near of the definitive necessity of death that
negates any and all possibility of life. A phenomenology of death would
then see the human situation as suspended between extremes, on one side
the human impossibility of life and the other the inhuman necessity of
death. And each perhaps doubles the other, as the first gathers as a trace of
life receding and the other approaches as inevitability of life ending. It is
this desperate double state of abandonment and engulfment that may
express the basic quality of death for human consciousness, its very abyss.
At the same time, and crucially for the event of the cross, we may also suggest that there is entirely no metaphysical necessity that avails here, no
presence of an eternal idea or foundation, no divine or messianic project,
that can stand as truth between the two overwhelming poles. On the contrary, Christ's loss of actuality is also the loss of his own people, of his relationship to them, replaced instead by the eruption of generative violence
upon his body and person. The event is the abyss, constituted by persecution redoubling the loss of everything, redoubled by absolute loss itself.
We might even imagine a fourfold shape of extremes, the horizontal crisis
of personal death crossed by the vertical sacrificial crisis of the community represented in this very particular person, the surrogate for its own conflictive impossibility. Crucifixion shapes the cross and constructs Jesus'
moment of the abyss both in a personal and singular historical sense. As
we saw in the last chapter, Jesus deliberately placed himself at the break
point of an apocalyptic crisis in first-century Judaea, at the impossible
juncture of intense expectation of God's deliverance and the brutal reality of Roman power. The personal impossibility of his approaching death
becomes existentially infinite through the religiohistorical impossibility
that he had personally assumed. Heavenly possibilities have become
earthly impossibility, the very fabric of the human abyss. The shape of the
cross crosses the vector of Jesus' personal crisis with the terrifying vector
of absolute historical crisis.

At this abysmal point we might also imagine the compounded crisis as
creating an infinitesimal moment of "weightlessness" right at its crux, if

---

41. We may remember Kierkegaard's precision that actuality is the combination of possibility and necessity, of the endless opportunities of freedom together with the exigencies
of human life; see, for example, *The Sickness Unto Death*, ed. and trans. Howard V. Hong
and Edna H. Hong (Princeton, N.J.: Princeton University Press, 1980), 36.

perhaps an individual might summon the will to choose this extreme condition for itself, in an act of profound choice precisely at that point. On the horizontal, the impossibility of life is not impossibility in itself, for it is not yet the brute necessity of death. The loss of actuality may in fact be seen to produce an excess of possibility, an absolute, empty, pure possibility. On the vertical, the impossible crisis of the times into which the community is plunged might too become possibility if the victim himself may respond with unfathomable forgiveness, a forgiveness without end. Paradoxically, therefore, what may be seen to remain is an abyss of sheer possibility itself, a moment that might truly become, in separation from all human support, and in contrast to the last, desperate retention of the persecuted self in defiance, despair, or collusion, a moment of unimaginable surrender and gift of love. Perhaps it is only a heart of unparalleled generosity, and in a specific relationship of absolute trust in the Father in the midst of the abyss, that could discover this tiny moment and constitute it uniquely as a moment of giving, a gift of life, to life, to the other, for the other. Only such an immense freedom could distinguish the times, not surrendering to loss and persecution, but transforming the very moment as contingency, as free act of unbounded giving into the abyss. This freedom, in this moment, is to be understood as contingency in itself.

Here is a point of intrinsic difficulty in presentation. Unlike "the gift of death" that can be evidenced ultimately by death itself, the gift of the cross arises in a singular moment that is not in fact death, but can only be told about in its foundering at the moment of death. It is more secret, more cryptic, than any sacrificial death, which as a ritual event is always a matter of public, objective appearance. Or, rather, it takes the interior of sacrifice, that which is structurally hidden, which is the resolution of others' violence in the victim, and turns it inside out, making it an event of freedom, of infinite subjective forgiveness by the victim. But as this freedom, as abyssal subjectivity, it absolutely cannot be recovered in a concept, an idea, an eidetic demonstration. It cannot be made "present." It can only be communicated in the undecidability of compassion, in the story of the Christ that may or may not bring alteration to the soul of the hearer. In presentation, therefore, it can only be hazarded, sketched, and suggested. Its truth belongs properly to the leap, to a choice to move abyssally with Christ, to an "imitation" of Christ that responds to an abyssal moment of the self where the Christ is sensed abyssally. The contingency of the cross is true contingency; it can never become a rational necessity (*pace* Anselm), which in fact would remove the very movement of abyssal love, which is always without ground. Is there any other place for mimetic humanity to leap from its burning foundations of rivalry and murder, except into the abyss?

At the same time, in virtue of this pure contingency, if granted in this abyssal way, we could also say that, paradoxically, it meets the theological doctrine of God as *actus purus*, pure act. This tells that God is absolute, sovereign freedom, acting unconditionally without necessity in any sense.[42] Here, however, this reflection is met not in abstract, philosophical terms, but in the facticity of Christ's death communicated in the kerygma, a proclamation repeated again and again in its very lack of necessity. Thus what in a high doctrine of God is divine contingent freedom as absolute metaphysical necessity becomes in the gospel narrative an absolute historical contingency without metaphysical guarantee. Where indeed would it be possible to meet pure act in historical terms? Would it not precisely require the abyss, a compassionate freedom and freedom of compassion that takes place in the abyss? And in this context it is at once evident that the particularity of the cross is pure act not because it is absolute, untrammeled power, but entirely the reverse. The cross grants life precisely where its own finite potency, its own room for maneuver, is reduced to zero plus one and the one is given away. This is *actus purus* as revealed by the cross, and it is far removed from the cold sovereignty of action that belongs to metaphysics.[43]

The heralded yet unheralded, an-archic beginning of the cross arises within the story of the Gospels, and it begins the universe anew and for the first time. It does so from within the splintering difference of existence, not from some remote court of inscrutable power. Only a truly human contingency such as this, a particularity that may or may not move, can approach another human particular, in its lack of movement, its lack of freedom, and through the event of compassion offer it the movement of alteration or repetition. By an act of unimaginable freedom one has posited itself for the other. Is this not the eschatological now, a moment that breaks into the doomed continuum of history to reconstitute it with hope? The kerygma is by definition an apocalyptic determination of time; it relativizes all time by eschatological interruption. Merging the reading we are giving here with this New Testament sense of the work of Christ—rather than the subsequent "normal time" cosmic-legal interpretations— we intelligibly posit a radical Christian transformation of the meaning of time. Abyssal compassion, vindicated in resurrection and set forth in the preaching, enters before

---

42. Karl Barth, *Church Dogmatics*, vol. II, part 1 (Edinburgh: T. & T. Clark, 1957, 257–321.

43. The nature of this historical-contingent *actus purus* also explains the methodology that turns to stories of the abyss, for example in Dostoyevsky and Wilde. The method needs to be adequate to the message (the abyssal Christ), not vice versa—i.e., the message conformed to systematic concepts.

the givenness of time and its terrible legacy of violence, in order to anticipate and subvert all its structures with new, an-archic future. The factual-kerygmatic past that comes to anticipate all given time with mercy does so because it subverts every human particular locked in violence with the absolute contingency of compassion. It is fore-given the moment it plunges in its own abyss and meets there the Crucified.

Everything happens within an intelligible scheme of anthropology. Indeed from this perspective we may reflect that the "foundation of the world" is the foundation of cultural, historical time in and through violence. It is a consistent assumption that its exposure and reversal will alter time's human phenomenology, and at a radical level. In a profound way, therefore, both past and future no longer exist. The event of the gospel is a kind of bottomless "future past" that presses on all known time in the manner of ultimate re-creation or palingenesis, the scriptural figure of which is universal resurrection. This perhaps is also the sense of Irenaeus's recapitulation of the whole human story in Christ. An anthropological account of the renewal of time gives sense to this doctrine. But it seeks to do so without the metaphysical, eidetic certainty attached to such traditional formulation. For although everything happens within a scheme of intelligibility, I would also stress that this intelligibility is exceeded, or rather undermined, from within that scheme. We see the person of Christ given over to mimetic human possibility, but the very seeing always trembles on the edge of an abyssal fall, and always at that point it is a matter of two contingent particulars—myself and Christ. The response of faith is undecidable, just as there is no absolute scheme that could ever capture the undecidability of abyssal compassion. Both contingencies are in themselves beyond final comprehension. In this sense eschatological interruption is itself contingent and undecidable; it beats as open possibility in the heart of the believer, precipitated there by the abyssal message of the cross, and therefore without metaphysical certainty. Re-creation is rooted in the alteration of humanity as such, which is always a matter of the particular, one by one.

However, at the same time, in an astonishing paradox, it only takes one to enter the an-archic future of Christ to make the whole universe topple into the new, to be sensed in that person decisively reconstituted.[44] Normal

44. See Dostoyevsky's figure of the elder Zossima, described in the response of his disciple. Alyosha "was not at all troubled by the fact that his elder stood before him as a solitary example: 'It doesn't matter, he is holy, his heart contains the secret of a renewal for all, the power which will finally establish truth on earth, and all will be holy, and will love each other, and there will be no more rich, nor poor, exalted nor humbled, but all men will be as the children of God and the real kingdom of Christ will come'" (*The Brothers Karamazov*, trans. with intro. by David Magarshack [Harmondsworth, UK and New York: Penguin Books, 1958, reprinted 1984], 32).

time continues unabated, one day succeeds another, kingdoms rise and fall accompanied by relentless violence, human life traverses the inevitable span of birth and death. Yet the now of the New Testament enters the individual as grace, the presence within ongoing time of the an-archism of the cross, something that seeks in the very body of that individual to come around to the front of ongoing time and bring it to life-filled conclusion. Because for the believer everything has "already" happened, and yet its truth is not yet the truth of given time, the "already" seeks to enter again and again into the structure of chronology in the believer's deep personal response. This is not simply so as to fill up given time, as if by gaining a certain mathematical balance of works everything would be historically transformed. Rather, I think, there is something intrinsically "again and again" about this time. Unlike time founded in violence, which seals everything in sacred order, in the same, in a succession where the act of generative violence permeates the world both with the security of threat and the threat of security, the time of the cross is a matter of infinite repetition, of renewal in each instant of abyssal giving. It depends intimately on the clock-tick of the heart, each beat of which repeats every other beat of the kerygmatic past, simultaneously the same and yet utterly new. The time of love is inherently instantaneous, rooted in the undecidable, free giving of each moment of the heart. Thus it is always "again." Yet the power is precisely in the "again," absolutely undetermined by chronology, by given time. Because of the abyssal contingency of love, because of its paradoxical "pure act," it is able to interrupt any possible moment of the given with the an-archic future of the cross. The grace of the cross in the life of the believer makes the whole universe tremble with the utterly new. This is the freedom of the children of God, a terrible, disturbing freedom in respect to all given history.

And there is gratitude! Gratitude, even as a cultural practice in ordinary time, is perhaps always at the edge of the possibility of the "again." I give thanks for each new gift exactly as I gave thanks in the past for other gifts, but also each time totally afresh, without mediation of the past. The new gift evokes in me a completely fresh thanksgiving. Of course our philosophers—who at this point seem to be bidding goodbye to the disciples, scandalized finally by the ridiculous contingency of the cross—would insist one more time that gratitude belongs fully in the circle of the gift, in the circle of given time. Gratitude simply rehearses, proves, recirculates the economic meaning of the gift. My thanks for your gift displays uncontrovertibly the way the gift is not a gift, that it returns at once to you even as you give it. But is this completely true? Does not gratitude itself leak outside, overflow the circle of the gift, absolutely, and so evince for a moment, in a barely detectable instant, the rupture of this circle? So, perhaps, an-archic time is traced, sketched in the structure of human relationships itself, in their abyssal possibilities? What about "sincere thanks" when we are not uttering something formal, but what we owe, or sense we owe, is the essence of our whole being to the other; when the gift-giver has consistently and without apparent self-interest continued to help us and so changed our lives for the better, for the good, the good of life, and therewith this felt goodness returns to the giver? What about a "heartfelt thanks," a thanks that is wrung from us spontaneously by the overwhelming nature of the gift, by its reprieve, its liberation, by the gift of our lives that suddenly changes a situation and possibility of disaster into one of freedom, life, hope? When we say "Thank you, thank you, thank you …" in these instances and say it again and again, is there not an attempt by the heart and the voice, at the borders of the possible, to break out of themselves, out of their reserve that still exists, and pour themselves out without remainder for and to the other?

This perhaps is another "structure of experience" and "groundless ground" upon which the meaning of the messianic may be built, but again the distance between such a structural possibility and the actual messi-ahship of Jesus is so qualitatively immense that there is no question of ontological disclosure. It is only the concrete singularity of Judaism and then of Jesus himself that makes a difference. To establish a sense of this one more time—again!—and yet also to retain the link with the limit possibil-ity of gratitude, to which the message of Jesus speaks, let me conclude with another word on the thanksgiving of Jesus himself, his *eucharistein*. "The night in which he was betrayed [Jesus] took bread and having given thanks broke [it] and said, 'This is my body which is on behalf of you. Do this remembrance of me.'"[45] How could Jesus say thanks in that night and by means of a proleptic symbol of his death? What does this mean about the human gesture of thanks, giving thanks from the bottom of a desperately unfolding experience of abandonment and suffering, to render the heart back even and precisely in this moment? What is overflowing here, what is wrung from the heart in helpless gratitude for a gift? Only the night stares in his eyes. And yet he gives thanks. Here again is the fully abyssal move-ment of heart pouring itself out into a degree zero of reciprocity, but now precisely as gesture, as meaning, as the creation of a language of thanksgiv-ing that breaks with every circle of exchange, an abyssal rupture of language itself. It is the gesture, with its concrete signifier in the breaking of the bread, by which he is recognized in the inn at Emmaus. Such is the power

---

45. 1 Cor. 11:23b–24, partly *Revised Standard Version* and partly from *Interlinear* text.

of this interruptive gesture, this thanksgiving in the night, that suddenly at the inn it explodes in the faces of two dejected disciples locked in the circle of time. And all is new. What else was this thanks when imitated, assimilated, allowed primitively to alter the disciples, but in-breaking of the kingdom, the free flowing of the heart in endless gift, and with that an understanding of the law and the prophets plunged suddenly in the abyss? The romance languages that give thanks in the etymologically linked forms of *grace/gratia/grazie/gracias* have been under the pressure of this "grace" for near two thousand years, through its again-and-again rehearsal in evangelical word and sacramental gesture. An an-archism in the meaning of language that arises from Emmaus, so much more profoundly than from Athens. As we bid farewell to our philosophers, we dare perhaps to say "Thanks be to God for our meeting." How much future grace may yet be revealed in that thanks, as it echoes on the road long after the disciples have taken their separate ways?

CONCLUSION

Christ comes to us as a person and subjectivity, whose singularity in a specific time and place gives rise to an event that changes the meaning of all place and time. This is a messianic event, founded not in ontology but in the narrative of a history and a history that arises dynamically out of a narrative. The event is the product of a particular culture at a critical juncture appropriated and mobilized by a single individual. Its messianic quality is this combination of history, narrative, and the concrete praxis of that individual projecting the history and narrative forward into an incommensurable future. The life of this individual contains all the dynamic force of this convinced leap, such that it announces its authority and recreative momentum from the beginning of his public engagement. But the moment in which it becomes truly recognizable and fulfills the promise previously contained in word and action is the generative moment of the cross. This is the point at which Jesus' radical meditation on his own Scriptures, particularly Isaiah and Daniel, and the depths of the Wisdom tradition, together with his unbounded prayer to the Father, is plunged into the abyss of human crisis.

It is the abyss of human crisis in a very particular circumstance of history, yet thereby also the abyss of human crisis itself. When humanity senses its lack of foundations, its own chaos, it seeks to halt its free fall in the expenditure of life, at least one. The blood of the victim becomes a foundation of cultural order, just as Cain the fratricide was the founder of the first city. Jesus' death follows the age-old pattern; but this time a limitless response of trust and surrender on part of the victim broke the pattern, provoking something entirely new in the repertoire of human possibility, and at the same time pushing the repressed pattern to the surface, like the sea giving up its dead. What forms the utter exceptionality of Jesus is his fidelity to his redemptive project in the midst of lethal persecution, achieved not in bitter defiance but in fathomless yielding. Here the majesty of his person is revealed, its integrity reaching and sounding pre-viously unsoundable depths. Here is the paradox. History in all its contin-gency is held to a universal re-creative possibility by the measureless gift of one man's spirit. The fixed world turns on its fused axis, and the future of life falls like rain into the pit of annihilation.

What I am pressing toward is a Christology without essence, a Christology that seriously resists the removal of Christ into essential eidetic categories. The message itself demands it, in its contingency and particular-ity, and the trembling of the new in a world in crisis, a world without foun-dations. This does not mean that dogmatic formulae are not valuable, or lack truth; but they are not the place to begin, or end. They act as a regula-tory fence around the memory of Jesus, saving it on the one hand from docetism, the speculation of a nonhuman Christ, and on the other from Arianism, a heroic version of Jesus that avoids the gospel's most radical moment, the revelation of God in the abyss. We can in fact also affirm the norms of dogma from within the hermeneutic of biblical anthropology. The gospel event does not start with calling Jesus God, but such is the fathom-less movement of life he provokes that both a scriptural and human logic begin to require it. The abyss is the place where the biblical Creator God first acted to separate a world out of primeval waters or chaos. Jesus' powerful creativity in the chaotic depths of the human world is claimed and pro-claimed as the Sabbath work of God, the seventh day of re-creation that only God could author. Who but God, or the Son of Man endowed with the dominion of God, can claim dominion of the Sabbath, doing so in the work of liberating and healing on the Sabbath? Who but God can forgive sin, cre-ating life in the depth of the human condition? And crucially, for the mis-sion among the Gentiles, what else is the movement generated by the cross, which leaps beyond the human destiny of death into an experienced end-lessness or eternity of love, but the hand of immortal divinity plunged into the wretched finitude of life?

But the irreducible factor to bear in mind is that this hand does not arrive from a vertical heaven, even thought it has almost inevitably been pictured as doing so. It arises in the contingency and particularity of one man's life and death, interrupting from within the essential order of the world, emptying this into its own deep contingency and particularity, the bottomless abyss of human uncertainty. It is here alone that love can begin to speak endlessly, without guarantees either of eternal ideas or cosmic exchange. Here alone can love change from possessive desire, from its lega-cy of violence, into a freedom and unconditionality before unknown, needing the New Testament redefinition of the little-used Greek word, *agape*, to give it a name. In this light all the brilliant apparatus of Greek thought, of mind, being, substance, and nature, is rendered relative, provisional, and secondary to the anthropological challenge of the Gospels.

Georges Bataille sees the general meaning of religion as a tendency toward an experience of fusion or continuity, overcoming the isolation or discontinuity of "our random and ephemeral individuality."[1] The ritual act of transgression through violence has the dual function of evoking a primordial experience of continuity and yet also reaffirming the taboos on which it is based. However, in Christianity "the wish was to open the door to a completely unquestioning love. According to Christian belief, lost continuity found again in God demanded from the faithful boundless and uncalculated love, transcending the regulated violence of ritual frenzy.... Christianity has never relinquished the hope of finally reducing this world of selfish discontinuity to the realm of continuity afire with love. The initial movement of transgression was thus steered by Christianity towards the vision of violence transcended and transformed into its opposite."[2] At the same time Christianity undoes its good intentions by reducing the divine "to a discontinuous and personal God," thus breaking the chain of sacred continuity into infinite fragments of individuality in his image. "Love itself made sure of the final isolation."[3] This at once is the protest of the violent sacred against Christianity and a near complete failure to recognize the meaning of the cross. It is the compassionate response of Jesus in his abyssal discontinuity, the impossibility that he makes possibility, that opens the doors of boundless love between individuals through mimesis of that response. It is precisely discontinuity, or human contingency and particularity, and to an extreme degree, that provides the place for the revelation of a God of love, and with that of an infinite repetition, or continuity, of love between individuals. It is only when we view the matter within the context of the violent sacred, of the abyss of violence on which humanity is based, that the issue becomes so clear. Thus anthropology, and specifically the biblical narrative both disclosing and constructing anthropology, makes credible the Christian discourse of love, while doctrine expressed in terms of essence freezes its movement in conceptual form, thereby making possible precisely the error into which Bataille falls.

It is discontinuity that is the heart of Christianity, the abyssal isolation of Jesus where the time-shattering possibility of love, of absolute gift, is generated. From the discontinuity of the Christ arises the gift of continuity

---

1. Georges Bataille, *Eroticism*, trans. Mary Dalwood (London: John Calder, 1962), 15.
2. Ibid., 118.
3. Ibid., 120.

for all others, by his breath, his spirit, the bottomless gift of life. The discontinuous Christ comes to us as testimony and faith, and with that the radically new continuity of love becomes possible, as opposed to that of sacred violence. The believer is called into abyssal continuity to embrace fully the quality of love revealed by Christ, which is at once also discontinuity. Abyssal subjectivity made possible by Christ, both continuous and discontinuous, becomes the mode of personal existence called love. Thus Christian continuity is more radical, provocative, and consistent than the modalities of death and a-subjective continuity promised by violence. It is the endlessness of love, founded in the very undecidability of compassion, its risk, its lack of guarantee, its discontinuity, but thereby also open to the an-archic future that reconstitutes time itself and all relationality within time. That is why Christ at Emmaus appears and disappears in the same instant, leaving the disciples suddenly discontinuous, and yet at the same time filled with abyssal continuity, able to challenge all given history. Continuity arises from discontinuity, and discontinuity again from continuity. An endless abyssal testimony and pattern of love are generated. The Christian image and doctrine of the Trinity is the nature of God given by this pattern. Because the Crucified provokes absolute newness of life as both continuity and discontinuity, he no less reshapes the very meaning and identity of God. When Christ breathes his final breath on the cross, without asking God to avenge him, he plunges God into the abyss of non-retaliatory love and, with that, announces discontinuity as the Father's essential condition. When Christ goes in order that the Spirit may come, he establishes that the experience of love among his disciples is determined by discontinuity, and then the Spirit as Christ's continuity of love is itself experienced as discontinuous! Through the abyssal praxis of the Christ the Spirit too becomes a person. Here, then, is the intense radicalism of the Christian project, the glory of the individual sustained in the self-surrender of love stretching out endlessly, and projected at once both anthropologically and theologically.

Testimony, not the eternity of ideas, is the mode by which this truth is declared, is its true modality. In the twentieth century the testimony of one man perhaps stood out more than any other as declaration of the abyssal compassion of Christ over against the sacred fascination of violence. It is that of Dietrich Bonhoeffer, the German theologian martyred by the Nazis at Flossenbürg concentration camp on 9 April 1945. Although Bonhoeffer took active part in a plot to assassinate Hitler, both the very circumstances of this choice, its abject failure, and then his whole career as theologian, pastor, and then prisoner mark him out as witness to the Crucified in and for the abyss. Bonhoeffer returned to Germany from America in July 1939, when he could have remained there as an intellectual and righteous critic of the beast ravening for prey in Europe. He belonged to an elite German family, a member of a privileged intelligentsia, and many of his statements and personal attitudes betray a sense of rank that goes with such a background. But at Christmas in 1942 he wrote: "One may ask whether there have ever before in human history been people with so little ground under there feet—people to whom every available alternative seemed equally intolerable, repugnant, and futile. . . ." And a little later: "There remains an experience of incomparable value, that we have learned to see the great events of world history for once from below, from the perspective of those who are excluded, suspected, maltreated, powerless, oppressed, and scorned, in short the sufferers."[4] Bonhoeffer had entered the abyss.

He had looked desperately for an authentic locus of Christian resistance in the conditions of the Nazi regime, a place from which to counter the grotesque distortions in the national German church. And in the end he was reduced virtually to a church of one, witnessing consistently against the catastrophic co-option of Christianity by Hitler. In the Tegel prison not long before his execution, he concluded that such was the alienation of both the world and the church that even a Christian had to proceed as if there were indeed no God, *etsi Deus non daretur*. As a kind of dual explanation he wrote that the world was abandoned by God and that Christ was excluded by the world. But the true character of this writing is a theological realization of the abyss, in which Bonhoeffer is able to intuit the deep nature of gospel passion, and then seeks to sketch it in outline as the scene of future Christian thought.

[We] cannot be honest unless we recognize that we have to live in the world *etsi deus non daretur*. . . . God himself compels us to recognize it. So our coming of age leads us to a true recognition of our situation before God. God would have us know that we must live as men who manage our lives without him. The God who is with us is the God who forsakes us. The God who lets us live in the world without the working hypothesis of God is the God before whom we stand continually. Before God and with God we live without God. God lets himself be pushed out of the world on to the cross. He is weak and powerless in the world, and

---

4. Biography from Renate Wind, *Dietrich Bonhoeffer, A Spoke in the Wheel*, trans. John Bowden (Grand Rapids: Eerdmans, 1992). Quotations from *After Ten Years* in *Dietrich Bonhoeffer, Letters and Papers from Prison*, ed. Eberhard Bethge, 16 July 1944 (New York: Collier Books, 1953; paperback 1972), 3, 17.

that is precisely the way, the only way, in which he is with us and help us. . . . The Bible directs man to God's powerlessness and suffering; only the suffering God can help. To that extent we may say that the development towards the world's coming of age outlined above, which has done away with a false conception of God, opens up a way of seeing the God of the Bible, who wins power and space in the world by his weakness. This will probably be the starting-point for our "secular interpretation."[5]

Bonhoeffer's testimony as a theologian has grasped the world as a place forsaken by God, the very abyss itself. And it is pushed to the limit of seeing God himself as an element of elimination from this world, through the cross. The two aspects sit side by side and are not fully integrated; Bonhoeffer perhaps misses the way in which the cross has been the agent of the whole process, the disclosure of the abyss both as absence of the God of the sacred and the revelation of the biblical God fully in and through the abyss. The key point, however, is the way in which his thought as a theologian implodes under the pressure of the twentieth century maelstrom in which he finds himself. Standing alongside Bonhoeffer's testimony are the six million Jews exterminated in the camps, and the many millions more eliminated by the Nazi political and war machine. How can the witness of one Christian counter the crushing weight of these deaths, and along with them the countless other systematic killings of our epoch? There can be no doubt that the Holocaust, and its profound reverberations in and through all the other mass killings of our time, constitutes an "end point" for Western culture and for its theological confidence.[6] The abyss becomes unmistakable, unavoidable as a gaping hole in the continuum of spirituality the West has claimed. But Bonhoeffer's testimony echoes more powerfully for that very reason. Not that it offers a cheap alternative hope, that we can reread and bring new closure to everything through it. Rather, because in the very circumstances of the abyss it makes the meaning of the cross emerge ever more starkly and urgently. It reveals the cross in the abyss, and tells us that the Crucified's challenge to time in the circumstances of our time becomes more and more actual and inescapable, first and foremost for Christians themselves. There is less and less room for a Christian to walk on earth other than in the valley of desolation, there

---

5. *Dietrich Bonhoeffer, Letters and Papers from Prison*, 360–61.
6. See Johann Baptist Metz, *The Emergent Church*, trans. Peter Mann (New York: Crossroad, 1987), 18.

to transform it into a place of spring rains. Bonhoeffer's testimony, exactly as he wished, opens up the scene of a secular theology, one that does not hide but affirms the crisis of Christianity turned irreversibly toward the abyss. That we are dealing with one man over against millions is in a way precisely the point. Testimony in the abyss is always the case of the single individual, of the discontinuous proclaiming the continuous without foundations. The testimony of Bonhoeffer recommences theology from the abyss, for it returns us, as it were for the first time, to the testimony of Christ from that place.

This is very different from the overwhelming image of Christ in the Middle Ages, the hero-victim of the cross, negotiating a settlement of salvation for humanity with God or the Devil, the Devil or God. Through the biblical hermeneutic of mimetic anthropology the face of the victim of human violence is declared to us, and the New Testament proclaims that God has assumed that face himself. The virtue of the work that here comes to a close is not simply that it recognizes the image of Christ consistently in the anthropology of the victim, but that simultaneously it discovers the scene of the abyssal Christ as the locus of human transformation. What is presented here may provide perhaps some realization of the theology that Bonhoeffer sketched out of his abyssal experience. If this work has helped clarify and amplify his testimony, and behind that the fathomless testimony of the Crucified, a possibility may emerge that Bonhoeffer in his predicament could only dream of. It is the event of a Christian congregation that precisely from the hermeneutic of biblical anthropology becomes an authentic secular Christianity, for it begins to understand itself as the appropriation of the abyssal redemption of Christ. What, simply, are the questions of faith for such a congregation? What are they but forgiveness, nonretaliation, compassion, and the movement of surrender in the Spirit of Christ leading endlessly to the endless life of love?

Index